The One Year® Book of
DEVOTIONS FOR MEN

DEVOTIONS

FOR *men*

TYNDALE HOUSE PUBLISHERS, INC.
WHEATON, ILLINOIS

Visit Tyndale's exciting Web site at www.tyndale.com

The One Year Book of Devotions for Men copyright © 2000 by Stuart Briscoe. All rights reserved.

The One Year is a registered trademark of Tyndale House Publishers, Inc.

Cover photograph copyright © 2000 by Fuste Raga/The Stock Market. All rights reserved.

Eagle cover photograph copyright © 2000 by Pictor, International. All rights reserved.

Edited by S. A. Harrison

Designed by Dean H. Renninger

Scripture quotations are taken from the *Holy Bible,* New Living Translation, copyright © 1996. Used by permission of Tyndale House Publishers, Inc., Wheaton, Illinois 60189. All rights reserved.

Material in this book was previously published in *The Daily Study Bible for Men* © 1999 by Tyndale House Publishers.

ISBN 0-8423-1920-4

Printed in the United States of America

05   04   03
7   6   5

Introduction

This morning I asked my six-year-old grandson, "Stephen, why do you think we should learn to read?" He thought for a moment and replied, "Because if you learn to read, it helps you to be smart and know words." Stephen, having been born in a country with a very high literacy rate, has an enormous advantage in this regard over those who have been born into circumstances where literacy is not available.

Mark Twain once said, "He who does not read good books has no advantage over he who cannot read them." In saying this, he pointed to a sad situation in many Western countries: People have learned to read but lack the time, interest, or discipline to avail themselves of the opportunity to read and to be smart and learn words.

I am particularly concerned about people who do not read the Scriptures on a regular basis. The Scriptures were written and preserved for us in order that we might "be smart" about the things of God and "learn words" about life and death, eternity and time, this world and the world to come, who God is and what he has done, what he plans to do and where we fit in his plans. These are things that we cannot learn anywhere else. It is my conviction that the Bible was given to us in our own language in order that we should read it and learn from it all the things God wants us to know and which we desperately need to know. But he who does not read it has no advantage over he who cannot read.

There are different ways of reading the Bible. Some do it as a purely academic exercise, others for no other reason than to try to prove or disprove its authenticity. But my concern is that we read it with a view to benefiting from it in our daily lives. We call this reading the Scriptures *devotionally*. It is reading with an inquiring mind and a thirsty spirit, longing to know God better and to live more in keeping with His principles. When the Bible is read in this fashion, it becomes a source of joy and delight, of encouragement and direction, of correction and instruction.

This book is designed to encourage daily, devotional Bible reading. It was written with the busy man in mind, hence the relatively short readings. It was designed for the modern man, hence the contemporary applications of the ancient Scriptures. And it was produced with the fervent hope and prayer that in reading it, modern men will be encouraged and challenged to become smart about the things of God and learn words which will enable them to express their appreciation to God for all his mercies and to articulate to others what they have discovered of God that has transformed their lives.

May it never be said of us that we had the ability to read, we had the most priceless book available for reading, but we lived our lives without becoming biblically literate.

Stuart Briscoe
December 2000

JANUARY

WHAT GOD WANTS

*What I want instead is your true thanks to God; I want you to fulfill
your vows to the Most High. Trust me in your times of trouble,
and I will rescue you, and you will give me glory.*

PSALM 50:14-15

A lot of men have problems relating to their wives. When they discover there is a problem they hadn't been aware of and then try to find out what it is, they might be told, "You should know what the problem is! The fact that you don't know is part of the problem!" Often the wife's complaint is that her husband does not give her enough attention. She longs for him to relate to her. She is not unappreciative of the things he gives her and the work he does for her. But even more she wants *him*.

God had a similar complaint about his people, Israel. His people were active in religious observance, meticulously offering animal sacrifices. God said, "I have no complaint about your sacrifices or the burnt offerings you constantly bring to my altar" (Ps. 50:8). But he was not looking for the bulls and goats from their barns and pens. He had no need of anything from them at all. In fact, even if he did have a need (which he didn't!), he certainly would not have told them, because his resources were greater than any need. More than their gifts, he wanted *them!* God's people had forgotten to relate to him, and he wanted them back.

God wanted his people to thank him (Ps. 50:14). He wanted to be thanked because saying "thank you" is evidence of a healthy relationship with him. Those who recognize who God is in their lives and know how much they depend on him to intervene in their experiences are people who know that all they are and have come from him. As they recognize this imperative connection with God, they overflow with gratitude.

God also wanted his people to fulfill their promises (Ps. 50:14b). It was God who took the initiative and told the people of Israel that he would be their faithful God. In response, they assured him that they would be his faithful people. The closest of relationships was born, but the people tended to forget—the vows lay unfulfilled, the promises were ignored, and the relationship deteriorated. But God longed to have his people back again.

God also wanted his people to trust him (Ps. 50:15). Imagine God's pain when his children get themselves into trouble and then turn away from him to find help in other people and things. He wants them to turn to him and ask him for *his* help. He is more than ready to give it.

What God wants is no mystery—he wants thankful, trusting, faithful children. He wants people who will keep their promises to him and live in active relationship with him. He wants people he can delight in and who delight in him. He wants *us*.

TO READ: *Isaiah 1:1-20*

WHY INVITE TROUBLE?

Why do you continue to invite punishment? Must you rebel forever?
Your head is injured, and your heart is sick.

ISAIAH 1:5

T om Sawyer's cousin, Sid, "had no adventurous, troublesome ways."[1] He went quietly about his business, did his chores, and caused no ripples. Tom, however, was different. He had a nose for trouble. Occasionally, very occasionally, he "stumbled into obedient conduct," much to the delight of his long-suffering Aunt Polly. But even then things were not always as they appeared.

It is impossible to imagine a book called *The Adventures of Sid Sawyer*. Who would want to read about a good kid who never got into trouble, never rocked a boat, never finagled his way out of a fix? We prefer the escapades and scrapes of an adventurous rascal. But as appealing as these characters are, their mischievousness can be disruptive.

Why do some people seek out trouble and home in on it like a heat-seeking missile? Perhaps it's the thrill of matching wits with authority. Maybe it's an indication of a restlessness of spirit that seeks a satisfaction not found in legitimate activities.

In the days of Isaiah the prophet, God asked his chosen people, "Why do you continue to invite punishment? Must you rebel for ever?" (Isa. 1:5). The people's rebellion and unacceptable behavior were inviting God's punishment. In fact, the Lord was so disgusted by their behavior that he even told them that the donkey and ox recognize and appreciate their master, but his people's behavior didn't even reach the standard of those servile animals!

God is the one who defines acceptable and unacceptable behavior, and he is the one who metes out the appropriate punishment when his laws are contravened. If we doubt the reality of judgment by God, or if we question whether a man should concern himself with the eternal consequences of his actions, a brief reading of God's dealings with Israel will show the facts. God displays his righteousness by dealing rightly with his people. That includes ensuring that they live with the consequences of their actions.

But the question remains. Why do people continue to invite punishment? Why do we persist in rebelling against God? The answer is found in Isaiah's statement. We invite punishment when we take from God all he provides but do not "appreciate his care." We invite trouble when, after years of instruction, we "still do not understand." We continue to rebel when, prompted by our wicked hearts, we willfully turn "away from the Lord." We behave like God's ancient people when we cut ourselves off "from his help" (Isa. 1:3-4).

People who persist in rebelling and inviting God's punishment are asking for trouble. And there's nothing appealing about that!

---

[1] Mark Twain, *The Adventures of Tom Sawyer.*

TO READ: *Isaiah 1:21-31*

WATERED DOWN WINE

Once like pure silver, you have become like worthless slag.
Once so pure, you are now like watered-down wine.

ISAIAH 1:22

J esus of Nazareth unveiled his miraculous powers at a wedding where, to the intense discomfiture of the wedding hosts, the consumption of wine had far exceeded the supply. So the wine ran out, which was going to be a matter of great social consternation. Then Jesus stepped forward and, to his disciples' amazement, he turned water into wine (see John 2:1-11). Jesus transformed the ordinary and mundane into something extraordinary and delightful. He saved the day.

The people of ancient Jerusalem, centuries earlier, had done the opposite. They had turned their wine into water: "Once like pure silver, you have become like worthless slag. Once so pure, you are now like watered-down wine" (Isa. 1:22). Morally and spiritually the people of Jerusalem were no longer what they used to be. In their heyday they were known for being "faithful," they were "the home of justice and righteousness"—they were "once like pure silver" (1:21-22). But slag had polluted their silver, and water had seeped into their wine. They had become morally impure and spiritually corrupt.

It probably did not happen all at once. It was not as if the inhabitants of Jerusalem had woken up one morning and decided to become unfaithful, unjust, and unrighteous. In all probability there had been a slow erosion of standards, a growing carelessness about details, and a gradual blurring of distinctives. Murderers were not dealt with summarily, thieves attained social standing, bribery was excused, and caring for the needy ran a poor second to paying attention to the greedy (1:22-23). It started at the top and worked its way down, until the whole culture was polluted and diluted.

God was outraged. He took decisive action and announced that he would deal with the corruption personally. God's purpose was to restore his people's purity: "I will melt you down and skim off your slag. I will remove all your impurities. Afterward I will give you good judges and wise counselors like the ones you used to have. Then Jerusalem will again be called the Home of Justice and the Faithful City" (1:25-26). These promises, of course, would be fulfilled only when the Messianic kingdom was finally established.

What God promised long ago to do for the city of Jerusalem he promises today to do for the individual. When God sees silver turning to slag and wine to water through the erosion of standards, spiritual carelessness, and poor moral discipline, he speaks out. He promises to deal firmly in order to cleanse and then restore. His discipline is not vindictive; it is restorative. His judgment is not spawned through anger; it is born from love. His intention is to redeem the repentant (1:27)—those who turn away from sin and turn to God with new trust. For those people, God will de-slag the silver and re-wine the water. But the unrepentant never experience it. Their silver remains slag, and their wine turns to water.

3

TO READ: *Isaiah 2:6-22*

THE HELP OF HUMANS

Stop putting your trust in mere humans. They are as frail as breath.
How can they be of help to anyone?

ISAIAH 2:22

A midst all the euphoria of the new millennium, some advertisers did get a little carried away. One credit card company, for instance, announced that we would soon have a cure for all illnesses, live to be 200 but look like 30, and spend our vacations on Mars. All paid for with credit, courtesy of the credit card company.

Clearly the developments of the last century have been stupendous, and the possibilities for further development are superb. Human ingenuity is impressive. But why live to be 200 if I'm miserable being 50? And what good is looking like 30 if I feel like garbage? And what's so exciting about a vacation on Mars if there's nothing to do but look at red rocks and I'm not sure that I'll have a job and a family when I get back? All this needs to be addressed. Fortunately, God did address it—many years ago!

Pride is a perennial human problem. The more we achieve, the more self-sufficient we become. The more ingenuity we display, the more arrogant we become. God is not impressed, because he knows that everything comes from him and without him we are nothing, can do nothing, and will achieve nothing. But we don't believe it, so sometimes God has to take strong measures to get our attention and drive the lesson home.

This is what he did through Isaiah the prophet. Isaiah promised, "The arrogance of all people will be brought low. Their pride will lie in the dust. The Lord alone will be exalted" (Isa. 2:17). Of course, Isaiah was speaking primarily to his contemporaries. What he was predicting came true when God's people were humbled in defeat and led into exile (see 2 Kings 25:1-21).

On a broader scale, though, the lesson applies to "all people." And what precisely is the lesson? That "humans are as frail as breath" (Isa. 2:22). Accordingly, people should "stop putting [their] trust in mere humans . . . how can they be of help to anyone?" Human help is severely limited and unreliable. So, ultimately, we need to swallow our pride and rely on God. Then we will receive his help. He will be of help to everyone who trusts in him!

If your ambition is to live till you're 200 and look like 30, your credit card may be able to help. But if your goal is to live forever and be like Jesus, it will be no help at all!

TO READ: *Isaiah 3:25–4:6*

A FEW GOOD MEN

In the future, Israel—the branch of the LORD—will be lush and beautiful,
and the fruit of the land will be the pride of its people.

ISAIAH 4:2

On the eleventh hour of the eleventh day of the eleventh month of 1918, the guns finally fell silent in Europe. World War I was mercifully over. Ten million soldiers had been slaughtered, most of them bachelors or young married men. Young officers had suffered disproportionately high casualties. They were called "the lost generation."

Then the battle to cope with the future began. This was particularly difficult for young women. The "lost generation" had been their husbands, fiancés, and boyfriends—and the wives, fiancées, and girlfriends knew that their "life chance of a partner had disappeared with their loved ones in the mud of the trenches."[2]

A similar tragedy had happened before. When Isaiah foretold Jerusalem's collapse, which occurred in 586 B.C., he wrote, "The men of the city will die in battle. . . . Few men will be left alive" (Isaiah 3:25–4:1). And the result? "Seven women will fight over them and say, 'Let us all marry you! We will provide our own food and clothing. Only let us be called by your name, so we won't be mocked as old maids'" (4:1). The scene of humiliation and desperation is hard to imagine!

Anyone traveling to Europe today can see that the continent has recovered. Men, women, and children are there in abundance. But it took time! It took time for Jerusalem, too. The prophet said the city would recover. In fact, Isaiah spoke in glowing terms of the future even before the tragedy happened: "But in the future, Israel—the branch of the Lord—will be lush and beautiful, and the fruit of the land will be the pride of its people" (4:2). Isaiah, with a prophet's vision, was looking down through the centuries to the Messiah—to the kingdom of Jesus Christ.

The survivors of the tragedy in Jerusalem were called to be a "holy people" whose "moral filth" had been washed away (4:5). It was not just a matter of survival and then a return to life as usual. Their devastating experience had served a purpose, opening up new vistas of hope and blessing. The promise was that their once-devastated city would receive "shelter from daytime heat and a hiding place from storms and rain" (4:6).

Life's devastating traumas can bring about ultimate blessing. The traumas allow God to deal with our sin, cleanse us from iniquity, call us to commitment, deepen our faith, strengthen our moral principles, and set us apart for holy living. When these things happen, blessing follows. It doesn't happen overnight, any more than a lost generation is immediately replaced. It takes time. But by God's grace, it does happen.

[2] Norman Davies, *Europe—A History*, p. 926

TO READ: *Isaiah 5:8–25*

THE UNHOLY CITY

The grave is licking its chops in anticipation of Jerusalem, this delicious morsel.
Her great and lowly will be swallowed up, with all her drunken crowds. . . .
But the LORD Almighty is exalted by his justice.
The holiness of God is displayed by his righteousness.

ISAIAH 5:14, 16

Jerusalem is rarely out of the news. We have become familiar with pictures of ambulances and fire trucks at the scene of bombings and of roadblocks where Israeli soldiers frisk and question Arab or Palestinian workers. We see cabinet members shirt-sleeved and chain smoking, sitting and discussing obstinate problems, and diplomats scurrying in and out of the King David Hotel.

More than 2,700 years ago, Isaiah wrote about Jerusalem. Even then the city was of great interest to the known world. More significantly, it was the focus of God's attention.

And God did not like what he saw there. In fact he predicted "destruction" for the city and its inhabitants. The inhabitants of Jerusalem were engaging in egregious business abuses, particularly in real estate (Isa. 5:8). They were a partying community given over to hedonistic lifestyles (5:11-12). They were so captivated by their own sin that they failed to see how far they had fallen, and they mocked God for not intervening in their lives (5:18-19). Public morality had been stood on its head, and private morality had been restructured to fit each person's tastes (5:20). The inhabitants of Jerusalem considered themselves clever enough to outsmart God. In reality, many of them were living in alcoholic confusion (5:21-22). And Jehovah had chosen this city as the place to make himself known to his special people, in order that they might spread their knowledge of God from the beautiful city to all the nations of the world (see Psalm 48).

But God had seen enough of Jerusalem's revelry, and he was ready to deal severely with his beloved city and her people. He had no alternative! God is "the Holy One of Israel" (Isa. 5:19), and his holiness had to be demonstrated and recognized. But how?

Isaiah knew the answer to that. He wrote, "The Lord Almighty is exalted by his justice. The holiness of God is displayed by his righteousness" (5:16). "Holiness" means "separateness" or "set-apartness." Alec Motyer, in his commentary on Isaiah, says holiness means "belonging to another [the divine] order of things."[3] What sets God apart from humanity is his moral purity, his righteousness. But this righteousness has to be displayed. It is displayed through God's justice in dealing with humanity. So God had to deal with Jerusalem. His own holiness, righteousness, and justice demanded it.

These are solemn words for any city-dweller to ponder! While in the countryside men may still be reminded of the God of nature and revere him, in the concrete jungles of the city God can be lost in the clamor and the glamour. So men frequently live divorced from Him and married to their sin.

---

[3] Alec Motyer, *The Prophecy of Isaiah.*

TO READ: *Isaiah 7:1-9*

DON'T PANIC, KEEP CALM

"Israel is no stronger than its capital, Samaria. And Samaria is no stronger than its king, Pekah son of Remaliah. You do not believe me? If you want me to protect you, learn to believe what I say."

ISAIAH 7:9

When King David and his son, King Solomon, had passed away, their magnificent kingdom split in two—Israel to the north, and Judah to the south. During that period, the Assyrians became the dominant force in the region. To combat them, Israel formed an alliance with Aram (Syria). But Judah declined to go along and actually showed signs of siding with Assyria. This prompted Israel and Aram to attack Judah, but they were unable to capture Jerusalem. The inhabitants of Jerusalem "trembled with fear, just as trees shake in a storm" (Isa. 7:2). And with good reason, because the northern allies threatened to attack again, intent on capturing Jerusalem, overthrowing the king, and installing their own ruler.

Isaiah lived in Jerusalem, and he was instructed to go speak to Ahaz, the frightened king of Judah. He took with him his son, whose odd name (Shear-jashub) meant "a remnant shall return." The boy's name was a message of both good news and bad news. The good news was that whatever happened a remnant would *survive*. The bad news? It would be a *remnant*, and it would be *returning!*

The Lord gave Isaiah a message for Ahaz: "Tell him to stop worrying. Tell him he doesn't need to fear the fierce anger of those two burned-out embers" (7:4). The embers in question were the king of Israel and the king of Aram, along with their forces. No doubt not worrying was easier said than done, but it was God's message nevertheless. So King Ahaz was presented with two alternatives: He could seek a political solution to his predicament—a treaty with Assyria, which would frighten off the northern kings and preserve him from Assyrian attack. Or he could choose a spiritual solution and trust that the Lord would intervene on his behalf and protect Ahaz's kingdom from harm.

Should he seek a political solution or a spiritual solution? Probably none of us is called to make such a decision about such an important matter—the fate of the state— but we do find ourselves in predicaments where a decision needs to be made. The choices often appear to be either to make a deal or to trust the Lord! Easy answers are usually not available in such situations. Yet there is one thing that we can learn from Ahaz's predicament. The Lord told him through Isaiah, "If you want me to protect you, learn to believe what I say" (7:9). The key is knowing what the Lord is saying, or has said, about a situation. If there are clear instructions, do what God says. If he says "do nothing except trust me," then that is the way to go. In other cases, God's instruction may be to take a certain course of action.

Trusting God to act on our behalf may seem more heavenly-minded than of earthly use, but it does have the advantage of turning out right every time!

TO READ: *Psalm 111*

REVERENCE

Reverence for the LORD is the foundation of true wisdom.
The rewards of wisdom come to all who obey him. Praise his name forever!

PSALM 111:10

C omedians often make a living by being irreverent. They capitalize on the foolish
adage "nothing is sacred!" Some even advertise their humor as "irreverent" and
thereby attract a following of people who like to demean that with which they do not agree
and diminish that which they possibly do not even understand. There is no doubt some
justification for humorists to point out the foibles of pompous people and to generate the
kind of humor that will help us see the alarming gap between our pretentiousness and our
actual performance. But they cross the line when they deprecate legitimate authority and
lampoon holiness. There is a place for reverence, and he is a poor man who fails to recognize
it and acknowledge it.

The psalm writer recognized the need for reverence, particularly reverence for God. The
writer of Psalm 111 concluded his beautiful and intricate poem with the following lines:

> *Reverence for the LORD is the foundation of true wisdom.*
> *The rewards of wisdom come to all who obey him.*
> *Praise his name forever! (Ps. 111:10)*

As the psalmist contemplated the Lord, he knew that reverence for God is the only
appropriate response to his existence—not only in public worship, but in the day-to-day
matters of the heart.

First of all, the psalmist recounted the amazing deeds of the Lord and instructed his
hearers to "ponder them." As a citizen of God's covenant nation, Israel, he was referring
particularly to the events in the nation's history that clearly demonstrated the power and
majesty of the Lord. God had wonderfully rescued Israel from their Egyptian oppressors
(111:4); had fed them in the wilderness (111:5); had "shown his great power to his people
by giving them the lands of other nations" (111:6), meaning the Promised Land; and all this
because "he always remembers his covenant" (111:5). When God makes promises, as he did
to Israel, he keeps them! The recollection of these events—which actually happened in time
and space—generated a sense of reverence in the psalmist's heart, which he encouraged the
other worshipers to share.

The psalm writer then turned his attention to the giving of the Law to the people
of Israel. This was instruction of the highest order, the means whereby the people would
know how to conduct themselves as God's people. The law was a revelation of God's
character and purposes and an exposition of the Most High's expectations, promises, and
warnings. He is the God who graciously communicates with his creatures who revere and
obey him.

It is noteworthy that this psalm was composed for use when "godly people"
gathered for worship (111:1). In the psalmist's mind, reverence in worship was of prime
importance. We should ponder this—it might get us to church regularly and on time, with
our hearts prepared and with a spirit of expectancy, awe, and reverence. This is, after all,
"the foundation of true wisdom" (111:10). Irreverence may come across as witty and
sharp, but in the end it is reverence that shows we are wise!

TO READ: *Mark 2:23–3:6*

THANK GOD IT'S MONDAY!

Then [Jesus] said to them, "The Sabbath was made to benefit people, and not people to benefit the Sabbath. And I, the Son of Man, am master even of the Sabbath!"

MARK 2:27-28

T hank God it's Friday" is a common sentiment in the workplace. Not that Fridays are any different from other days; the sun rises and sets as usual! It's just that on Friday the work weekends and the weekend begins.

It was not always like this. The Scriptures say, "Six days a week are set apart for your daily duties and regular work but the seventh day is a day of rest dedicated to the Lord your God" (Exod. 20:9-10). This is one of the Ten Commandments, and the Jewish people understood the reasoning behind it: God created the world in six days but rested on the seventh, and man should do the same. Accordingly, they were forbidden to do any work on the Sabbath, and they defined work by listing thirty-nine prohibited actions. The penalty for breaking this law was death!

One Sabbath day, while Jesus and his disciples were busy about the work of the kingdom, the disciples picked some wheat and ate it as they traveled. This was technically "reaping"—one of the thirty-nine activities prohibited by the rabbis. So he was in contravention of basic Jewish law, and his opponents challenged him. He replied that the Sabbath was made for the benefit of man and, therefore, it was appropriate for his hungry disciples to be fed. Then, to the anger of his opponents, he said, "And I, the Son of Man, am master even of the Sabbath" (Mark 2:28).

Christians now celebrate a "sabbath," a day of rest and worship, on the first day of the week, rather than on the last day, in commemoration of Christ's resurrection (see Matt. 28:1; Mark 16:1-9; Luke 24:1; John 20:1, 19; Acts 20:7; 1 Cor. 16:2). The first day of the week was called "the Lord's Day" in New Testament times (see Rev. 1:10). But what matters to secular people is not a day of rest in honor of the Creator who rested from his work, but a weekend away from work and freedom to do whatever they wish.

Jesus said that he is master even of the Sabbath, and the Sabbath is made for man's well-being. If Jesus' words are to be applied for modern people, surely they mean that our times of rest from work should be lived in conscious recognition not only of the Creator who rested, but also of his Son who rose again. Such recognition would lead to worship and service as a prime weekend activity. This would not only serve to renew weary people after the struggles of the previous week, but also would refresh them with spiritual energy with which to face the new week. When that happens, the refreshed and renewed can't wait to get back to work. They may even be heard saying as they go, "Thank God it's Monday"!

TO READ: *Mark 3:7–19*

THE CROWD
AND THE CORE

*Afterward Jesus went up on a mountain and called the ones
he wanted to go with him. And they came to him.*

MARK 3:13

When crowds are drawn together, either by something sensational or by the offer of something free, they can be extremely difficult to handle! Then the inner drive of the individual to be first, to see all there is to see, or to get all there is to get, multiplied by a few thousand becomes a practically irresistible force. They can be very fickle, too. If they receive what they are seeking, they can be adulatory, while if they are denied or disappointed, they may become ugly in a flash.

The "huge crowd" (Mark 3:7) that followed Jesus as he headed for the lake was liable to get out of hand, and Jesus knew it. People were eager to touch him in a quest for healing, but there were also many deranged people and people driven by demonic forces. No doubt some of Jesus' avowed enemies were in the crowd, too. In other words, the situation was potentially explosive. So Jesus quietly asked the disciples to ensure that a boat was made available "in case he was crowded off the beach" (3:9).

When the day's ministry passed without incident, Jesus made his way into the hills and "called the ones he wanted to go with him" (3:13), so that they might become "his regular companions" (3:14). In all probability they had little idea what Jesus expected of them, but they soon found out. First and foremost, he was looking for "a few good men" who would put a personal relationship with him at the top of their agenda. So "they came to him" (3:13)—not to an institution, not to a movement, but to a person who would capture their hearts, change their lives, and become their reason for being. He became their Savior, their Lord, their friend, their leader—their very life. This was their calling, and to this they responded.

The center of the disciples' call was to companionship with Jesus, but the circumference was a commission to serve the world. They would be given the task of spreading the message of Christ, fired by their personal experience of him, preaching his kingdom in ever widening circles to the ends of the earth (see Matt. 28:18-20; Acts 1:8). This commission was not without cost, however, since many of them died a martyr's death.

Jesus had his crowds, but he worked primarily through a core group. There is fickleness in a crowd, but faithfulness in the core—with the sad exception of Judas Iscariot. There is momentum in a mob that can easily get out of control, while there is drive and direction in a dedicated nucleus that is not easily diverted from its purpose. Where there is no dedicated core, the crowd rules—how unruly! Where there is a committed core, the core controls the action. Jesus showed us that truth and the church dare not forget it! In a world where bigger is often automatically regarded as better, the church should not forget that it is not difficult to attract a crowd of spectators. The real challenge is to call out a core of committed believers.

THE BALANCED LIFE

When Jesus returned to the house where he was staying, the crowds began to gather again, and soon he and his disciples couldn't even find time to eat. . . . [Then Jesus said,] "Anyone who does God's will is my brother and sister and mother."

MARK 3:20, 35

V ince Lombardi, the legendary coach of the Green Bay Packers, once told his players that they should order their lives by establishing the following priorities:

1. God
2. Family
3. Green Bay Packers

Lombardi's priorities are often recounted with great approval, and it is certainly refreshing to hear of a football coach telling professional athletes to "put God first" and to be concerned for their families, when so often the professional athlete shows little regard for his family and less for his Creator. Many men struggle to balance all the demands of work, family, and worship. But I do have a problem with Lombardi's list.

What, I wonder, would have happened if one of the Packers had said to coach Lombardi, "Sorry, coach, that I won't be able to play in the Super Bowl on Sunday. I feel I need to take my family to church. I'm putting God and family ahead of the Packers, like you said!" I suspect that player would not have been a Green Bay Packer for long! Making lists of priorities is commendable, and Lombardi's list is much better than most, but life does not fit so conveniently into compartments. A neatly balanced life is not easily achieved.

Perhaps the desire itself is misplaced. How "balanced" was the life of Jesus and his disciples? We are told that the crowds demanding their attention were so vast and the needs so great that "he and his disciples couldn't even find time to eat" (Mark 3:20). Jesus and his disciples knew the pressure of life. In their case, it was not the pressure to make more money or the pressure to climb to the top of the corporate ladder by sacrificing family and worship on the way. They knew the pressure of being aware of the needs of a crying world and being prepared to address them. This kind of pressure pushes people away from the equilibrium of a neatly balanced life. You miss meals.

Jesus' own family did not approve of his lifestyle. In fact, "they tried to make him come home with them. 'He's out of his mind,' they said" (3:21). The religious leaders went further and attributed his lifestyle to Satan (3:22). This raises another point. Not only were Jesus and his disciples driven by their world's need, they also recognized they were in a spiritual battle for the souls of men and women. Fighting this spiritual battle required more than balance—it took everything they had.

Perhaps the desire for a balanced life is not as balanced as it appears. A little divine imbalance may not be wrong!

TO READ: *Mark 4:1-20*

TELL US A STORY

"Anyone who is willing to hear should listen and understand! . . . 'They see what I do, but they don't perceive its meaning. They hear my words, but they don't understand. So they will not turn from their sins and be forgiven.'"

MARK 4:9, 12

E verybody, young and old, loves a story. My grandchildren have a few favorites that they ask me to tell them over and over again. Like the one about my grandfather who was accused by a neighbor of throwing a brick through his window. He denied it, so his father punished him twice—once for breaking the window and the second time for denying it. There was only one problem: He had not thrown the brick. So, having been punished for what he did not do, he promptly went to the neighbor's house and threw the brick through the window! I have been trying to find the moral of this story for the benefit of my grandchildren, but I'm not sure that I have succeeded!

There is a problem, of course, with repeating the same stories. The hearers can become so acquainted with them, so familiar with their twists and turns, and so aware of their conclusion that the stories lose their impact, even though they are nice to hear. Familiarity seems to deaden the senses, rather like what happens to young people who spend endless hours listening to music played at an alarming decibel level. Their hearing is deadened, and their perceptions are dulled.

When God commissioned Isaiah to go and preach to his people, God gave him the strangest orders. Isaiah was apparently required to proclaim God's message to the people, knowing full well that they would not listen or respond (see Isaiah 6:9-10). It looks at first sight as if God was setting his people up—sending a prophet but knowing full well that they would not pay any attention. But that was not the case. Isaiah preached in unmistakably simple terms, with great passion and concern. God's attempt to reach his people's hearts was genuine. At the same time, God knew in advance how they would respond: their hearts were callused to the message.

When Jesus embarked on his ministry in Galilee he found a similar situation (Mark 4:12). He said that when he preached, it was like a sower sowing seed on hard ground, in shallow soil, or among thorns. The seed did not germinate and reproduce as intended. Only a few seeds fell on good soil and grew to maturity. No wonder Jesus told his hearers, "Anyone who is willing to hear should listen and understand" (4:9).

There is a warning here for those of us who have ample access to God's Word, who have Bibles we can read regularly, who attend services where the word is preached faithfully. We can become so familiar with the message, we can so enjoy the sound of it and bask in the beauty of it, that we become desensitized to the meaning and impact of it.

God's Word is supposed to bring forth abundant fruit, and the harvest of a changed life should be plain to see. If we are willing to hear the story, we should listen and understand.

TO READ: *Mark 4:21-25*

NEVER STOP LEARNING

"To those who are open to my teaching, more understanding will be given. But to those who are not listening, even what they have will be taken away from them."

MARK 4:25

P eople often talk about "where they received their education." They usually mean "where they went to school." Speaking of receiving an education in these terms suggests that an education is complete once graduation has been achieved. It also assumes that while people are in college they are busy being educated, while quite often they have insufficient time to attend classes without interrupting their social life! Peter Drucker, the management expert, said that an educated person is someone who has learned how to learn and never stops learning. Perhaps we should not talk about where we received an education but about how our education is progressing.

This was the thrust of Jesus' teaching about the lamp, the basket, and the bed (Mark 4:21). When a light "comes" into a room it is not promptly placed under a basket or a bed. The purpose of light is to be seen and to make sight possible. To hide a lamp would be counterproductive. It would not only fail in its objective of lighting the room, but the law of unintended consequences would apply: The lamp would light the *house*—on fire!

Jesus' next saying is "Everything that is now hidden or secret will eventually be brought to light" (4:22). This suggests that while the objective of bringing light is not to hide it, that is precisely what happened in his ministry! The hidden things will be revealed, but only to those who take the trouble to listen.

There is no problem in ascertaining what Jesus expected people to listen to and what the secret is that would be revealed: "the secret about the Kingdom of God" (4:11). Jesus was telling his disciples that, in his own coming into the world, there had been a great revelation of God's purposes and his kingdom, but there was still much more to be revealed—the lamp was still under the bucket and the bed. His disciples must constantly be open to new discoveries of his plans and purposes. In other words, they must not stop learning!

Jesus promised, "To those who are open to my teaching, more understanding will be given" (4:25). In other words, those who listen to what Jesus tells them receive even more insight into God's eternal purposes. But Jesus also warned, "To those who are not listening, even what they have will be taken away from them." Those who do not pursue God's self-revelation find the little they had learned slowly disappears.

God has no intention of leaving the message of the kingdom under a bed. He puts it out in the open where Christian disciples never stop learning. And they never graduate.

TO READ: *Mark 4:26-34*

KNOWING YOUR LIMITATIONS

Here is another illustration of what the Kingdom of God is like:
A farmer planted seeds in a field, and then he went on with his other activities.
As the days went by, the seeds sprouted and grew without the farmer's help,
because the earth produces crops on its own.

MARK 4:26-28

A famous organist was visiting a number of small towns giving recitals in the local churches. At each stop he hired the services of a small boy to pump the organ manually. After a highly successful recital, the boy who had been pumping said to the organist, "We had a great recital tonight, didn't we?" The organist replied, "*I* had a great recital. Not we! I! *I* had a great recital tonight!" The following night, halfway through the repeat recital, the organ ceased to function. Then a small face appeared from behind the screen where the pump was. With a grin, the boy announced, "We aren't having such a great recital tonight, are we?" The organist had developed such confidence in his own skills that he had overlooked his dependency and forgotten his limitations.

Jesus made sure that his disciples were aware of their limitations. He spoke about a farmer who sowed his seed and then went on with his normal activities while the seed germinated, developed, and matured—all without his help or even his understanding how the procedure worked! Jesus told his disciples, "As the days went by, the seeds sprouted and grew without the farmer's help, because the earth produces crops on its own" (Mark 4:27-28).

The disciples certainly had a role to play in scattering the seed of the word, but they were totally incapable of producing the lasting effects of the Word in people's lives. Only God can do that. The mysterious power hidden in the most unprepossessing, dry, little seed, when planted in good soil, has the ability to grow and produce in remarkable ways. Even in our enlightened scientific world there are still great mysteries about life that the finest brains have not fathomed. That is how it is with the work of God's kingdom, too. God's people must recognize what they are called to do—and do it. Then they must depend upon God to do what only he can do. And he will.

There's something wonderfully humbling about knowing your limitations—and liberating, too. Once the disciples had presented the message, they were free from responsibility for the response of the hearers. They had to plant the seed, but they didn't have to make the seed grow. And they could watch with amazement as it did.

One word of caution is in order. The farmer, despite his limitations, was still called upon to put in the sickle and harvest the crop (4:29). Knowing your limitations is no excuse for laziness. Knowing what you cannot do does not allow you to fail to do what you are called to do!

TO READ: *Psalm 85*

LISTEN CAREFULLY

I listen carefully to what God the LORD is saying, for he speaks peace to his people, his faithful ones. But let them not return to their foolish ways.

PSALM 85:8

W illiam Wordsworth, in his poem "The Excursion," talked about meeting a small boy holding to his ear a seashell "to which, in silence hushed, his very soul listened intensely." Even though the boy lived far from the sea, as he listened he "heard murmurings" which "expressed mysterious union" with the ocean. As a result "his countenance soon brightened with joy."

Getting some boys to listen to anything, whether intensely or otherwise, is a challenge. Activity, rather than contemplation, is their rhythm. And yet if they could be persuaded to, as the railway crossing signs command, "Stop, Look, Listen," they would be surprised by what they heard.

Men, like small boys, also find it hard to stop, look, and listen. We don't like to stop what we're doing—we think it wastes time. We don't find it necessary to look—we think we already know. We find it difficult to listen because as another speaks, we are formulating a rebuttal. But failure to listen intensely can mean missing the message entirely, or it can lead to hearing the message only partially. To miss the message entirely means living in ignorance; to grasp it only partially can mean living with confusion.

The psalm writer, on the other hand, had decided to "listen carefully to what the Lord is saying," because he had learned that the Lord "speaks peace to his people, his faithful ones" (Ps. 85:8). In those days, the Lord spoke directly and powerfully through the prophets who had responded to his call to "listen carefully" to the message God was delivering to them. Then they had to get the message across. But it was a difficult task. The people either didn't listen or they listened only halfheartedly, and they ignored the warnings, predictions, pleadings, and promises of the prophets. Because they did so, disaster overtook them. They had lived in such turmoil that their question to God was, "Will you be angry with us always? Will you prolong your wrath to distant generations?" (85:5). Those who had taken the trouble to listen had learned that God's "salvation is near to those who honor him" (85:9). They knew about unfailing love, truth, righteousness, and peace—"the amazing blessings" (85:1) which the Lord delighted to pour out on his people. But they also knew better than "to return to their foolish ways" (85:8).

Men today have the Bible, godly preachers, and gifted authors on every hand speaking God's message. If these men will try listening attentively to what God is saying, they will find that he is still offering "peace" and warning against "foolish ways." And, like small boys with sea shells, their countenances will be "brightened with joy."

TO READ: *Isaiah 29:1-14*

THE CITY OF DAVID

"These people say they are mine. They honor me with their lips, but their hearts are
far away. And their worship of me amounts to nothing more
than human laws learned by rote."

ISAIAH 29:13

"T he house that Ruth built" is Yankee Stadium in New York city. Babe Ruth was neither the architect who designed the imposing structure nor the contractor who built it. But his baseball exploits put the stadium on the map. Not that the fans entering "the house that Ruth built" talk about New York City. It's "The Big Apple." In the same way, New Orleans is "The Big Easy" and London, England, is "the Smoke."

"The City of David," as every Old Testament scholar knows, is Jerusalem. But King David didn't design or found the city. The Jebusites did that before Israel arrived from Egypt. But David conquered them, occupied the city, and put Jerusalem on the front pages of history (see 2 Sam. 5:6-7).

In keeping with the tendency to give major cities nicknames, Isaiah called Jerusalem, the City of David, "Ariel." He explained that Ariel means "an altar covered with blood" (Isa. 29:2)—certainly an odd name for a city!

In the temple, the altar was a constant reminder of the need for sin to be confessed and dealt with by sacrifice—a clear pointer to the eventual death of Christ as a sacrifice for our sin. But the altar was also a continual source of encouragement because it spoke of divine forgiveness and restoration. In the same way "Ariel"—that is, Jerusalem—would be a historical reminder of both divine judgment and heavenly restoration.

Unfortunately, the people of Jerusalem in Isaiah's time had rejected the Lord's constant reminders of their sin and his offers of forgiveness for so long that they had become stupefied. You can only reject truth for so long before you become hardened and blinded to it. "Ariel" was about to see the judgment of God, yet it was in no mood to welcome the forgiveness of God. The promises of God were "a sealed book to them" (29:11). They continued with their worship activities but they were "nothing more than human laws learned by rote" (29:13). The people of Jerusalem were practicing religious rites devoid of reality, and they were professing a faith without performing it. The Lord complained, "They honor me with their lips, but their hearts are far away" (29:13).

The judgment promised for Jerusalem finally came, but the promised blessing came, too. Seven hundred years after Isaiah, the angels announced Christ's birth "in Bethlehem, the city of David!" (Luke 2:11). Bethlehem was the "city of David." It was there that David had been born and there that, in Christ's coming, hope for promised blessings was born anew.

QUIETNESS AND CONFIDENCE

The Sovereign LORD, *the Holy One of Israel, says, "Only in returning to me and waiting for me will you be saved. In quietness and confidence is your strength. But you would have none of it."*

ISAIAH 30:15

When activists see that something needs fixing, they fix it. They see a problem, identify a solution, establish a strategic plan, create a budget and goals, and move into action. Obstacles are defined as problems to be solved and problems are seen as opportunities. The can-do spirit reigns, and optimism is the only legitimate attitude. In less time than it actually takes, everything will be on track.

Jerusalem in Isaiah's time had its share of activists. The problem was a man called Sennacherib who had a mighty Assyrian army at his disposal. And Jerusalem was in his sights! The solution to the problem was the amassing of enough power to counter the Assyrians. The Egyptians were close at hand, and a strategic alliance with them was suggested. This would be costly, but pack animals could be sent immediately with the necessary bribes and gifts (Isa. 30:6-7). If Egypt could be counted on to cooperate, the problem was solved. No problem!

Meanwhile, back in Jerusalem, Isaiah was holding forth! Isaiah was convinced that Egypt was worthless as a source of help—a "Harmless Dragon" with big teeth but no bite. Isaiah warned that sending ambassadors with pack animals loaded with gifts was a waste of time and money and that, if Judah persisted in this "solution," it was only a matter of time until everything would collapse "like a bulging wall that bursts and falls" (30:13). Isaiah's strategic plan, by contrast, was very simple. He had received it from the Lord, who said, "Only in returning to me and waiting for me will you be saved. In quietness and confidence is your strength" (30:15).

Activists do not see the wisdom of "quietness and confidence." Their doctrine is, "God helps those who help themselves," even though they are usually so confident in their own abilities that the help of God is rarely seen as significant unless things get really out of hand! The Jerusalem activists were not at all responsive! "Shut up! We don't want any more of your reports," they shouted at Isaiah (30:10). They added, "We have heard more than enough about your 'Holy One of Israel.' We are tired of listening to what he has to say" (30:11).

Is any of this relevant? The Lord certainly thought so, because he told Isaiah, "Write down these words concerning Egypt. They will then stand until the end of time as a witness" (30:8). In other words, look at what eventually happened to Jerusalem, as Isaiah said it would, and learn the lesson which applies "to the end of time."

The lesson is this: In every situation, turn to the Lord, quietly and confidently, and expect him to work! And he will!

TO READ: *Luke 12:35-48*

ACCOUNTABILITY

But people who are not aware that they are doing wrong will be punished only lightly.
Much is required from those to whom much is given, and much more
is required from those to whom much more is given.

LUKE 12:48

I n the so-called "Gender Wars," some women have made harsh statements about men, and the men have not exactly taken it lying down! Having said that, both sides did get some things right. For instance, the women who said that men needed to "get in touch with their feminine side" were making a fair point, even though they went overboard in making it. Men do need to recognize that masculinity is not all about muscular machos making mayhem. Men can and should be gentle and considerate! The women also said that men should stop being cowboys and lone rangers, and that they should be willing to be vulnerable enough to make intimate friendships—even to be accountable to others for their actions! Vulnerability, gentleness, consideration, and accountability are not purely feminine traits, though. They are masculine traits as well.

During his earthly ministry, Jesus referred to accountability more than once. He predicted both his departure to his Father and his coming again to establish his eternal kingdom. Using the analogy of a rich landowner who had gone away, leaving his affairs in the care of a trusted servant, Jesus said his disciples were his servants and, like the landowner, he would return and evaluate their lives. Jesus' coming again would not be advertised in advance any more than a thief would advertise his arrival to divest an owner of his property. It was incumbent on the servant to be ready. Jesus explained, "Be dressed for service and well prepared, as though you were waiting for your master to return from the wedding feast" (Luke 12:35-36).

The thought of being held accountable by their master is a challenge to Christ's disciples. It serves as a powerful motivating factor. But it is not designed to strike fear into their hearts. The Lord said standards of evaluation would be based on opportunities presented and responses to opportunity. Using dramatic hyperbolic language, Jesus described the lot of the servants who blatantly abuse their positions (12:46-47). He also explained, "Much is required from those to whom much is given, and much more is required from those to whom much more is given" (12:48).

That raises a question: How much is much and how much more is much more? Perhaps the answer is found in the Lord's description of the kind of servant he is looking for. He had in mind a "faithful, sensible servant" (12:42)—"faithful" in the steady, consistent fulfilling of duties and obligations with joy and delight; and "sensible" in that the servant is very much aware of the impact of grace, the bestowal of privilege, and the embracing of opportunity.

Faithful, sensible servants have nothing to fear—their Lord is faithful and sensible, too!

HEROES AND CELEBRITIES

Look, a righteous king is coming! And honest princes will rule under him. . . .
In that day ungodly fools will not be heroes. Wealthy cheaters will not be respected
as outstanding citizens. Everyone will recognize ungodly fools for what they are.

ISAIAH 32:1, 5-6A

W here have all the heroes gone? What happened to the Lincolns and the
Washingtons, the Roosevelts and the Churchills? Where are men of courage,
principle, and integrity, who operate with vision, drive, and initiative, and whose
achievements are plain to see, beneficial, and far-reaching? What happened to the great
athletes who played through their pain, who believed they were role models to the young,
and who invested their lives in their communities, playing for one team all their careers?
People talk about the death of God. But what about the death of heroes?

Os Guinness, in his book *The Call,* cites three reasons for the conspicuous absence of
heroes. First, we live in a cynical age that respects nothing and reveres nobody. Guinness
wrote, "As modern people, we look not for the golden aura but for the feet of clay, not for
the stirring example but for the cynical motive."[4] Second, we see fewer heroes for the very
simple reason that there aren't as many around! We have traded heroes for celebrities. As
everybody knows, celebrities are just people who are famous for being well-known. It is not
that they have achieved anything of profound significance or have invested their lives in
some noble venture that will change the lot of humanity for the better. They just happened
to be around doing something when the lights came on and the cameras started to roll.
Third, we are lacking in heroes because we have lost sight of God as an active participant in
human lives. So we lack the ability to see God calling men to live for him and his cause,
which transcends anything humans can envisage. Having such a calling gave men's lives
grandeur and nobility of purpose, with the result that many became true heroes.

In Isaiah's time it wasn't so much that they lacked heroes. It was a matter of the
people regarding "ungodly fools" as heroes. Perhaps that is nearer the truth of the
situation in our culture. There is no shortage of celebrities who are considered "heroes,"
whose words are recorded with awe and whose actions are followed with slavish devotion.
It is just that so many of them are such incredibly ungodly fools! And people haven't
realized it yet!

The prophet looked forward to a day in the future when "ungodly fools will no
longer be heroes. Wealthy cheaters will not be respected as outstanding citizens" (Isa.
32:5). It would be a time when their society would be turned right side up! Good would
be recognized as good and evil as evil, and foolishness would be recognized as foolishness
and accomplishment as accomplishment.

That day will finally come when the "Righteous King" (32:1) arrives to establish his
kingdom. In the interim, God's people need to recognize that in today's world, any fool
can become a "hero," but in God's economy a real hero is no fool!

---

[4] Os Guinness, *The Call.*

TO READ: *Jeremiah 23:23-32*

DREAM AND DREAMERS

"Let these false prophets tell their dreams, but let my true messengers faithfully proclaim my every word. There is a difference between chaff and wheat!"

JEREMIAH 23:28

A young man was preparing to assist missionaries in Europe. Shortly before he was due to leave for his assignment, he had a dream so vivid that he could describe it in detail. He had seen a beach with a boat drawn up on the sand and a young man sitting in the shade of the boat. The dreamer was so impressed that he felt constrained to change his plans and spend the summer in another country. This he did, and one day that summer he came across a beach that he recognized as the one in his dream. There on the beach was the boat and the young man who was in his dream. They engaged in conversation. The young man by the boat asked questions concerning spiritual matters and that day professed faith in Christ. The last report of him was that he was actively involved in a local fellowship of believers. God can and does communicate to us in dreams!

But beware! Jeremiah knew only too well that dreamers who profess to have a message from the Lord should not necessarily be accepted at face value. There are some who claim to have a message from God who, in actuality, have no such thing. Instead, they are seeking to authenticate their own imaginations and investing their own ideas with divine sanction. If we believe the fabrications, it can result in profound spiritual confusion when it is later discovered that they were lies.

The problem is, how do you differentiate between a genuine, revealed message from God and the product of a wicked or vain imagination? The key is to test what is said against Scripture. Jeremiah was told by the Lord, "Let these false prophets tell their dreams, but let my true messengers faithfully proclaim my every word. There is a difference between chaff and wheat" (Jer. 23:28).

The more familiar we are with what God has to say in the Bible, the less likelihood there will be of our being led astray by "smooth-tongued prophets" (23:31). Once you've tasted wheat, you'll quickly recognize chaff. (Once you've tasted corn, you'll quickly recognize the cob!) Carefully studying Scripture and deliberately applying its truths to our lives may seem unglamorous and mundane compared to receiving dramatic revelations and making imaginative predictions. But there are enough warnings in Scripture about false prophets, their lies, and their ultimate fate (23:39-40) to put us constantly on guard.

The Scriptures are so powerful and winsome, so life-giving and refreshing that we will relish them as the staple diet for spiritual nourishment. And should the Lord on occasion give a special dream—that's dessert!

TO READ: *Malachi 2:1-12*

THE CALL
TO FAITHFULNESS

*"The priests' lips should guard knowledge, and people should go to them for
instruction, for the priests are the messengers of the LORD Almighty. But not you!
You have left God's paths. Your 'guidance' has caused many to stumble into sin. You
have corrupted the covenant I made with the Levites," says the LORD Almighty.*

MALACHI 2:7-8

The only mutiny in the long, illustrious history of England's Royal Navy took place in
1933. The seamen's wages had been cut in a desperate political move to head off the
effects of the nationwide depression. In retaliation, the seamen attacked their officers. But the
men of the Royal Marines defended their officers against the rest of the crew. As a result, to
this day the Marines are quartered on board ship between the officers and the crew, to act as
the officers' guards and to maintain the security of the ship. In Britain's navy today, this is
mainly symbolic, but it symbolizes a reward for faithfulness. It is a source of pride and a
great factor in the unusual *esprit de corps* of the Royal Marines.

When King David's son Absalom staged a mutiny against his father, many of the king's
men went over to the side of the young revolutionary. But Zadok the priest remained faithful
and protected the king (see 2 Sam. 15:1-37). As a result, he and his descendants were
rewarded by being appointed as the priests in Jerusalem right up through the time of the
Exile (see Ezek. 44:15ff). No doubt they accepted this position with great pride and, as
faithful men, they endeavored to fulfill their roles.

It comes as a great surprise, therefore, to read what Malachi had to say about the
priests in his day, after Israel returned from exile. He reminded the priests of their
privileged position and their profound responsibilities. They had been called to greatly
reverence the Lord, to stand "in awe" of him, to pass on to the people "all the truth they
received," to live "good and righteous lives" before the people, and to turn "many from
lives of sin." They were called "to guard knowledge" and to function as "messengers of the
Lord Almighty" (Mal. 2:5-7).

But something had gone wrong. They had "corrupted the covenant" (2:8), they had
failed to live in obedience, and they had "shown partiality in [their] interpretation of the
law" (2:9). As a result, their "'guidance' [had] caused many to stumble into sin" (2:8). This
was a monumental disaster for Israel, and God did not treat it lightly. The faithful men
had become unfaithful.

Peter wrote that Christians are now "a kingdom of priests" (1 Pet. 2:9). That means
that we have access to the Father through the Son, that we should offer sacrifices to God
consisting of praise, and that we are called to live in a manner befitting our high standing.
This requires faithfulness—like Marines standing at their posts.

TO READ: *Psalm 77*

A PATH NOT KNOWN

Your road led through the sea, your pathway through the mighty waters—
a pathway no one knew was there!

PSALM 77:19

A dolf Hitler believed that the European Jews were diabolical, that they were evil incarnate, part of a great conspiracy behind all the troubles of Europe. So he planned their extermination. He called it the "Final Solution." At first the Jews were rounded up into labor camps where they were systematically starved and worked to death. The archway over the entrance to the infamous Auschwitz camp bore the words "Arbeit Machts Frei"—"Work makes free." But in Nazi code "makes free" meant "kills." As the Allied forces were strengthened by the entrance of the United States of America into the War, the Nazis realized that they were facing possible defeat. So they expedited the killings by herding the Jews into gas chambers. It is estimated that 67% of European Jews were exterminated by the Nazis.

Still, many escaped through the help of a network of incredibly brave, committed individuals who managed to whisk the terrified Jews to safety. They were hidden under the noses of the Nazis and then, under cover of darkness, they were led along highways and byways known only to the rescuers, from one safe house to another, until finally they reached safety.

Psalm 77 was written by Asaph in the depths of despair. He couldn't sleep, and he couldn't pray. He couldn't get a response from God; he couldn't get answers to his questions. He even came to the conclusion that it was his fate "that the blessings of the most High have changed to hatred" (Ps. 77:10). But then he recalled the great events of Jewish history. And no Jew of his time would think on such matters without contemplating the Exodus from Egypt and the miraculous escape through the Red Sea. Asaph remembered, "Your road led through the sea, your pathway through the mighty waters—a pathway no one knew was there!" (77:19).

It is always good for the Lord's people in all situations to remember that, when the night is dark and all hope is lost, God knows a path of rescue and mercy that no one else knows is there. Many of God's people have lived in less dramatic circumstances than those marching through the waters of the Red Sea or the terrors of the Holocaust. They can testify to having been led through the dangers and the despair by the unerring hand of God. Always, when God is leading, the path not known leads eventually to the safe house of his loving embrace.

TO READ: *Luke 1:5-25*

ONCE IN A LIFETIME

*But the angel said, "Don't be afraid, Zechariah! For God has heard your prayer,
and your wife, Elizabeth, will bear you a son! And you are to name him John. . . .
He will precede the coming of the Lord, preparing the people for his arrival."*

LUKE 1:13, 17B

Most people never get to meet the President or the Queen. Most athletes never make it to the Super Bowl, the World Cup Final, the Wimbledon Championship, or the Olympics. Should they be fortunate enough to receive that kind of opportunity, they savor it, for they know it may be a once-in-a-lifetime experience.

Zechariah the priest had one of those experiences when he was picked to burn incense on the altar in Jerusalem's temple. There were approximately eight thousand priests in Israel at the time. They were divided into "divisions" that rotated the duties of the Temple, including the burning of incense morning and evening—part of a tradition dating back to the days of Aaron, the first high priest (see Exod. 30:7-8). Individual priests were chosen out of the division by casting lots. One day, old Zechariah's name was called for this most sacred of tasks. It was his once-in-a-lifetime opportunity. No doubt Zechariah entered the holy place with a mix of exhilaration and trepidation. He was part of a venerable tradition, and he was as close to the Holy of Holies as any man other than the High Priest would ever be allowed to go. The awesomeness of God's presence would be well nigh overpowering for him. And then it happened!

The angel Gabriel met him beside the altar and said, "God has heard your prayer" (Luke 1:13). Zechariah could have been forgiven if he had asked "Which prayer?" but immediately he was told about the impending birth of a son in his old age. Now a once-in-a-lifetime experience had suddenly turned into a once-in-a-hundred-lifetimes experience! This son's dramatic birth was only the prelude to a dramatic life devoted to a ministry which would "make ready a people prepared for the Lord" (1:17).

Zechariah asked what probably seem to us to be perfectly understandable questions, but the angel interpreted them as evidence of unbelief (1:18-21)! Then he was made mute, presumably so that he could not express his unbelief until it was obvious that God had done what he had promised to do.

Most people haven't seen angels—or at least they haven't recognized them as such. And most have not received as direct a message from the Lord as did Zechariah. But all God's people have been called to a relationship with the Lord and to an avenue of service for him. For some, the experience was dramatic and unforgettable; for others, less so. But for all it is a once-in-a-lifetime experience, never to be forgotten, always to be cherished.

TO READ: *Luke 1:26-38*

OMNIPOTENCE

Nothing is impossible with God.

LUKE 1:37

D uring World War II, England's Royal Navy commissioned three aircraft carriers called the "Illustrious" (renowned), the "Indefatigable" (tireless), and the "Indomitable" (unconquerable). Difficult as the names were, it is not difficult to catch the spirit behind them. These were the brave words the Royal Navy used to describe her pride and tradition even in the darkest days of the War.

Theologians use a trio of similarly difficult but noble words to describe God. They talk about him being omnipotent (all-powerful), omniscient (all-knowing), and omnipresent (everywhere present).

In a startling conversation with Abraham, God claimed to be all-powerful. He announced, "About this time next year I will return, and your wife Sarah will have a son" (Gen. 18:10). We don't know how Abraham reacted, but Sarah simply laughed at the ludicrous idea, because both she and her husband were well past childbearing age. Reading Sarah's unspoken thoughts, God challenged the old man: "Why did she say, 'Can an old woman like me have a baby?' Is anything too hard for the Lord?" (Gen. 18:13-14). The implied answer: No, nothing is too hard for the Lord. God was affirming his omnipotence.

A similar message was delivered loud and clear to a young woman called Mary in the city of Nazareth centuries later. She, too, was startled to hear the news. But there was a difference. Sarah reacted because of her antiquity, Mary because of her virginity! Mary's questions were answered by the firm assuring statement, "Nothing is impossible with God" (Luke 1:37).

The doctrine of divine omnipotence is not without its perplexities. Some people say, "If God was omnipotent he could destroy all evil. He doesn't, so he must be either impotent or immoral." And others wonder if the Bible is not contradicting itself when it says, on the one hand, "nothing is impossible with God," but on the other hand, that it is impossible for him to lie (Heb. 6:18).

The statements to Sarah and Mary about divine omnipotence need to be seen in the context of the divine will. God was stating that nothing would hinder him from doing what he willed to do. And they needed to believe it!

There is a great challenge and wonderful comfort in these words. The challenge lies in the fact that resistance to God is little short of suicidal. The comfort inherent in God's omnipotence means that he will come through in the end. Like a majestic ship sailing through storm, tempest, and battle, God is Illustrious, Indefatigable, Indomitable—and Omnipotent!

TO READ: *Luke 1:38-45*

BELIEVING AND BLESSED

"You are blessed, because you believed that the Lord would do what he said."

LUKE 1:45

T he emperor Constantine chose as a tutor for his son a learned man named Lactantius. Lactantius said this about the idea that the earth is not flat:

> *Is there any one so senseless as to believe that there are men whose footsteps are higher than their heads? or that the things which with us are in a recumbent position, with them hang in an inverted direction? that the crops and trees grow downwards? that the rains, and snow, and hail fall upwards to the earth? And does any one wonder that hanging gardens are mentioned among the seven wonders of the world, when philosophers make hanging fields, and seas, and cities, and mountains? The origin of this error must also be set forth by us.[5]*

Clearly, geography was Lactantius's weakest subject! That the earth was flat was an article of faith in those days, and it was a long time before some intrepid men believed otherwise. Those who did believe set sail, and they discovered the bounty of an undiscovered world. They believed and were blessed.

Zechariah had difficulty believing his aged wife would conceive, and he was struck with silence until the promised child was born. But when Mary was told that she, even though a virgin, would bear a son, her response was, "I am the Lord's servant and I am willing to accept whatever he wants" (Luke 1:38). Mary's faith was no doubt strengthened by the knowledge of Elizabeth's pregnancy, and she went to visit her friend. In some remarkable way, Elizabeth's baby *in utero* leaped for joy when he recognized the arrival of Mary and the significance of the baby she carried. Elizabeth said to Mary, "You are blessed, because you believed that the Lord would do what he said" (1:45). Mary, like the explorers of the new world, believed and was blessed.

Of course, there is a major difference between believing in a hunch and believing in God's Word. And there is little similarity between believing a scientifically proven hypothesis and trusting a God-given promise. Yet that is what God calls his people to do. To the extent that we believe God, we experience the blessings of his promises.

The belief of the global circumnavigators required purchasing ships, fitting them out, recruiting a crew, and setting sail in a westerly direction with a view to arriving in the east! It was nothing short of lunacy to many of their friends and foes! But they were right. And they were blessed!

Men who wish to know the blessing of God need to believe what they profess to believe, trim their sails, and set out on a voyage of discovery. Should they feel a failure of nerve, the young woman of Nazareth may offer a role model!

---

[5] Lactantius, *Divine Institutes*, Book III, Chapter 24.

TO READ: *Luke 1:46–56*

THE HOLY
AND THE LOWLY

How I rejoice in God my Savior! For he took notice of his lowly servant girl. . . .
For he, the Mighty One, is holy, and he has done great things for me.

LUKE 1:47-49

Modern society rewards its celebrities handsomely. They are welcome in the best hotels, and they are forgiven the worst behavior. The longest limousines await them, the shortest waiting lines confront them, and the fattest bank accounts provide for them. Their fans press to intercept them, and the media mass to interview them. Young people imitate them, while older people tolerate them. Fame and fortune are lavished upon them, but maturity and responsibility are not expected of them. They live charmed lives—if not always charming, they become accustomed to enjoying life's luxuries and unaccustomed to dealing with life's necessities. For many of their admirers, their status is something to be aspired to, and their exalted position something to be longed for.

Mary, the mother of Jesus, is known the world over. She has been the model for a million works of art, the topic of theological debates, the subject of encyclicals, the object of veneration. Dogmas have been attached to her, superstitions and mystical beliefs have clustered around her. But how did she view herself?

Her song of praise was directed away from herself. The topic of her heart was "Oh how I praise the Lord. How I rejoice in God my Savior!" (Luke 1:46-47). The reason for her adoration was this: "For he took notice of his lowly servant girl" (v. 48). She had no illusions about herself and no confusion about the Lord: "He, the Mighty One, is holy," she affirmed (1:49). The Holy One had taken note of the lowly one. She interpreted the "great things" he had done for her in the context of something far greater and grander than her own interests. She knew it had to do with his mercy extended "from generation to generation" (1:50)—what he had done for her he had done for "his servant Israel," in accord with what he had promised (1:54).

There was no trace of haughtiness in Mary. Her only claim to fame was that the Lord had "exalted the lowly" (1:52). Mary had no room for self-congratulation, because she knew that the Lord "scatters the proud and haughty ones" (1:51). She had no reservation in praising the Holy One and no desire to see herself other than as a blessed lowly one.

How sobering it is to realize that the Lord takes notice of the "lowly" and that it is the "hungry" who are satisfied with good things from his hand. How sad it is to think that the Lord will send "away with empty hands" many of today's "rich" (1:53). Better to be a lowly one before the Holy One!

TO READ: *Luke 1:57–66*

FAMILY PRESSURE

He motioned for a writing tablet, and to everyone's surprise he wrote,
"His name is John!"

LUKE 1:63

O n Thanksgiving Day, 1999, the crew of a Florida fishing boat plucked 6-year-old Elian Gonzalez from the Atlantic Ocean. The Cuban child was lashed to an inner tube on which he had floated for two days. The small boat in which he and thirteen other people were trying to escape from Cuba had capsized, and Elian's mother and ten others had perished in the ocean. Once on dry land and cared for by relatives in Miami, Elian's problems seemed to be over. But he soon became the key person in a massive tug-of-war that started between his father, who wanted him returned to him in Cuba, and his Cuban-American family members in Florida, who insisted that, as his mother obviously had wished him to live in America, he should be allowed to stay. Elian's welfare sparked an international incident. Presidents became involved, flag-waving patriots demonstrated, politicians postured, and Elian learned how to wear a baseball cap backwards. Fortunately, not all family disagreements reach such proportions!

Centuries-old tradition required that Zechariah and Elizabeth's newborn son should be circumcised as evidence that he had been introduced into the privileges and responsibilities of God's covenant with his people, and the family happily gathered to witness the event (Luke 1:59). But trouble started when the topic of the boy's name was introduced. The family insisted that he should be named after his father, Zechariah, who unfortunately had lost his voice during the spiritual encounter in which the announcement of the boy's birth was made (1:8-20).

To everyone's surprise, Elizabeth insisted that the boy should be called John, and his father wrote his agreement on a tablet (1:63). And so it was, for this is what the angelic messenger had instructed (1:13).

John means "God has shown favor." The significance of the unusual name, the remarkable circumstances of John's birth, and the instantaneous recovery of his father's voice were not lost on the family. They recognized something big was in the air, and so they asked, "I wonder what this child will turn out to be?" (1:66). What John turned out to be is history, but his parents' courage and commitment to follow divine instructions played a major role in John's development.

Parents should never underestimate the importance of their obedience to the Lord in the training and development of their children. Sometimes this requires taking a stand even against loved ones. What matters in the long term is not keeping the family happy but ensuring that the child knows that "the hand of the Lord is surely upon him" (1:66).

TO READ: *Luke 1:67–80*

FATHER AND SON

*"And you, my little son, will be called the prophet of the Most High,
because you will prepare the way for the Lord. You will tell his people
how to find salvation through forgiveness of their sins."*

LUKE 1:76-77

S tock car racing is one of the major spectator sports in America. But it was born in the days of Prohibition, when the bootleggers, in order to deliver their illicit liquor to the speakeasies, "souped up" the engines of their cars so that they could outrun the police. When the need for such vehicles vanished with the repeal of Prohibition in 1933, the hot rods were raced on the sands of Florida, and eventually NASCAR was born. Some of today's superstar racers are the grandsons of the drivers who outran the police years ago. Paternal influence is more significant than we sometimes realize.

Wise fathers believe that the Lord has a plan for their boys and that their parental role is to help the boys discover and do it. This was Zechariah's approach to his "little son" John. Speaking under the prompting of the Holy Spirit, Zechariah prophesied that John would "prepare the way for the Lord" and "tell his people how to find salvation through the forgiveness of their sins" (Luke 1:76-77). He saw the role that John was to play as only one part of a colossal plan that was born in the days of Abraham (1:73). This plan could only be described adequately as "the light from heaven is about to break upon us" (1:78).

If a father believes that his parental role has been fulfilled once he provides a roof over the child's head, puts food in his stomach, and gets him through school while watching most of his ball games, that father should reconsider. The child, from the divine perspective, is part of a grand plan in which the father has an important role. A father's life is to be lived with due consideration being given not only to temporal and material dimensions of human existence, but also to eternal and spiritual aspects, which not only serve to form the character of the young person but also make an impact on others for their eternal good.

Clearly, not everybody is a John and not every father has Zechariah's prophetic gift. But by the same token, no son is purely a creature of time and space, and no father is only a provider of material substance. Fathers are called to be involved in the lives of their children, to "bring them up with the discipline and instruction approved by the Lord" (Eph. 6:4). This may not mean putting them behind the wheel of a very fast NASCAR race car, but it will involve putting them on the road to a very full life.

TO READ: *Psalm 89*

THE THRONE

"I will establish your descendants as kings forever;
they will sit on your throne from now until eternity."

PSALM 89:4

In the year 1215, King John of England traveled outside London to Runnymede, on the banks of the River Thames, and signed the Magna Carta. He had to! His barons had told him that if he did not sign, he would be in big trouble. They were tired of his heavy taxes, his ineffective leadership, and his less than spectacular rule. So they forced him to sign. In doing so, King John severely curtailed the traditional powers of the monarchy. Many people date monarchical decline from 1215.

Political systems now favor democracies over monarchies. Given the abuses of power by the latter, there is much to be said for the former. But as thrones and empires have been toppled, respect for the majestic has all but disappeared. This may not be politically significant, but it does have spiritual implications.

In the days of the Old Testament, kings were anointed by prophets and the trappings of their reign and the splendor of their person were often seen as reflections of the glory of the Lord. Even the extravagance of their palaces, their vestments, and their inordinate wealth were regarded as evidence of divine favor. The queen of Sheba was overwhelmed by Solomon's splendor. He had built for himself "a huge ivory throne and overlaid it with pure gold. . . . No other throne in all the world could be compared with it" (2 Chron. 9:17-19). From this splendid platform, Solomon ruled his vast empire. He was powerful, splendid, and majestic.

Solomon's reign, part of David's dynasty, came to an end. His throne is lost, and his empire has long been divided. But God's throne is "founded on two strong pillars—righteousness and justice" (Ps. 89:14), and he promised King David, "I will establish your descendants as kings forever; they will sit on your throne from now until eternity" (89:4).

When David's dynasty collapsed, was the promise rendered null and void? Not at all! Hundreds of years later, a humble girl in Nazareth was told by an angel, "You will become pregnant and have a son, and you are to name him Jesus. . . . The Lord God will give him the throne of his ancestor David. And he will reign over Israel forever; his Kingdom will never end!" (Luke 1:31-33). One day, Mary's son Jesus will sit on his everlasting throne in his eternal kingdom. Unlike Solomon's throne, we do not know what Jesus' throne is made of—but we do know that it is majestic! Even more important, though, is the one sitting on the throne—he will be the focus of attention! He will be marvelous, majestic, and magnificent. And we will be overwhelmed with the glory and the majesty (see Rev. 4).

TO READ: *Luke 2:1-20*

SIT AND THINK

But Mary quietly treasured these things in her heart and thought about them often.

LUKE 2:19

A farmer's wife, concerned about the young man who worked out in the fields, asked him, "What do you do in your spare time, John?" He thought for a moment and replied, "Sometimes I sits and thinks, and other times I just sits!" This incident occurred long before the advent of television. Had the young man lived in the television age, he might have become an accomplished "couch potato." Few things in the modern world are more effectively designed than the TV to pass the time without the achievement of anything while cramming the mind with emptiness.

But there is a place for quietness. Silence and solitude are great blessings to the overwrought human soul. And they are rare commodities! Blaise Pascal, the brilliant French scientist and philosopher, observed, "I have discovered that all the unhappiness of men arises from one single fact, that they cannot stay quietly in their own chamber."[6]

Mary, however, knew how to stay quietly in her own room. She and Joseph traveled to Bethlehem for the census that Caesar had ordered. So did everybody else whose family came from that town. As a result, there was no room in the inn, so Joseph and Mary camped out in a stable. There she gave birth to a boy and was visited by a group of rowdy shepherds who brought stories of vast angelic choirs in the vicinity. The story attracted great attention from the crowds in Bethlehem, and all the people were astonished. The town was in a state of excitement and wonder. Yet Mary found silence and solitude. She "quietly treasured these things in her heart and thought about them often" (Luke 2:19).

Blaise Pascal would have approved. And no doubt the Lord did, too. Mary was probably limited in what she could do by her new duties as a mother and by the aftermath of the birth. But she could have just sat there—staring, dazed and blank—her mind crammed with emptiness. She resisted that impulse. Mary didn't just sit—she sat and thought!

And what momentous topics filled her heart! The shepherds had given her all the details and these she "quietly treasured." She treasured thoughts about the child, the angels, the Messiah, the Lord, peace on earth, the favor of God (vv. 11-14), and her own role in these momentous events.

There's a place for silence and solitude. Search for it. When you find it, don't just sit—sit and think. Think about such things as Mary thought. You'll find treasures for your heart.

[6] Blaise Pascal, *Pensées.*

TO READ: *Hebrews 2:5–15*

A PERFECT LEADER

It was only right that God—who made everything and for whom everything was made—should bring his many children into glory. Through the suffering of Jesus, God made him a perfect leader, one fit to bring them into their salvation.

HEBREWS 2:10

After Nazi Germany surrendered in 1945, the war in Europe came to an end amid scenes of well-earned jubilation. Shortly thereafter, a general election was held in the United Kingdom. Winston Churchill and his Conservative party were roundly defeated in that election—Churchill was ousted from office. Given his exemplary leadership during the war, Churchill's defeat was a stunning reversal. Many in the British electorate had been swayed by a cartoon in one of the major newspapers which showed a pistol with a finger on the trigger and the caption, "Whose finger on the trigger?" The unmistakable inference people drew was that Churchill was a great wartime leader but he could not lead in peacetime. The man in the street was saying, "Don't put Winnie back in power. He'll get us into another war." He was seen as the perfect leader for war but not for peace. They may have been right, because the demands on a leader vary according to circumstances. A lot depends on who is being led and what they are being led into.

"God—who made everything and for whom everything was made—" saw his creation ruined by the Fall (see Gen. 3). He determined, nevertheless, that he should "bring his many children into glory" (Heb. 2:10). Doing so involved dealing with their sin, defeating the awesome power of the devil, and leading people into eternal salvation. For that, "a perfect leader" was needed.

For these objectives to be achieved, a perfect sacrifice for sins had to be made. So a leader without blemish, with all the necessary attributes of leadership, who was willing to suffer death for us (2:9), had to be found. Jesus, the perfect Son of God, was the one. It was necessary that he "became flesh and blood by being born in human form. For only as a human being could he die, and only by dying could he break the power of the Devil who had the power of death" (2:14). This is why Jesus was born. "Only in this way could he deliver those who have lived all their lives as slaves to the fear of dying" (2:15).

Churchill was regarded by many as a perfect leader for wartime but not for times of peace. But Jesus was a perfect leader for all time. He was the right leader for the greatest of all wars, fought and won at the Cross. And he is certainly the only one who can lead people into the eternal peace that comes through being rescued from the fear of death. Jesus is the perfect leader. Follow him!

FEBRUARY

TO READ: *1 John 1:1-4*

TESTIFYING TO THE TRUTH

The one who existed from the beginning is the one we have heard and seen.
We saw him with our own eyes and touched him with our own hands.
He is Jesus Christ, the Word of life.

1 JOHN 1:1

When Marlon Brando, the renowned actor, was called as a witness in the murder trial of his son, Christian, he refused to take the oath promising to "tell the truth, the whole truth, and nothing but the truth, so help me God." Citing religious scruples (or the lack thereof!), Brando refused to call on God as a witness that he was telling the truth. He was allowed to promise without swearing an oath, and he took the witness stand to testify to what he had seen and heard.

When religious sensitivities were more sharply focused than they are today, the very thought of swearing on oath invoking God's judgment was enough to ensure that the witness would not lie. For many people those days are long gone, but the person who lies on the witness stand is still committing perjury and is still subject to prosecution.

John's first epistle opens with a statement of personal testimony. True, John swore no oath. But given the seriousness of the statement being made, the purpose for which it was given, and the churchwide credibility of the witness, there can be no doubt that this is a piece of evidence concerning Jesus Christ that is of the first magnitude.

There is no hearsay here. Concerning Jesus, John said, "We saw him with our own eyes and touched him with our own hands" (1 John 1:1). It was common knowledge among believers that John and his colleagues had lived in close proximity to Jesus during his ministry. On the basis of his personal experience, John testified without hesitation that Jesus' life was so exemplary, his works so miraculous, his words so powerful, and his teaching so life-changing that John had no doubts that Jesus was "the one who existed from the beginning . . . the Word of Life . . . the one who is eternal life" (1:1-2). John had been a witness to Jesus' death on the cross, Jesus' appearances after his resurrection, and Jesus' ascent into heaven. There was not a doubt in John's mind—he had seen it, heard it, felt it, and lived in the good of it. So he testified.

John's goal in testifying was "that you may have fellowship with us. And our fellowship is with the Father and with his Son, Jesus Christ" (1:3). John not only wanted his readers to believe as he did, but he also longed for them to enjoy Jesus as he had. This would make his joy "complete."

Sharing truth is a joy, and experiencing reality is a delight.

33

TO READ: *1 John 2:1-6*

CHEAP GRACE

My dear children, I am writing this to you so that you will not sin.
But if you do sin, there is someone to plead for you before the Father.
He is Jesus Christ, the one who pleases God completely.

1 JOHN 2:1

Dietrich Bonhoeffer, a young Lutheran pastor in Germany before World War II, fiercely opposed the policies of the Nazis out of profound Christian conviction. Because of this, he was captured by the Gestapo, imprisoned, and eventually executed in April, 1945, shortly before the prison camp where he was held (Flossenburg) was liberated by the Allied forces. He died a martyr.

In his well-known book *The Cost of Discipleship*, Bonhoeffer deplored what he termed "cheap grace." He defined "cheap grace" as "the preaching of forgiveness without requiring repentance, baptism without church discipline, Communion without confession, absolution without personal confession. Cheap grace is grace without discipleship, grace without the cross, grace without Jesus Christ, living and incarnate."[7] Bonhoeffer recognized this as an abuse of the biblical doctrine of grace—that most wonderful truth that God, out of a heart of love, reaches out to lost and sinful people, favors them in ways that they do not deserve, and grants them blessings that they could never earn. Bonhoeffer's concern about cheap grace was right on target, and he lived and died in accordance with his convictions.

The apostle John expressed similar concerns when he wrote, "I am writing this to you so that you will not sin" (1 John 2:1). John was not promoting sinless perfection—he immediately added, "But if you do sin, there is someone to plead for you before the Father." John wanted to remind believers that their sins are not forgiven in order that they may casually and contentedly continue in them. He wanted them to experience the freedom of victory over the sins that had formerly held them captive.

A reminder that Jesus "is the sacrifice for our sins" (2:2) should be sufficient to encourage believers to view sin seriously and to seek freedom from its bondage. Who can sin without remorse when he remembers that the penalty for sin is death and that Jesus assumed our penalty in that most horrendous of deaths, crucifixion?

But how do we enjoy this freedom and victory over sin? John suggests two foolproof methods. First, out of love for the Lord Jesus we embark on a lifestyle characterized by obedience. "Those who obey God's word really do love him" (2:5). Second, we intentionally adopt the Lord Jesus as our role model. "Those who say they live in God should live their lives as Christ did" (2:6).

No one, least of all Dietrich Bonhoeffer, would suggest that doing these things is easy. Look where obedience and following Jesus took Bonhoeffer! But if we are to avoid the abuse of God's grace, we must accept the disciplines of discipleship.

There is nothing cheap about God's grace—it is costly, both for Christ and for us! Yet it has great worth.

---

[7] Dietrich Bonhoeffer, *The Cost of Discipleship*.

TO READ: *1 John 2:15-25*

THE LAST HOUR

Dear children, the last hour is here. You have heard that the Antichrist is coming,
and already many such antichrists have appeared.
From this we know that the end of the world has come.

1 JOHN 2:18

I n the waning hours of 1999, many people were preparing for the end of the world. They believed that the world was created in 4004 B.C. Adding the 2000 years A.D., they calculated that the world had been in existence for just over 6000 years. As a thousand years are like a day in God's reckoning, and as God worked for only six days in creation, it was obvious to them that the world would end when the clock struck midnight, January 1, 2000. They were wrong, of course.

Then there was the Y2K problem. There was great concern that computers would not know whether it was 1900 or 2000, so murderers might be released early from prison, nuclear warheads could take off of their own accord, and electrical plants the world over might shut down. Predictions of a nuclear holocaust, a new ice age, or rampant anarchy abounded. In fact, nothing cataclysmic happened. Very little happened at all except for a larger-than-usual New Year's celebration (and, for many, a larger-than-ordinary headache!). It was a monumental non-event.

Predictions of the end of the world have come and gone, only to be proved inaccurate time and again. A degree of skepticism about end-of-the-world scenarios has settled in.

Toward the end of the first century, the apostle John wrote, "Dear children, the last hour is here. You have heard that the Antichrist is coming, and already many such antichrists have appeared. From this we know that the end of the world has come" (1 John 2:18). John was addressing the belief, commonly held by Christians, that human history would not go on indefinitely, that God would terminate this world as we know it and eventually create "new heavens and a new earth." Before that would happen, a major political figure, the Antichrist, would arrive on the world scene. He would epitomize everything that is anti-God and would attempt to replace God with himself. But he would be defeated, and Christ's eternal kingdom would be established (see 2 Thess. 2:3-12; Rev. 11:7-13; 13:1-18; 19:11-21).

"Many such antichrists" were already abroad in John's day, and he saw it as the beginning of the end. The subsequent 1900 years have served only to add to their number, so prudent people avoid skepticism, thank God for his mercy in allowing things to continue, but do not forget for a moment that one day the "last hour" will strike. They live their lives fully aware that anti-God forces are at work and that this state of affairs will not continue indefinitely. They anticipate the impending showdown and Christ's ultimate victory.

Since we survived the recent millennial transition, human self-confidence received an enormous boost. Optimism abounds, much of it misplaced. Things *will* come to an end. The coming of the "last hour" is only a matter of time.

TO READ: *Ephesians 2:11-18*

EXTERNAL RELIGION

Don't forget that you Gentiles used to be outsiders by birth. You were called "the uncircumcised ones" by the Jews, who were proud of their circumcision, even though it affected only their bodies and not their hearts.

EPHESIANS 2:11

Things aren't always what they appear to be. We used to say, "A picture is worth a thousand words," but we now know that, through modern technology, a picture may not be worth the film on which it was exposed. For example, when one television network broadcasting the New Year's celebration in Times Square at the end of 1999 realized that the picture being broadcast included the massive logo of a competitor, they simply erased the logo from the screen and superimposed their own. Millions "saw" the new logo on their screens, even though it was not really there.

The ability to project what is palpably false has been developed into a fine art—and not just in the realm of advertising. It has been going on in religion for thousands of years. For instance, the classic definition of a sacrament is "an outward and visible sign of an inward and spiritual grace." What appears is intended to convey what is actual. But historically, this has always been a problem. One example was in ancient Jewish culture.

The ancient Jewish people were rightly proud of their special place in God's plan. He had established a covenant of love with them, initiated unique lines of communication with them, and had determined that through them all the nations of the world would be blessed (see Gen. 12:1-3; Rom. 3:1-2). They were given special promises, they received special mandates, they were granted special privileges. They were special, they knew it, and they did not hesitate to let other people know.

In some instances, their pride got the better of them. They demeaned others in order to exalt themselves. This was nowhere more apparent than in their attitude toward non-Jews, whom they called "the uncircumcised ones" (Eph. 2:11). Circumcision is hardly a topic of conversation for polite company, but they were referring to the fact that circumcision was both a sign and a seal of their special relationship with God. It was a *sign* that "signified" that they had "cut off" all that was displeasing to God. It was a *seal* that reminded them of God's covenant promises and instilled confidence and assurance. It was an outward sign of an inward grace.

And therein lay the problem, for things were not always as they appeared—that is, the inward grace was not always present. Paul told the Ephesians that the Jews were "proud of their circumcision, even though it affected only their bodies and not their hearts" (2:11).

The believer is called to practice the externals of Christian faith as a symbol of the internal realities of faith in Christ. Signs signify, and symbols symbolize. Signs that signify nothing and symbols that symbolize a fiction are contradictions. Congruence is required between the symbol and the reality. The alternative is hypocrisy.

JOY—OR FUN?

What joy for those you choose to bring near, those who live in your holy courts. What joys await us inside your holy Temple.

PSALM 65:4

S ome people say they are not interested in religion because they're having too much fun. Should you, by chance, catch them in a somber moment, they may admit there is value to a faith life, but they don't want it to interfere with their fun life. They may even concede that, toward the end of their days, they will probably take religion a little more seriously. After they've had their fun!

It isn't that they are against a life of faith, it's just that they see it as a hindrance to having fun. They do not necessarily deny the existence of God; in fact, they may even call on him when they're in a fix. It's his reputation as a somber old spoilsport that bothers them. They think he's no fun!

God is certainly serious, and he warrants serious thought and deep devotion. Furthermore, the issues of life and death that God speaks to us about demand that we stop playing around and start getting our lives on track. But to imagine that these serious issues are antithetical to the deepest joy and enjoyment is to seriously misunderstand the essence of who God is and what he offers to his people.

The psalm writer, speaking realistically about his life, said, "Though our hearts are filled with sins, you forgive them all. What joy for those you choose to bring near" (Ps. 65:3-4). Indeed, there is no deep joy for people who have a guilty conscience, no matter how much fun they are having! There is unspeakable joy, though, for the person who knows release from guilt and the relief of forgiveness. And while many people have the impression that church is boring, the psalmist exclaimed, "What joys await us inside your holy Temple" (65:4). Ironically, it is the people who take God seriously enough to learn the serious deficiencies of the fun life who discover the joy of the forgiven life.

The joy that God gives is infinitely more durable and enjoyable than the "fun" that is available apart from him. Those who are forgiven discover that the world is full of people just like them who rejoice in the Lord's goodness. The psalm writer celebrated this fact: "Those who live at the ends of the earth stand in awe of your wonders. From where the sun rises to where it sets, you inspire shouts of joy" (65:8).

When you have experienced God's forgiveness and release from a guilty conscience, there is no shortage of people with whom to share your joy! And there is not a place on earth where you will not find reasons for rejoicing. Observe creation and you will see that created things "all shout and sing for joy" (65:13). That's much better than just having fun!

TO READ: *Isaiah 63:7-14*

THE SUFFERING GOD

In all their suffering he also suffered, and he personally rescued them. In his love and mercy he redeemed them. He lifted them up and carried them through all the years.

ISAIAH 63:9

I n the old days fathers were allowed to spank their children without being charged with child abuse. As those fathers prepared to administer whatever punishment they deemed necessary, they would tell the offending child, "This is going to hurt me more than it hurts you!" No child ever believed it. But years later these children became parents, and they began to understand the pain a father feels.

Throughout her troubled history, Israel had frequently felt the Lord's displeasure and had been subjected to his discipline. It was Israel's fault entirely. God's "unfailing love," His "great goodness," and His "mercy" were abundantly evident (Isa. 63:7)—so much so that the Lord had said, "They are my very own people. Surely they will not be false again" (63:8). But they were—and he was obliged to discipline them once again.

In their distress, God's people complained. They questioned him, wanting to know where he was during their affliction (63:11-13). They recounted the ways that he had saved and led, provided and cared for them, and they wondered where their great Savior had gone (63:18-19). It apparently did not occur to them to ask, "What have we done to cause such a sad situation?" They preferred to ask, "Where has he gone? What is he doing?"

The answer to that question was that he was not distant, although he had withdrawn from them. In case they thought he might be remote, they needed to know that "in all their suffering he also suffered" (63:9). The Lord was certainly a father who disciplined, but it hurt him more than it hurt them! Not that his children believed it—but it was true!

Discipline is not designed for the benefit of the one handing it out. It is not a God-given means of venting frustration. When properly administered, it is supposed to bring about the disciplined person's reformation. The heart of the one doing the disciplining should be set on the well-being of those being disciplined. Without it, they would continue in their mistaken ways. A father's love requires that they be reproved. But a father's loving heart cannot help but feel the anguish of their suffering.

Remember: Next time you receive the Lord's discipline, don't complain. It hurts him more than it hurts you.

TO READ: *Isaiah 64:1-12*

REGRETS

We are all infected and impure with sin. When we proudly display our righteous deeds, we find they are but filthy rags. Like autumn leaves, we wither and fall. And our sins, like the wind, sweep us away.

ISAIAH 64:6

B enjamin Disraeli was both a novelist and a brilliant twentieth century statesman who twice served as Prime Minister of Britain. He wrote, "Youth is a blunder; Manhood a struggle; Old Age a regret." Looking back over his tumultuous life, he no doubt could see plenty of reasons for regret. His disastrous venture into speculative investments saddled him with crippling debt, his questionable relationship with a society lady tarnished him with scandal, his critical writings about colleagues created major disruptions in business, and his policy of "never complain and never explain" did not always endear him to the political world. Regrets there could be aplenty!

Regrets also dominated Isaiah's thoughts as he surveyed his social landscape. He recalled with joy the days when the Lord "came down" and "did awesome things beyond our highest expectations." "Oh, how the mountains quaked!" Isaiah exclaimed (Isa. 64:3). But those days were gone, and now he longed to see them return (64:1-2).

Isaiah lived in days when the people were ungodly. He confessed, "We are not godly. We are constant sinners, so your anger is heavy on us. . . . No one calls on your name or pleads with you for mercy. Therefore, you have turned away from us and turned us over to our sins" (64:5, 7).

The people had been privileged beyond measure. "Since the world began, no ear has heard, and no eye has seen a God like you, who works for those who wait for him!" (64:4). But they had not "waited for" God. The Lord "welcome[s] those who cheerfully do good, who follow godly ways" (64:5). But this they had refused to do. As a result, they were like "autumn leaves" that "wither and fall" (64:6).

But the Lord had not changed, he was still their Father, still the potter who had formed them. If their regret matured into repentance, the mountains could quake again.

Not all men wait until old age to engage in regrets. Circumstances catch up with some of them much earlier in life, leading to solemn contemplation and reevaluation—and deep regret. Thoughts of what-might-have-been flood the mind. "If only" dominates reflection, past mistakes are recognized, and missed opportunities are mourned. Sometimes, but not always, it is not too late to undo some of the damage and restore some of the hope of earlier years.

To avoid an old age of regret, learn to regret and repent early. And if it's too late for that, repent now anyway. Better late than never. It's never too late for hope.

TO READ: *Isaiah 65:1-10*

I AM HERE!

*The LORD says, "People who never before inquired about me are now
asking about me. I am being found by people who were not looking for me.
To them I have said, 'I am here!'"*

ISAIAH 65:1

I n 1999, *Christian History* magazine surveyed its readers and Christian historians. Respondents to the survey were invited to name the five most influential well-known Christians. By a substantial margin, C.S. Lewis was most often named.

Born in Belfast, Ireland, in 1898 to parents who loved books, young "Jack" Lewis became a book lover during childhood, embarked on a scholarly career at Oxford, and became a convinced atheist. Strange beginnings for a man voted the most influential in spiritual growth!

In 1929, Lewis discarded his atheism and became a theist—but not happily. He described himself as "a prodigal who is brought in kicking, struggling, resentful, and darting his eyes in every direction for a chance of escape."[8] Jack Lewis was experiencing the love of God drawing him.

Two years later, Lewis converted to Christianity. He had been meeting people he admired, only to discover (to his horror) that they were Christians. He had been reading his favorite authors, whom he liked except for their Christianity. But through their influence, his understanding of God grew. He was led to recognize that if God is God, he must be obeyed—not for the sake of reward but simply because he is God. Lewis wrote, "If you ask why we should obey God, in the last resort the answer is, [because God says,] 'I am.'" Lewis insisted that he was no more seeking God than a mouse seeks a cat. But God was seeking him. And he responded, he submitted, and the rest (as they say) is history.

We must always remember that the impulse to think about God comes from him, and that the desire to discover truth and beauty and reality is born from him. Jesus said, "People can't come to me unless the Father who sent me draws them to me" (John 6:44). The Lord said through Isaiah, "People who never before inquired about me are now asking about me. I am being found by people who were not looking for me. To them I have said, 'I am here!'" (Isa. 65:1).

Through the people Jack Lewis met, the books he read, the beauty he saw on his long country walks, and the longing in his own heart for which he found no satisfaction, Lewis eventually heard the Lord say, "I am here." For years he wasn't looking and listening. But once he did, his life became a vehicle through which the Lord began to speak.

Every converted life is supposed to be a pulpit from which the Lord proclaims, clearly, to people who may not be listening, "I am here!"

---

[8] C.S. Lewis, *Surprised by Joy.*

TO READ: *Isaiah 66:17-23*

A STARTLING FACT

*I will perform a sign among them. And I will send those who survive to be messengers
to the nations . . . and to all the lands beyond the sea that have not heard of my fame
or seen my glory. There they will declare my glory to the nations.*

ISAIAH 66:19

John R. Mott was born in Livingston, New York, in 1865. While studying at Cornell University, he met the English missionary, J.K. Studd, who led him into "a reasonable and vital faith." Shortly thereafter, Mott attended a conference led by the famous American evangelist Dwight L. Moody. During that conference, Mott joined one hundred other men who volunteered to commit their lives to foreign missionary service.

In 1910, when Mott was forty-five years old, he chaired the Edinburgh Missionary Conference. In his opening address Mott said, "It is a startling and solemnizing fact that even as late as the twentieth century, the Great Command of Jesus Christ to carry the Gospel to all mankind is still so largely unfulfilled."

Mott's influence dramatically changed the church's involvement in world missions. He traveled the world tirelessly, convening conferences where the needs and opportunities for worldwide mission were presented, and recruiting and training the many young people who responded to his challenge. Yet almost a century later it is still "a startling and solemnizing fact" that there are billions of people about whom the Lord would say, "[they] have not heard of my fame or seen my glory" (Isa. 66:19).

The Lord intended that his people should "declare [his] glory to the nations," and he promised a day when missionaries would bring "people back from every nation"(66:20). These people would become worshipers "from week to week, from month to month" (66:23), and some of them would function as "priests and Levites"—servants of the living God (66:21).

This ancient picture of the people of God in action needs to be studied by the church. In so much of the world, men and women still have not heard of God's fame or seen his glory. What is the problem? Why is this the case?

The Lord told Isaiah, "I will gather all nations and peoples together, and they will see my glory. I will perform a sign among them. And I will send those who survive to be messengers to the nations" (66:18-19). First, God gathers people to himself. Then, he shows them a "sign"—the cross and the empty tomb—and "sends" those who, because of the Cross, "survive" God's judgment to be his messengers. But those who never see the significance of the Cross never understand the need of men and women to survive the judgment and accordingly see no reason to be sent as messengers.

There's another "startling and solemnizing fact." There are millions who have seen the sign of the cross and have survived the judgment. But when they were sent, they never went. And that is why so many have not heard of the Lord's fame. That's a shame!

TO READ: *Isaiah 60:1-9*

RISE AND SHINE

"Arise, Jerusalem! Let your light shine for all the nations to see!
For the glory of the LORD is shining upon you."

ISAIAH 60:1

Any man who has been in boot camp will never forget the sound of a bugle blowing reveille. The harsh, jarring tones dragged him into the challenging reality of another day's coping with drill sergeants, those delightful gentlemen who followed hard on the bugle, rattling bunks and shouting, "Come on, you lazy good-for-nothings. Rise and shine!" Ironically, the two things most recruits are reluctant at that moment to do are to rise and to shine.

Isaiah was no drill sergeant, and he didn't use a bugle. But he did have a message for Jerusalem: "Arise, Jerusalem! Let your light shine for all the nations to see! For the glory of the Lord is shining upon you" (Isa. 60:1). Jerusalem, the city whose history was a succession of tragedies and trials, was being promised better days. These days came, in part, after the return from the Babylonian exile. Then, centuries later, in A.D. 70, the Romans came and devastated the city once more.

Isaiah was looking down the centuries to something more than the physical restoration of the beleaguered city. He could see with the farsighted vision of a prophet what the apostle John saw much later and with greater clarity: "The holy city, the new Jerusalem, coming down from God out of heaven like a beautiful bride prepared for her husband" (Rev. 21:2). The new Jerusalem—the church, the community of believers, the company of the redeemed. The contrast with the ungodly, who are living in "darkness as black as night" (60:2), is stark and startling.

The call to the church is to "rise and shine," and the rationale for the call is that "the glory of the Lord is shining upon you" (Isa. 60:1). God does not expect anybody to rise and shine with heaven's glow on their faces without first shining his own radiance into their lives.

What does God's radiance look like? When the load of guilt is removed from a man's shoulders, the frowns of worry begin to disappear. When the promise of life eternal is embraced, the light of hope fills the eyes. When the beauty of grace is apprehended, a quiet smile of inner satisfaction lightens the countenance. When the Lord becomes a present reality in the believer's life, the heart begins to glow with his passion.

When this happens, people notice and are attracted. Isaiah said, "All nations will come to your light. Mighty kings will come to see your radiance" (60:3). People from all walks of life will be drawn to the people who have risen and are shining. For they, too, are looking for life and beauty, hope and gladness. But first, the church must rise and shine.

TO READ: *Isaiah 42:1-9*

LIGHT IN DARK DUNGEONS

"I, the LORD, have called you to demonstrate my righteousness. . . . I have given you to my people as the personal confirmation of my covenant with them. And you will be a light to guide all nations to me. You will open the eyes of the blind and free the captives from prison. You will release those who sit in dark dungeons."

ISAIAH 42:6-7

As Charles Wesley was lying ill in the home of his friend John Bray, he read Luther's *Commentary on Galatians.* His eyes were opened to the wonders of God's saving grace, and he wrote in his journal, "This I know, I have 'now peace with God.'"[9] He immediately composed a hymn of thanksgiving to the Lord entitled, "Where shall my wondering soul begin?" In it he expressed amazed delight at the love of Christ. More than 7,200 other hymns flowed from Charles Wesley's pen. Many of them were composed on horseback as he traveled tirelessly around Britain, preaching the good news. He was frequently known to arrive at his destination, jump off his horse, and, without greeting anyone, rush into the house shouting, "Pen and paper, pen and paper!" in order that he might record the hymn that had been born in his imagination while riding.

The lyrics of Wesley's hymns were poetic reflections on the great truths of the Bible. One of his best loved compositions, "And can it be," is one of his greatest reflections on spiritual truth. In this hymn Wesley wrote the following testimony of God's grace in his life:

> *Long my imprisoned spirit lay*
> *Fast bound in sin and nature's night,*
> *Thine eye diffused a quickening ray,*
> *I woke, the dungeon flamed with light;*
> *My chains fell off, my heart was free,*
> *I rose, went forth and followed thee.*

It seems quite likely that when Charles Wesley wrote these lines he had been meditating on Isaiah's great prophecy about the Lord's servant, who would "be a light to guide all nations," would "open the eyes of the blind and free the captives from prison," and would "release those who sit in dark dungeons" (Isa. 42:6-7).

Even as a young student at Oxford, Charles Wesley was known for his piety and his commitment to serious living. He helped found the "Holy Club" and, a few years later, sailed to Georgia as a missionary. But it was many years before he made his peace with God. His "dark dungeons" were not populated by overt egregious sins of the flesh. But in the years before he personally trusted Christ, his soul was dark nevertheless with doubt and fear, with striving and despair.

Every man has his own dark dungeons, some darker than others. All men need a "quickening ray" from God—perhaps a shaft of blinding insight or maybe the gift of grace quietly dawning in the heart. The result of God's light is a new life, which in Wesley's case "rose, went forth, and followed." That is the result God desires.

A man who follows Christ is called to be "a light to guide" (42:6). It is unlikely a modern man will be called to write hymns on horseback as a means of enlightenment for others. But it is highly probable that being a light will involve clearly testifying to God's powerful grace at work in the hustle and bustle of the office or the factory.

[9] John Wesley, *The Journal of John Wesley.*

TO READ: *Psalm 92*

A SONG FOR MORNING AND EVENING

It is good to proclaim your unfailing love in the morning,
your faithfulness in the evening.

PSALM 92:2

Composer Franz Schubert died destitute in Vienna at the age of thirty-one, leaving nothing but his clothes and what his brother called "some old music." It transpired that this "old music" contained a series of beautiful songs (*lieder*) which are still performed today. One of his best known song series was based on twenty poems written by a traveling horn player. We know nothing of the horn player's travails, but we know enough of Schubert's life to marvel that a man experiencing such pain and sadness could write such beautiful music. Schubert wrote to a friend, "I feel myself to be the most unhappy, unfortunate creature in the world. . . . Every night, when I go to sleep, I hope I will not wake again, and every morning reminds me only of yesterday's unhappiness."[10]

The ancient book of Psalms is another song series. The psalms have been in use for millennia in the liturgy and life of the people of Israel. Psalm 92, for instance, is a song "to be sung on the Lord's day" (Ps. 92:TITLE). This does not mean that ancient worshipers sang praises only on the Lord's day. Those who follow the psalmist's thinking know that "it is good to proclaim [the Lord's] unfailing love in the morning, [his] faithfulness in the evening" (92:2). Every morning, every evening.

Morning and evening thankfulness is good, not only because it lifts the downcast soul and makes the godly "flourish like palm trees" (92:12), but also because it is an expression that comes from the satisfied soul. That soul can say, "You thrill me, Lord, with all you have done for me!" (92:4), and marvels, "Lord, . . . how deep are your thoughts" (92:5). The thankful heart is made "strong as a wild bull" and exclaims, "How refreshed I am by your power!" (92:10).

By contrast, the miserable soul compounds its own pain. Schubert went to sleep dreading the next morning, and woke reliving the previous day's unhappiness. But if a man cannot recount the Lord's goodness, if he cannot recognize it in what is common, in good times and in bad, he will not think to "give thanks to the Lord, to sing praises to the Most High" (92:1).

If you go to bed miserable, you stand a good chance of waking up sad, but if you lay your head on the pillow with thanksgiving, you are more likely to greet the morning with joy. And you may even sing as you shave!

[10]Carter Harman, *A Popular History of Music.*

TO READ: *Ephesians 1:3-14*

HEAVENLY REALMS

*How we praise God, the Father of our Lord Jesus Christ, who has blessed us with
every spiritual blessing in the heavenly realms because we belong to Christ.*

EPHESIANS 1:3

A woman was asked by her husband, "Will there be golf in heaven?" She wisely
replied, "If it is necessary for your eternal bliss—Yes!" His question and her
response suggest that our idea of heaven is everything we enjoy on earth, only more so! So
if the boss gives you 50-yard-line seats at the Super Bowl, you think you've "died and gone
to heaven," while your wife's idea of heaven might be a few days on a tropical island with
blue sky, white sand, azure ocean, warm sun, and candlelit dinners for two. Who knows?
But Scripture speaks of heaven in a way that should not be left to speculation or relegated
to somewhere in "the sweet bye-and-bye."

God "has blessed us with every spiritual blessing in the heavenly realms because we
belong to Christ" (Eph. 1:3). It is clear that this is not reserved for the future, because God
"raised us from the dead along with Christ, and we are seated with him in the heavenly
realms" (2:6). The tenses say it all: "he *raised* us;" "we *are* seated;" "we *are* one with Christ
Jesus." We're already there!

When God saves people, he transports them from where they were to where they
will be. They were "dead," now they are alive. They were "under God's anger" (2:3), now
they are seated "in the heavenly realms." So in one sense, heaven is not something we
anticipate to be like the best of earth but better. Instead, it is something that we experience
now while we may be going through some of the worst of earth!

What then are these "heavenly realms" (1:3)? John Stott helpfully suggests that the
heavenly realms are "the unseen world of spiritual reality."[11] It is there that we experience
"every spiritual blessing," and it is there that the "rulers and authorities in the heavenly
realms" are being educated by God (3:10). The emphasis is on spiritual reality.

Experiencing life in the heavenly realms is all about being related to the risen Christ,
having immediate access to him in his glory, and enjoying security in his love. It is in this
invisible realm of spiritual reality that you have all that you need to live wisely,
winsomely, and well. So rather than thinking longingly of something like pristine beaches
or 50-yard-line Super Bowl seats, why not rejoice in the abundance of blessings that make
the invisible realm as real as the material? Enjoy where you are right now, while you're on
the way to where you're going sooner or later.

---

[11]John R.W. Stott, *God's New Society.*

READ: *Ephesians 2:1–10*

UNSINKABLE MAN

God saved you by his special favor when you believed. And you can't take credit for this; it is a gift from God. Salvation is not a reward for the good things we have done, so none of us can boast about it.

EPHESIANS 2:8-9

The *Titanic*, the largest and the most luxurious ship of its time, was a shipbuilder's delight. Because the ship featured a double hull that included sixteen watertight compartments, the *Titanic's* builder boasted that the ship was unsinkable, that "not even God could sink this ship." But at midnight on April 14, 1912, the great ship, with 2,224 souls aboard, ploughed into a huge iceberg at twenty-two knots, and two and a half hours later lay at the bottom of the Atlantic. The unthinkable had happened—the unsinkable had sunk. The builders of the *Titanic* had good reason to be proud of their workmanship—but no grounds for their boasting. Majestic though the *Titanic* undoubtedly was, God was more than her match.

So it is with mankind. There is an undeniable majesty about man, the pinnacle of God's creation—a uniqueness that is undeniable. Nothing else in creation comes close. Man knows it, there's no point in denying it, and it is perfectly appropriate for mankind to rejoice in it. But when man boasts of abilities that he does not possess, he gets into trouble. Like the *Titanic*, man is far from unsinkable.

It is precisely when man comes up against God that he discovers the awesome grandeur of divine law and the majestic glory of divine standards. It is then that he begins to take on water and sink under the weight of divine indignation and the burden of human failure. No amount of effort on man's part can bail him out. He may boast of his superiority, claim invincibility, and believe in his own sufficiency, but he will sink nevertheless. He can't sail on as he should, and he can't save himself either.

This is where God's grace comes in. God is willing to do for man what he cannot do for himself. Salvation will not happen for man because of his efforts but because of God's intervention. Paul explained, "God saved you by his special favor when you believed. And you can't take credit for this; it is a gift from God. . . . so none of us can boast about it" (Eph. 2:8-9).

Perhaps it is hardest for a man to admit that he needs saving at all, and that, if he does need saving, he can't save himself. Proud boasts drip too easily from a man's lips when a call for help is more appropriate.

Another ship, the *California*, was within twenty miles of the distressed *Titanic*, but her radio operator was not listening, so the calls for help were never heard. But God is always listening.

TO READ: *Ephesians 2:11-22*

ETHNIC CLEANSING

For Christ himself has made peace between us Jews and you Gentiles by making us all one people. He has broken down the wall of hostility that used to separate us. . . . Together as one body, Christ reconciled both groups to God by means of his death, and our hostility toward each other was put to death.

EPHESIANS 2:14, 16

A t first sight, the term "ethnic cleansing" appears to be wholesome and welcome. Why not engage in "cleansing" in order to get rid of dirt and garbage, and recover that which is beautiful and pure? But ethnic cleansing is not what it purports to be; it is not at all wholesome and welcome. Ethnic cleansing presupposes that it is the *people* of a particular ethnicity who are the dirt and garbage, and the cleansing called for is to get rid of those people.

The former People's Federal Republic of Yugoslavia is a case in point. Created in 1945, it consisted of Serbia, Croatia, Slovenia, Bosnia, Herzegovina, and Macedonia, plus the regions of Vojvodina and Kosovo. But in 1992, after the collapse of Communism, all the constituent republics declared independence and turned on each other. A vicious, bloody, murderous season of rape, pillage, and mass slaughter erupted. They called it "ethnic cleansing." It was actually an attempt at ethnic extermination, and there was nothing clean about it.

At the time the New Testament was written, there had been ethnic tensions between Jews and Gentiles for centuries. The Jews accurately believed that they were a special people—God had told them so. But he had not told them that they were superior to all the other peoples. In fact, they were called to be servants, not superiors, as they carried God's good news to the world. But they became supercilious. So the Gentiles became enraged and, over the years, ethnic tensions flared into outrageous acts of cruelty between the two groups.

Then came Jesus, a Jew, followed by Paul, another Jew. Paul wrote this about Jesus: "Christ himself has made peace between us Jews and you Gentiles by making us all one people. He has broken down the wall of hostility that used to separate us. . . . Together as one body, Christ reconciled both groups to God by means of his death, and our hostility toward each other was put to death" (Eph. 2:14, 16).

People involved in ethnic cleansing will angrily explain that they are avenging historic atrocities. But both the atrocities and the anger, both the brutality and the revenge, have another name—sin. And the only way to deal with sin is by the death of Christ and the willingness of the sinners to humbly come to him for forgiveness in order to know his transforming power. That cleanses their souls and begins to clean up their relationships. That is *real* ethnic cleansing.

We all have ethnic prejudices and tensions that could use some cleansing. And there's only one place to find it—the cross of Christ.

47

TO READ: *Ephesians 3:1-13*

POINT OF VIEW

I, Paul, am a prisoner of Christ Jesus because of my preaching to you Gentiles.

EPHESIANS 3:1

When three ships docked in Boston harbor on December 16th, 1773, with a valuable cargo of tea, the Bostonians were furious, and the tea finished up in the harbor. The Americans were exhilarated by this act of defiance, the British outraged. Samuel Johnson, the British man of letters, said, "Patriotism is the last refuge of the scoundrel." A few months later, Patrick Henry, the Virginian legislator, dramatically encouraged patriotic fervor. As he knelt before the Continental Congress he said, "Is life so dear, our peace so sweet, as to be purchased at the price of chains and slavery? Forbid it, Almighty God!" Then leaping to his feet he threw wide his arms, shouting, "Give me liberty," and then, holding an imaginary dagger to his chest, he added, "or give me death!" Johnson and Henry held two entirely different views of the American Revolution!

When the Apostle Paul arrived in Rome, it appeared to all who knew him that he was a prisoner of Caesar, bound for death. But Paul thought otherwise. He said, "I, Paul, am a prisoner of Christ Jesus because of my preaching to you Gentiles" (Eph. 3:1). Paul was not foolish enough to ignore the fact that he was being held at the mercy of a tyrannical Caesar. But in his mind he was the prisoner of Jesus. If Jesus wanted him free, even Caesar could not hold him; and if he was not freed, then Jesus wanted him in captivity. Paul's point of view and that of others were clearly at odds!

Paul added that he was also a prisoner because of his "preaching to you Gentiles" (3:1). In actual fact, Paul was in Rome because, as a Roman citizen, he had the right to appeal to Caesar and he had exercised this right. But that was not important to Paul. What mattered was that he had been the given the task of preaching the gospel to the Gentiles. This had upset the Jews who had stirred up trouble for him, which led to his near lynching, his rescue by the Roman garrison, and his eventual trip to Rome (see Acts 21–28). In Paul's view, he was in Rome simply because Christ wanted him to preach to the Gentiles there.

In Rome, Paul was in deep trouble—but it did not bother him at all. Not only was he confident in the lordship of Christ—even over Caesar—he also was convinced that his ministry of the gospel was more important than life itself.

So who was right? Was he an unfortunate wretch under a death sentence or Jesus' triumphant servant, bound for glory? You decide!

THE PLAN

When I think of the wisdom and scope of God's plan,
I fall to my knees and pray to the Father.

EPHESIANS 3:14

When General George Marshall, Secretary of State in the Truman Administration, gave the commencement address at Harvard University on June 5, 1947, he said, "It is logical that the United States should do whatever it is able to do to assist in the return of economic health in the world, without which there can be no political stability and no assured peace." Europe at that time was, in Winston Churchill's words, "A rubble heap, a charnel house, a breeding ground for pestilence and hate." It was clear to Truman, Churchill, and Marshall that unless America became involved in the restoration of Europe, World War III was not far distant. So the Marshall Plan, to invest twelve and a half billion dollars in the shattered states of Europe, of both friend and foe, was born. There had never been a plan like the Marshall Plan.

With one exception! Paul talked about "the wisdom and scope of God's plan" (Eph. 3:14). This "unchanging plan" was born "long ago, even before he made the world." This plan was all about God establishing "his own family," which "gave him great pleasure" (1:4-5). "It is a plan centered on Christ. . . . And this is his plan: At the right time he will bring everything together under the authority of Christ—everything in heaven and on earth" (1:9-10). So before the creation of the world God was busy planning that the world, which would eventually turn against him, should be brought back under his gracious, sovereign control through the activity of Christ in time and space.

But there is more. The church would play a significant role in the plan, too. For it is "his body" (1:23), through which (as is the case in all bodies) the wishes and promptings of "the head" will come to pass. This church, an integral part of God's plan, would be made up of the most unlikely material—those who "were dead, . . . full of sin, obeying Satan, . . . following the passions and desires of our evil nature," and "under God's anger" (2:1-3). Not only that, Christ also would reconcile traditional enemies to God and each other "by means of his death" (2:16), and they would become the church!

So God has a plan, an eternal plan, born before the world began, centered in Christ and his church, which is made up of redeemed sinners! No wonder Paul marveled at "the wisdom and scope" of it all! God has a plan—and we're part of it!

TO READ: *Ephesians 4:1–16*

A HEALTHY BODY

Under his direction, the whole body is fitted together perfectly.
As each part does its own special work, it helps the other parts grow,
so that the whole body is healthy and growing and full of love.

EPHESIANS 4:16

W hat do Florence Nightingale, Richard Simmons, and Hillary Clinton have in common? In the nineteenth century, long before soldiers wounded in battle received anything but minimal medical care, Florence Nightingale and a group of "gentlewomen" traveled out to the Crimean battlefield to care for the wounded. As a result of her heroism and compassion, the first school for training nurses was established in her name. Richard Simmons is the television celebrity who specializes in getting sedentary people out of their armchairs and into a regimen of vigorous aerobic exercise. And Hillary Clinton is well-known for her advocacy of government-sponsored health care. So what do they have in common? A concern for healthy bodies, which is highly popular in the western world. This is not surprising, in light of the fact that this world is teeming with things that are hazardous to our health!

Paul was concerned about health issues, too. He not only said, "the church is [Christ's] body" (Eph. 1:23), but he also worked hard to see that "the whole body is healthy and growing and full of love" (4:16). Careful attention to the well-being of the church—the "body of Christ"—is necessary if it is to be vigorous and healthy. Paul explained how this will be achieved.

First we must recognize that "we are all one body, we have the same Spirit, and we have all been called to the same glorious future" (4:4). There is no place in Paul's gospel for rugged individualism. Believers must take their place in the community of believers, those with whom they hold the most precious truths in common.

Second, we recognize that in the church there will inevitably be major and minor differences, but the way we handle them is crucial. So we are called to "be humble and gentle. Be patient with each other, making allowance for each other's faults" (4:2).

Third, we must recognize that the Lord has given gifted leaders to the church and that those leaders are responsible to "equip God's people to do his work and build up the church, the body of Christ" (4:12). This means that each of us should acknowledge the leaders' role and identify and fulfill our own. This is the way to develop a healthy body.

The man who is aware that he is part of the body of believers, whose attitudes contribute to a loving, caring atmosphere, and who actively exercises his gifts in the ministry contributes to the church's health. And he'll be healthy, too!

VICTORY CELEBRATIONS

This is the day the LORD has made. We will rejoice and be glad in it. . . .
Give thanks to the LORD, for he is good! His faithful love endures forever.

PSALM 118:24, 29

W hen the Green Bay Packers defeated the New England Patriots in the Super Bowl
in New Orleans, the streets of the French Quarter were soon filled with joyous
fans celebrating the victory. It was striking, therefore, at the end of the game to see Reggie
White, the All-Pro defensive end of the Packers, and a number of other players kneeling
in the stadium and giving thanks to the Lord. Not everybody appreciated this show of
devotion; some people wondered aloud if God would have been thanked if the Packers
had lost. But there is a marked contrast between those who celebrate victory with partying
and those who celebrate with thanksgiving.

Psalm 118 records the celebration of a military victory. The triumphant leader has
brought his troops to the Temple, and the priest calls the people of Israel to give thanks to
the Lord (Ps. 118:1-3). Then the leader addresses the people: "In my distress I prayed to the
Lord, and the Lord answered me and rescued me" (118:5). As a result of this experience, he
exclaims, "It is better to trust the Lord than put confidence in people . . . [or] princes" (118:8-
9). The "strong right arm of the Lord," says the leader of the triumphant army, "has done
glorious things . . . [and] is raised in triumph" (118:15-16).

The leader asks permission to enter the Temple (118:19), and as the gates are
opened, he says, "those gates lead to the presence of the Lord, and the godly enter there"
(118:20). Upon this, the choirs burst into song, praising the Lord for the wonders he has
done in snatching the leader from the jaws of defeat and giving him the victory. "This is
the Lord's doing, and it is marvelous to see," they sing (118:23). This day of celebration "is
the day the Lord has made." So they proclaim, "we will rejoice and be glad in it" (118:24).
The victorious leader asks for a blessing from the priests, who respond, "We bless you from
the house of the Lord" (118:26). The psalm ends with the leader honoring the Lord by
encouraging the people to "give thanks to the Lord" (118:29).

Most men will never win a battle or even play in a Super Bowl, but all men can win
smaller victories in life. What they do then speaks volumes about the kind of men they are.
If they go out to get drunk, they lack perspective—as well as balance! If they take a knee
and thank the Lord, they stand tall.

TO READ: *Proverbs 4:1-22*

PAYING ATTENTION

Pay attention, my child, to what I say. Listen carefully. Don't lose sight of my words.
Let them penetrate deep within your heart, for they bring life and
radiant health to anyone who discovers their meaning.

PROVERBS 4:20-22

I n his utopian novel "Island," Aldous Huxley wrote, "You forget to pay attention to what's happening. And that's the same as not being here and now." To pay attention, we need to be aware of and concentrating upon the data that are being supplied to us by our senses at any given moment. But it is possible for us to be in a situation which is so familiar that we can "switch off" the data and concentrate on something that is neither here nor now. For instance, driving a car is so familiar and so repetitive that it is possible for the driver on the way home to have no conscious recollection of the journey but to be deeply aware of the discussion with his passenger.

Our attention can also be distracted from the "here and now" experience because our pre-attentive processes have already determined that the data are weird, boring, or too familiar. Any insignificant event can appear more significant because it is unfamiliar or unusual. So when listening to a profound sermon on eternal issues, an inattentive listener will be easily distracted by a child crying—or a cell phone ringing! With all the possibilities for attention wandering, the need to give "wake up" signals is profoundly important. So imperatives such as "Look out!" or "Listen!" and instructions to pay attention need to be utilized regularly.

The writer of Proverbs certainly thought so. He wrote, "Pay attention, my child, to what I say. Listen carefully. Don't lose sight of my words. Let them penetrate deep within your heart, for they bring life and radiant health to anyone who discovers their meaning" (Prov. 4:20-22).

Like the writer of Proverbs, God is a father who calls his people "my children" (4:1). God our father, in his gracious will, has brought us into existence and is deeply concerned about our well-being. We, being human, are prone, like children, to allow our attention to wander. We find matters of prime importance too familiar to warrant our concentrated awareness and issues of little import so fascinating that they dominate our thinking and captivate our desires.

It takes a disciplined mind to concentrate on what God is saying in his Word, and to allow the truth of the Word to find a deep resting place in the affections, desires, and aspirations of the human spirit. Failure to pay attention may mean you miss the point. That could mean you miss your way. Listening is of prime importance.

TO READ: *Proverbs 6:1-23*

THE TROUBLEMAKER

There are six things the LORD hates—no, seven things he detests: haughty eyes, a lying tongue, hands that kill the innocent, a heart that plots evil, feet that race to do wrong, a false witness who pours out lies, a person who sows discord among brothers.

PROVERBS 6:16-19

S ome people seem to have a nose for trouble. Their lives lurch from one crisis to the next. Those who live within the sphere of their influence find their own lives being drawn into the vortex of stress and strife. They are often gifted people who have all the tools to contribute greatly to society, but their penchant for trouble undoes all they could productively do.

There once was a star on the Chicago Bulls' National Basketball Association championship team. Year after year he led the league in rebounding, and he played a key role on one of the greatest basketball teams in the history of the game. His bizarre appearance and his unorthodox lifestyle, at first, made him a darling of the media, and his on-court and off-court antics propelled his name into the headlines and spectators into the seats. But as time wore on his welcome wore out. Teams that desperately needed a player with his rebounding abilities passed up the opportunity to sign him and eventually he could not find a place to play. He caused too much trouble. A promising career crashed.

There are troublemakers in all walks of life—in the office, at the church, in the Congress, and on professional sports teams. And Scripture has some trenchant things to say about them, particularly with regard to the Lord's evaluation of them.

The troublemaker's root problem is attitude—"haughty eyes" that reveal a person's thoughts, and "a heart that plots evil," which shows up in words. The underlying attitude shows itself in actions—"a lying tongue"; "lies"; "hands that kill the innocent"; and "feet that race to do wrong" (Prov. 6:17-19). All of this eventually and inevitably led to discord among brothers.

Where will it all end? One day the troublemaker will have to meet with his boss, his coach, or his constituents and face the music. But a far more somber fate awaits him. For the Lord "hates" what he does and detests what he stands for. At the final judgment, the troublemaker will be in deep trouble when he discovers that his overriding achievement in life was to make deep trouble for himself.

But the Lord specializes in turning troublemakers around. They just need to admit that the envy, the jealousy, the insecurity, the anger—or whatever other deep-rooted dynamic led to their behavior—is sinful, and turn to him for forgiveness and strength to live in newness of life. There's nothing quite so refreshing as seeing a troublemaker converted into a peacemaker!

TO READ: *Proverbs 8:1–11*

AT THE CROSSROADS

Listen as wisdom calls out! Hear as understanding raises her voice!
She stands on the hilltop and at the crossroads.

PROVERBS 8:1-2

A bright red sports car screeched to a halt at a country crossroads, and the driver shouted to an old man sitting on a bench, "Can you direct me to London, please?" "No, I can't," he replied. "Then which road to Oxford?" he asked. "Can't rightly say," answered the old man. "You don't know much, do you?" asked the young man sarcastically. "No, I don't know much," replied the uncommunicative local man. "But I'm not lost!"

The problem with crossroads is that they present choices and require that they be made, and unless you make the right choice you end up being hopelessly lost. It is at the crossroads that we need somebody who, unlike the old man, has a word of wisdom to impart.

Life is full of crossroads; it is all about choices. When we are young they are made for us, hopefully by wise, loving parents. As young people grow up they need to learn how to make good choices. Often they fail to do this, and they suffer the consequences for a lifetime. Even in the golden years, there are still crossroads to be faced—choices which become increasingly difficult as faculties decline and fears increase. The need to make choices never ends; there's a crossroads just around the corner.

Fortunately, there is a word from the Lord on the subject: "Listen as wisdom calls out! Hear as understanding raises her voice! She stands on the hilltop and at the crossroads" (Prov. 8:1-2). This wisdom is also called "common sense" and "understanding" (8:5), "excellent things" and "right" (8:6), "truth" (8:7), and "advice [that] is wholesome and good" (8:8). This wisdom is more than knowledge. There are learned people who lack wisdom, and uneducated people who display the wisdom of which Scripture speaks.

The key is found in Proverbs 9:10: "Fear of the Lord is the beginning of wisdom. Knowledge of the Holy One results in understanding" (9:10). True wisdom is available to those who "fear the Lord." This does not mean living in mortal terror of a cold, merciless Deity, but rather loving with reverence and awe a great and gracious God who longs to be deeply involved in life's journey and consulted at life's crossroads.

The Lord does not even wait for us to ask directions. "Wisdom calls out. . . . understanding raises her voice" (8:1); "Listen to me! For I have excellent things to tell you" (8:6). It takes a wise man to listen to the right voice and make the right choices. This way he'll find the right road. This way he takes the high road.

PRIVATE AND PUBLIC MORALITY

"I, Wisdom, live together with good judgment.
I know where to discover knowledge and discernment."

PROVERBS 8:12

Presidential candidates usually start out talking about "the issues." As the competition becomes tighter and the stakes get higher, though, such noble concepts as "issues" tend to get lost in a welter of more *personal* issues. Then attack ads fill our television screens, charges and countercharges fill the air. It doesn't take long before matters of private behavior are "leaked" and indignant rebuttals are voiced. Usually the rebuttals claim that what a man does in his private life is of no concern to the public.

The idea that a line can be drawn between what a man is in private and what he does in public is worth exploring. It has its roots in the majority opinion in America that there are no absolute truths—72% of young Americans think so! They overlook, of course, the nonsense in this self-defeating statement—the statement purports to be an absolute truth!

If there is no such thing as absolute truth, then everyone can make his own truth and develop his own morality. It may be necessary for the sake of appearances and social integration to have some nebulous public standards, but private standards are just that—private. Since there are no absolutes, this can mean that what is morally acceptable in private is morally wrong in public!

Proverbs would beg to differ. There is in biblical truth an inescapable link between private and public morality. "All who fear the Lord will hate evil. That is why I hate pride, arrogance, corruption, and perverted speech" (Prov. 8:13). Pride and arrogance are private issues—they are all about what a man is in his heart when he is on his own. Corruption and perverted speech can be either private or public. But Wisdom goes on to say, "Because of me, kings reign, and rulers make just laws. Rulers lead with my help, and nobles make righteous judgments" (8:15). These are public actions.

Both the private motivations and the public actions spring from the same root—wisdom. There is no dichotomy here. For what is right is right, whether in public or private. What is evil is evil, whether anyone sees it or not.

Politicians are sitting ducks in such matters, but the average man needs to search his own heart concerning the possible contradictions between what he does in public and what he is in private. The aim of the godly man is to "walk in righteousness, in paths of justice" (8:20), both in the darkness of his inner sanctum and in the blaze of public scrutiny. One standard fits all.

TO READ: *Proverbs 8:22-36*

APPROVAL

"Whoever finds me finds life and wins approval from the LORD.
But those who miss me have injured themselves. All who hate me love death."

PROVERBS 8:35-36

The story is told of a young pianist who was making his professional debut in a famous concert hall in one of the capitals of Europe. The fashionable audience were most responsive to his playing, and at the end of the concert they gave him a resounding, standing ovation and called for an encore. Backstage, the young man refused to return to the platform despite the pleas of the stage manager and the concert sponsors. "But they love you!" they expostulated. "They're on their feet." The young man replied, "I know they are, but there's one man sitting in his seat. He isn't standing." "What's one man in a concert hall full of people?" they replied. Quietly he responded, "He's the master—my teacher!" The approval that really mattered to the young pianist was missing.

In the human heart there is a thirst for approval, a longing for belonging, a hunger for acceptance. Children seek to please their parents and are insecure if they sense disapproval. Teenagers move from seeking to please parents to seeking peer approval. They must be with the "in" crowd, dress as they dress, listen to what they listen to, and conform to their patterns of behavior—all in order that they might have their peers' approval.

Men do not easily grow out of this longing for others' approval. No one likes to be thought weird, to be socially outcast, to be ignored or discounted. The tragedy is that sometimes the applause of the crowd drowns out the approval of the Master.

Wisdom says, "Happy are those who listen to me, watching for me daily at my gates, waiting for me outside my home! For whoever finds me finds life and wins approval from the Lord" (8:35). Approval from the Lord is what matters. No matter how many peers stand and applaud or how many bosses issue good reports, if the Master is not pleased, all is in vain. The whole world can stand, but if the Lord stays seated, all is lost.

How do we gain the Lord's approval? By listening attentively to what he is telling us, absorbing the truth he proclaims, and making practical application. Problems arise when what he says does not agree with the audience that we wish to impress. Teenagers vacillate between doing what is right and behaving in a way that is "cool." Businessmen wrestle with doing what is right and doing "what it takes" to close a deal, knowing full well that the Lord does not approve of the methods used.

It comes down to this: Whom do we wish to please? Whose approval do we crave?

TO READ: *Proverbs 9:1–18*

TEACHING THE TEACHABLE

Teach the wise, and they will be wiser. Teach the righteous, and they will learn more.

PROVERBS 9:9

The late Tom Landry, legendary football coach of the Dallas Cowboys, used to tell his players that the coach's job is to teach grown men how to do what they don't want to do in order for them to become what they've always wanted to become. Anyone who has gone through the rigors of training has no difficulty remembering the things they didn't want to do that the coach required them to do. Many aspiring athletes have dreamed of holding the championship trophy but have had nightmares remembering the aching muscles, the torn ligaments, the endless repetitions, and the long hours on the treatment tables. There have been some whose natural talents were so huge that they thought they could make the grade on ability alone, only to discover that ability was not enough to carry them to the top.

So it is in life. Proverbs says, "Teach the wise, and they will be wiser. Teach the righteous, and they will learn more" (Prov. 9:9). The wise man is wise enough to know his own weaknesses, while the foolish man either refuses to acknowledge his faults or assumes he can succeed in life without paying attention to them. The wise man in his wisdom has learned so much that he recognizes how much there is to learn and how much he doesn't know. By contrast, the foolish man either thinks he knows it all or assumes that he knows enough, and what he doesn't know won't hurt him. Wise men are open to correction; in fact, "the wise, when rebuked, will love you all the more." That is not the case with those who mock at learning: "Don't bother rebuking mockers; they will only hate you" (9:8).

Of course, wise men aren't born wise. Somewhere they heeded and responded to the invitation, "Leave your foolish ways behind, and begin to live; learn how to be wise" (9:6). No doubt many of them had formerly subscribed to Folly's enticements and believed, "Stolen water is refreshing; food eaten in secret tastes the best" (9:17). The adventure of eating forbidden fruit was so exhilarating, the joy of cutting corners to achieve easy results so smart, the dishonest practices that had outwitted the honest paid such rich dividends, that the foolish didn't see the deadening of the soul, the downward spiral of character.

But where to start being smart? "Fear of the Lord is the beginning of wisdom. Knowledge of the Holy One results in understanding" (9:10). Get to know the Lord, and you get to know yourself. In so doing, you learn how to learn and you never stop learning.

TO READ: *Psalm 12:1-8*

ENDANGERED SPECIES

Help, O LORD, for the godly are fast disappearing!
The faithful have vanished from the earth!

PSALM 12:1

W hen Portuguese sailors arrived at the island of Mauritius in the Indian Ocean in 1507, they saw a large, rather clumsy bird called the dodo. It weighed approximately fifty pounds, had a huge black bill and blue-gray plumage. But it had one fatal shortcoming—it couldn't fly. Its short stubby wings were not made for aviation. This may well have contributed to its demise. Long before we began to think about endangered species, the dodo had disappeared entirely and only fragmented remains of the bird are to be found as relics in European museums. Hence the expression, "As dead as the dodo."

The dodo was not one of the most beautiful birds in God's creation, but it is sad that it became extinct. It had a role to play, and in its demise the whole of creation is a little poorer. While environmentalists have worked hard to preserve disappearing species, often to the chagrin of land developers, the steady march of "progress" has contributed to the relentless trend of environmental regress. The dodo is not the only thing that is dead for ever.

David worried about another possible endangered species. He called out, "Help, O Lord, for the godly are fast disappearing! The faithful have vanished from the earth!" (Ps. 12:1). No doubt we can grant David some poetic license here—the faithful have not completely vanished from the earth. But from where he was standing, he was beginning to wonder. The trends were all in the wrong direction.

David specifically mentioned the issue of lying. "Neighbors lie to each other, speaking with flattering lips and insincere hearts" (12:2). He talked about "this lying generation" and grieved not only that the people thought truth was irrelevant, but also that they brazenly said, "We will lie to our hearts' content. Our lips are our own—who can stop us?" (12:4).

Godly people don't lie, because they believe that truth is precious and that people are important. The person who lies demeans the one lied to. Lying is designed to gain an advantage or to avoid valid repercussions of wrongdoing. Godly people think too highly of others to want to gain an unfair advantage over them, and they know that wrongdoing has consequences which they should rightfully bear. So they don't lie.

In our day, as in David's, truth is not honored, lying is endemic, relationships are being destroyed, society is fragmenting, godliness is discounted, and the future looks bleak. We should pray, "Help, O Lord, the godly are an endangered species!" And we should seek to live truthfully ourselves.

TO READ: *Philippians 1:27—2:4*

GET A LIFE

*But whatever happens to me, you must live in a manner worthy of the Good News
about Christ, as citizens of heaven. Then, whether I come and see you again or only
hear about you, I will know that you are standing side by side,
fighting together for the Good News.*

PHILIPPIANS 1:27

I t is possible to make a good living without putting together a great life, to work hard
at providing all the ingredients of a comfortable existence without bringing them all
together in a life of purpose and significance. It is possible to spend a major part of your
life asking, "What is the point of all this?" and waiting to retire with the hope, "Now I can
get a life." A real life starts long before that!

A good life, like a classical symphony, has a major theme. This theme will work its
way throughout the piece of music in a variety of forms. Sometimes it fades into the
background, only to reappear later with renewed force and fresh expression.

Paul's basic theme for the Philippians was, "You must live in a manner worthy of
the Good News about Christ, as citizens of heaven" (Phil. 1:27). At that time, many of the
people living in Philippi were Romans. Rome was their home; Philippi was a distant
colony in which they were required to work and live. These people would have had no
difficulty recognizing Paul's analogy. Since they had embraced the Good News, they had
become "citizens of heaven," with temporary residence in the colony of earth. Their hearts
belonged to heaven although their homes were on earth. Their longings and aspirations,
their goals and their affections were rooted in eternity, although of necessity they were
residing in time.

This core allegiance showed in the Philippians' willingness to take a stand for what
they believed. Paul expected to find them "standing side by side, fighting together for the
Good News" (1:27). He wanted them to be willing to put their lives on the line and to
recognize that in Christ they had found a cause worth living for and, accordingly, one worth
dying for. They understood the "privilege of suffering" for Christ (1:29). They were not
alone—they lived constantly in the presence of the risen Christ. They experienced great
"encouragement from belonging to Christ," much "comfort from his love," and "fellowship
together in the Spirit" (2:1). They were learning not to be "selfish" or concerned about
making an "impression," and what it means to be genuinely "humble" and "interested in
others, too, and what they are doing" (2:3-4).

All this was because the Philippians had grasped the wonder of Christ's self-humbling
to the point of the Cross, which provided for them the wonderful model of how to get a life.
You give your life to God, as Jesus did, and then he gives it back filled with himself. That's
the difference between making a living and getting a life.

TO READ: *Philippians 2:5-18*

A DARK WORLD

You are to live clean, innocent lives as children of God in a dark world full of crooked and perverse people. Let your lives shine brightly before them.

PHILIPPIANS 2:15

A lexander Pope, the crippled eighteenth-century poet, wrote gloomy verse describing his world as he saw it.

Religion blushing veils her sacred fires,
And unawares Morality expires.
Not public flame, nor private dares to shine;
Nor human spark is left, nor glimpse divine!
Lo! thy dread empire, Chaos! is restored;
Light dies before thy uncreated word;
Thy hand, great Anarch! lets the curtain fall,
And universal darkness buries all.[12]

The apostle Paul and Alexander Pope possibly held similar views of the world's darkness, but Paul did not content himself with writing gloomy verse about it. He saw the darkness as a chance to shine! Paul encouraged his friends, "You are to live clean, innocent lives as children of God in a dark world full of crooked and perverse people. Let your lives shine brightly before them" (Phil. 2:15). Some men content themselves with cursing the darkness, but Paul challenged it.

How are men to shine in a dark world? First of all, it is matter of downright obedience. "Let your lives shine" is not a suggestion—it is an order! In his absence from them, Paul instructed his friends, "Be even more careful to put into action God's saving work in your lives, obeying God with deep reverence and fear" (2:12). The problem for many people is that the fear of perverse people outweighs the fear of the Lord, and the pull of the darkness is more powerful than the "desire to obey him" (2:13). Even if the fear of people and the pull of darkness can be overcome, how does one find the strength to live "clean, innocent lives" in such a polluted atmosphere?

Paul's words address this issue in masterly fashion. The key to all spiritual life is found in the indwelling presence of the Lord. The believer needs to know that "God is working in you," imparting both "the desire to obey him and the power to do what pleases him" (2:13). This does not excuse a passive approach to life which says, "If he's living in me and he's going to do it, let him!" Rather, it inspires the discouraged, the fearful, and the inadequate to obey, knowing that God not only inspires the desire, but also empowers the action. And the light shines brightly.

---

[12]Alexander Pope, "The Triumph of Dulness," from *The Dunciad.*

MARCH

TO READ: *Philippians 2:19-30*

THE SUPPORTING ROLE

I have no one else like Timothy, who genuinely cares about your welfare. All the others care only for themselves and not for what matters to Jesus Christ.

PHILIPPIANS 2:20-21

One thing to be said in favor of the Academy Awards, the Oscars, is that while they acknowledge star quality and have probably done as much as anything to elevate people to superstar status, they do not overlook the value of the supporting role. Oscars are awarded for "best picture" and "best actor," but "best costumes" and "best actor in a supporting role" are also recognized.

This is not just a matter of even-handedness—it is a recognition of the fact that there would be no superstars without someone playing the supporting role. There are no superstar quarterbacks without offensive linemen! Violin virtuosos need someone playing the second fiddle well.

Paul would have been horrified at the thought that he would eventually achieve superstar status in the worldwide church. Nevertheless, it is a fact. It is widely recognized, as far as we are able to ascertain, that no man, with the obvious exception of the Lord Jesus, has done more than Paul to establish the eternal kingdom. And yet even a casual glance at Paul's letters reveals his deep indebtedness to his supporting cast.

Take Timothy, for instance. This young man was exemplary. Paul said, "I have no one else like Timothy, who genuinely cares about your welfare. All the others care only for themselves and not for what matters to Jesus Christ" (Phil. 2:20-21). Paul had found in Timothy a kindred spirit. Paul, who was never reluctant to admit his times of discouragement, actually looked to this young man to cheer him up (2:19) and considered him a "son" to him in his advancing years.

Then there was Epaphroditus, "a true brother, a faithful worker, and a courageous soldier" (2:25). When Paul was lonely, he needed a brother alongside. When the work was overwhelming, he needed another pair of hands. And when the battle was raging, he needed someone watching his flank. And young Epaphroditus was there—a brother, worker, and soldier.

The Philippians knew their apostle well, and when they were concerned about him, they sent Epaphroditus. Paul acknowledged gratefully that Epaphroditus had come "to help me in my need" (2:25). Despite his serious illness, Epaphroditus, who was more concerned about his family worrying about him than he was concerned about his illness, carried on faithfully. Even mortal illness did not deter him.

Paul managed wonderfully well without the Web, the cell phone, the fax, or the computer. But I doubt if he could have managed without his Timothys and Epaphrodituses! Neither can men today.

TO READ: *Philippians 3:1–16*

BRAGGING RIGHTS

For we who worship God in the Spirit are the only ones who are truly circumcised.
We put no confidence in human effort. Instead,
we boast about what Christ Jesus has done for us.

PHILIPPIANS 3:3

M en love to brag. Old men regale their grandchildren with "war stories" of daring exploits in foreign lands, while younger fathers tell their children of athletic prowess and dazzling performances in years long gone. Males of inferior morality brag about sexual conquests, men of superior intellect of academic honors. The need to impress seems to flow in the testosterone.

When it comes to their spiritual lives, men tend to be more reticent. If pushed to talk about their religion, they may fall back on bragging about a heritage they no longer pursue and about rituals to which they no longer relate. They may wish to suggest that they are living lives that, while far from perfection, are close enough to a passing grade.

There was a time when the apostle Paul had a right to brag about religious matters. His response to the religious tradition into which he was born had been extraordinary. He dared to say, regarding his religious status and practice, "I could have confidence in myself if anyone could. If others have reason for confidence in their own efforts, I have even more!" (Phil. 3:4). Paul then listed heritage, commitment, and activities that would impress anyone.

But then, Paul disavowed them all! "I once thought all these things were so very important, but now I consider them worthless because of what Christ has done" (3:7). Paul quit bragging! In its place, a humble, trusting attitude was born. It was his discovery of Christ that made the difference. Paul stated simply, "I trust Christ to save me" (3:9). He began to see boundless possibilities in his new relationship with the Lord: "I can really know Christ and experience the mighty power that raised him from the dead. I can learn what it means to suffer with him" (3:10). And he looked forward to eventually experiencing "resurrection from the dead" (3:11). All because of Christ—and not because of himself!

Lest he should fall into the trap of bragging about his new found faith, however, Paul quickly added, "I don't mean to say that I have already achieved these things or that I have already reached perfection. But I keep working toward that day when I will finally be all that Christ Jesus saved me for and wants me to be" (3:12).

Apparently Paul suspected that some of his readers might not "agree on these things" (3:15), so he added, "We must be sure to obey the truth we have learned already" (3:16).

Perhaps the men among Paul's readers still wanted to brag. The habit dies hard. But die it must.

TO READ: *Philippians 3:17–4:3*

ENEMIES OF THE CROSS

For I have told you often before, and I say it again with tears in my eyes,
that there are many whose conduct shows they are really enemies of the cross
of Christ. Their future is eternal destruction. Their god is their appetite,
they brag about shameful things, and all they think about is this life here on earth.

PHILIPPIANS 3:18-19

O n the banks of the river Neva in St. Petersburg (formerly Leningrad), Russia, stands the massive green, gold, and white building called the Winter Palace, which includes the Hermitage Museum. The priceless art collection of the Empress Catherine II that is displayed there includes numerous fine religious works by the great masters. Prominent among them are depictions of Christ's crucifixion.

It is ironic that during the days of the Marxist regime, these artistic masterpieces bore dramatic silent testimony to the crucified Savior whom those in authority in the land were at great pains to disavow. The men who were at heart "enemies of the cross of Christ" (Phil. 3:18) were confronted by heartrending images of Christ's anguish and of his followers' devastation and despair. But their hearts remained unchanged.

It is hard to imagine how anyone looking at depictions of the cross could feel anything less than pity and sorrow for the one hanging there. And yet down through the centuries there has been no shortage of detractors and rejecters of the cross.

Paul certainly encountered "enemies of the cross" in his day, and he knew how to recognize them, even when they tried to project a love for Christ and his cross in the Christian community. Paul said, "There are many whose conduct shows they are really enemies of the cross of Christ" (3:18). It was their conduct that gave them away.

The behavior of the enemies of the cross need not be overtly antagonistic, like the Marxists in authority in Leningrad were. Paul described how enemies often behave. He wrote, "Their god is their appetite, they brag about shameful things, and all they think about is this life here on earth" (3:19). They are purely sensual, utterly shameless, and totally secular. In modern society, they are regarded as totally acceptable and perfectly normal. What, then, is the problem?

Christ died on the cross to deal with man's sin. Sin is the power that perverts man's sensuality, deadens his sense of shame, and fools him into thinking this world is the reality, rather than a shadow, of existence. But enemies of the cross see no need for forgiveness, and they resent those who suggest they do! They prefer self-indulgence to self-sacrifice as modeled on the cross, and they regard Christ's followers as sadly misguided individuals who are missing out on life. They may even endeavor to convert the Christian from the "error" of his ways.

Tragically, "their future is eternal destruction" (3:19). No wonder Paul spoke of them "with tears in [his] eyes" (3:18).

TO READ: *Philippians 4:4-9*

ENJOYING JOY

Always be full of joy in the Lord. I say it again—rejoice!
PHILIPPIANS 4:4

C hurch leaders are well aware that disagreements among participants in church life are not uncommon. Music is one of the most controversial areas. One minister had a problem with his choir, who decided to withdraw their services unless their demands were met. He responded by writing a hymn which included the line "Let those refuse to sing who never knew our Lord!" This may have helped the minister feel better, but it probably did little to resolve the conflict. Styles of music vary so dramatically and musical tastes have been nurtured by such widely divergent experiences that music too easily becomes a battleground, a test of spiritual orthodoxy, or a determinant as to what constitutes worship. No wonder someone said, "When the devil was thrown out of heaven, he landed in the choir loft."

Notwithstanding the struggles and pain surrounding music in the church, it is still one of the greatest means of expressing praise, giving thanks, and generating joy in the company of God's people. And praise, joy, thanks, and delight are integral parts of the believer's life.

This should not surprise us, because God is a joyful God! Zephaniah tells us, "For the LORD your God has arrived to live among you. He is a mighty savior. He will rejoice over you with great gladness. With his love, he will calm all your fears. He will exult over you by singing a happy song" (Zeph. 3:17). A singing God? A joyful God? Undoubtedly! So, of course his people should be a joyful people.

Paul, writing from prison, insisted, "Always be full of joy in the Lord. I say it again— rejoice!" (Phil. 4:4). It adds poignancy to this instruction to realize that these words were penned in a dismal prison cell by a man under sentence of death. "Always" in Paul's mind apparently meant *always*! But isn't this unrealistic? Aren't we allowed "down days"? In fact, didn't Paul get discouraged and depressed and even despair of life itself on occasion? Yes, he did, but he was not contradicting himself. Note carefully what he actually said: "Always be full of joy *in the Lord*." To be "in the Lord" is to be conscious of being part of his salvation, kept in his love, guarded by his grace, comforted with his compassion, convinced of his faithfulness, and secure in his hand.

It is not in our circumstances that we find the ability to be "full of joy." Circumstances often won't allow it. Joy resides "in the Lord" in the midst of our circumstances. This is worth singing about—and agreeing on!

TO READ: *Psalm 18:1-25*

WORDS ARE WORDS

I love you, LORD; you are my strength.

PSALM 18:1

In Shakespeare's play *Othello*, when the wealthy senator of Venice learned that his beloved daughter had secretly married a Moor (a man of African descent), he was outraged. But realizing that he was powerless to undo what she had done, the senator listened to the advice of the Duke, who said, "The robb'd that smiles steals something from the thief." So, as we would say, he decided to "grin and bear it!" But then his daughter said that her allegiance was now to her husband rather than her father. No doubt smarting, the senator said,

> Words are words; I never yet did hear
> That the bruis'd heart was pierced through the ear.

Recognizing the emotional state the senator was in, we must cut him some slack. But can we agree that "words are words" in the sense that they are merely sounds that emanate from the larynx? That the heart is not touched, bruised, lifted, or smitten by words? Surely not. Words can be weapons to wound, medicine to heal, a messenger to convey good news, or an instrument to play a happy tune.

David, the psalmist, knew this when, in a high state of emotion on the day he was finally rescued from his relentless enemies, he wrote in simple, plain, unambiguous words, "I love you, Lord" (Ps. 18:1). Not content with that, however, David then used words— picturesque, pointed words—to explain what he thought of the Lord: "The Lord is my rock, my fortress, and my savior, my God is my rock, in whom I find protection. He is my shield, the strength of my salvation, and my stronghold" (18:2).

David could simply have stated that he had gone through hard times. Instead, he wrote, "The ropes of death surrounded me; the floods of destruction swept over me. The grave wrapped its ropes around me; death itself stared me in the face" (18:4-5). And his description of the Lord's response was dramatic and memorable, written in terms of an earthquake, fire, storm clouds, lightning, and thunder (18:7-19). David used such words so that the choir could sing them to the people. Then they, too, would have their hearts inflamed with love for the Lord as they envisioned him, the invisible one, as a rock, a shield, a stronghold, a fortress. They would be moved as they "felt" the pain David had endured and "saw" the Lord's earth-moving response.

We use words, too. But to what effect? To praise, to wound, to heal, to enthuse? Watch your words. Say "words are words" if you will. But words are wonderful.

TO READ: *Proverbs 20:1-21*

THE GIFT
OF EYES AND EARS

Ears to hear and eyes to see—both are gifts from the LORD.

PROVERBS 20:12

H elen Keller was born in 1880. When she was not yet two years old, she had a fever in which she lost both her hearing and her sight. Think of it, she was unable to see, hear, or speak! Yet she excelled to such an extent that she graduated *cum laude* from Radcliffe College. She said, "the problems of deafness are deeper and more complex, if not more important, than those of blindness. Deafness is a much worse misfortune for it means the loss of the most vital stimulus—the sound of the voice—that brings language, sets thoughts astir, and keeps us in the intellectual company of man."[13]

The little lady might find herself in an argument if she returned to the world today. Now we say, "A picture is worth a thousand words," and we are told that with the advent of television people are more visually oriented. We can say, though, that to lose either sight or hearing has momentous effects on human life.

The writer of Proverbs did not get into comparisons of the relative worth of eye and ear because he believed, "Ears to hear and eyes to see—both are gifts from the Lord" (Prov. 20:12). We need to appreciate these gifts. We need to make use of our God-given opportunity to enjoy the wonders of the created world laid out in such profusion and grandeur before our eyes. We need to listen to the wealth of knowledge, beauty, and experience available to our ears.

Rather than taking sight and hearing for granted, these sensory faculties and what they provide for us should take on even greater significance when seen as gifts from God. We are as accustomed to seeing and hearing as we are to breathing and to the operation of the cardiovascular system. So we pay no attention to any of them—until something goes wrong, of course. But to embark on a day with eyes literally wide open and ears pricked so as not to miss a sight or a sound is to live at a higher level. Doing so from time to time will enrich the life, because God planned for it to be so enriched. At the end of the day, to reflect on what you have heard and seen and to give thanks to the Giver of gifts who made it possible is to live with a sharpened sense of enjoyment and a richer sense of worship.

Not everything you hear is profitable, "so don't hang around with someone who talks too much" (20:19), and "haughty eyes" along with other things "are all sin" (21:4). Remember the three monkeys? "Hear no evil, see no evil, say no evil!" They got it right.

---

[13] *Encyclopaedia Britannica* 5:1131.

TO READ: *Proverbs 21:17-31*

THE PURSUIT OF GODLINESS

Whoever pursues godliness and unfailing love will find life, godliness, and honor.

PROVERBS 21:21

Benjamin Franklin, the wise and witty son of a Philadelphia candle maker, looked up after signing his name on the parchment and said, "Well, gentlemen, we must now hang together, or we shall most assuredly hang separately." It was August 2, 1776. Franklin and the other members of the Continental Congress had just signed the Declaration of Independence, which they had passed on July 4.

Despite his jocular tone, Franklin was well aware that what he and his colleagues had done would be seen by many in the British government as an act of treason and rebellion, and they might well suffer deeply for their actions. But they were convinced of the rightness of their cause and the necessity of overthrowing the tyrannical regime of George III, in order that the men and women of the thirteen states might be free to enjoy "life, liberty, and the pursuit of happiness."

Everybody is pursuing something, with varying degrees of intensity and success. Most of them long for happiness. Sadly, for many happiness proves desperately elusive. As the modern world produces a vast array of toys for people to play with and assures people that being happy is their noblest goal in life, the pursuit of happiness has become a national obsession, and providing the means to attain it has become a lucrative industry. But in spite of it all, unhappiness abounds.

Proverbs suggests a better way. "Whoever pursues godliness and unfailing love will find life, godliness, and honor" (21:21). If we pursue "godliness" instead of "happiness," the direction of the pursuit changes immediately. Godliness is the quality of life that seeks to please God. Happiness is often absorbed with pleasing self. While happiness is concerned with *feeling* good, godliness is committed to *being* good and *doing* good. This is a major difference, since it is possible to feel good while being bad.

Being good and doing good are directed, respectively, toward heaven and toward earth. Being good brings delight to the Father, while doing good brings blessing to the needy. Proverbs calls it "godliness and unfailing love," and when they are pursued with diligence and perseverance, they bring their own reward: The pursuer actually catches up with what he aims for and he will "find life, godliness, and honor."

While Thomas Jefferson wrote in the Declaration of Independence of a God-given right to pursue happiness, the writer of Proverbs stipulated a God-given requirement to pursue godliness. Pursue happiness, and you may or may not find it. Pursue godliness, and you will find it—and much, much more. And you probably won't hang for it—so hang onto it!

TO READ: *Proverbs 22:1-16*

RICH MAN, POOR MAN

The rich and the poor have this in common: The LORD made them both.

PROVERBS 22:2

In 1999, Kevin Brown was the ace pitcher of the Los Angeles Dodgers baseball team. That season, Brown started 35 games. His salary for that year was $10,714,286. Assuming that he threw, on average, 100 pitches per game, he earned over $3,000 every time he threw a pitch in earnest! For comparison, a young man earning minimum wage in 1999 needed to work approximately 600 hours to earn the same amount. Rich man, poor man!

Yet by the standards of people living in parts of the Third World, the young man flipping hamburgers is relatively well off. The World Bank, as long ago as 1978, defined "absolute poverty"—the condition in which close to a billion people were living at the time—as "a condition of life so characterized by malnutrition, illiteracy, disease, squalid surroundings, high infant mortality, and low life expectancy as to be beneath any reasonable definition of human decency." John Stott says that while more than a fifth of the world's population "lack the basic necessities for survival," about the same number "live in affluence and consume about four-fifths of the world's income." Some economists and politicians advocate the redistribution of wealth, which means they tax the wealthy and give it to the poor. Critics of this approach point out that it often serves to trap the poor in a dependency from which they cannot escape.

In bygone days, some commentators stated confidently that God had intentionally made some poor and some rich, so everybody should be satisfied with his or her lot. More recently, the chronic poverty from which many precious people whom the Lord made are suffering has been condemned as a profound "social evil" that should concern every child of God.

The writer of Proverbs had an insight often lacking in such political-economic-social debates. He wrote, "The rich and the poor have this in common: The Lord made them both" (Prov. 22:2). One consequence of the fact that the rich and the poor are both made by God is that no one—rich or poor—is either unloved or insignificant in the Lord's eyes. It also means that no one, regardless of economic status, is outside the reach and purpose of God's redemption. And it means that no one should be forced to live in degradation and starvation when those who live in luxury could help to alleviate their state.

Once a man embraces these truths, he will seek practical ways to implement them. How it works out will vary from case to case, but one thing will be constant—the recognition that "if God made me, and he made them, we're in this together." The Lord made us all!

TO READ: *Proverbs 23:19-35*

GOD AND GENES

My child, listen and be wise. Keep your heart on the right course.

PROVERBS 23:19

T he dawn of the twenty-first century has seen another dawn—the first rough draft of the complete human genome. The genetic code, we are learning, determines our physical shape, the number of our fingers, the color of our eyes, our capacity for languages, and our ability to store information and recall it. While we are only on the fringes of discovering the wonders of this aspect of our creation, there are those who have already decided that some of our genes determine our behavioral tendencies. That has led them to conclude that man is not responsible for his actions—he is simply an unfortunate repository of genes which determine his behavior and map out his destiny.

Whatever influence our genetic makeup has on our behavior, it certainly does not negate the clear biblical teaching that we are responsible people, to whom God has clearly outlined acceptable behaviors for which we are ultimately accountable. So Proverbs says, "My child, listen and be wise. Keep your heart on the right course" (Prov. 23:19). Proverbs is not denying that we have behavioral tendencies, but it is affirming that we have behavioral responsibilities.

Preachers used to talk about "besetting sins," based on an expression found in Hebrews 12:1 in the King James Version of the Bible: "Let us lay aside . . . the sin which doth so easily beset us" (Heb. 12:1, KJV). The preachers were referring to the habitual sins that people find particularly hard to overcome. In more recent times, under the influence of psychology, the tendency is to talk about "addictive behavior." This can show up in many forms. Proverbs, while not using this term, certainly speaks about it when it insists: "Do not carouse with drunkards and gluttons" (23:20); "Too much sleep clothes a person with rags" (23:21); and "A prostitute is a deep pit; an adulterous woman is treacherous" (23:27-28). Drunkenness, gluttony, laziness, and sexual aberrations may be described either as "besetting sins" or as "addictive behavior"—either way, they are wrong.

Being a captive to a besetting sin or being bound by an addictive behavior is frightening—it leads to "anguish," "sorrow," and "unnecessary bruises" (23:29). But there is hope. The man who responds to God's invitation, "O my son, give me your heart" (23:26), and is careful to "get the truth, . . . wisdom, discipline, and discernment" (23:23), will find the iron bands of addictive behavior and besetting sin snapped. God promises that he can give a man the power to do what is right even when his natural inclination is wrong. And whatever a man's genes may say, that is what his God declares.

TO READ: *Proverbs 24:23-34*

LOOKING AND LEARNING

*Then, as I looked and thought about it, I learned this lesson: A little extra sleep,
a little more slumber, a little folding of the hands to rest—and poverty will pounce
on you like a bandit; scarcity will attack you like an armed robber.*

PROVERBS 24:32-34

There is a famous engraving by J.W. Steel of a young boy sitting with his chin cupped in his hands, staring at a boiling kettle on the open fire. The boy is James Watt, and he is sitting in his parents' home in Greenock, Scotland, early in the eighteenth century, watching with fascination as the steam from the boiling water lifts the lid of the kettle with a rattling sound. His mother is chatting with a friend, unaware of what her son is seeing. But the boy is keenly observing what is going on—and he's thinking about it! He is looking and learning, observing and contemplating. He is recognizing the power of steam to generate energy and the possibilities of harnessing this energy and channeling it into useful activity.

A hundred miles south of Greenock and twenty-four years after James Watt's birth in 1736, William Wordsworth was born in the English Lake District. Left to his own devices as a boy in his rustic home, Wordsworth wandered over the hills and beside the lakes, looking and learning. In his mature years he wrote,

> For I have learned
> To look on nature, not as in the hour
> Of thoughtless youth; but hearing oftentimes
> The still, sad music of humanity,
> Nor harsh nor grating, though of ample power
> To chasten and subdue.[14]

Wordsworth, the poet, had learned to look and learn far differently from Watt, the engineer. But both stood out from their peers, who walked through life as if blindfolded to its visual lessons. Both were able to observe the world, ponder the meaning of what they saw, and learn from it.

The writer of Proverbs wrote about passing an overgrown vineyard. What had once been well cared for and productive now lay wasted and barren. He thought about what he saw, and he learned a lesson from it: "A little extra sleep, a little more slumber, a little folding of the hands to rest—and poverty will pounce on you like a bandit; scarcity will attack you like an armed robber" (Prov. 24:33-34).

Watt observed, and his practical mind translated the data into scientific principles. Wordsworth looked, and he drew from what he saw lessons about the inner workings of the human heart. The writer of Proverbs observed an abandoned field, saw the folly of another man's actions, and learned from the other's mistakes.

It has been said that an educated man is one who has learned how to learn and never stops learning. He has also learned how to look and never stops looking. So if you learn to look, you'll look and learn. And then you, like Watt, Wordsworth, and the writer of Proverbs, will pass on to others the lessons of looking and learning.

[14]William Wordsworth, from "Lines Composed a Few Miles above Tintern Abbey.

TO READ: *Proverbs 25:11-28*

THE THINGS PEOPLE SAY!

Telling lies about others is as harmful as hitting them with an ax,
wounding them with a sword, or shooting them with a sharp arrow.

PROVERBS 25:18

E vents during the American War of Independence had convinced the Federalists that bigger government was necessary for the security and well-being of the fledgling nation. Their opponents in the debate over the Constitution thought otherwise, and pressed for recognition of the rights of individuals. A compromise was reached when the opponents were assured that, if they helped pass the Constitution, one of the first acts of the government would be to pass a Bill of Rights. This was done, and the right to religious freedom, the freedom of assembly, and the freedom of speech was written into the Constitution. The freedom to express an opinion, to share a conviction, and to communicate an idea should be cherished!

However, these freedoms are not freedoms to be abused. Proverbs is full of helpful teaching on the subject. For example, "Timely advice is as lovely as golden apples in a silver basket" (Prov. 25:11). The right word spoken in the right way at the right time is a gift to be treasured. A word that points the way forward in the moment of despair, a truth that corrects a misapprehension, an explanation that dispels the fog of confusion, and a reminder that buoys the flagging spirit and replenishes the drained soul—all these are "lovely as golden apples."

Or, "Valid criticism is as treasured by the one who heeds it as jewelry made from finest gold" (25:12). Criticism that is invalid is destructive and demeaning, but the right kind is to be embraced and acted upon. Left alone in an uncorrected error, a man will drift into further mistakes. Unexamined actions may contain elements that negate their worth. Bad habits unconsciously formed inexorably imprison the unaware. But valid criticism, properly heeded, is a boon and a blessing in such circumstances.

On the other hand, "Telling lies about others is as harmful as hitting them with an ax, wounding them with a sword, or shooting them with a sharp arrow" (25:18). While both speaking in error and telling a lie communicate something that is not true, the difference is that the former is unintentional, while the latter is intentional. A lie is designed to mislead, to demean, or to unfairly put another at a disadvantage. An error in speech is nothing more than a mistake. It is in the intent behind the untruth that the damaging impact of the lie is to be found. So words can contain "timely advice," "valid criticism," or downright "lies." They can encourage or deflate, build up or destroy.

It is good to cherish your freedom of speech. It is even better to be careful what you say.

ATTENTION TO ATTENDANCE

Who may worship in your sanctuary, LORD?
Who may enter your presence on your holy hill?

PSALM 15:1

S ome churches are cold and correct, decorous and dead. In such places of worship the emphasis is placed on God's awesomeness, his holiness, and the reverence due to him. Worshipers enter with silent tread and downcast eye as they make their way to sacred pew, where they kneel in solemn reflection.

Other churches advertise what they have to offer in the Yellow Pages, with exuberant claims like, "The end of your search for a friendly church!" Should the man whose fingers have done the walking arrive at the entrance to such a place of worship, he would find himself swept along by a hurrying crowd, greeted warmly by a strategically placed "greeter," led personally to the youth center to park the children, and then shown to an inviting pew where his hand is warmly shaken and he is engaged in animated conversation. Meanwhile, the musical prelude tries desperately to be heard.

Only God knows the heart, so he alone can say who is truly worshiping. But one thing can be said with confidence: Before the worshiper arrives at the sanctuary entrance, he should ask, "Who may worship in your sanctuary, Lord? Who may enter your presence on your holy hill?" (Ps. 15:1). In the formalized worship of the Jerusalem sanctuary, worshipers would ask that question at the entrance to the temple, and the priest would reply with a list of ten qualifying requirements which can be summarized as follows:

1. Taking God's law seriously
2. Ordering their lives accordingly
3. Engaging in practical good works
4. Being known for integrity of speech
5. Having warm neighborliness and helpfulness that is well attested
6. Avoiding being entrapped in ungodly liaisons
7. Supporting those who serve the Lord
8. Saying what they mean and meaning what they say
9. Fulfilling "their promises even when it hurts"
10. Having business dealings that are beyond reproach

Taken seriously, these requirements could cause the biggest and most precipitous decline in church attendance in church history. But they are not designed to keep people away from worship—they are intended to draw prepared people into worship. The key word is "prepared."

The Lord wants his people to spend time searching their hearts to identify the things they have done that they should not have done and the things they have failed to do that they should have done. In this way, a humble, repentant attitude is ensured, a longing for forgiveness is born, and a sense of delight in God's grace is fostered all over again. And then worship begins.

Church attendance requires careful attention!

TO READ: *1 Peter 1:1–12*

FIERY TRIALS

These trials are only to test your faith, to show that it is strong and pure.
It is being tested as fire tests and purifies gold—and your faith is far more precious to
God than mere gold. So if your faith remains strong after being tried by fiery trials,
it will bring you much praise and glory and honor on the day when
Jesus Christ is revealed to the whole world.

1 PETER 1:7

O n July 18, A.D. 64, a fire broke out in the ancient city of Rome, destroying more than half the city. Great numbers of citizens lost their lives. Even though the emperor was out of town at the time, rumors circulated that he had ordered the blaze to accomplish his own purposes. Tacitus, the Roman historian, tells us that Nero "put forward as guilty, and afflicted with the most exquisite punishments, those who were hated for their abominations and called 'Christians' by the populace." "After scenes of great cruelty," Tacitus continues, the Roman people began to feel sorry for the Christians whom, they believed, were suffering unjustly "to gratify the cruelty of Nero."

News of these events no doubt traveled rapidly throughout the provinces of the empire, where many Christians were living. So the apostle Peter, who, along with Paul, would die at the hands of the murderous Nero, wrote a letter of encouragement, perhaps assuming that similar persecution would break out in the provinces. Peter wrote, "If your faith remains strong after being tried by fiery trials, it will bring you much praise and glory and honor on the day when Jesus Christ is revealed to the whole world" (1 Pet. 1:7).

The thought of being torn by dogs, crucified, or "burned as torches to light the night," as Tacitus reported, was enough to panic the bravest soul. So Peter reminded his readers of three principal Christian truths that would serve to strengthen them for the ordeal.

First, Christians must not forget *what God had done* in their lives. Peter wrote, "God the Father chose you, . . . the Spirit has made you holy, . . . and [you] are cleansed by [Jesus'] blood" (1:2). Including himself, Peter added, "God has given us the privilege of being born again" (1:3). Father, Son, and Holy Spirit had all been actively involved in their salvation. So they should take heart, for they were safe in the keeping of the triune God.

Second, Peter's readers needed to remember *what God had promised to do.* "God has reserved a priceless inheritance for his children . . . beyond the reach of change or decay" (1:4). Should their circumstances change dramatically and should they suffer death and their bodies decay, nothing would change their promised eternal inheritance.

Third, they must bear in mind *what God was doing.* He was permitting the trials so that their faith would be "tested as fire tests and purifies gold" (1:7). It is possible that Peter's readers might have preferred to save their skins rather than test their faith, but Peter reminded them that "faith is far more precious to God than mere gold" (1:7). Their faith was even more valuable than their skin!

The thought of persecution can cause one's heart to miss a beat. Knowing what God is doing through the trials helps God's people not to miss a step.

TO READ: *1 Peter 1:13-22*

GOD HAS NO FAVORITES

And remember that the heavenly Father to whom you pray has no favorites when
he judges. He will judge or reward you according to what you do. So you must live
in reverent fear of him during your time as foreigners here on earth.

1 PETER 1:17

W hen artists portray Justice, she wears a pure white robe, stands erect and
blindfolded, and holds a pair of scales in one hand and a drawn sword in the
other. The symbolism is clear. Justice is pure, straight, and impartial, and she only
punishes those whom the weight of evidence condemns. She plays no favorites, she
tolerates no injustice, she accepts only truth, and her fairness is impeccable.

When many people look at the kind of justice meted out in the modern world,
however, they see a different picture. Justice, at times, seems to be able to peer over her
blindfold and recognize ethnicity, for there is no doubt that a disproportionately high
number of minorities feel Justice's sword. And her scales do seem weighted in favor of the
wealthy, since the best lawyer money can buy is usually much more adept at persuading
her than a public defender fresh out of law school. And this is the state of affairs in lands
where Justice is revered! In lands where Justice is not admired, little or no attempt to
administer true justice is attempted. No wonder, then, that many oppressed and
mistreated peoples are crying out for justice.

There is good news about God's justice, though: "Remember," wrote the apostle
Peter, "that the heavenly Father to whom you pray has no favorites when he judges. He
will judge or reward you according to what you do" (1:17). Peter was not speaking, in this
context, about the judgment of God that will determine whether a sinner's eternal destiny
is heaven or hell. Rather, Peter was referring to the type of life expected of the one whose
sins have been forgiven through God's action. As Peter reminded his readers, "You know
that God paid a ransom to save you from the empty life you inherited from your ancestors.
. . . He paid for you with the precious lifeblood of Christ, the sinless, spotless Lamb of
God" (1:18-19). And so Peter assured them, "You were cleansed from your sins when you
accepted the truth of the Good News" (1:22).

God's impartial evaluation here discussed is all about life after we "have been born
again" (1:23). God rightly expects a life of obedience from his child. The life of God's child
should reflect the family likeness! That is why God tells his children, "You must be holy
because I am holy" (1:16).

The believer need not fear that his sins will be judged. They have been dealt with by
Christ's death. But the believer's redeemed life will be examined by a Judge who has no
favorites—but who calls those he examines his children, and who loves us without end.

TO READ: *1 Peter 1:23–2:8*

BORN AGAIN LIVING

You have been born again. Your new life did not come from your earthly parents because the life they gave you will end in death. But this new life will last forever because it comes from the eternal, living word of God.

1 PETER 1:23

J immy Carter was relatively unknown outside his native state of Georgia when he announced that he wanted to run for President of the United States. Many people were surprised, not only because they didn't know who he was, but because he also told reporters that he had been "born again." Often, when people don't understand something, they ridicule it, and this is precisely what happened in Carter's case. Talk about being "born again" spread like wildfire, though, and in a very short time everybody was using the term. An athlete returning from injury became a "born again" athlete, a businessman recovering from bankruptcy was "born again" when he started up a new business. And so on. The more people talked about being born again, the less they meant by it, and as a result a superlative spiritual truth has been devalued in the popular understanding.

When Peter wrote "You have been born again" (1 Pet. 1:23), he was referring to something that God does in a man's life that determines his eternal destiny and changes his daily life. It is a "new life" both as it transcends death and qualifies the person for heaven, and as it transforms his life on earth on the way to heaven.

In the same way that a "baby cries for milk" (2:2), so the born-again man, having "had a taste of the Lord's kindness" (2:3), craves spiritual nourishment so that he "can grow into the fullness of [his] salvation" (2:2). One of the evidences that a man is getting the right kind of nourishment is that his behavior changes. This is not a matter of putting on a religious cloak or a spiritual performance, but rather a deep work of the Spirit that changes attitudes and actions. A born-again man does not simply "pretend to be good," because he is "done with hypocrisy and jealousy and backstabbing" and all kinds of "malicious behavior and deceit" (2:1).

Jimmy Carter's presidency was beset with problems, and he was not reelected to a second term, but he is widely regarded as the best ex-president America has ever had because of his godly approach to people, his gracious concern for those in need, and his humble walk in high places. Men may ridicule a claim to be born again—but they respect a man who lives it.

TO READ: *1 Peter 2:9-17*

FOREIGN TRAVEL

*Be careful how you live among your unbelieving neighbors. Even if they accuse you
of doing wrong, they will see your honorable behavior, and they will believe
and give honor to God when he comes to judge the world.*

1 PETER 2:12

Traveling overseas can be nerve-racking for those who are inexperienced. Communication is difficult, customs are strange, and currency is confusing. The U.S. State Department regularly publishes bulletins explaining the conditions prevailing in various countries, warning people against traveling in some of them and advising them how to behave in others. Careful attention to what these bulletins say can save the traveler a lot of grief.

The apostle Peter wrote similar instructions to his friends living in the Roman Empire in circumstances that were less than convivial and, at times, downright dangerous. He said, "Dear brothers and sisters, you are foreigners and aliens here. So I warn you to keep away from evil desires because they fight against your very souls" (1 Pet. 2:11). Peter was aware of very real physical dangers, but his primary concern was to warn his people about spiritual evils to which they would be exposed. He was concerned for the safety of their souls more than the safety of their bodies.

The enemies Peter identified first were enemies within, not without. Peter's readers would undoubtedly run into people full of evil designs, but he was primarily concerned about the dangers posed by evil desires in their own hearts. No doubt Peter agreed with his friend James, who explained, "God is never tempted to do wrong, and he never tempts anyone else either. Temptation comes from the lure of our own evil desires. These evil desires lead to evil actions, and evil actions to death. So don't be misled, my dear brothers and sisters" (James 1:13-16).

But there were outside dangers, too. So Peter added, "Be careful how you live among your unbelieving neighbors. Even if they accuse you of doing wrong, they will see your honorable behavior, and they will believe and give honor to God when he comes to judge the world" (1 Pet. 2:12). Perhaps Peter was being optimistic when he assured his friends that their unbelieving neighbors would "give honor to God." Not all citizens of a country take kindly to foreigners, and not all unbelievers in the world respond positively to the faithful!

The authorities put Peter to death not long after he penned these words. As a result, his statement that state officials exist to "punish all who do wrong and to honor those who do right" (2:14) must have raised questions from the young believers living in perilous times. But it is just another example of the trials about which Peter earlier spoke (1:5-7) and of the "unfair treatment" that believers sometimes have to face (2:19).

Whether the enemies are within our own hearts, in government offices, or next door, the calling of the Christian is clear: Live "good lives," "show respect for all" and exhibit "honorable behavior." This will go a long way for God's kingdom—whether "at home" or "abroad."

TO READ: *1 Peter 2:18–25*

SUFFERING
FOR DOING RIGHT

God is pleased with you when, for the sake of your conscience,
you patiently endure unfair treatment.

1 PETER 2:19

T homas Jefferson, in writing the Declaration of Independence, identified a number of "truths," namely, "that all men are created equal, that they are endowed by their Creator with certain unalienable Rights, that among these are Life, Liberty, and the pursuit of Happiness." Yet Jefferson owned, traded, and even bred slaves all his life! He stated that slavery corrupted the owner even more than it oppressed the slave, but he did nothing to emancipate his own slaves. It is generally believed that he quieted his conscience for purely economic reasons—he could not afford to release the slaves! People today find it difficult to balance such inconsistencies.

The New Testament's attitude toward slavery raises similar problems in modern minds. It needs to be understood, however, that slavery in Roman times was drastically different from that experienced by slaves in Colonial America. Many Roman slaves rose to positions of authority and power; others owned slaves themselves. Many, when they were released, achieved Roman citizenship—yet they were still slaves.

In this context, the New Testament writers did not advocate the abolition of slavery. They did, however, elevate the status of slaves as men and women created in the divine image, loved by God, and redeemable by Christ. Many Roman slaves became ardent believers, and some even rose to positions of leadership in the early church.

It was against this background that Peter wrote, "You who are slaves must accept the authority of your masters. Do whatever they tell you—not only if they are kind and reasonable, but even if they are harsh" (1 Pet. 2:18). Peter was not advocating a groveling subservience, both demeaning and soul-destroying. He explained, "God is pleased with you when, for the sake of your conscience, you patiently endure unfair treatment" (2:19). A slave would have little option but to "endure" unfair treatment. He had little or no recourse, as there was no one looking out for his civil liberties! But to endure patiently as a matter of conscience was unique. A willing, submitting spirit was to spring from a moral conviction that to retaliate, to curse, to "get even" (2:23) was fundamentally wrong. However appealing it might have been to harbor resentment, as a matter of principle the Christian slave would refrain, for no other reason than it was wrong in God's eyes.

Should the slave believe this was an unattainable ideal, he was referred to the example of Jesus, who "did not retaliate when he was insulted. When he suffered, he did not threaten to get even. He left his case in the hands of God, who always judges fairly" (2:23). If the Master suffered mistreatment patiently, how much more should the slave!

There are no slaves in modern business, but there are plenty of opportunities to be mistreated and to respond in a way that is either pleasing or not pleasing to God. "The blows" (2:20) employees experience are not physical, but they do hurt. They bring us pain—but our reaction can bring God pleasure.

TO READ: *1 Peter 3:1-12*

A HAPPY LIFE

The Scriptures say, "If you want a happy life and good days, keep your tongue from speaking evil, and keep your lips from telling lies. Turn away from evil and do good. Work hard at living in peace with others."

1 PETER 3:10-11

O n one occasion strikers on a picket line were asked, "Why are you on strike? What exactly do you want?" They replied, "We're not sure, but we're not going back to work until we get it!" They probably wanted what all men want—"a happy life and good days" (1 Pet. 3:10). Peter had some advice for them on the subject.

Some men think that being happy and being godly are mutually exclusive. Their perceptions of a life lived doing "what God wants you to do" (3:9) are negative in the extreme. But since God created us to live, he is the one who knows how life is to be lived and enjoyed. So a wise man accepts that there are certain things that God wants us to do, and in doing them true happiness is to be found.

This happiness is related to the fact that "the eyes of the Lord watch over those who do right, and his ears are open to their prayers" (3:12). Knowing this serves to produce a great sense of peace and well-being. Conversely, should a man choose to go against what God wants, he finds "the Lord turns his face against those who do evil." The resultant sense of loss and emptiness is the antithesis of "a happy life and good days."

God wants a man to establish moral principles based on his Word, and to "work hard" at human relationships. In the modern world, men often think that they alone can determine what is right or wrong for themselves, that what God has to say is fundamentally irrelevant. This is not the way to a happy life. God alone is the one who determines what is good and what is evil, and man is expected to know the difference and choose to "turn away from evil and do good" (3:11).

Since life is lived out in terms of relationships, the quality of one's life is directly related to the quality of one's relationships. Relationships are fragile, and the possibilities for fragmentation and resultant frustration are immense. But "loving one another with tender hearts and humble minds," refusing to "repay evil for evil," and "living in peace with others" will contribute greatly to a full life (3:8-9, 11).

The man who is not sure what he wants should realize that, deep down, what he wants is to be happy. So he should go about finding happiness God's way. That way he'll know what he wants *and* how to get it. That should make him really happy!

TO READ: *Psalm 138*

DON'T ABANDON ME

The LORD will work out his plans for my life—for your faithful love,
O LORD, endures forever. Don't abandon me, for you made me.

PSALM 138:8

I n 1463, the authorities of the cathedral of Florence, Italy, purchased a huge, sixteen-foot-tall piece of white marble. They commissioned a sculptor from Sienna to carve a figure that would be displayed prominently. The marble was so faulty, though, that the sculptor abandoned the task. Another Florentine artist was commissioned, but he, too, found the task impossible and gave up. The marble was placed in a warehouse, where it remained for almost forty years before a twenty-six-year-old prodigy was asked if he could make the abandoned and mutilated marble into anything significant. He said he could. Four years later, the masterpiece statue "David" was unveiled. Michelangelo had transformed the "worthless" marble into something majestic.

The original David, the king of Israel after whom the statue was named, once wrote, "The Lord will work out his plans for my life—for your faithful love, O Lord, endures forever. Don't abandon me, for you made me" (Ps. 138:8). In the same way that Michelangelo had worked on a faulty piece of marble until he completed the task others had abandoned, so the Lord looked at the flawed David and knew what he wanted to make of him.

David knew it, too, so he could say, "The Lord will work out his plans for my life." The assurance that the Lord had a plan and that he was capable of bringing it to fulfillment was the bedrock of David's life. It came from a solid conviction expressed in the words "for you made me." David reasoned that his Creator had a purpose in creating him—the divine artist had a vision of what he could be—and, accordingly, was not about to give up on him. This was not just wishful thinking, because the Lord had shown his "faithful love" that "endures forever."

This did not mean that David's life was a bed of roses. On the contrary, David testified that he was "surrounded by troubles." But his confidence in the Lord's "unfailing love and faithfulness" (138:2) was such that he continued to count on the Lord finishing what he had started.

In the dark days of life, it is not unusual to feel abandoned, as though one were left in life's warehouse unheeded, unfulfilled, and unfinished. At times like this, it is appropriate to cry out like David, "Don't abandon me," but we must do so with the assurance that David articulated based on his conviction: "Your promises are backed by all the honor of your name" (138:2).

As the statue of David silently testifies to Michelangelo's skill, so the confident, consistent believer speaks loudly of the Master's faithfulness.

TO READ: *Proverbs 26:1-12*

ARGUMENTS

When arguing with fools, don't answer their foolish arguments, or you will become as foolish as they are. When arguing with fools, be sure to answer their foolish arguments, or they will become wise in their own estimation.

PROVERBS 26:4-5

O n June 14, 1643, the English Parliament passed a law limiting the publication of books and requiring that all printing presses be licensed. The honorable members of parliament were concerned about the number of "scandalous, seditious, and libelous" books that were being published, including a pamphlet on divorce by the great poet John Milton. He responded to this governmental action by publishing—unlicensed—an article called "Areopagitica," in which he challenged the ruling on the grounds that learning should be encouraged, that the free exchange of ideas is necessary, and that attempts to stop books from being published without a license would be no more successful than attempts to lock up crows by shutting the park gates! Milton said, "give me liberty to know, to utter, and to argue freely according to conscience, above all liberties." The freedom to argue!

But not all arguing is profitable. Proverbs states, "When arguing with fools, don't answer their foolish arguments, or you will become as foolish as they are." If we agree with Milton that we should be free to argue, we must also bear in mind that certain standards of argument must be followed. Otherwise, arguing will be an exercise in futility. Furthermore, thinking and expression might be dragged down to the level of foolish people. Better to pass by your freedom to argue than to argue and be degraded in the process!

But the next statement in Proverbs apparently contradicts the first statement: "When arguing with fools, be sure to answer their foolish arguments, or they will become wise in their own estimation." So the question now is, "Should you argue with a fool or not argue with a fool?" And the answer is "Both!"

Perhaps the best way of synchronizing the two statements is to say this: In matters of relative unimportance, don't bother getting into a debate that may deteriorate into a shouting match. But in matters of profound significance, you must not allow foolish statements to go unchallenged. A foolish statement uncorrected may bolster the fool in his folly and release dangerous nonsense into the thinking of unsuspecting—and unthinking—people. Not to argue in such cases is to be guilty of encouraging ignorance.

The key to successful argument is to know what is worth arguing about, to be sure of what you're talking about, to know when to speak and when to be silent, to express yourself graciously, and to be willing to be proved wrong. That is a good argument for good arguing.

TO READ: *Proverbs 27:1-10*

FRIENDS

Wounds from a friend are better than many kisses from an enemy.

PROVERBS 27:6

J ulius Caesar was attacked by sixty conspirators in the entrance to the Roman Senate on March 15, 44 B.C. As this was happening, he saw Marcus Junius Brutus rush at him with drawn dagger. He was shocked and in anguish cried out, "Et tu, Brute?"—"You, too, Brutus?" Brutus, a former enemy, had been forgiven, trusted, and genuinely loved by Caesar. But he had joined the assassins, and he plunged his dagger into the dictator's breast. While Caesar had forgiven many of his defeated opponents, he had not made genuine friends.

Harry S. Truman, the thirty-third President of the United States, had a similar problem. He said, "If you want a friend in Washington, D.C., get a dog!" While emperors and presidents face special problems in making friends, most men find difficulty in establishing and maintaining genuine friendships. The reason may be that friendships require time, effort, and vulnerability. Work demands a great part of a man's time and effort, and vulnerability is seen by many men as unmanly. So men tend to settle for acquaintances and colleagues, and friendships remain undeveloped.

That this is a serious omission in a man's life can be seen from the teaching of Proverbs: "Wounds from a friend are better than many kisses from an enemy" (Prov. 27:6). The kiss of Judas in the Garden of Gethsemane was, on first appearances, a greeting and a blessing, but in fact it was the infamous act of an unscrupulous enemy. Better to have been wounded by Peter's flailing sword than betrayed by Judas's deceitful kiss.

Not that a friend's wounding has to come from a sword; it can come from being told hard truths—things we need to hear, that only those who love us enough to be more concerned about our well-being than about our good feelings and their own status as friends would be willing to tell us. But "the heartfelt counsel of a friend is as sweet as perfume and incense" (27:9). Unpalatable counsel from a true friend is "heartfelt," genuine, and therefore sweet. Only one who trusts and has been trusted knows the motives behind the critical evaluation and the corrective advice.

A genuine friend is of inestimable worth. So "never abandon a friend—either yours or your father's" (27:10). The time will come in the uncertainties of life when support, encouragement, counsel, and help are in short supply. That is the time when long-standing friendships pay off. In Washington, and elsewhere, a dog is okay—he will lick your face and bring your slippers. But only a friend will deliver what you really need.

TO READ: *Proverbs 28:1-13*

HONESTY—
THE BEST *POLICY*?

It is better to be poor and honest than rich and crooked.

PROVERBS 28:6

onesty is the best policy" is a well-known aphorism. But it does not convey what Richard Whately, the Archbishop of Dublin, actually meant. The complete quotation is as follows: "Honesty is the best policy; but he who is governed by that maxim is not an honest man."[15] In the Archbishop's mind, to say "Honesty is the best policy" is to speak from a purely pragmatic point of view, not necessarily to be guided by the principle that honesty is intrinsically right and dishonesty is innately wrong!

It is true that "honesty is the best policy" can be nothing more than a hard-nosed, calculating conclusion. The person who believes "honesty is the best policy" may not be making a moral statement at all, and he may even be ready to engage in dishonest behavior if he thinks it will pay dividends. That is how a fundamentally dishonest man can subscribe to the idea that "honesty is the best policy."

Proverbs says, "It is better to be poor and honest than rich and crooked" (Prov. 28:6). This is not to suggest that all the poor are honest or that all the rich are crooked. But, all things being equal, being crooked has been known to lead to economic advantage, and being honest has at times been a financial disadvantage.

The point at issue, however, is that the advantages gained by dishonesty demand a heavy price from the dishonest man. That price is the disturbance of conscience, the fear of disclosure, the compounding of the problem by cover-up and further lies, and the ultimate accounting to God. The honest man pays no such price—while he may be financially impoverished, he is morally rich.

Dishonesty in financial dealings is robbery, and dishonesty in business is arrogance. What could be more arrogant than the attitude of the liar who lies to gain advantage and says, in effect, "You do not deserve the truth and I am the one who determines what you deserve"?

Dishonesty in the marriage bond, though, is destruction. The adulterer uses the body of his paramour without thought for her person and destroys her self-esteem. He abuses the love of his wife without thought for her heartbreak and destroys her ability to trust. It is fundamentally wrong!

The honest man will pay his taxes and be poorer, will deal fairly in business and may miss a deal, and will be true to his wife and never taste forbidden fruit. But he will know that in the eyes of his God he did right, that he did not contribute to the "moral rot" (28:2) of his society, and he did not lead "the upright into sin" (28:10). For him, it is not a matter of pragmatic policy—it is a matter of spiritual integrity.

---

[15] *Oxford Dictionary of Quotations*, second ed., p. 565.

TO READ: *Proverbs 29:11-18*

CHILDREN AND DISCIPLINE

Discipline your children, and they will give you happiness and peace of mind.
When people do not accept divine guidance, they run wild.
But whoever obeys the law is happy.

PROVERBS 29:17-18

The cultivated rose, that most fragrant and most beautiful of flowers, has captured the imaginations of poets and songwriters down through the centuries. But roses left to themselves soon run wild. They lose their fragrance, the blooms deteriorate, thorns and brambles take over, and no one writes of their beauty. They need the pruner's knife to cultivate them and make them beautiful again.

Children "run wild" when they are not exposed to helpful discipline (Prov. 29:18). This creates problems for their parents, for themselves, and for anyone else who crosses their paths. Their parents experience embarrassment and public disgrace by their behavior (29:15). The children themselves, not obeying God's law or even their parents', are not happy (29:18). So if parents want to do the right thing for their children, and at the same time save themselves some grief, they should listen to Scripture, which says, "to discipline and reprimand a child produces wisdom" (29:15) and "discipline your children, and they will give you happiness and peace of mind" (29:17).

Discipline is not designed for the benefit of parents, so that they can work out their frustrations—it is for the good of the children. It is intended to save young people from foolishness and lead them into wisdom. It is meant to show them the right way and encourage them to follow it.

Many children appear to have a nose for folly and an aversion to wisdom. This is because they have a built-in bias toward doing their own thing, being their own person, and satisfying their own desires. Discipline is designed to help them see that, as responsible members of the human race, they cannot live wisely and well if they become absorbed with themselves, focused on getting their own way, and determined to brook no opposition. That kind of living is an affront to God, an embarrassment to parents, and, ultimately, destructive of the young person.

A big question in modern Western culture is "What is the right way to discipline a child?" In Old Testament times, the answer was to use the "rod of correction"—to apply physical punishment to the anatomy of the offending youngster. In recent times, this has been frowned upon as a form of child abuse. Some would respond, "That is why we have created a permissive society." Both have a point!

More recently, the emphasis in child-rearing has been on explaining to the child what is unacceptable, pointing out the natural consequences, and appealing to the child's better nature. Perhaps a paraphrase of Proverbs would be a suitable response to this approach: "For a [child], mere words are not enough—discipline is needed. For the words may be understood, but they are not heeded" (29:19).

Parents who are careful to show children what they need to heed will find that they themselves are blessed with what they desperately need—peace of mind! More importantly, the child will have peace of heart and life.

TO READ: *Proverbs 30:1–16*

SATISFACTION

O God, I beg two favors from you before I die. First, help me never to tell a lie.
Second, give me neither poverty nor riches! Give me just enough to satisfy my needs.

PROVERBS 30:7-8

As late as the nineteenth century, leeches were used by physicians in the treatment of a variety of ailments. The green and brown worms were attached to the patient, and the sucker at each end of the leech's anatomy went to work. The leech's saliva contains an anticoagulant to stop the blood clotting, an anesthetic so the patient (victim!) feels no discomfort, and a substance which dilates the vessels to facilitate the blood flow. Leeches are highly sophisticated suckers!

Dissatisfaction is a leech. Agur, a writer of proverbs, said, "The leech has two suckers that cry out, 'More, more!' There are three other things—no, four!—that are never satisfied: the grave, the barren womb, the thirsty desert, the blazing fire" (Prov. 30:15-16). The person who is never satisfied, who cries out continually for "more, more" is probably anesthetized to the fact that, because he concentrates on what he *doesn't* have, he is incapable of enjoying what he *does* have. And all the time, joy, delight, contentment, and thanksgiving flow freely away from his thoughts, leaving him depleted and spiritually anemic.

The picture of the leech is sufficient to portray the attitudes and condition of the dissatisfied man. But the further analogies of grave, barren womb, thirsty desert, and blazing fire serve to underline his serious condition. Not only does his dissatisfied soul find no satisfaction, but his dissatisfaction creates further dissatisfaction and he sinks into the grave of deadened delight while the fires of insatiable longings consume him. His life becomes barren like a desert, and the inner longings of his soul cry out unheeded, unanswered, and unmet. So what can be done about it?

Agur prayed a mature prayer, which should be echoed by every person concerning his financial status and spiritual condition: "O God, I beg two favors from you before I die. First, help me never to tell a lie. Second, give me neither poverty nor riches! Give me just enough to satisfy my needs. For if I grow rich, I may deny you and say, 'Who is the Lord?' and if I am too poor, I may steal and thus insult God's holy name" (30:7-9). The poor man, who, understandably, is not satisfied with his poverty, may be tempted to steal in order to have enough to survive. His dissatisfaction can lead him into an endless cycle of trouble. So Agur wisely prays to be delivered from poverty. But the pathologies of abundance need to be addressed as well. For abundance and affluence not only create a desire for more, but also a dangerous tendency to self-sufficiency. For the man who has everything—even if he wants more—may decide he doesn't need God. So Agur prays to be delivered from abundance, and asks for just enough to satisfy his needs (30:8).

The leeches of dissatisfaction will drain you—but the vitamins of contentment will sustain you.

TO READ: *Proverbs 31:10-31*

A VIRTUOUS WOMAN

Who can find a virtuous and capable wife? She is worth more than precious rubies.

PROVERBS 31:10

N aomi Wolf wrote in a recent book, "There are no good girls; we are all bad girls." She went on to suggest that, since this is the case, women should admit it, society should accept it, and everybody should get on with their lives. Presumably, traditional thoughts of feminine virtue and decorum, grace, and beauty should be jettisoned, and women should be allowed to behave like—well, like men!

Should that happen, the search for a virtuous woman will become even more of a challenge than it apparently was in the days that the book of Proverbs was written. There we read, "Who can find a virtuous and capable wife?" (Prov. 31:10). Given her stated worth as being "more precious than rubies," it appears that there were not enough "virtuous and capable" women to go around. But men were nevertheless well-advised to search for such a woman, because a virtuous and capable woman's "husband can trust her, and she will greatly enrich his life. She will not hinder him but help him all her life" (31:12).

As this "Proverbs 31" woman is described, her virtues and capabilities come clearly to the fore. In fact, she appears to be a superwoman. It is no wonder that such a woman, once discovered, would be a precious treasure! Perhaps no one woman is expected to display all the characteristics of the woman described here. Her trustworthiness, her industry, her foresight, her wisdom, her generosity, her reputation, her faith, her wisdom, her kindness, her childcare, and her love for her husband are the characteristics that a man should look for in a wife and virtues that he should nurture and nourish once she has agreed to share her life with him.

Unfortunately, men often tend to look on the physical attractiveness of a woman as her most significant asset, and they may overlook more important aspects of her person. They should remember that "charm is deceptive, and beauty does not last; but a woman who fears the Lord will be greatly praised" (31:30). In other words, a woman's outward appearance is not insignificant, but her inward disposition is profoundly more significant. And this disposition stems from a heart for the Lord. In other words, her faith matters more than her face!

Feminists like Naomi Wolf may be convinced that all girls are bad, but they're wrong. God has his women, and a wise man who has sought one of them, wooed her, won her, and cherished her will never let her go—and he will treat her in such a way that she'll never want to stray.

TO READ: *Psalm 121*

MOUNTAINS

I look up to the mountains— does my help come from there?
My help comes from the LORD, who made the heavens and the earth!

PSALM 121:1-2

Some men regard mountains as sacred residences of spiritual beings. They treat the peaks with deference. So a British expedition stopped just short of the summit of Kanchenjunga at the request of the Sikkim government because it was believed the gods lived there. Other men, like the great military leader Hannibal, see the mountains as a hindrance to be overcome. In the third century B.C. he marshaled his army and led them over the Alps from Spain into northern Italy—a spectacular feat made even more dramatic by the fact that the army's supplies were carried over the mountains by elephants! Still other men, when they look at the soaring peaks, see a challenge to be accepted. So when a mountaineer was asked why he tried to climb Everest, he said simply, "Because it was there."

The psalm writer, on viewing the mountains, asked the question, "Does my help come from there?" (Ps. 121:1). As he was on a pilgrimage journey, climbing the rough road to Jerusalem, which lies nestled in the mountains, perhaps the psalm writer asked himself whether Jerusalem, and all it stood for, was the answer to his feelings of insecurity. Or perhaps the psalm writer had just completed a time of festival worship in the Holy City, and as he contemplated the mountainous terrain lying between him and his home, this question came to mind.

The answer is forthcoming, and serves to direct the psalm writer's attention to the Lord, who made the mountains—in fact, he is the one "who made the heavens and the earth!" (121:2). The Lord is the one from whom all things come, in whom all things consist, and because of whom all things continue to be.

As we face life's mountains, our help comes from the Lord. The mountains are austere, forbidding, and immovable. Because of this, men may be excused if they gain the impression that the One who made the mountains—and everything else—is similarly austere, forbidding, and immovable. But the psalm writer insists otherwise. The Lord himself is the one who "watches over you" (121:5). He is not remote; he is "at hand." He is not uncaring; he is alert to our condition and aware of our needs. He is not callous and indifferent; his ears are attentive to our cries.

The mountains of life may hold promise of adventure or cast grim shadows of foreboding, but nothing they offer or threaten can alter the fact that "The Lord keeps watch over you as you come and go, both now and forever" (121:8). Hannibal crossed his mountains with the help of elephants. To cross our mountains, we have the Lord!

TO READ: *Mark 6:6b-13*

LEARNING BY DOING

*Then Jesus went out from village to village, teaching. And he called his twelve
disciples together and sent them out two by two, with authority to cast out evil spirits.*

MARK 6:6-7

W hen Socrates taught his pupils in ancient Greece, he did not stand on a podium
while they sat in quiet rows assiduously taking notes. Instead, he engaged them
in a structured dialogue. Nowadays, graduate students in the Harvard Business School do
case studies, students in junior high classes are given team projects, and medical students
learn through practical residencies. There are many different ways of learning.

Jesus, the master teacher, sometimes used monologue, while at other times he
engaged in dialogue. Occasionally he told parables, which were basically case studies. But
the most surprising thing about Jesus' teaching methods was his commitment to learning
by doing.

In the training of the twelve disciples, there came a time when Jesus decided it
was time to send them out on a mission. At that juncture, the disciples were clearly not
polished preachers or teachers. In fact, they didn't even have a firm grasp of their subject—
as evidenced by their total surprise when Jesus was crucified, and even greater amazement
when he rose from the dead, despite the fact that he had been telling them throughout
their training that this would happen! And they certainly were not always proficient when
they were called upon to confront evil spirits, or even capable of handling the squabbles
that arose in their own fellowship. But Jesus sent them out anyway!

The disciples were told to travel in pairs, presumably for mutual support, and were
given detailed instructions about traveling light and being content with their lodgings.
Because of the urgency of their mission, they would not have time to bother about creature
comforts, and since they would need to be constantly on the move in order to reach as
many people as possible, they should not be encumbered by unnecessary baggage.

The disciples were charged to "cast out evil spirits" (Mark 6:7). This may have caused
them some consternation, but they were given Jesus' own authority, which was as powerful
as the one who delegated it to them. And they were instructed not to waste time talking to
people who had no intention of listening to them, even to the point of shaking the dust
off their feet as they left an unresponsive village—an action usually done by Jews as they
left a pagan environment.

So with a sense of mission, urgency, dependency, apprehension, and expectation
they went forth. Uncertain in their own minds, unprepared in their own strength, they
went in obedience to Jesus and in dependence on Jesus. They were a blessing—and they
were blessed. Ministering as they went, they learned as they worked. God's teaching
methods have not changed.

TO READ: *Mark 6:14–29*

CONSCIENCE

*And Herod respected John, knowing that he was a good and holy man, so he kept
him under his protection. Herod was disturbed whenever he talked with John, but
even so, he liked to listen to him.*

MARK 6:20

A llan Bloom, in his book *The Closing of the American Mind*, probably borrowed from
Shakespeare's famous line, "Conscience doth make cowards of us all." Bloom wrote,
"Conscience is a coward and those faults it has not strength enough to prevent, it seldom
has justice enough to punish by accusing."[16]

The story of John the Baptist and Herod Antipas is a fascinating commentary on
Bloom's observation. Herod and John knew each other well. As a matter of conscience,
John had been outspoken in opposing Herod's marriage to "his brother Philip's wife,
Herodias" (Mark 6:17). Herodias was understandably upset by this public condemnation
and persuaded Herod to imprison John. But even in prison John would not be silenced.
He "kept telling Herod, 'It is illegal for you to marry your brother's wife'" (6:18). There was
something about John's integrity which appealed to Herod, and he "liked to listen to him"
(6:20), even though John said things he didn't like to hear. But Herodias did not like it,
and when Herod (no doubt in a rash, unguarded, and possibly wine-induced moment)
offered Herodias's daughter anything she wanted—"up to half my kingdom"—she asked
for John's head on a platter. And she got it, much to Herod's chagrin, because of his fear
of losing face (6:26).

When Jesus appeared on the scene, superstitious people said, "This must be John the
Baptist come back to life again" (6:14). The gossip reached Herod's ears, and this powerful
man "was worried and puzzled" because of what he heard (Luke 9:7). The ruler of all
Galilee and Perea was troubled by a guilty conscience. John, whom he had executed, "was
a good and holy man" (Mark 6:20). While Herod sat on his royal throne with a troubled
conscience, John had gone to his grave with a clear conscience.

John undoubtedly had his faults, but cowardice was not one of them. Herod was full
of faults, but his conscience did not have strength enough to prevent them. Whether or not
Herod's conscience had the justice to accuse his faults, we cannot be sure. At least he was
worried and puzzled!

The issue for me, and every modern man, is how to keep the conscience alive, and
where to find the courage to respond. In John's case, the answer was found in his
commitment to truth and his relationship to God's Spirit. It comes down to whether my
conscience makes me a coward or my commitment to truth gives me the courage of
conviction—whether I'm a Herod or a John.

[16]Allan Bloom, *The Closing of the American Mind*.

TO READ: *Mark 6:30-44*

NOT BY BREAD ALONE

A vast crowd was there as he stepped from the boat, and he had compassion on them
because they were like sheep without a shepherd. So he taught them many things.

MARK 6:34

At the beginning of the twentieth century, a serious issue split the American church. Some of the "liberal" ministers, who had been influenced by German theologians, preached that the church's mission was to deal with society's ills and thus to bring in God's kingdom. On the other hand, more traditional, or "conservative," Christians believed that the church's task was not so much to change man's lot on earth but rather to make man fit for heaven. The latter, conservative approach was called "pie in the sky when you die" by those who opposed it, while the former, liberal approach was called "the social gospel" by its detractors.

The attempts to bring in God's kingdom by social engineering in the name of Christ fell on hard times during the great World Wars of the twentieth century, as the atrocities perpetrated by so-called Christian nations became known. So, as the twentieth century ran its course, the liberal churches, which had espoused the social gospel, went into serious decline, while conservative churches, which preached the gospel of salvation from sin and the hope of eternal life, flourished.

However, toward the end of the twentieth century, many of the same churches that had reacted negatively to the social gospel of the liberals began to rethink their understanding of the church's mission. They read passages such as the "Feeding of the Five Thousand" and could not overlook the fact that Jesus dealt with physical as well as spiritual needs.

When Jesus saw the "vast crowd . . . he had compassion on them because they were like sheep without a shepherd. So he taught them many things" (Mark 6:34). Jesus addressed people's spiritual needs by proclaiming the truth of God's kingdom to them. But it soon became apparent that the people were hungry. So, to the surprise of his disciples, Jesus said, "You feed them" (6:37). The disciples doubted whether the hungry throng was their responsibility, but Jesus had no doubts! So he sent his men scurrying around, and they mustered pitifully inadequate resources. These Jesus gladly accepted and wonderfully blessed, and the people were fed—physically!

There is now general agreement that the church's mission involves concern for both the physical and the spiritual needs of the crowds, but there the consensus ends. Some say we should feed the crowds to get them to listen to the gospel. Others say we should feed them because they're hungry, whether they listen or not. And still others say we only need to feed those who respond to the gospel.

Every man who eats should remember those who starve. And each man who rejoices in the gospel should have compassion for those who have never heard it once. Jesus did!

TO READ: *Mark 6:45-56*

SLOW LEARNERS

*They still didn't understand the significance of the miracle of the multiplied loaves,
for their hearts were hard and they did not believe.*

MARK 6:52

I t has been said that a professional football game is an event where eleven men in
desperate need of rest are criticized by a crowd of people in desperate need of exercise.
Criticizing is considerably easier than participating. And it is a whole lot easier to criticize
the first disciples than it would have been to live their lives. But their story is included in
Scripture for our edification, so we must be careful not to miss the lessons we should learn
from their mistakes. After all, learning by making mistakes is a common educational
method, and it is least painful when based on the mistakes of another!

Jesus sent the disciples on ahead of him after feeding the five thousand. But while
crossing the Sea of Galilee, they ran into a major storm and feared for their lives. Jesus
decided to walk home by the quickest route—over water. As he drew level with their boat
and "started to go past them" (Mark 6:48), his disciples saw him but thought they saw an
apparition of some kind. When "they screamed in terror, thinking he was a ghost," he
turned to them and said, "'It's all right. . . . I am here! Don't be afraid.' Then he climbed
into the boat and the wind stopped" (6:49-51).

Clearly, the disciples had been eyewitnesses to another miracle, but there are two
strange aspects to this story that require exploration. First, why did Jesus "start to go past
them" in their hour of need? Second, why does Mark record that "they still didn't understand the significance of the miracle of the multiplied loaves, for their hearts were hard
and they did not believe" (6:52)?

The psalm writer, talking about the Lord's dealing with his people in the wilderness,
wrote, "[God] gave them bread from heaven. They ate the food of angels! God gave them
all they could hold" (Ps. 78:24-25). The psalmist also wrote, "Your road led through the
sea, your pathway through the mighty waters—a pathway no one knew was there" (Ps.
77:19). Jesus, by his actions, was living out what these Scriptures write about God! He
walked "through the mighty waters" and gave them "food of angels . . . all they could
hold." Jesus was actually performing before their eyes the incredible things their Scriptures
told them were the activities of God!

But the disciples did not yet believe that Jesus was actually God with them. Their
understanding of him was still in embryonic form. That's why their faith still needed to be
stretched. The disciples had no shortage of data about Jesus—just a shortage of application.
They were thoroughly conversant with what the Scriptures say about God. They believed that
God could do marvelous things. Their history told them that he had regularly shown himself
strong on behalf of their forefathers. But they had trouble believing he was actually with
them in the storm and that his presence should banish their fears and infuse them with
confidence.

But let's criticize them gently and learn from them quickly. Which of us does not
struggle at this point?

TO READ: *Mark 7:1-13*

CEREMONIES
AND TRADITIONS

*"These people honor me with their lips, but their hearts are far away. Their worship is
a farce, for they replace God's commands with their own man-made teachings."*

MARK 7:7

M ost parents require their children to wash their hands before mealtime. In many
instances, this appears to create great hardship for the children, if their reluctance
to obey is anything to go by. But basic hygiene demands that the ritual be fulfilled before
food is handled. It's a matter of hygiene—and nothing more.

In Jesus' day, what had started out as basic hygiene had developed into something
quite different. Simple hand washing before eating or after returning home from the
market had developed into an elaborate ceremony with purported spiritual significance.
Instead of simply eradicating unpleasant dirt when they followed "the usual Jewish ritual
of hand washing before eating" (Mark 7:2), the religious Jews believed that they were
ensuring a religious purity before God by their action. By their ablutions on returning
home from market, they believed they were underlining their divinely-approved
separation from the contaminating world.

As time went by, these "ancient traditions" (7:3) took on such importance that a
person's spiritual standing was evaluated by his adherence to the ritual—or lack thereof.
In some instances, a person who failed to go through the ritual, for any reason whatever,
would be regarded as ceremonially unclean and therefore be banned from worship.

This was what lay behind the question asked by the Jerusalem leaders when they
traveled to confront Jesus: "Why don't your disciples follow our age-old customs? For
they eat without first performing the hand-washing ceremony" (7:5). Jesus replied with
surprising vehemence. "You hypocrites! Isaiah was prophesying about you when he said,
'These people honor me with their lips, but their hearts are far away. Their worship is a
farce, for they replace God's commands with their own man-made teachings'" (7:6-7).

Jesus was exposing the age-old problem of religious ritual devoid of spiritual reality.
The charge of hypocrisy was well-founded. In those days, a hypocrite was literally an actor
who would convey an emotion by holding a mask over his face. Religious externalism does
just that: it portrays on the outside that which may not be present on the inside. That was the
problem—the Jerusalem religious leaders lacked a real spirituality. They were faking it!

Adherence to religious rituals such as baptism or communion is to be encouraged,
provided that the external act represents an inner reality. But if the familiar act has
degenerated into an empty symbol, that which claims to be a spiritual experience may be
nothing more than a gross distortion. What outwardly purports to demonstrate a deep
spirituality may be nothing more than a blatant lie. Religious ritual is intended to portray
spiritual reality, not to become a substitute for it.

So here's a healthy exercise. Check on the religious rituals in which you have
participated in the past or in which you still participate, explore their hidden significance,
and see if the significance is as real in your heart as the participation is part of your life.

APRIL

TO READ: *Mark 7:14-23*

THOUGHT-LIFE

It is the thought-life that defiles you.

MARK 7:20

W hether the world is getting better or worse is a subject for debate about which you will not find agreement. But there is no argument that there are many things sadly wrong with our world. The evidence is unmistakable. The debate on this issue is, "Why?" Some say that Western culture is polluted, and its insidious corrupting influence is responsible for personal ethics and behaviors which are so deplorable. The solution then becomes a matter of reforming culture. Others say that as culture is created by humans, it is the humans who are corrupted. Therefore, the solution lies in the human heart.

This debate was raging, in a slightly different form, during the earthly ministry of Jesus. The religious people of the day were adamant that it was external things that were responsible for moral and spiritual corruption and that, if proper care was taken to avoid the corrupt externals, moral and spiritual purity was assured. On this premise, they had established elaborate codes of behavior. The result was a meticulous observance of religious rituals designed to guarantee right behavior and a sound society.

Then along came Jesus. He challenged this viewpoint and told the people, "You are not defiled by what you eat; you are defiled by what you say and do" (Mark 7:15). Even his disciples were confused by this radical statement, so they asked him privately to explain further. This Jesus did, in graphic terms. He pointed out that food, which in their minds was an example of an external polluting influence, could not possibly be responsible for polluting a person's character and behavior, because it enters the stomach and passes through the body (7:19). Instead, "You are defiled by what you say and do. . . . It is the thought-life that defiles you" (7:15, 20).

Jesus taught that the ills of society are born in the human heart. "From within, out of a person's heart, come evil thoughts, sexual immorality, theft, murder, adultery, greed, wickedness, deceit, eagerness for lustful pleasure, envy, slander, pride, and foolishness" (7:22). A modern way of expressing similar sentiments is this:

> *Watch your thoughts, they become words.*
> *Watch your words, they become actions.*
> *Watch your actions, they become habits.*
> *Watch your habits, they become character.*
> *Watch your character, it becomes your destiny.*

Speaking of destiny, Jesus not only said that thoughts corrupt, but he added that the thought-life "make[s] you unacceptable to God" (7:23).

The social ramifications of aberrant behavior that is born in the human heart are desperately serious. But the seriousness pales in comparison to the eternal consequences of sin. Your thought-life can corrupt your society but, more significantly, it can condemn your soul.

TO READ: *Psalm 33:1-22*

NEW SONGS OF PRAISE

Let the godly sing with joy to the LORD, for it is fitting to praise him. . . .
Sing new songs of praise to him; play skillfully on the harp and sing with joy.

PSALM 33:1, 3

W orship wars" is a sad new term in Christian dialogue. It is hard to imagine anything more discouraging than Christians actually fighting over the subject of worship. But it happens. "War" may be too emotive a word to describe what has happened, but "skirmish" is a little on the weak side, given the emotion generated by the issue.

The problem has its roots in the tendency to equate music with worship. Not many years ago, song leaders gave way to worship leaders—with little discernible difference in function. People old enough to remember song leaders may sometimes wonder about their metamorphosis into worship leaders and all that is involved in the change. Of course, music has been and continues to be a powerful means of expressing praise and of communicating a message. It is a legitimate aspect of worship. But worship is much more than music and involves more than praise.

Perhaps the central question, and the biggest cause of strife, is, "What precisely constitutes worshipful music?" To a large extent, the differences of opinion on this issue are generational. Younger people have been raised in an era dominated by a powerful music industry that fills every waking moment with music, most of it contemporary. So their musical tastes have been firmly fixed in place, and they often have little knowledge of, or interest in, music that is not contemporary in style. Meanwhile, the older people, having been raised on "church music," view the new styles with varying degrees of suspicion and rejection.

So what to do? The psalm writer gives us some clues. First, he said, "Let the godly sing with joy to the Lord" (Ps. 33:1). Music has a mandatory place in worship, and it must be addressed to the Lord. Second, the psalmist encouraged the people to "sing new songs of praise to him" (33:3). So there is a place for contemporary music. But third, the music should be done well—musicians who aspire to lead worship should learn to "play skillfully" (33:3). Fourth, song (or worship!) leaders should constantly bear in mind that their songs and everything else in their worship should be based on "the word of the Lord" that "holds true" for everyone regardless of musical taste or generational preferences (33:4).

The only war the church is commissioned to fight is the war against evil. The only restriction on the church's style of worship is that it be compatible with truth. The only explanation for worship wars is that the evil one has deflected our focus. So let's get back on track.

TO READ: *Genesis 7:1-24*

NOAH AND THE FLOOD

Finally, the day came when the LORD said to Noah, "Go into the boat with all your family, for among all the people of the earth, I consider you alone to be righteous."

GENESIS 7:1

O ne of the most ancient pieces of literature known to man is called the *Gilgamesh Epic*. Gilgamesh, the hero of the story, was a king who did not want to die. So he traveled to see a man named Utnapishtim, who had reputedly survived a flood. According to the story, this tragic flood had been brought about by the gods, who were angry that the human race was multiplying so rapidly and was so noisy that the gods' peace and quiet was being disturbed. However, not all the gods were in favor of this "final solution" to the problem of noise. One of them, Ea, broke ranks and warned Utnapishtim of the impending tragedy. Forewarned, Utnapishtim built a boat and with his family escaped destruction.

This ancient story has been preserved for millennia on clay tablets. The interesting thing about the story is its remarkable similarities to the Noah account—and the striking dissimilarities to it. No one knows which version of the flood story was written down first. Clearly, though, these stories reflect a historical event, which was handed down verbally and then recorded. But there the similarity ends! The Gilgamesh story is all about squabbling, petty, selfish deities who reflect the sordid actions and attitudes of the men whose imagination created them. The biblical account records the gracious actions of the holy God, who is deeply distressed at human sin, and how he reaches out in grace, saves Noah and his family, and makes a solemn pledge never again to destroy the earth with a flood.

According to the *Gilgamesh Epic*, when Utnapishtim saw the weather worsening, he got into his boat and battened down the hatches. But according to the biblical account, Noah heard the Lord command, "Go into the boat with all your family, for among all the people of the earth, I consider you alone to be righteous" (Gen. 7:1). When Noah was inside with his family and the animals, "the Lord shut them in" (7:16).

Noah's salvation was based on the grace of the Lord, who had seen in Noah a man who walked before God in righteousness. Noah was not perfect, but he was obedient, loving, and trusting. He was instructed by the Lord to make the ark, and he did it. When he was invited by the Lord to enter the boat, he responded. And once inside, he was secured by the Lord, who personally battened down the hatches!

When the calamities of life overtake us, there are those who have nowhere to turn. Like Gilgamesh, who did not know how to cope with life, they turn to people whose luck has held and seek comfort from them. But those who know the Lord, like Noah, trust him and find him sufficient in their hour of need. They float when others sink.

AFTER THE DELUGE

*But God remembered Noah and all the animals in the boat. He sent a wind
to blow across the waters, and the floods began to disappear.*

GENESIS 8:1

The floods which swept over Mozambique in March 2000 were described by veteran relief workers as the worst natural disaster they had ever witnessed. After many days of cyclonic rainfall, the River Limpopo burst its banks. Mozambique, which is virtually the flood plain of southeast Africa, was inundated. Tens of thousands of helpless people were swept away, villages disappeared, and crops were devastated. Those who survived found precarious refuge in the tops of trees or on rooftops, which occasionally collapsed under the weight of the people. Rescue efforts were hindered by bureaucratic red tape, corruption, and lack of supplies. In the aftermath of the flooding, outbreaks of malaria and typhoid fever took many lives. The specter of starvation loomed over the troubled land. Hopelessness and helplessness prevailed.

The devastation in Mozambique no doubt prompted some people to think about the Flood recorded in Scripture. In that flood, the devastation was unprecedented and has never been repeated. While no theological cause and effect can be attributed to the Mozambique inundation, we do know the cause of the biblical flood. God, on observing "the extent of the people's wickedness," had specifically said, "I will completely wipe out this human race that I have created" (Gen. 6:5-6).

In Mozambique, the treetop survivors waited endlessly in hope that one of the few helicopters brought into action would see their plight and rescue them. In Noah's case, "God remembered [him] and all the animals in the boat. He sent a wind to blow across the waters, and the floods began to disappear" (Gen. 8:1). After careful reconnaissance with a raven and a dove, Noah and his family, the Flood's sole human survivors, disembarked in direct response to the divine command, "Leave the boat, all of you" (8:16). Then Noah promptly "built an altar to the Lord and sacrificed on it the animals and birds that had been approved for that purpose. And the Lord was pleased with the sacrifice" (8:20-21). Then the Lord promised that the normal course of seasonal and diurnal life would never again be disrupted. For no other reason than God's own grace, mankind was given a chance to start again, to be born anew.

The devastation caused by the floods in Mozambique reminds us of the horrors of Noah's flood, which, in turn, points to the seriousness of human sin and divine judgment. The shortage of relief in southeast Africa contrasts vividly with the gracious divine rescue of Noah. It is against the dark backdrop of sin and judgment that grace shines most brightly.

TO READ: *Genesis 9:8–17*

THE RAINBOW

*"I have placed my rainbow in the clouds. It is the sign of my permanent promise
to you and to all the earth. . . . Yes, this is the sign of my covenant
with all the creatures of the earth."*

GENESIS 9:13, 17

William Wordsworth, the poet, lived in the English Lake District. There, because of a damp climate and steady rainfall, rainbows regularly appear in the dark skies. He wrote,

"My heart leaps up when I behold
A rainbow in the sky,
So was it when my life began;
So is it now I am a man
So be it when I shall grow old
Or let me die."[17]

Wordsworth did not identify the reasons for his heart-leap. Given his love of nature and his poetic vision, he no doubt rejoiced in the rainbow's beauty and drew profound lessons from the sight.

The scientist, looking at the same rainbow, recognizes that light refracted through moisture produces a colored ray. In a shower of rain, many rays refracted at slightly different angles through many raindrops produce all the colors of the spectrum, which then form concentric arcs around the common center, the sun. And that's all that a rainbow is!

Two totally different viewpoints—one poetic, the other scientific. But there is another way of looking at the rainbow. God told Noah, "I have placed my rainbow in the clouds. It is the sign of my permanent promise to you and to all the earth. . . . Yes, this is the sign of my covenant with all the creatures of the earth" (Gen. 9:13, 17).

Scientific observation has enabled man to explore the world, to probe its mysteries, to mine its treasures, and to harness its power, more often than not to man's greater good. And poetic imagination has done much to enrich our souls. But only divine revelation can introduce man to the deepest, richest dimensions of life and the knowledge of eternity. Without God telling us, we would never have guessed that the rainbow is a message from the Creator of the universe, proclaiming his loving faithfulness and unending commitment to the covenant he freely made with man.

Some men who engage in scientific observation of the world fail to see evidence of the Creator in that which he created. And others whose poetic imaginations take them into flights of fancy frequently land in regions far from the Lord. But the scientist who knows and understands the things of God worships as he observes creation's wonders, and the believing poet's imagination soars to unimagined heights as he recognizes evidences of God on every hand.

Next time you see a rainbow, don't just see moist refractions or look for a pot of gold. Instead, worship God. And thank him for his promises.

[17]William Wordsworth, "My Heart Leaps Up."

TO READ: *Genesis 11:1-9*

CONVERSATION AND CONFUSION

In that way, the LORD scattered them all over the earth; and that ended the building of the city. That is why the city was called Babel, because it was there that the LORD confused the people by giving them many languages, thus scattering them across the earth.

GENESIS 11:8-9

Deborah Tannen has written a couple of books on the subject of conversation.[18] In the first, she explained the difficulties that people experience in communicating with each other. In the second, she pinpointed a particularly difficult area—the communication between men and women! There isn't a man or woman alive who has not experienced problems in that area. And Dr. Tannen was talking about communication difficulties between people using the same language!

The problems associated with people speaking different languages are even greater. Ask anyone who has tried to reason with a customs official in a foreign country, or any sick person who tried to explain his symptoms to a physician in another language!

The confusion among languages, however, is intentional. God did it! Genesis records, "At one time the whole world spoke a single language and used the same words" (Gen. 11:1).

So far, so good. But as the human race multiplied, they not only put up big numbers, they also began to have big ideas. They declared, "Let's build a great city with a tower that reaches to the skies—a monument to our greatness. This will bring us together and keep us from scattering all over the world" (11:4). Apparently, there were already signs of fragmentation among people, which they found disconcerting. So they decided to take steps to reverse the trend. The means that they chose to achieve this objective were both spectacular and self-serving. They would draw attention to their own greatness by building an edifice breathtaking in its design and execution—a temple to worship themselves. Everybody seeing it would recognize its message: "As long as we stick together, we're unbeatable. Nothing is beyond our ability. The sky's the limit."

There is nothing intrinsically wrong with ambition, and there is no doubt that God delights to see his creatures using the powers of imagination and ingenuity he gave them. But imagination and ingenuity have their limits. When man becomes so enraptured with his own greatness that he overlooks the incontrovertible truth that he is an infinitesimal fragment of a vast creation, utterly dependent upon God's grace for survival and salvation, then he needs to be stopped. Otherwise, he will not so much build edifices declaring his greatness as he will erect monuments displaying his folly.

God decided to keep the human race off balance, so he gave us a multitude of languages to keep us from communicating clearly with one another (11:7). The result has been both infuriating and illuminating. The downside of language confusion is misunderstanding, which causes friction and division. The upside is that misunderstanding is a constant reminder that we're not as smart as we think we are! There should be no confusion about that!

---

[18]Deborah Tannen, *That's Not What I Meant!* and *You Really Don't Understand.*

TO READ: *Genesis 11:27–12:8*

STAKING THE CLAIM

Then the LORD *appeared to Abram and said, "I am going to give this land to your offspring." And Abram built an altar there to commemorate the Lord's visit.*

GENESIS 12:7

In the days of the California gold rush, the miners rushed to stake claims to land that they believed held their fortune. Before them, in the days of the colonizers, the explorers arrived at foreign shores and, in front of the curious glances of the indigenous people, they planted the flag of their sovereigns. In more recent times, after great battles the victorious troops raised their standard over hard-won territory—for instance, the U.S. Marines on Iwo Jima, an event captured in the famous photograph (and subsequent statue) which was taken the day after the actual event took place!

Millennia earlier, Abram received instructions from the Lord that he was to leave his home in Ur of the Chaldees and head toward a destination that would be shown to him *en route*. In a remarkable display of obedience and faith, he did so. The enterprise stalled in Haran until Abram's father died. The Lord then gave his instructions directly to Abram: "Leave your country, your relatives, and your father's house, and go to the land I will show you" (12:1). So he did. When he eventually arrived at Shechem, the place to which he had been traveling unknowingly, the Lord visited him and confirmed that it was the place of his choice, telling Abram, "I am going to give this land to your offspring" (12:7).

Abram had no flag, and there was no office to which he could rush to stake a claim, but he left his mark at the place: He "built an altar there to commemorate the Lord's visit" (12:7). Then he traveled on to Bethel and "there he built an altar and worshiped the Lord" (12:8). When the colonial explorers planted their flags and staked their claims to vast territories, they had little to go on to justify their claims but their own arrogance and gunpowder. In Abram's case, the Canaanites were in possession of the land when he arrived, but it was because the Lord (whose land it was in the first place) had ceded it to Abram's heirs that Abram took his action in trust and obedience.

When we look at the promises that God gave Abram, it is remarkable that not one of them could be substantiated with any degree of certainty. Becoming the "father of a great nation" (12:2) seemed highly unlikely, being blessed and becoming famous and becoming a "blessing to others" were far removed from anything that he was experiencing at that time (12:3). There was nothing tangible except altars, bearing silent witness to Abram's faith and obedience.

Everybody believes something. Along the path of our lives, we have each erected silent witnesses to what we hold dear—a business, a building, a boat, or a book. Sit down sometime, and look back and see the things you've left along the way. They'll speak volumes about the journey you've taken and the place where you've arrived.

TO READ: *Genesis 13:1-18*

STAYING ON TRACK

"I'll tell you what we'll do. Take your choice of any section of the land you want,
and we will separate. If you want that area over there, then I'll stay here.
If you want to stay in this area, then I'll move on to another place."

GENESIS 13:9

When a plane leaves the runway, or a train jumps the tracks, or a ship drifts off course, disaster looms large. And when men lose their vision, they can quickly lose direction and make big mistakes. Reputations are easily tarnished and hard-earned positions of influence quickly forfeited. When these men are the Lord's servants, the cause of the Lord suffers setback. The people of God become easy targets for ridicule and abuse.

After Abram had arrived in Canaan, severe famine necessitated his moving once again, this time to Egypt (Gen. 12:10). There is no indication that he should not have gone there—common sense dictated he should. But once there, Abram got off course. He lost sight of the Lord's care, and his triumphant faith was conquered by fear—fear that led him to tell half-truths that amounted to lies, which, in turn, embarrassed and enraged Pharaoh and led to Abram's ignominious expulsion from Egypt.

Sadder and wiser, Abram and his entourage "traveled north into the Negev. . . . They continued traveling by stages toward Bethel . . . the place where Abram had built the altar, and there he again worshiped the Lord" (13:1-4).

Back on track worshiping the Lord, Abram was immediately confronted with a test. It soon became obvious that the area where he was living lacked the means to support both his herds and those of Lot. Arguments erupted between their employees, and Abram stepped forward with a wise and selfless proposal to Lot. He told him, "I'll tell you what we'll do. Take your choice of any section of the land you want, and we will separate. If you want that area over there, then I'll stay here. If you want to stay in this area, then I'll move to another place" (13:9).

Lot promptly chose the prime land for himself, so Abram settled in the inferior territory. He could have pulled rank. He could have reminded Lot that he, Abram, was the Lord's chosen one and Lot was along for the ride. But he didn't. He knew in his heart that even when the Promised Land didn't look promising, the Lord of the promise was faithful, and the correct response to faithfulness is a fullness of faith.

Abram's failure of nerve in Egypt had taken him to the brink of disaster. He had learned a bitter lesson. But even his embarrassing expulsion had proved a blessing, because it had propelled him back to the place of worship.

Any man is capable of jumping the rails. The wise man knows how to get back on track.

TO READ: *Psalm 23*

ALL THE DAYS
OF MY LIFE

The LORD is my shepherd; I have everything I need.

PSALM 23:1

When Isaiah the prophet lamented that "All of us have strayed away like sheep. We have left God's paths to follow our own" (Isa. 53:6), it was not a compliment to be compared to sheep. Sheep have an infuriating tendency to wander and, not infrequently, to end up in deep trouble. Men have the same tendency. But not all sheep wander. Some seem to find an antidote to their restlessness—they settle down with a watchful shepherd. That is precisely what men need as well.

David, as we know, was no stranger to sheep. He spent many long and lonely hours shepherding on the hills surrounding Bethlehem, guarding against lions and bears and leading his charges to water and pasture. The simple words of David's most famous psalm capture the beauty of a sheep's life under the gracious care of a shepherd—or more accurately, the splendor of a man's life lived under the shepherding of the Lord.

The ability to say "I have everything I need" (23:1) is a rarity in today's consumer-oriented society. We are bombarded by skillfully-directed advertising that plays on our innermost fears and longings and blurs the distinction between needs and wants, necessities and luxuries. It is becoming harder to find "rest in green meadows" and peace "beside peaceful streams" (23:2). Men are fighting the rush of modern life in the concrete jungle.

The man who can testify truthfully "The Lord is my shepherd" (23:1) can also speak of how this fundamental truth has made an impact on his life. And not just occasionally, but "all the days of [his] life" (23:6). To know the place where "strength" can be renewed and guidance along "right paths" (23:3) can be found is to be assured and encouraged in the midst of modern uncertainty. A man can have this confidence even when called upon by life's vicissitudes to "walk through the dark valley" (23:4) and to live "in the presence of [one's] enemies" (23:5). When the Lord is our shepherd, he gives the grace "not [to] be afraid" and to testify, "My cup overflows with blessings" (23:4-5). To experience this is to live at a level not known by many a man.

Should it be objected that all this sounds too good to be true, the response must be—it is! That is, unless the Lord is shepherding. Then his "goodness and unfailing love" (23:6) will pursue even the potentially wayward sheep, like divinely directed sheepdogs.

And that is not the end of it. When "all the days of [his] life" are over, the well-shepherded man will "live in the house of the Lord forever" (23:6). What a way to go!

TO READ: *Mark 9:38-50*

HEART TO HEART

[Jesus] sat down and called the twelve disciples over to him. Then he said, "Anyone who wants to be the first must take last place and be the servant of everyone else."

MARK 9:35

Good coaches know that when things are going badly, it is necessary to call a team meeting. It happens in families, too; Father decides it is time to call everybody together to go over basic family rules. And businesses do the same thing; management closes down the operation for a day, calls the staff together, and addresses the issues that need to be confronted.

There is a great precedent for this approach. Jesus did it with his disciples: "He sat down and called the twelve disciples over to him" (Mark 9:35), and he began to go over some of the things that he had decided needed special emphasis!

Jesus started with the issue of spiritual pecking order, which the disciples were apparently concerned about. He said, "Anyone who wants to be the first must take last place and be the servant of everyone else" (9:35). They couldn't argue, because Jesus modeled it! Then he addressed their elitist attitude toward their ministry. They had come across somebody who was using the name of Jesus to cast out demons, but because he did not belong to the twelve they "told him to stop" (9:38). Jesus said that was the wrong thing to do. If the man was genuinely operating in the name of Jesus—that is, out of a genuine relationship with Christ—there was no problem with him doing the same type of ministry as Christ and his twelve disciples were doing.

Then Jesus turned his attention to the subject of causing people to be hindered in their spiritual lives. He told them, "If anyone causes one of these little ones who trusts in me to lose faith, it would be better for that person to be thrown into the sea with a large millstone around the neck" (9:42). Harsh words indeed. The little ones to whom he referred could have been either the children who were gathered around or young believers like the man who was casting out demons. Either way, the message was clear. Using dramatic, symbolic language to make his point, Jesus warned of the consequences of sin, not only in terms of the harm it does to others but also with regard to the eternal destiny of the sinner. The point of the heart-to-heart talk was to remind his disciples that they were called to be special—"salty"—and that they were in danger of becoming ordinary—of losing their flavor!

Attitudes and actions speak loudly and make a profound, sometimes detrimental, impact on other people. Rather than be responsible for causing someone else "to lose faith," strict discipline should be self-imposed. That way, men who follow Jesus can keep their Christlike flavor. Jesus likes his salt salty!

TO READ: *Mark 10:1-16*

MARRIAGE AND DIVORCE

God's plan was seen from the beginning of creation, for "He made them male and female." This explains why a man leaves his father and mother and is joined to his wife, and the two are united into one.

MARK 10:6-8

F rom the beginning of creation God ordained physical laws for the universe. The law of gravity and the laws of thermodynamics are well-established realities. When we acknowledge and adhere to them in our daily lives, they prove highly beneficial and ensure that life proceeds smoothly. However, should we attempt to contravene natural laws, for instance by stepping off a skyscraper or sitting on a hot stove, then negative things happen and consequences are incurred.

In the same way, God ordained societal laws for the well-being of those of us who are privileged to live in his wonderful world. Jesus reminded his questioners of some of these fundamental laws when he was challenged by a question. The question, designed "to trap him," was, "Should a man be allowed to divorce his wife?" (Mark 10:2-3). In our own society, given the high incidence of divorce, it is almost assumed that a man can divorce his wife whenever and why-ever he wishes.

But it was not so in Jesus' day. In fact, divorce was the subject of heated debate. Some rabbis, like Hillel, taught that divorce was legitimate for the most trivial, flippant reasons—but only for men! Others, like Shammai, adopted a conservative stance about divorce and condemned the teachings and attitudes of men like Hillel.

Jesus' questioners were trying to get him to say something on the subject that they could later use against him. Jesus replied, as he so often did, by asking a question, "What did Moses say about divorce?" (10:3). To this they replied, "Well, he permitted it" (10:4). Jesus established that divorce was permissible during Moses' time, but only as a "concession" to people's "hard-hearted wickedness" (10:5). In other words, it was not God's ideal. Jesus immediately explained, "But God's plan was seen from the beginning of creation, for, 'He made them male and female.' This explains why a man leaves his father and mother and is joined to his wife, and the two are united into one" (10:6-8).

God's ideal is very clear. A man and a woman come together in marriage, they have children whom they raise in the safety and love of a home, the children eventually leave home, they get married, they have children, and the cycle of human life and well-being continues. Like divinely ordained natural laws, these societal principles are designed for mankind's well-being. And like the physical laws, negative consequences are incurred when we attempt to contravene them.

Society needs to obey God's laws of marriage and family. But what about people who disobey and finish up divorced? They need care, too. In fact, one of the greatest challenges facing the contemporary church is, "How do we uphold the divine principles of marriage and family while at the same time caring for those whose marriages have failed and whose families are in shambles?" That is a question we need to think seriously about!

TO READ: *Hebrews 12:1-13*

RUNNING THE RACE

Therefore, since we are surrounded by such a huge crowd of witnesses to the life of faith,
let us strip off every weight that slows us down, especially the sin that so easily hinders our
progress. And let us run with endurance the race that God has set before us. We do this by
keeping our eyes on Jesus, on whom our faith depends from start to finish.

HEBREWS 12:1-2

When, in 490 B.C., the Greeks won a mighty victory over the Persians, one of the victorious soldiers reputedly ran the 25 miles from Marathon to Athens to bring the good news to his compatriots. Many years later, in 1896, the modern Olympic Committee introduced a long distance footrace, which they called the "marathon." In 1924, the distance of the race was standardized at 26 miles 385 yards. This race has now become the final event of the modern Olympic games—a fitting climax to many athletic achievements. At the end of their grueling race, the competitors circle the track to the cheers of the people in the crowded stands.

The original readers of the New Testament letters were familiar with the ancient Olympic games—the precursors of the modern Olympics. So they had no difficulty getting the message when they read, "Therefore, since we are surrounded by such a huge crowd of witnesses to the life of faith, let us strip off every weight that slows us down, especially the sin that so easily hinders our progress. And let us run with endurance the race that God has set before us" (Heb. 12:1). We, too, should have no trouble getting the message! Strict training, suitable clothing, skillful tactics, and enormous self-control and self-discipline are all critical factors in modern distance running. And the fact that the race is being run before huge viewing audiences adds to the intensity of the event for the competitors.

So the modern believer is exhorted to "run" the life of faith seriously. He is not to enter the race casually, nor to participate in it halfheartedly. He is to run it with intensity and endurance.

The modern distance runner can look back to the feats of such great athletes as the Czech runner Emil Zatopek, who won the five thousand meters, the ten thousand meters, and the marathon at the 1952 Olympics. In the same way, the modern believer is encouraged to remember the feats of faith of such men as Abraham and Noah, Paul and Stephen, and to be encouraged and challenged by their examples.

Above all, believers are to focus on Jesus, "the Originator and Perfecter of our faith" (Heb. 12:2, NLT note), who sits at the finishing line. It was he who showed us the way: enduring the pain, steadfastly completing his task, and finally triumphing over the enemy. And it is following him that we run, under his watchful eye and loving care. It is for him we compete, and it is to him that we speed our way through life. He will not award us a physical gold medal, but we can anticipate a glorious welcome at the end of our race. Finishing well and seeing him will be reward enough!

TO READ: *1 Corinthians 1:1–18*

THE MAIN THING

Now, dear brothers and sisters, I appeal to you by the authority of the Lord Jesus Christ to stop arguing among yourselves. Let there be real harmony so there won't be divisions in the church. I plead with you to be of one mind, united in thought and purpose.

1 CORINTHIANS 1:10

The Vietnam War remains one of the most troubling and exasperating chapters in American history. Having been drawn into what General De Gaulle warned President Kennedy would be a "quagmire," the mightiest nation in the world was soundly defeated by a relatively small group of peasant-guerrillas. Endless postmortems have been held since those sad days, but it is widely believed that disagreement between the politicians and the generals was a major part of the problem. The U.S. military had the means and the will to demolish the Vietnamese infrastructure—but the politicians did not have the will. Discord resulted, and uncertainty prevailed. In stark contrast to the American ambivalence to the war, Ho Chi Minh won the day through sheer determination and unwavering objectives.

Lack of focus and inner turmoil spell defeat for any organization, not least the church. Take, for instance, the church in Corinth. The Corinthian believers were blessed with "the generous gifts" God had given them, "enriched . . . with the gifts of eloquence and every kind of knowledge" (1 Cor. 1:4-5); they were strategically positioned in one of the most influential parts of the ancient world; and they had been taught and trained by the great apostle Paul himself. Yet this church had failed miserably to reach her potential. There were a number of reasons, but heading the list were the deadly twins: lack of focus and inner turmoil.

The church in Corinth had been blessed by good ministry, not only from Paul but also from such luminaries as Peter and Apollos. Peter, Paul, and Apollos were, of course, unique—they had differing temperaments and personalities, and no doubt each of them appealed to different segments of the church. There is nothing wrong—or unusual—about that. What *was* wrong, however, was the divisive partisanship that had developed in the community of believers. Some said, "I am a follower of Paul." Others said, "I follow Apollos," or "I follow Peter," or "I follow only Christ" (1:12). The result was lack of harmony, the dissipation of spiritual energy on internal struggles, and a reputation for conflict and turmoil. What a singularly unattractive image to project to a skeptical and needy city!

Lost in the partisan struggles was any sense of the "main thing." But not by Paul. He reminded the Corinthians, "Christ didn't send me to baptize, but to preach the Good News—not with clever speeches and high-sounding ideas, for fear that the cross of Christ would lose its power" (1:17). The main things—"Good News" and the "cross of Christ"— were the focus that the church had lost. The main things were no longer the main things.

Look wherever you will, and the same principle holds true: Focus, cohesion, and commitment spell victory. Turmoil, strife, and confusion promise defeat.

WISDOM AND NONSENSE

Since God in his wisdom saw to it that the world would never find him through human wisdom, he has used our foolish preaching to save all who believe.

1 CORINTHIANS 1:21

When man needs insight into life's mysteries, it is understandable that he often turns to great minds in the search for answers. Occasionally he gets help, but more often than not, his confusion is compounded and his dismay deepened. One of the great minds of the twentieth century belonged to Lord Bertrand Russell, a philosopher. He wrote,

> *Man is the product of causes which had no prevision [foresight] of the end they were achieving. . . . His origin, his growth, his hopes and fears, his loves and his beliefs, are but the outcome of accidental collocations of atoms. . . . No fire, no heroism, no intensity of thought and feeling, can preserve an individual life beyond the grave. . . . All these things, if not quite beyond dispute, are yet so nearly certain that no philosophy that rejects them can hope to stand."[19]*

How could the brilliant Lord Russell be so sure that no individual life can be preserved beyond the grave? He did not explain. Of course not—he could not! Such information does not belong to the philosopher. It belongs to the one who inhabits eternity and who reveals his truth to man in Christ. In fact, philosophers who ignore the Good News need to heed the word of the Lord, which actually reveals what they cannot know on the basis of unaided human reason. As Paul wrote, "God has made them all look foolish and has shown their wisdom to be useless nonsense" (1 Cor. 1:20).

It was kind of God to determine "that the world would never find him through human reason" (1:21), because that would have given the genius an advantage and put the ordinary man in an unfair position. A heaven populated exclusively by the brilliant was not part of the divine plan. On the contrary, in order that all might be blessed, God determined to use "foolish preaching to save all who believe" (1:21). Everybody, whether brilliant or backward, is capable of believing.

Of course, it is not simply believing that brings salvation. A man can fervently believe lies and sincerely trust error. Salvation comes through believing the message "that Christ was crucified" (1:23) and that "he is the one who made us acceptable to God," who can make us "pure and holy" and is able through his death and resurrection to "purchase our freedom" (1:30). It is faith in Christ and his work that introduces us into the eternal blessings that God has in store.

Bertrand Russell offers this tidbit of advice: "Only on the firm foundation of unyielding despair can the soul's habitation henceforth be safely built."[20] Christ offers the assurance of eternal salvation. Who do you believe? Think about it!

---

[19]Bertrand Russell, "A Free Man's Worship."
[20]*ibid.*

TO READ: *1 Corinthians 2:1–16*

THE CROSS

For I decided to concentrate only on Jesus Christ and his death on the cross. . . . The wisdom we speak of is the secret wisdom of God, which was hidden in former times, though he made it for our benefit before the world began.

1 CORINTHIANS 2:2, 7

T he Union Jack, the flag of the United Kingdom, is made up of the flags of England, Northern Ireland, and Scotland superimposed on each other. Each of these flags represents the country's patron saint—George of England, Patrick of Ireland, David and Andrew of Scotland. Each saint is represented by a cross.

The cross has become a well-known symbol often pictured on flags, incorporated into church architecture, or simply worn as a piece of jewelry. But its original significance is largely overlooked, which is not surprising when we remember what the cross was. During the days of the Roman Empire, the cross was a means of execution so torturous, vile, and cruel that no Roman citizen could ever be crucified. It is remarkable that such a horrendous instrument of torture could become such a precious symbol to so many. But how?

The answer is to be found not in the cross itself, but in a particular execution, that of a humble young craftsman, Jesus of Nazareth, whose bold preaching challenged the religious status quo in Jerusalem almost two millennia ago. But even his crucifixion does not account for the widespread respect for crosses—until we remember that the underlying reason for the religious establishment's antipathy toward him was that he claimed to be God. His claims took on undeniable force when his tomb became empty, his body disappeared, and many people reported seeing him risen from the dead.

The disciples of Jesus, who originally deserted him during the terrifying hours of his arrest, trial, and execution, were remarkably transformed after the reported sightings. They began to preach loudly and clearly that Jesus was the promised Messiah, that he had died for the sins of the world, had risen again, and was triumphant over sin, death, and hell. This dramatic message spread throughout the Roman Empire.

The apostle Paul, whose activities were significant for the spread of this message, said that his task was to "concentrate only on Jesus Christ and his death on the cross" (1 Cor. 2:2). Paul said that, if those who killed Jesus had understood what they were doing, "they would never have crucified our glorious Lord" (2:8). Although they did not know it, one of "God's deep secrets" (2:10) was becoming a reality. For it was at the cross that Jesus died for all men's sins and made forgiveness and eternal life available to all who believe.

The secret is no longer hidden. The word is out, and today many men see beyond the symbolism to the significance of the cross. They, having been forgiven, love him, and serve him. They rightly revere the cross and the one about whom it speaks.

WAITING QUIETLY

I wait quietly before God, for my salvation comes from him.

PSALM 62:1

W hen men go shopping, they usually know what they want, they pick it up, they take it to the checkout counter, they pay for it, and they leave. Mission accomplished. When women go shopping. they are not necessarily looking for something specific. They enjoy seeing what's available, trying it on, comparing it, buying it, taking it home, trying it on again, and then returning it. No doubt there are exceptions to these stereotypes, but not many!

Should a man find himself going shopping with his wife, he will have plenty of time to contemplate his fate as he waits for what seems an endless amount of time. But it will seem to be only a few minutes to his wife! In such scenarios, men are usually impatient. Should another hapless male come by in a similar situation, they will share their pain and commiserate with each other. Men are not very good at waiting!

But David was good at waiting. He said, "I waited quietly before God, for my salvation comes from him" (Ps. 62:1). The difference is striking. On the one hand, a man waits impatiently *for* his wife to do something in which he has no interest. In fact, he may even actively disapprove. On the other hand, a man waits *before* God to intervene in affairs that are vitally important to him.

Waiting "before God" suggests waiting in a particular place in a particular posture. It is waiting in an attitude of worship and dependence rather than hanging around hoping something will happen. Waiting before God involves actively focusing upon who he is and what he is doing in the world while waiting for his answers to arrive.

Those men who are used to being in control of their own lives, and the lives of others, find waiting before God particularly difficult. They will tell you that "time is money," and while they are supposed to be waiting they expect answers to be forthcoming. But David had come to the point of admitting that he could not fix his problem—"so many enemies against one man" (62:3). He knew that his only hope was in the Lord's intervention.

God works at his own pace and in his own way. No amount of impatience will alter the speed or the manner in which God will work out his purposes. So when the only direction you can turn is to the Lord, and the only way to look is up, remember to wait *before* him as you wait for him. He will act. And don't be impatient, because his clock keeps perfect time.

TO READ: *Genesis 24:1-27*

RIGHT HAND MAN

"O LORD, God of my master," he prayed. "Give me success and show kindness to my master, Abraham. Help me to accomplish the purpose of my journey."

GENESIS 24:12

The special assistants of great men become accustomed to being given extraordinary tasks. So they need to be fine men, too. Frequently the great men draw all the attention, and the assistants fit conveniently into the background. Yet without the man behind the scenes, the main man would often have difficulty functioning.

Abraham was a great man. And he had a truly fine assistant. There is reason to believe that the name of Abraham's assistant was Eliezer (see Gen. 15:2). Whatever his name, Abraham's assistant was "the man in charge of [Abraham's] household" and "his oldest servant" (24:2).

Abraham charged his assistant with a very difficult assignment. The assistant was instructed to find a suitable wife for his boss's son. Imagine! He not only had to find a girl whom the boss would approve of, but no doubt he would want to find a girl whom the young man would be excited about, too.

It is worth noting that if the man was indeed Eliezer, the arrival of the boss's son on the scene had robbed him of the chance to inherit Abraham's vast fortunes. Reason enough in many situations to cause deep resentment on his part toward Abraham's son. But this man was a fine man!

His task was not made any easier by the specific instructions that he was given and the severe restrictions that were placed on his choice. He was not allowed to take the young man with him, and he could not look for a wife anywhere other than in Abraham's family. This necessitated his traveling a considerable distance from home, back to where Abraham had lived before God called him to the Promised Land.

When he asked for help from Abraham, the assistant was told, "The Lord, the God of heaven, . . . will send his angel ahead of you, and he will see to it that you find a young woman there to be my son's wife" (24:7). With that assurance, he began his walk of faith.

When he arrived in the vicinity of Abraham's extended family, he realized how slim his chances of finding the right girl were. So he prayed about it, asking God to do exactly what Abraham had told him God would do. And God did. Rebekah, the Lord's beautiful choice, arrived on the scene, proved herself a fine woman, and agreed to the proposal.

The star of this story is not the big man, Abraham. No, the star is the quiet, unassuming, faithful, prayerful, reliable man behind the scenes—the man who honored and served his earthly master and loved and trusted his heavenly Lord. Our world needs more like him.

TO READ: *Genesis 24:59-67*

MEDITATION

One evening . . . [Isaac] was taking a walk out in the fields, meditating.
GENESIS 24:63

B usy men live at a fast pace. Their time is precious, their tasks are numerous, and the demands on them are unrelenting. There are not enough hours in the day, and they suspect there may not be enough years in their lives to accomplish all that needs to be done. So business, productivity, time management, meeting deadlines, and "keeping all the balls in the air" serve to define the lifestyle of such a man. Health is neglected, marriage suffers from lack of attention, children become strangers, and spiritual life gets lost in the shuffle. Such a man is not unaware of the situation, and he is not unconcerned about it. In fact, he promises himself that he will make the necessary changes to make his life more meaningful and to restore some semblance of balance to his days. Such promises are, sadly, often unfulfilled. A heart attack, enforced retirement, or marital breakdown may thrust him into a position of contemplation and rumination. Better late than never, certainly. But how much better it would have been if he had seen the value of contemplation and meditation earlier in life.

Isaac knew the value of contemplation. Being the son of Abraham obviously had its advantages, and presumably being heir apparent had its responsibilities. With his father's advancing years and his mother's recent decease, Isaac could not avoid contemplating his future. Added to that was his impending marriage to a woman he had never met! No wonder "he was taking a walk out in the fields, meditating" (Gen. 24:63)!

No doubt Isaac had many things competing for his attention, and undoubtedly there were numerous things requiring careful thought and wise decisions. But unless he took the time to clear his mind, escape distractions, and concentrate his attention, there was a real possibility that his life would go the way of the busy, unthoughtful man—the way of inevitable confusion and ultimate disappointment.

Isaac needed to think through the significance of the covenant God had made with his father—a covenant that included him. He could profitably ponder the way his father had handled the difficult problem with Lot. And Lot's bad decisions and his hair-raising escape from the consequences certainly merited a degree of meditation.

Modern men should copy Isaac, factoring time into their lives for thoughtfulness and disciplining their thought-lives to concentrate on issues other than those dictated by immediacy. Urgent and pressing matters will demand attention and get it. But it takes times of meditation to deal with ultimate, eternal, spiritual, and moral issues. Strident and spectacular communications will arrest the attention. But it is in the quiet fields that meditation on matters of moment takes place.

TO READ: *Ezekiel 2:1-10*

MISSION: IMPOSSIBLE

"Son of man," he said, "I am sending you to the nation of Israel, a nation that is rebelling against me. Their ancestors have rebelled against me from the beginning, and they are still in revolt to this very day."

EZEKIEL 2:3

M ission: *Impossible* holds a special place in the annals of television drama. Mysterious assignments were handed out at the beginning of each program. and that which was billed as impossible became possible, however improbable, before the weekly installment ended.

Ezekiel's assignment came to him in a much more dramatic fashion than the way *Mission: Impossible*'s operators received theirs. He was given a vision of God's glory that was so overwhelming that he "fell face down in the dust" (Ezek. 1:28). In this undignified but perfectly understandable position, Ezekiel was ideally situated to hear from the Lord. It was there, in the posture of awestruck submission, that he was told, "Stand up, son of man. . . . I want to speak with you" (2:1). The voice, of course, was the voice of God. This was no ordinary voice, and the words spoken were no ordinary words. These words contained the very power necessary for obedience to them. Ezekiel testified, "The Spirit came into me as he spoke and set me on my feet" (2:2).

Men today rarely find themselves flat on their faces in reaction to hearing the voice of God. But they do have available to them the written word of God, which, when read, marked, learned, and inwardly digested, not only commands but empowers for obedience. The word heeded releases the power needed.

Ezekiel soon discovered he needed the unique empowering of the Spirit working through the word. Ezekiel was instructed, "I am sending you to the nation of Israel, a nation that is rebelling against me. . . . They are a hard-hearted and stubborn people. . . . They won't listen, for they are completely rebellious" (2:3-4, 7). The nature of Ezekiel's mission was essentially that he was to talk to people who would not listen and who, even if they listened, would not do what they were told. Mission impossible!

It might reasonably be asked, "What, then, was the point of sending Ezekiel to them?" God's rationale for sending him was that "whether they listen or not . . . at least they will know they have had a prophet among them" (2:5). The point of them knowing they had been listening to a prophet would not be immediately obvious. But later on when the things he had said came about, they would realize that what they were experiencing was no accident—it was what God had promised. It was exactly what he had determined should come to pass. In other words, they would learn that even when things go wrong, God is still in control.

Ezekiel's mission was impossible, but essentially practical. And his message was unmistakable: God is in control, he knows what he is doing, and he will bring it to pass. Just watch!

TO READ: *Genesis 25:28-34*

ACCEPTING RESPONSIBILITY

Then Jacob gave Esau some bread and lentil stew. Esau ate and drank and went on about his business, indifferent to the fact that he had given up his birthright.

GENESIS 25:34

The title "Prince of Wales" is traditionally given to the eldest son of the United Kingdom's reigning monarch. This prince is born to privilege. From birth he is prepared for the crown, while his brothers and sisters are merely prepared for life as royalty. On the death of his reigning parent, the crown prince will become King and enjoy all the trappings of majesty—and assume its responsibilities.

When George V died, his son, the Prince of Wales, became Edward VII. But he had fallen in love with a divorced American lady whom he wished to marry—a marriage which the British government would not permit. So the King had to decide between the throne or the lady, duty or desire. He chose the latter, abdicated, and married Mrs. Wallis Simpson. Together they lived out their lives in Paris as the Duke and Duchess of Windsor.

The ancient Hebrews had a system called "primogeniture." In some ways similar to the laws governing British royal succession, it guaranteed the special rights of the firstborn son and also stipulated his corresponding responsibilities. Esau was Isaac's firstborn; Jacob was Esau's twin brother. The younger brother was, in fact, "born with his hand grasping Esau's heel" (Gen. 25:26). Esau, in light of his birth-order position, was given the privilege of maintaining and sustaining the remarkable spiritual heritage that God had granted first to his grandfather, Abraham, and later to his father, Isaac. He was also eligible, on his father's death, to receive a double portion of his father's considerable estate.

But Esau had little interest either in the privileges or the responsibilities of his favored position in the family. Jacob had considerable interest in both. Knowing Esau's limited sense of calling or vision and his truncated sense of privilege and responsibility, Jacob set about accomplishing the amazingly simple task of taking the firstborn rights away from his older brother. One day, when Esau returned hungry from the hunt, he smelled Jacob's stew, and a deal was struck. Jacob ended up with the birthright and Esau with a plate of stew! So much for appreciating privilege and embracing responsibility. It was Esau's attitude, as well as his lack of priorities, which was so disconcerting. "Esau ate and drank and went on about his business, indifferent to the fact that he had given up his birthright" (25:34).

When a man's sensual appetites dominate him, he will trade eternal values to fulfill them. He will prefer the satisfying of the those appetites to the fulfilling of his responsibility before God. Such a man is like Esau—"immoral" and "godless." One day that man will weep "bitter tears" (Heb. 12:16). That's troubling.

TO READ: *Ezekiel 34:1-16*

WHEN LEADERSHIP IS LACKING

You drink the milk, wear the wool, and butcher the best animals,
but you let your flocks starve.

EZEKIEL 34:3

I t is a well-known fact that, during World War II, the Nazi leaders of the Third Reich, particularly Hermann Göring, "Die nummer Zwei"—number two man to Hitler—were busy robbing the occupied countries of their art treasures and storing them in secret hiding places for their personal collections. And it has been well-documented that more recent dictators have amassed great treasures for themselves in the vaults of Swiss banks, at the expense of their own people. In fact, many of them, as they have seen their own power and popularity diminishing, have turned their attention away from affairs of state to concentrate on securing their own position and providing for their own well-being.

There is nothing new about this abuse of power. Ezekiel complained, on behalf of the Lord, about the "the shepherds, the leaders of Israel" (Ezek. 34:2). In those days leaders were often called "shepherds," and in graphic language, Ezekiel detailed the Lord's objections to their behavior: "You shepherds . . . feed yourselves instead of your flocks. Shouldn't shepherds feed their sheep? You drink the milk, wear the wool, and butcher the best animals, but you let your flocks starve" (34:3). Concentrating on their own interests, Israel's leaders had neglected to go "looking for those who have wandered away and are lost. . . . No one has gone to search for them" (34:4, 6). The Lord's displeasure with the failed leadership was clear. He told them, "I now consider these shepherds my enemies, and I will hold them responsible for what has happened to my flock" (34:10).

If God places men in positions of leadership, he expects them to take their roles seriously and to perform them with integrity and grace. For them to show more interest in their own affairs than in those of their "flock," and to become so absorbed with their own lives that they fail to serve the needs and interests of those placed in their care, will merit divine displeasure.

Every man who has married a wife has been invested with a shepherding role in her life by God. The man who uses his wife for his own purposes, demanding of her sexual favors, expecting from her menial service, insisting that she meet his every whim and satisfy his every desire with little or no thought for her own well-being, should answer the question, "Shouldn't shepherds feed their sheep?" If he does not answer it now—he will answer for it later!

TO READ: *Ezekiel 34:11-31*

SHEEP AND GOATS

*I will search for my lost ones who strayed away, and I will bring them safely home
again. I will bind up the injured and strengthen the weak. But I will destroy those
who are fat and powerful. I will feed them, yes—feed them justice! . . . I will judge
between one sheep and another, separating the sheep from the goats.*

EZEKIEL 34:16-17

P eople who believe that they have been abused seek justice. The abused want wrong
to be punished and right to be rewarded. Where wrong has triumphed, they look
for restitution. Where right has been ignored, they look for recognition.

By contrast, people who have abused others seek mercy. When their wrongs go
unnoticed, they hope it will remain so. When their wrongs are exposed, they hope they
will not be caught. Should those people be brought to justice, they look for mercy. When
mercy is granted, the abused cry, "Where's the justice?" When abusers are dealt with firmly,
they complain, "Where's the mercy?"

There were similar complaints in Ezekiel's time, directed against the Lord! The
people were saying, "The Lord is not just." To this the Lord replied, "I will judge each of
you according to your deeds" (Ezek. 33:20). The "deeds" of which he spoke were the
dealings that the people of Israel were having with each other. They all belonged to the
same nation, were all beneficiaries of the same covenant, and were all suffering the same
punishment for unfaithfulness. But there the similarity ended. From a distance, they all
looked the same. But the Lord knew the difference and promised that he would separate
"the sheep from the goats" (34:17). The Lord would deal with the "fat and powerful" who
were abusing the "injured" and the "weak" (34:16). What would be the Lord's treatment of
the abusers? He promised to feed them—but to "feed them justice" (34:16).

The Lord's indignation and promised judgment were leveled at those whose behavior
showed scant regard for anyone other than themselves. Maintaining the sheep and goats
analogy, he complained, "Is it not enough for you to keep the best of the pastures for yourselves? Must you also trample down the rest? . . . All that is left for my flock to eat is what
you have trampled down. All they have to drink is water that you have fouled" (34:18-19).

Social justice is the name we give to concerns of this nature today. It has always been
a concern of the Lord's. But it has not necessarily been a concern of his people. The Lord
repeatedly sent his prophets to remind his people that they must treat their neighbors
justly. And he constantly reminded them that failure to exercise justice would mean they
would be subjected to divine justice! But they dished out injustice and craved mercy.
Nothing has changed.

Fortunately for us, our just and righteous Lord is full of compassion and grace.
When we appreciate this and appropriate his mercy, we will demonstrate a concern for
justice. This separates the sheep from the goats—and the men from the boys.

TO READ: *Psalm 30:1–12*

HEALTH AND WEALTH

O Lord my God, I cried out to you for help, and you restored my health.

PSALM 30:2

Benjamin Franklin's saying, "Early to bed, early to rise, makes a man healthy, wealthy, and wise," contains more than a grain of truth. Whether or not there is an exact correlation between good sleep habits and "the good life" is hard to say. But Franklin's epigram certainly identified three areas of concern for men in all ages: health, wealth, and wisdom.

Issues related to health, wealth, and wisdom are often discussed in the pages of Scripture. David, for example, said, "O Lord my God, I cried out to you for help, and you restored my health" (Ps. 30:2). We do not have details of his ailments, but they were serious enough for him to say, "You brought me up from the grave, O Lord. You kept me from falling into the pit of death" (30:3).

Many a man has been brought to his spiritual senses when his health failed. The healing of his body has led to a cleansing of his soul, and he has lived to thank God for illness. Some men only look up when they are put on their backs! But a little thought shows that, if we thank God for healing, we should praise him for health. Health is perpetual healing. Given the intricacies of our bodies, the prevalence of viruses, and the incidence of accidents, it is quite remarkable that we are ever well. Yet most of us are. We live our lives assuming that the robust health we enjoy will continue unabated. In fact, we assume that it is a right, not a privilege. The problem is that the more we enjoy good health, the less we depend on the Lord for it; the less we know of suffering, the less we turn to the Lord for help.

As it is with health, so it is with wealth. David's lost health, once restored, led him to worship and thanksgiving. And his lost wealth led to a similar conclusion. He said, "When I was prosperous I said, 'Nothing can stop me now!' Your favor, O Lord, made me as secure as a mountain'" (30:6-7). But sadly, the prosperity the Lord had granted him led him away from a life of trusting obedience: "Then you turned away from me, and I was shattered" (30:7).

Lost health can shatter us; so can lost wealth. It is drastic medicine, but men absorbed with their own lives respond to little else. When the Lord restores lost health and wealth, and men respond by praising the Lord, they get wise. So be wise—get to bed early, but rise up to bless the Lord.

TO READ: *1 Corinthians 5:1–13*

SEX SCANDALS

You must cast this man out of the church and into Satan's hands, so that his sinful nature will be destroyed and he himself will be saved when the Lord returns.

1 CORINTHIANS 5:5

T he pagan world in which Paul lived was similar to ours, not least in that it was a sex-saturated society. Corinth, in particular, was known for its sexual promiscuity. The Christian church had taken root all across the Roman Empire and was set apart from the rest of society by her convictions. Christians' view of sex as a divine gift to be enjoyed exclusively in the confines of monogamous, heterosexual marriage was well-known and widely disparaged.

The believers in the Corinthian church were an unfortunate exception. They prided themselves in their "freedom," which had taken a particularly unsavory turn. One of the men in the congregation was "living in sin with his father's wife" (1 Cor. 5:1). If this was not serious enough, the church was proud that they were "spiritual" enough to accept what was happening. Paul found it necessary to point out to them that even pagans would draw the line at that kind of behavior. The church was so out of step with spiritual reality that they had not only done nothing about the man's behavior, but also had taken pride in their failure to do so! He asked, "Why aren't you mourning in sorrow and shame?" (5:2).

Paul had no doubt about what action the church should take: The man should be removed from membership of the church for at least two reasons. First, his removal from the protective spiritual environment of the fellowship of believers would "cast" the man "into Satan's hands," not in order to destroy him but "so that his sinful nature will be destroyed and he himself will be saved when the Lord returns" (5:5). The drastic action was intended to be remedial, not vindictive. Second, his removal would counter the serious danger that his continued presence presented to the fellowship. Paul asked, "Don't you realize that if even one person is allowed to go on sinning, soon all will be affected?" (5:6). This is a serious consideration indeed!

This kind of teaching is rare in many churches, which usually has one of two results. In some churches, sexual scandals are either carefully ignored or promptly forgiven. In other churches, the church embarks on a witch hunt where the wounded are shot, the believers withdraw from all contact with sinners, and a hard, harsh, separatist, and irrelevant church emerges.

There is nothing new about scandalous sexual behavior inside and outside the church. And there is no shortage of teaching in Scripture about how to deal with it. Sadly, there is often a shortage of firm, loving discipline that prizes the church's integrity. And there is often a shortage of loving, caring concern for the erring person that prizes their redemption. Contrary to popular belief, love and discipline are not mutually exclusive. The church needs both.

TO READ: *1 Corinthians 6:1-11*

CONFLICT RESOLUTION

*Don't you know that those who do wrong will have no share in the Kingdom of God?
Don't fool yourselves. . . . There was a time when some of you were just like that,
but now your sins have been washed away, and you have been set apart for God.*

1 CORINTHIANS 6:9, 11

B umper stickers can communicate messages that might not otherwise be heard, but never take your theology from them! For example, consider this popular bumper sticker message: "Christians aren't perfect—just forgiven." The sentiment that Christians are painfully aware of their sinfulness is correct, and they know how necessary forgiveness is. Christians also affirm that while their sins are forgiven, that does not add up to an ongoing life of perfection. But to suggest that Christians are *just* forgiven is surely to miss the point. Christians are forgiven, they are not perfect, but they are more than "just forgiven"—they are called to and empowered for a new life.

Paul explained this truth quite bluntly and plainly. Having listed some of the common sinful behaviors of the day—behavior patterns that disqualify the behavors from participation in God's kingdom—he concluded: "There was a time when some of you were just like that, but"—and it was a big but—"now your sins have been washed away and you have been set apart for God. You have been made right with God because of what the Lord Jesus Christ and the Spirit of our God have done for you" (1 Cor. 6:11). The Corinthians were undoubtedly forgiven sinners, but in light of the fact that they had been "washed" and "set apart" and "made right with God," a higher standard was now expected from them in their lives.

For example, some of the Corinthian Christians were trying to resolve their differences by taking each other to court. There was nothing unusual about Corinthians suing each other, but Paul said it was not acceptable behavior for Christians. Christians will one day "judge the world" and also "judge angels" (6:2-3), so Paul argued that they ought to be capable of settling conflicts among themselves without seeking a legal remedy imposed by unbelievers.

How strictly modern Christians should apply this principle to their business lives is a subject of earnest debate and genuine disagreement. But Christians should, at least, be willing to "accept the injustice and leave it at that," and they should be willing to "let [them]selves be cheated" (6:7-8). Nobody likes to be treated unjustly or to be cheated. And rather than accept such treatment, the natural response is to take whatever action is available to avoid it. Paul's point is that Christians respond to life's injustices in ways that are not "normal." They have been "set apart" for something different. Their model, of course, is Jesus, who suffered monumental injustice on a cross without complaining. And their empowerment comes from the Holy Spirit. Christians are not "just forgiven," they're definitely different!

TO READ: *1 Corinthians 6:12-20*

FREEDOM'S LIMITS

Our bodies were not made for sexual immorality. They were made for the Lord,
and the Lord cares about our bodies. . . . God bought you with a high price.
So you must honor God with your body.

1 CORINTHIANS 6:13, 20

F reedom of speech does not allow you to shout "Fire!" in a crowded cinema. Freedom of religion does not grant you the right to make human sacrifices. Freedom of movement is limited, too: Your right to swing your fist ends where my nose begins. In other words, freedom has limits. So an intoxicating statement, like "I am allowed to do anything," is simply not true. Even if it were true, such freedom would have to be handled with extreme care. Sometimes freedom can mean freedom to do harm, and as Paul said, "Not everything is good for you" (1 Cor. 6:12). Not to mention whether it is good for others!

Moreover, the exercise of a freedom can dominate you. Ironically, you then become freedom's slave. Take the matter of sexual liberation, for instance. It is not uncommon for sexual freedom to become sexual addiction. This situation removes a man far from Paul's dictum, "I must not become a slave to anything" (6:12).

Even apart from the possibility of freedom leading to bondage, the limits of sexual freedom need to be clearly understood. It may be argued that, in the same way that when the body is hungry for food it is right to eat whatever is available, so when the body's sexual appetites are stirred, it is right to have sex. In fact, that was one Corinthian argument. But it contained a fatal flaw. For while it may be right to say "Food is for the stomach, and the stomach is for food," it is not correct to infer that our bodies were made for sex. On the contrary, the body was "made for the Lord, and the Lord cares about our bodies" (6:13).

Food and stomach will pass away, but not our bodies. "God will raise our bodies from the dead by his marvelous power, just as he raised our Lord from the dead" (6:14). Bodies are made for the Lord—and for eternity. In fact, Paul tells the Corinthians, "Your body is the temple of the Holy Spirit, who lives in you and was given to you by God" (6:19). As a result, it is possible to say, "Your bodies are actually parts of Christ" (6:15).

The Corinthian Christians who had freely engaged in sexual promiscuity prior to their conversions—sometimes in the name of religion—were being required to rethink their sexual morality. In summary, they needed to recognize that "sexual immorality is a sin against your own body," and they were told, "Honor God with your body" (6:18, 20). In practical terms that meant, "Run away from sexual sin"— for Christians, it is off limits.

TO READ: *1 Corinthians 7:1-16*

MARRIAGE MATTERS

Because there is so much sexual immorality, each man should have his own wife,
and each woman should have her own husband. . . . I wish everyone could get along
without marrying, just as I do. But we are not all the same. God gives some
the gift of marriage, and to others he gives the gift of singleness.

1 CORINTHIANS 7:2, 7

Marriage is a divine idea. Right from the beginning of creation, God ordained that a man and a woman should devote themselves to each other in a mutually loving, caring, marital relationship. He made it clear that marriage was to be a fundamental building block of society.

But in Corinthian society, as in our modern societies, there were some people who, for a variety of reasons, did not wish to be married. They glorified the unmarried state, and they believed that it was a superior lifestyle. They asked for Paul's opinion, and he agreed: "Yes, it is good to live a celibate life" (1 Cor. 7:1). Paul went even further and said, "I wish everyone could get along without marrying, just as I do" (7:7). But having said that, he stopped far short of advocating that being single was morally superior to being married. On the contrary, he insisted, "God gives some the gift of marriage, and to others he gives the gift of singleness" (7:7). To those who have the gift of being married, Paul says, "Each man should have his own wife, and each woman should have her own husband" (7:2).

The downside of singleness, from Paul's point of view, was that if natural sexual desires were not carefully controlled, single people—particularly those living in the sexually charged environment of Corinth—would be vulnerable to the blandishments of illicit sexual activity. Rather than allow that to happen, they should marry and enjoy mutually satisfying sexual relations.

But marriage is not without its difficulties either. Marriage is particularly difficult when one of the partners becomes a Christian subsequent to the marriage. Rather than working through the difficult tensions that such a situation created, people in Corinth were giving up on their marriages and settling for divorce. Christians who were contemplating taking this way out of difficult marriages were overlooking, or ignoring, the fact that a Christian marriage partner "brings holiness to" her or his marriage, and that the children of such a marriage live under a "godly influence" (7:14).

The Christian, bearing all this in mind, should not divorce. On the other hand, if the unbeliever decides to leave the marriage, the Christian partner "is not required to stay" with that person (7:15).

In marriage matters, modern western society bears striking similarities to ancient Greco-Roman society. So it is not too difficult to make an application of Paul's teachings and of Christ's specific commands.

Marriage is good, and in special circumstances, singleness is a blessing. But marriage is not easy. In certain limited circumstances divorce is permissible, but it also creates major problems. So honor marriage, respect singleness, and avoid divorce. And remember, "God wants his children to live in peace" (7:15).

TO READ: *1 Corinthians 8:1-13*

WHAT D'YOU KNOW?

While knowledge may make us feel important, it is love that really builds up the church. Anyone who claims to know all the answers doesn't really know very much. But the person who loves God is the one God knows and cares for.

1 CORINTHIANS 8:1-3

That the ancient Greeks were exceptionally clever goes without saying. Anyone who has read their philosophers, attended their plays, studied their buildings, learned their mathematics, or contemplated their art recognizes their unique skills. The problem was that some of them were so smart that they thought they knew it all!

Some of that kind of thinking has seeped into the church, too. In Corinth, there were church members who not only felt they had achieved "perfect knowledge," but they also thought that "everyone should agree" with it! (1 Cor. 8:1). The people who embraced this attitude felt very important. They were very impressed with themselves!

So bright as they undoubtedly were, the Corinthians had blind spots that needed to be pointed out. First, as Paul said, "Anyone who claims to know all the answers doesn't really know very much."(8:2). Second, "while knowledge may make us feel important, it is love that really builds up the church" (8:1). The Corinthians needed to learn that the person who is impressed with the heights of his knowledge should be alerted to the depth of his ignorance. They also needed to be reminded that, if knowledge is not mixed with love, it can become desperately destructive rather than impressive. Being smart is not the whole story.

Here is a case in point. Greek temples often doubled as restaurants, so that is where Corinthians went out to eat. The fact that part of the ritual in the temple included offering some of the food to an idol was of little or no concern to most of them. They were smart and liberated—remember? They knew that the idol was nothing more than a piece of wood or stone. So as long as the food was good, it was no big deal. The Christians were particularly aware of the irrelevance of idols. They, of all people, knew, "there is only one God and no other" (8:4). So they went to the temple for a good meal.

But some of them were not so sure. They reasoned that going to the temple meant that they were in some way associating with idol worship and, accordingly, it was wrong for them to be there. Not only was it wrong, in their minds, for them to attend such a social event, but they also didn't think other Christians should go! So the Corinthian church had a controversy on its hands. "To eat or not to eat?"—that was the question.

From a purely intellectual point of view, Paul apparently agreed with those who saw nothing wrong with eating at the temple. He said, "We all know that an idol is not really a god" (8:4). But he looked at the issue from another perspective. What happens when an intellectual conclusion is deeply offensive to a brother? Then love for the brother becomes an important factor—even more important, in this case, than knowledge about the issue.

Knowledge isn't everything. Love matters, too! So smart people who don't love have a lot to learn. They're not as smart as they thought!

TO READ: *1 Corinthians 9:1-14*

RIGHTS AND WRONGS

*Just as farm workers who plow fields and thresh the grain expect a share
of the harvest, Christian workers should be paid by those they serve. . . .
Yet we have never used this right. We would rather put up with anything
than put an obstacle in the way of the Good News about Christ.*

1 CORINTHIANS 9:10, 12

The more civilized a country becomes, the more civil its people tend to be. The more a culture acknowledges the significance of the individual, the more its people recognize the need to treat other people well. But because human beings have a great capacity for behaving badly, they do not always treat each other civilly. So the government steps in and begins to legislate behavior, predicated on real or perceived human and civil rights. Then individuals and businesses take great care not to transgress the law, because failure to observe such legislation can lead to severe penalties.

In the first century, there apparently was no legislation protecting the civil rights of preachers! Not that they did not have rights. They did, as much as anyone else. It was just that no one had gone to the trouble of protecting them from potential abuse. This meant that preachers could be wronged—the question was, "How should they respond?"

Paul spoke quite bluntly to the Corinthians on this subject of preachers' rights. What he had to say should be required reading for all church leaders! While some of the congregation were questioning his credentials and capabilities, there was no real questioning that he was a bona fide apostle. Even those who were not inclined to acknowledge this could not deny that the only reason they had come to faith was that Paul had exercised an apostolic ministry in their midst. "This is my answer to those who question my authority as an apostle," he said (1 Cor. 9:3).

Paul then asked the Corinthian church if he and the other apostles did not have certain basic rights, such as proper support, encouragement, and remuneration for their work. He cited the facts that soldiers don't pay their own way, that farmers get to eat some of their crops, and that shepherds drink milk from their flocks. So was it not obvious that a preacher should be cared for adequately by the congregations who benefited from his ministry? Should there be any doubt in the congregation's mind on the subject, Paul reminded them, "Doesn't God's law say the same thing?" (9:8-9). His conclusion was, "Christian workers should be paid by those they serve" (9:10). Christian workers have their rights!

But significantly, Paul then added, "We have never used this right. We would rather put up with anything than put an obstacle in the way of the Good News about Christ" (9:12). Paul believed it was wrong to deny rights, but that it was right to carry on when wronged. Right on, Paul!

ALL DAY LONG

Lead me by your truth and teach me, for you are the God who saves me.
All day long I put my hope in you.

PSALM 25:5

S ome people are morning people. They awake refreshed, renewed, and ready to meet the day, but by evening, the enthusiasm and energy begin to wear down. Others take a little longer to get going, but when the rest of their family and friends are ready to call it a day, they are hitting their stride, eager for more. But both kinds of people have to make it through the day—and do it well. The middle of the day can be the hardest time for both.

Among the early risers are those who have developed the discipline of a quiet time of devotional reading, meditation, and prayer before they face the challenges of the day. There is much to commend this approach—but not if you already have difficulty getting out of bed in time for work! The evening people can just as easily reserve time during the lunch hour or before they retire for the night to engage in specific spiritual exercises.

George Herbert, the sixteenth-century Anglican pastor and poet, gave some of the best advice. He wrote,

Sum up at night what thou hast done by day.
And in the morning what thou hast to do,
Dress and undress thy soul.[21]

The idea of dressing and undressing the soul, just as we dress and undress the body, has special appeal because it points to the fact that the whole day needs to be lived in the light and power of our relationship with the Lord. This requires both preparation and evaluation. The day will present many and varied challenges and opportunities for which we need to be prepared and about which we need to be concerned.

Perhaps David said it best—"All day long I put my hope in you" (Ps. 25:5). He stated no preference for morning devotion or evening reflection, but his commitment to daily communion with the Lord and concentration on him probably required both.

Spiritual preparation and evaluation should make spiritual concentration easier during the day. Spiritual concentration is a matter of putting our trust in the Lord "all day long." Should it be objected that the busy surgeon can't be thinking of the Lord when he is taking out a tumor or that a truck driver can't be praying when he's driving a huge eighteen-wheeler down the freeway at sixty-five miles per hour, the objection would, of course, stand. However, it is possible to have an awareness of the Lord, and an inner sense of reliance on him, while doing these tasks.

If all men, including truck drivers and surgeons, start their day with a conscious waiting on the Lord, and they bear in mind that they will talk with the Lord about it at day's end, they will be aware of living before the Lord "all day long." Should crisis hit, their instincts will turn them promptly to the Lord. And at the end of the day, when the patient is sewn up or the truck is parked, they'll hear the Lord saying, "Well done."

---

[21]George Herbert, "The Temple."

MAY

TO READ: *Genesis 37:1-36*

EMOTIONS

Now Jacob loved Joseph more than any of his other children because Joseph had been
born to him in his old age. So one day he gave Joseph a special gift—a beautiful robe.
But his brothers hated Joseph because of their father's partiality.
They couldn't say a kind word to him.

GENESIS 37:3-4

O f all the emotions, love is the greatest; but there is a dark side to love. Misdirected or misapplied, love can lead to the ugliness of jealousy, the heat of rage, or the cold relentlessness of hatred.

Jacob is a case in point. He "loved Joseph more than any of his other children because Joseph had been born to him in his old age" (Gen. 37:3). As an expression of his love, Jacob gave Joseph "a special gift—a beautiful robe." The reaction of the other brothers was as predictable as it was despicable. They "hated Joseph because of their father's partiality. They couldn't say a kind word to him" (37:4).

If his brothers had simply ostracized him, Joseph could probably have borne the brotherly hostility, and no further harm would have been done, but unrestrained emotions do not remain static. So when the brothers saw their chance to get rid of Joseph, they decided to take it. They said, "Come on, let's kill him and throw him into a deep pit" (37:19-20). What they didn't realize was how deep the pit they were digging for themselves was.

Reuben's secret plan to rescue his brother required the brothers to buy into his fatuous argument: "Why should we shed his blood? Let's just throw him alive into this pit here. That way he will die without our having to touch him" (37:22). In essence, the argument, which they warmly embraced, was, "Let's not kill him, let's leave him to die! That way we won't be guilty of killing him"—even though they would be guilty of callously, intentionally letting him die. When hatred takes over, clear thinking checks out. Callousness was clearly part of their hatred, because after depositing Joseph in his intended "grave," they went on with their lives unperturbed, even "sitting down to eat" (37:25).

Judah, meanwhile, was being slightly troubled by his conscience. "What can we gain by killing our brother? That would just give us a guilty conscience. Let's sell Joseph" (37:27). So now, instead of avoiding killing him by allowing him to die, they would banish him to oblivion, to die out of sight and out of mind. And they would be guilty of nothing. Hardly! Because now they trumped up a story of Joseph's death by wild animal attack. Then they told their father, who "mourned deeply for his son," while the "family tried to comfort him, but it was no use" (37:34-35). Comfort born of hypocrisy doesn't comfort.

Hatred masquerading as anything but hatred only digs pits for the hated and the haters. Hatred is the pits.

TO READ: *Genesis 40:1-23*

GOD'S BUSINESS

*They replied, "We both had dreams last night, but there is no one here to tell us what
they mean." "Interpreting dreams is God's business," Joseph replied.
"Tell me what you saw."*

GENESIS 40:8

As Sigmund Freud, the Viennese doctor, listened to his patients, he became increasingly
interested in the phenomena of dreams. Eventually, he wrote his book *The Interpretation of Dreams.* Freud's findings were both fascinating and controversial. To this day, he has
both admirers and detractors.

Joseph, too, was involved with people who recounted their dreams to him. While he
never wrote a book about it (so far as we know), he did make a strong statement about the
interpretation of dreams. "Interpreting dreams is God's business," he told two of his fellow
prisoners. "Tell me what you saw" (Gen 40:8). Freud would certainly have said, "Tell me
what you saw," but he would have scoffed at any suggestion that God should be involved
in the inner workings of a man's life.

The difference of outlook between a Freud and a Joseph could not be more basic or
far-reaching. It highlights the age-old question about whether or not God is actively involved
in people's lives, about whether or not God is in business in the world today. Freud was an
atheist, so he did not bother his mind with the question of God's involvement in the world.
He had already decided that, since God does not exist, there could be no thought of his
involvement. But many men who are not at all atheistic in their outlook doubt whether God
communicates with men today. They do not question his existence, but they are dubious
about his involvement—and, accordingly, about his relevance.

When Potiphar's wife tried to seduce Joseph, his response was "It would be a great
sin against God" (39:9). When he was confronted with interpreting Pharaoh's dreams, he
said, "It is beyond my power to do this . . . but God will tell you" (41:16). Later, looking
back over his life, Joseph said, "God has made me forget all my troubles," and, "God has
made me fruitful in this land of my suffering" (41:51-52). And when he finally confronted
his brothers and talked about their treatment of him, he told them, "It was God who sent
me here, not you!" (45:8). Joseph knew that his life was God's business.

The loving, faithful God is actively involved in a man's daily affairs. But the man who
lives his life without consciously knowing this must endeavor to find alternative ways of
making peace with life's eventualities. Blind fate and dumb luck come to mind as possible
salves for the mind. But it is better by far to trust the Lord of the universe, who sets up shop
in men's lives on a daily basis. And there he works his wonders.

BUT GOD . . .

*"I had a dream last night," Pharaoh told him, "and none of these men can tell me
what it means. But I have heard that you can interpret dreams, and that is why
I have called for you." "It is beyond my power to do this," Joseph replied.
"But God will tell you what it means and will set you at ease."*

GENESIS 41:15-16

S ome of the longest words in the English language mean very little to modern men,
while some of the shortest are packed with significance. For instance, there was a time
when "disestablishmentarianism" was a word of greatest importance in church affairs, but it
has since faded into obscurity. But the word *but* is still very much in vogue! Technically, *but*
is an adversative. It introduces something different, it poses a different point of view, it offers
a contrast. *But* can introduce right as opposed to wrong, good as opposed to evil, truth in
opposition to error. That is why *but* is such a significant word—life is full of contrasts,
differences, and differing points of view. Contrasts—between truth and error, good and evil,
right and wrong—highlight the differences.

Joseph was confronted with the task of interpreting Pharaoh's dreams. On being told
of Pharaoh's expectations of him, he was quick to point out that he was unable to do what
was expected of him since he was not an expert in the interpretation of dreams. "But God
will tell you . . . and will set you at ease," he added (Gen. 41:16).

If *but* is a big word, "But God" is an immense statement. In this instance it pointed
out the difference between human and divine capabilities. Where human effort and skill
fell short, God's abilities shone through. Where the inadequacy of men was apparent, the
superlative adequacy of God came into the fore.

Joseph was supremely confident of this. Many men come to the end of their resources
and give up. They see no hope of a solution to their problems and no alternatives to their
despair and discouragement. *But God* makes all the difference. The believing man knows
better than to give up when he reaches the end of himself. He is aware not only of his own
inadequacies, *but also* of God's presence, wisdom, power, and grace. He knows that he
cannot, *but God* can!

It is perfectly possible to believe in God's presence in daily life without crossing over
the *but God* bridge from despair to confidence. There is a difference between believing that
God is able to act and trusting that God will be active.

What set Joseph apart was the blend of a total lack of *self*-confidence *but* a complete
God-confidence. He had a sure and certain trust in God, but not in himself. The Egyptian
Pharaoh knew an extraordinary man when he saw one. And there's nothing more extraordinary than a man who knows his limits and the limitless God and blends the two
together. That man, like Joseph, uses the small-immense term, "But God." Man cannot,
but God can—and will!

TO READ: *Genesis 41:25-40*

FOREWARNED, FOREARMED

*"This will happen just as I have described it,
for God has shown you what he is about to do."*

GENESIS 41:28

When the annual hurricane season comes to the United States, the National Weather Service forecasters watch the developing systems carefully so that the coastal inhabitants of the southeastern states know what to expect. Over the years, more and more people have begun taking these forecasts seriously. This was not always the case. There have always been those who ignore warnings to evacuate areas prone to serious flooding or other natural disasters. In some instances they have paid for their folly with their lives. To be forewarned is to be forearmed, but the forearming is not automatic. Responsible action is required. Beforehand!

Joseph's interpretation of Pharaoh's dreams points out this truth very clearly. He told the ruler, "God has shown you what he is about to do" (Gen. 41:28). Then, after giving graphic details of the enormity of the impending problem, Joseph added, "My suggestion is that you find the wisest man in Egypt and put him in charge of a nationwide program" (41:33). First, there was the declarative statement concerning God's intentions. Then came the suggestion about appropriate action. Joseph also told Pharaoh what would happen if he followed through on the suggestions: "There will be enough to eat when the seven years of famine come. Otherwise disaster will surely strike the land, and all the people **will** die" (41:36). The options were abundantly clear; the choices were unmistakably spelled out.

Pharaoh was forewarned, but would he forearm himself? The record shows that he did, and that he chose Joseph, "the wisest man in Egypt," to head up the program!

One of the greatest mysteries of the relationship between God and humans is the matter of divine sovereignty and human responsibility. Scripture is full of references to God ruling supremely in the affairs of men, demonstrating unambiguously that he is truly the sovereign Lord. Yet at the same time, God instructs men how to respond to what he says, and he expects them to do so with glad obedience and joyful trust. And their actions are important and significant. Attempts to harmonize these aspects of God's revealed truth often prove notoriously difficult.

God is going to do what he says he is going to do. As God, he is perfectly free to do it. And he lets people know, hoping they will take the necessary action to be prepared.

Even when the intricacies of philosophical and theological debate lead to unanswerable questions, simple faith that God is as good as his word is possible. And wise, responsible, prompt responses are eminently practical! This does not mean that we should ignore the perplexing questions, but it does mean we should not spend time debating when the time for action is at hand—any more than an approaching hurricane heralds the occasion for a thorough debate on the accuracy of weather forecasters' predictions!

TO READ: *Genesis 42:1-38*

GOD AND GUILT

Speaking among themselves, they said, "This has all happened because of what we did to Joseph long ago. We saw his terror and anguish and heard his pleadings, but we wouldn't listen. That's why this trouble has come upon us."

GENESIS 42:21

Guilt feelings do not go away easily. They are perfectly capable of raising their heads throughout a lifetime.

This was certainly the case with Joseph's brothers. Years had passed since they had treated their brother so badly. While they continued to look after their flocks, battling the elements and coping with the vicissitudes of their rugged lifestyle, Joseph had gone on to become the prime minister of Egypt. Famine had spread to his brothers' land, and they were powerless to stop its ravages. In fact, they seemed to have become so totally depressed and immobilized that their aged father rebuked them: "Why are you standing around looking at one another? I have heard there is grain in Egypt. Go down and buy some for us before we all starve to death" (Gen. 42:2).

In desperation the brothers arrived at Pharaoh's court and unwittingly encountered their own brother. Joseph promptly recognized them, although they did not recognize him. Joseph's treatment of them, including a brief jail sentence and strident charges that they were spies, led them to say to each other, "This has all happened because of what we did to Joseph years ago. We saw his terror and anguish and heard his pleadings, but we wouldn't listen. That's why this trouble has come upon us" (42:21). Under the pressure of their circumstances, it did not take long for their guilt and shame to surface. And they quickly assumed that there was a real connection between their previous behavior and their subsequent difficulties, and that the link between the two must be God himself.

God was very much in the center of the brothers' thoughts when they eventually were allowed to return home, minus Simeon. On the way, they discovered to their horror that the money they had paid for the grain was still in the neck of their sacks (42:25). They realized that they would be charged with theft. Their immediate response was, "What has God done to us?" (42:28). They recognized their guilt before God, they felt his displeasure because of their actions, and they rightly saw their predicament before God as the consequence of their sin.

Guilty men are in deep trouble when they are no longer troubled by their misdeeds. They may have stuffed in their guilt feelings and gotten on with their lives to their own satisfaction, but the unresolved guilt will do its work in their souls nevertheless, haunting and harassing them at the most unexpected moments, depressing and debilitating them at others.

The only safe way to handle guilt is to face it, as Joseph's brothers faced their guilt. Then confess it to the Lord, who knows all about it, and ask for his forgiveness. Then see him lift the load of guilt and give you joy and peace.

TO READ: *Genesis 43:1–14*

GENERATION GAP

When the grain they had brought from Egypt was almost gone, Jacob said to his sons,
"Go again and buy us a little food." But Judah said, "The man wasn't joking when
he warned that we couldn't see him again unless Benjamin came along."

GENESIS 43:2-3

I n the turbulent 1960s people talked about the "generation gap." There have always been differences between generations. It is an old problem, but during the 1960s it was given a new name and a lot of attention. Young people decided not only to take issue with their elders, but to reject what those wielding authority said. The result was a standoff between those who held the power and those who resented it being used to their perceived detriment.

Even as far back as Jacob's time, the gap between the generations was clearly in evidence. Jacob had long been in control of his family. He was used to telling his sons what to do and expecting them to obey. But as the days and weeks of the famine wore on, and the food supply diminished, it was obvious that there was going to be a showdown between the old man and his sons.

Jacob wanted his boys to return to Egypt to buy more food (Gen. 43:2). Judah, the spokesman for the younger generation, said, "The man wasn't joking when he warned that we couldn't see him again unless Benjamin came along" (43:3). He then added forcefully, "If you don't let Benjamin go, we may as well stay at home" (43:5). For understandable reasons, Jacob was not prepared to listen to his son's explanation. Jacob said that Benjamin was not going, and Judah said, in effect, that if Benjamin didn't go, no one was going, with the probable result that they would all die.

Sensing that he was between a rock and a hard place, Jacob "moaned" about his own pain and grumbled about the brothers even mentioning their other brother to the Egyptian ruler. With startling self-centeredness, Jacob asked, "Why did you have to treat me with such cruelty?" (43:6). Judah, showing a lot of good sense, reasoned further with his father, gave personal guarantees, and reminded him that if they had acted when they ought to have, they could have made the journey several times over. Finally Jacob relented and yielded control to the younger men. He then gave them wise instructions for their journey, but Jacob's decision was hardly with great grace. "If it can't be avoided" set the tone of his surrender (43:11). "If I must bear the anguish of their deaths, so be it" dominated his thinking (43:14). This is not to suggest that the sons were always right and their father always wrong. Jacob understandably was having a bad day. Fortunately, his sons were doing better.

There comes a time for the older men to allow the younger generation to take the lead. If they hand over the reins with joy, they may watch with delight as the young men succeed. If they don't, they widen the generation gap into a gulf that becomes the grave for promising endeavors.

GENTLENESS
AND GREATNESS

You have given me the shield of your salvation. Your right hand supports me;
your gentleness has made me great.

PSALM 18:35

I n the long and illustrious history of the Jewish people, no man shines brighter than
King David. His mighty victories against overwhelming enemies, his administration of
the far-reaching kingdom, his concern for the true worship of Jehovah, his establishment
and development of Jerusalem as the nation's capital, not to mention his amazing spiritual
legacy in the Psalms—all these accomplishments point unerringly to his greatness, both as
a king and as a man.

David was always ready to speak most warmly of the ways in which the Lord had
intervened in his life. He wrote, "He delivered me from my powerful enemies, from those who
hated me and were too strong for me. They attacked me at a moment when I was weakest, but
the Lord upheld me" (Ps. 18:17-18). Men who are in the process of celebrating great victories,
as David was when he wrote this psalm, rarely speak about their weakest moments and how
they were delivered from them! Men who win are more inclined to talk about what they did
to accomplish their feats. David never downplayed the significant role he had played in the
victories he won, but he always returned to his main theme: giving God the credit for working
in and through him. "You gave me victory over my accusers. You appointed me as the ruler
over the nations; people I don't even know now serve me" (18:43).

The secret of David's success was in the way the Lord had worked in his life. But
Psalm 18 has a surprise for us. In the midst of all the dramatic language speaking of war
and victory in this psalm, David said, "Your gentleness has made me great" (18:35).
Gentleness? Making him *great*? That is a surprise! David testified to the amazing fact that
his own greatness was directly due to the Lord's gentleness.

When we look at David's life and the way God worked in it, gentleness is not the
first thing that comes to mind! But perhaps David's greatest moments were not when he
was triumphant on the fields of battle. It could be that the most influential moments in
David's experience of God were not when "the earth quaked and trembled," or when "the
foundations of mountains shook" (18:7). Perhaps David was at his greatest when he
spared Saul's life, not once but twice (1 Sam. 24 and 26). Or when he took Mephibosheth,
the crippled survivor of Saul's wrecked dynasty, into his own home (2 Sam. 9). Or when
he protected the survivor of one of Saul's senseless massacres with his own life (1 Sam.
22:23). This great warrior king had a great gentleness. It was a gentleness he had learned
from the great—and gentle—God.

To this day, great men are gentlemen. And gentle men are truly great!

TO READ: *1 Corinthians 12:1-31*

REFLECTIONS
OF THE CREATOR

A spiritual gift is given to each of us as a means of helping the entire church. . . .
Now all of you together are Christ's body, and each one of you
is a separate and necessary part of it.

1 CORINTHIANS 12:7, 27

P erhaps the greatest mystery in Christianity is the doctrine of the Trinity. Attempts to explain how God is one and yet exists in three persons—Father, Son and Holy Spirit—have usually been less than compelling. Part of the reason for this is that we explain something unknown by drawing an analogy with something known. But nothing adequately explains the Trinity—how God exists in a unity that is characterized by diversity. Yet it is true.

On the other hand, the created world in which we live is full of examples of unity in diversity and diversity in unity, and these examples are reflections of the Creator. Take, for example, the human body. As we know, it is made up of a great number of diverse parts. All of these parts have a special and unique place and function. In fact, the more we learn about the human body, the more complex and intricate we understand it to be. Paul observed, "The human body has many parts, but the many parts make up only one body" (1 Cor. 12:12). This is an obvious point, but Paul made this point for a very good reason. He wanted to show how the church—the body of Christ—reflects the unity-diversity characteristics of God. Using the human body as a starting place, Paul added, "So it is with the body of Christ" (12:12).

Just like the members of the human body, all the members of the body of Christ have a unique role to play in the life and health of the church. Paul stated this explicitly: "Now all of you together are Christ's body, and each one of you is a separate and necessary part of it" (12:27).

Not every member of the church has grasped that he or she is a "separate and necessary part" of the church. Many feel perfectly comfortable playing no discernible role in the church's life—except, perhaps, the role of spectator! But the fact remains that, as in the human body, each member of the church has been uniquely endowed not only with a role but also with the means to fulfill it. The enabling for service in the church is found in unique "spiritual gifts" given by the "Holy Spirit," and these gifts are granted to "each of us as a means of helping the entire church" (1 Cor. 12:4, 7).

If the body, both physical and spiritual, is to remain healthy and function effectively, then each part of the body must fulfill its task. A church is healthy when all its members function as they were designed to function. Christ works best through his body!

TO READ: *1 Corinthians 13:1-13*

THE GREATEST THING

*There are three things that will endure—faith, hope, and love—
and the greatest of these is love.*

1 CORINTHIANS 13:13

M odern psychology does not always see eye-to-eye with the Bible, but in one area there is some agreement. Psychologists tell us that there are two main things that people need for full and effective lives. The first is the ability to express love, and the second is the opportunity to experience love. The person who cannot or will not love will be shriveled in his relationships. The man who is not loved, or who does not know what being loved is like, will be stunted in his own soul. We are made for relationships, so to be stunted relationally is to be impoverished personally, shriveled emotionally, and impaired socially.

The Bible uses different terminology but makes a similar point. The Corinthian Christians were very excited about their ability to use exotic spiritual gifts and engage in many exciting spiritual exercises. Yet Paul told them, "If I could speak in any language in heaven or on earth but didn't love others, I would only be making meaningless noise like a loud gong or a clanging cymbal" (1 Cor. 13:1). Paul reinforced this point by asking, "If I had the gift of prophecy, and if I knew all the mysteries of the future and knew everything about everything, but didn't love others, what good would I be?" (13:2). He recognized that he would "be no good to anybody," even if he could move mountains simply by speaking to them, if he did it without love (13:2).

Paul concluded, "There are three things that will endure—faith, hope, and love— and the greatest of these is love" (13:13). The "things that will endure" are the timeless, fundamental factors of experience without which humans cease to function as they should. Faith is an instinctive part of our make up—we cannot survive without trusting. Hope is also necessary—it is what keeps us going in times of despair and despondency. And there will never come a time when love is not paramount. Because love is the language of our relationships, both with God and with others, love is the greatest!

That being the case, a man is well-advised to acquaint himself with the Bible's teaching on love—what love is and how it functions. Then a man should take seriously the apostle's instruction: "Let love be your highest goal" (14:1). This does not mean, of course, that the gifts are insignificant, or that ministry is unimportant. It just means that love is what makes them effective. For that matter, love is what makes the world go round and our lives go forward—forever.

TO READ: *1 Corinthians 14:1-12*

COMMUNICATION

Dear brothers and sisters, if I should come to you talking in an unknown language,
how would that help you? But if I bring you some revelation or some special
knowledge or some prophecy or some teaching—that is what will help you.

1 CORINTHIANS 14:6

I recently read about an old gentleman who had traveled out to the West Coast of the United States by oxcart as a boy who would return to the East Coast, at the end of his life, by plane. During his lifetime, dramatic changes had taken place in the Western world. It has not been so long since America was an agrarian society, where people lived on the land and from the land. Then came the Industrial Revolution, when steam and electricity were harnessed. In time, life became considerably easier. In recent years, we have moved into the communications era—information is power and wealth, and fortunes are made and lost in a matter of moments. Although times are changing, some things never change. Even though the means of communication change, the basic rules of communication remain the same.

That is why the things that Paul told the Corinthians about communication two millennia ago are relevant today. In the Corinthian church, the issue was speaking in tongues. It still is an issue today. On the day of Pentecost (see Acts 2), the disciples spoke about Christ in such a way that people who spoke all kinds of different languages were able to understand them. A miracle of some kind took place—either a miracle of speaking or one of hearing (Acts 2:7-13). Subsequently, the Corinthian Christians discovered that they had a spiritual gift—"the ability to speak in tongues" (1 Cor. 14:2). Some believe it was the same gift that was in evidence at Pentecost. Others suggest that this ability was not related to earthly languages but that it was a gift of ecstatic utterance used in worship, understandable only by God and a person with the corresponding spiritual gift of interpretation. Whatever the nature of the gift of tongues, as it is often called, Paul was concerned about unbelievers coming in to the worship service where people were using it: "If I should come to you talking in an unknown language, how would that help you?" (14:6). The first and greatest rule in communication has not changed through the centuries. If you want to get your message across, speak the language of your target audience!

One of the criticisms of the church is that it spends time answering questions no one is asking in a language no one is speaking. That is a contravention of the basic rule of communication. It is also an exercise in futility. Effective communication requires clear enunciation and perceptive listening. Without clarity, perception will not happen. Without perception, the clear enunciation may as well not happen. The church's challenge is to use modern means of communication, to which modern people will listen, to speak the ancient message clearly.

TO READ: *1 Corinthians 14:13-25*

CRAZY CHRISTIANS

Even so, if unbelievers or people who don't understand these things come into your meeting and hear everyone talking in an unknown language, they will think you are crazy.

1 CORINTHIANS 14:23

B eing a Christian has never been easy. In the early days, Christians were treated cruelly, and large numbers lost their lives. Even when they were not physically assaulted, Christians were often grossly misunderstood and misrepresented. For instance, they were accused of being cannibals because when they took communion they talked about eating the flesh and drinking the blood of the Lord Jesus (see 1 Cor. 11:23-26). They were also accused of being atheists because they did not worship the pagan gods. Perhaps worst of all, they were charged with incest because "brothers" were marrying "sisters." Christians were basically defenseless against such charges. They lacked both the means and the power to stand against the authorities arraigned against them.

But in other situations, Christians could do something about the charges leveled at them. For example, people visiting the worship services where Christians were behaving in an apparently unrestrained and eccentric manner, were understandably confused and offended by what they saw. Paul said, "If unbelievers or people who don't understand these things come into your meeting and hear everyone talking in an unknown language, they will think you are crazy" (1 Cor. 14:23). In situations such as that obtained for the early Christians living in a hostile environment, there may not be a lot that Christians can do about charges of being wicked on the basis of misunderstanding or malicious misrepresentation. But they can respond to accusations of being "crazy" when they conduct their worship without a thought of how they appear to unbelievers in their midst!

Paul's solution was straightforward. First, if God has given you the gift of ecstatic speech, then use it in worship, but not in such a way that unbelievers will think you are crazy. One way to do this, of course, is to exercise the gift in private devotion, but if the gifts are to be exercised in a public worship service and unbelievers are present, then at least explain to them what is going on. In modern parlance that means to be "seeker-sensitive." Second, ensure that your worship services are conducted in such a way that unbelievers will be ministered to, so that "as they listen, their secret thoughts will be laid bare, and they will fall down on their knees and worship God, declaring, 'God is really here among you'" (14:25).

Paul had unprecedented experiences of the Lord (see 2 Cor. 12:1-10), yet he was remarkably level-headed about corporate worship: "In a church meeting I would much rather speak five understandable words that will help others than ten thousand words in an unknown language" (1 Cor. 14:19). These twenty-four words should be borne in mind at all times in the contemporary church.

There is a place for private worship. There is also a place for public proclamation. Both should be dear to the hearts of God's people and integral parts of their Christian walk. If people call you crazy for that kind of lifestyle—so be it. If they call you crazy for anything else—make changes!

TO READ: *1 Corinthians 14:26-40*

ORDERLY WORSHIP

Remember that people who prophesy are in control of their spirit and can
wait their turn. For God is not a God of disorder but of peace. . . .
Be sure that everything is done properly and in order.

1 CORINTHIANS 14:32-33, 40

I n sports there are those who know the plays and perform their roles meticulously. Then there are those who, with a flash of unrehearsed brilliance, can win a game. Or lose it! In business, there are people who manage the details and give order to the enterprise, while others chafe at the daily grind but have the ability to win the contract. Some people thrive on details and structure. Others love spontaneity and inspiration.

In an ideal world, form and freedom coexist cooperatively. They complement each other and produce a congenial atmosphere in which to function and an effective result toward their intended goals. In the real world, it is not always so straightforward. For instance, look at the church. Most church people would agree that the church's privilege and responsibility is to engage in worship that praises and serves God, that honors his name, that proclaims his worth, and that furthers his cause. But when it comes to agreeing on what constitutes "worshipful" worship, major differences rise to the surface, and often stay there! In fact, the differences are often so sharp that there is a term for these differences—"worship wars," an oxymoron if ever there was one!

The Corinthians provide us with an ancient example of this recurring problem. By temperament, inclination, and preference they were in the camp of the spontaneous and the free. A worship service in the Corinthian church would have been lively and animated, unstructured, and unpredictable, even bordering on the chaotic. Worshipers were encouraged to participate and lead in the service, but sadly, this often took place without appropriate courtesy and decorum. As a result, there was strife among the members of the church over the conduct of their worship services.

So Paul spelled out some "rules of worship" for the Corinthian Christians. "No more than two or three should speak in an unknown language. They must speak one at a time, and someone must be ready to interpret. . . . Let two or three prophesy, and let the others evaluate what is said. . . . Women should be silent during the church meetings" (14:27, 29, 34). All three groups mentioned were required to exercise "control of their spirit," which meant that they had to be as ready to be silent as to speak. If prophets were prophesying all at once, if tongues-speakers were speaking without interpretation, and if women were asking questions aloud, then the result would be noise and chaos. A situation like that did not honor God or enrich the church. So Paul instructed, "Be sure that everything is done properly and in order" (14:40).

Paul was neither an opponent of spontaneity nor a control freak. His only desire was to see form embracing freedom and structure allowing spontaneity. This is a noble goal for the church today. It's a challenging goal, too.

TO READ: *1 Corinthians 15:1-11*

THE MAIN THING

Now let me remind you, dear brothers and sisters, of the Good News
I preached to you before. You welcomed it then and still do now,
for your faith is built on this wonderful message.

1 CORINTHIANS 15:1

S hould the players on a sports team begin to experience difficulties with each other off the field, the chances of their performing well on the field will be jeopardized. The same thing applies to a business, a family, or a church. Good leaders know this and, therefore, spend considerable time and effort seeking to maximize good relations and minimize personal frictions. Good leaders do this by constantly reminding the group about their objectives and helping them to focus on what is of prime importance. Good leaders teach their people that "the main thing is to keep the main thing the main thing."[22]

Paul, as we have seen, was dealing with a particularly fractious group of people in the church of Corinth. They were divided on a number of issues. All of these issues, in Paul's view, were less significant than the "main thing." So, having dealt with some of the issues that were dividing them, and having reminded them that they were called to love each other, Paul turned his attention to sharpening their focus once more on the main thing. He wrote, "Now let me remind you, dear brothers and sisters, of the Good News I preached to you before. You welcomed it then and still do now, for your faith is built on this wonderful message" (1 Cor. 15:1). The main thing was not who was the best leader, or who exercised which gift, or which ministry was most important. The main thing was that God had done something in human history to change their lives for time and eternity, and that he had alerted the people of Corinth to what he had done through the preaching of the Good News. Without the Good News there would be no church, no gifts, no ministry, no apostles, no salvation, and no forgiveness. In fact, without the Good News, there would be no Corinthian church at all to get worked up over these less-than-main things!

What precisely *is* this Good News? "That Christ died for our sins, . . . he was buried, and he was raised from the dead on the third day" (15:3-4)—that is the Good News. Many men have died bravely, some even voluntarily and vicariously. But no one has ever died with the intention of raising himself from the dead. No one, that is, except Jesus (see John 10:17-18), which demonstrates that his death was unique. It was so unique that it alone could be the basis for the forgiveness of sins.

The main thing is that Christ died to bring forgiveness and rose from the dead, conquering sin, death, the devil, and hell. As long as Paul was alive he would never cease to remind people.

When the risen Christ is central, you know what is peripheral. Never confuse the two.

[22]Source unknown.

TO READ: *Psalm 81*

OPEN YOUR MOUTH WIDE

It was I, the LORD your God, who rescued you from the land of Egypt. Open your mouth wide, and I will fill it with good things.

PSALM 81:10

G. K. Chesterton, one of Britain's great writers, was of the opinion that an open mind is like an open mouth: It is only useful when closed on something of substance. Sadly, some people only seem to open their mouths in order to put their feet in them.

The psalm writer had a better idea. He exhorted the people in the name of the Lord, "Open your mouth wide, and I will fill it with good things" (Ps. 81:10). The instruction was given in the context of a religious celebration. The people of God were "required by the laws of Israel" to participate in "a sacred feast when the moon is new, when the moon is full" (81:3-4). The purpose of the regular cycle of feasts and celebrations was to remind the people about what God had done in the experiences of their forefathers, so that they would remember who the Lord is and not deviate from his ways.

The Lord never tired of reminding his people, "It was I, the Lord your God, who rescued you from the land of Egypt" (81:10). And he found it necessary to give them "stern warnings" constantly telling them, "You must never have a foreign god" (81:8, 9). But tragically, the history of the people was full of examples of willful disobedience. The Lord said sadly, "But no, my people wouldn't listen. Israel did not want me around" (81:11).

The feasts and festivals were factored into the life of the nation, to bring them back to basics and to stir their hearts to worship and obedience. But there was something about God's people that periodically caused them to refuse to believe that their security and joy rested in the Lord. They found other ways of living, more to their liking. So they had to be brought back repeatedly to a position of remembering God.

It was in that position that they were told to open their mouths wide. This certainly referred to them joining in singing "praises to God" (81:1)—a practice that warms the coldest heart and cheers the downcast spirit. But it also meant that they should "open their mouths," spiritually speaking, to feed on the truth being presented to them and inwardly digest the Good News of God's salvation.

Unlike ancient Israel, the law of our land does not legislate regular worship. But the most fundamental spiritual law insists that regular worship is necessary for all-around well-being. And it is not burdensome—in fact, regular worship is like being fed with "the best of foods" (81:16). It tastes good! It is something on which to close an open mouth.

MAY I HAVE
YOUR ATTENTION?

"Amazing!" Moses said to himself. "Why isn't that bush burning up?
I must go over to see this."

EXODUS 3:3

The busier a man is, the more difficult it is to get his attention. The higher he climbs on the corporate ladder, the more hoops one must jump through to talk to him. When he is asked at the beginning of a flight to pay attention to the announcements concerning safety regulations, he, having heard it all before, continues to read the financial page of his paper. When he returns home and his teenage daughter tries to speak to him, he is too busy downloading the latest news about his stock portfolio and favorite sports teams. And once the ball game starts on TV, his wife knows it is useless to try to get him to listen to her concerns about a leaky faucet or a troubled child. Very often, in this world, when the question is, "May I have your attention?" the answer is "No."

Although the pace of life was slower—much slower—in biblical times, it was not always easy to get people's attention in those days, either. In particular, if God wanted to say something, he often resorted to doing something dramatic—like appearing to Moses in a bush that burned without burning up. "'Amazing!' Moses said to himself. 'Why isn't that bush burning up? I must go over to see this'" (Exod. 3:3). Having gained Moses' attention, the Lord then began to communicate to him what he wanted to say: that he was well aware of the predicament of his people in Egypt, that he had every intention of rescuing them, and that Moses was to spearhead the rescue!

Assuming that the Lord wants to communicate with modern man, and knowing that it is not always easy to get his attention, the question is, "How does the Lord get our attention today?" No one testifies to seeing burning bushes that are not burned up. But some of God's men burn brightly without burning out. They exhibit unusual resources that enable them to stand tall under pressure, to stand firm through temptation, to exhibit cheerfulness in the face of trouble, and to exude equanimity in the teeth of disaster. They are inveterate encouragers, tireless supporters, and consistent examples to all. And they don't burn out!

Seeing one of God's brightly-shining men in action causes other men to stop and wonder. That is the time to explain that while there is nothing special about the bush that burns, there is something unusually special about the fire that burns within. The essence of the believer's life is, as Paul explained, "I myself no longer live, but Christ lives in me" (Gal. 2:20). Being a burning bush without being bushed (or burned) draws attention.

TO READ: *Exodus 4:10-18*

THE IMPATIENCE
OF GOD

*"Now go, and do as I have told you. I will help you speak well, and I will tell you
what to say." But Moses again pleaded, "Lord, please! Send someone else."
Then the LORD became angry with Moses.*

EXODUS 4:12-14

S hakespeare said that there was never a philosopher who could bear a toothache patiently. Even a philosopher has his limits. There is only so much that he will endure. It was the same in Job's case. His patience was legendary, but there came a time when he had heard enough from his "comforters," whose comfort he did not need. Most men have little difficulty identifying (or at least responding to) the limits of their own tolerance and patience. But what about God? Are there limits to his patience?

This is a disturbing question, because God's patience is not only clearly taught in Scripture but it has been widely experienced by those who have received his forgiveness and embraced his grace. God's patience is often assumed by those who do not love God. Where is the man, whatever his religious convictions, or lack of them, who does not assume that God, if he is there, has a boundless supply of patience? So the ungodly man will continue in a lifestyle that he knows in his heart is not right, on the assumption—or hope—that he will get away with it in the end. He either thinks that God isn't there or that God is so patient that anything goes.

Disturbing or not, the question about the limits of God's patience deserves an answer. The answer is in the ongoing discussion that Moses had with the Lord concerning his call to go to Egypt and confront Pharaoh. Moses had raised question after question, excuse after excuse, until finally he said in desperation, "Lord, please! Send someone else!" (Exod. 4:13).

That did it! God had heard enough! "Then the Lord became angry with Moses" (4:14). The limit of God's patience was reached when Moses obdurately refused to do what the Lord told him to do. Moses had been attracted to God's presence in the bush, had heard God's voice, had received God's assurances, had seen God's miracles, and had been told that God didn't mind that he was "clumsy with words" but would give him words to speak! Still Moses resisted God's call and tried with all his might to avoid being what God wanted him to be. That is what brought on God's impatience.

Even though Moses was impatient, the Lord gave him Aaron as a spokesman, and he still sent Moses to Pharaoh. And Moses went. Perhaps, through the display of divine impatience, Moses finally got the message!

The patience of God is legendary. Where would we be without it? But it is not inexhaustible, and it should not be abused or taken for granted. Better to seek to bring him pleasure than to try his patience!

TO READ: *Exodus 5:1-23*

BRICKS
WITHOUT STRAW

"Do not supply the people with any more straw for making bricks. Let them get it themselves! But don't reduce their production quotas by a single brick. They obviously don't have enough to do. If they did, they wouldn't be talking about going into the wilderness to offer sacrifices to their God.

EXODUS 5:7-8

Nelson Mandela, in his book *Long Walk to Freedom*, wrote about his years as a prisoner on Robben Island, South Africa. Each morning the prisoners were marched into the courtyard wearing light shirts and shorts—no underwear or socks— where they were required to hammer boulders the size of volleyballs into gravel. The first week, they were ordered to fill a giant skid half full. The second week it had to be three quarters full, and the third week completely full. The task finally became impossible. They were being driven intentionally to the breaking point. But instead of breaking, the prisoners decided to stage a go-slow strike. Despite dire threats from the wardens, the strike continued until the the wardens were forced to relent.

Pharaoh's prisoners, the Israelites, were pushed to the breaking point, too. They were required to produce a quota of bricks each day. Raw materials, including chopped straw, were provided. Then Moses and Aaron appeared before Pharaoh and said, "This is what the Lord, the God of Israel, says: 'Let my people go, for they must go out into the wilderness to hold a religious festival in my honor'" (Exod. 5:1). Pharaoh retorted that he did not know the God of Israel and could see no reason why the people should stop working in order to worship him! To show his displeasure, Pharaoh ordered, "Do not supply the people with any more straw for making bricks. Let them get it themselves! But don't reduce their production quota by a single brick" (5:7-8). Pharaoh's prisoners, however, dared not stage a go-slow strike. Unlike the South African prisoners, the Hebrews were as likely to be killed as to be kicked. So their sufferings simply increased. If they complained, they were whipped into submission.

The Israelites blamed Moses and Aaron for adding to their pain: "May the Lord judge you for getting us into this terrible situation" (5:21). But Moses knew that he and Aaron were obeying God's orders, so he complained to God: "Why have you mistreated your own people like this, Lord? Why did you send me?" (5:22). On the surface, everybody's complaints seem quite reasonable. Yet behind the scenes, God was at work. He was setting the stage for Pharaoh to learn a major lesson about God's sovereign lordship! It was not going to be easy; a lot of people were going to get hurt.

In the struggle between good and evil, it often seems that evil is winning and that good people are bearing the brunt of the struggle unjustly. But remember, Mandela was eventually released and became the president of South Africa, and the children of Israel went free and headed for the Promised Land. The Pharaoh who ordered bricks made without straw turned out to be a man of straw himself.

No matter how hard the struggle, we can be confident that, in the end, God wins!

TO READ: *Exodus 11:1-10*

TURNING THINGS AROUND

Now the LORD had caused the Egyptians to look favorably on the people of Israel, and Moses was considered a very great man in the land of Egypt. He was respected by Pharaoh's officials and the Egyptian people alike.

EXODUS 11:3

W hatever you think of Fidel Castro, the communist leader of Cuba, you have to admit that he has had staying power. Despite all the efforts of the United States to overthrow him, including the ill-fated Bay of Pigs episode and more than forty years of economic sanctions, he has remained in control. Meanwhile, Presidents Kennedy, Johnson, Nixon, Ford, Carter, Bush, and Clinton have moved on from the presidency. Even though doctrinaire communism no longer holds sway in former strongholds, this fact has not deterred Castro. Nothing has appeared to move him or change him! No doubt his enemies—and there is no shortage of them—wonder what it will take to remove him and bring freedom to the Cuban people.

The Israelites must have wondered how anything could change the heart of Pharaoh, the cruel tyrant who dominated their lives during their captivity in Egypt. Even a series of divinely inspired disasters had served only to strengthen Pharaoh's resolve to oppress them and had stoked his antipathy to the Lord and his people. The Lord said, "Pharaoh is very stubborn, and he continues to refuse to let the people go" (Exod. 7:14). With each succeeding disaster, Pharaoh's pattern of stubbornness and heart-hardening made further confrontation necessary. But through it all, the Lord was at work, determined to turn things around so completely that eventually Pharaoh would beg the children of Israel to leave.

The Lord was already turning things around for Moses. Despised even by his own people at one point (see 6:9-12), Moses was now "considered a great man in the land of Egypt. He was respected by Pharaoh's officials and the Egyptian people alike" (11:3). The Egyptians' attitude toward the rest of the Israelites had gone through a remarkable transformation, as well: "The Lord had caused the Egyptians to look favorably on the people of Israel."

That God is fully capable of intervening in human affairs is without question, and that he does so is amply documented. The methods that God employs are sometimes hard for us to take or even to understand, but his objectives are always right, and his means of achieving them are just. That the prisoners should be freed from Pharaoh's control was right, and that Pharaoh should be punished for his intransigence was equally correct. But Pharaoh's ongoing obduracy and his unrelenting antipathy necessitated ever increasing disasters until he finally yielded.

God is committed to turning things around the way they ought to be, and he will. Even Castro's regime will fall one day. Pharaoh's did! This being the case, we who live neither under Pharaoh's tyranny nor Castro's regime, yet find our work situations onerous or our social climate challenging, should take heart. God is at work, and ultimately, he will see that right is rewarded and wrong is punished. But he works at his speed, not ours, and he is not limited by time—he has eternity at his disposal!

TO READ: *Exodus 12:1-28*

PASSOVER

"Then your children will ask, 'What does all this mean? What is this ceremony about?' And you will reply, 'It is the celebration of the Lord's Passover, for he passed over the homes of the Israelites in Egypt. And though he killed the Egyptians, he spared our families and did not destroy us.'"

EXODUS 12:26-27

There are many elements of educating children in addition to sending them to school. Parental example, for instance, has a profound impact on the formation of a young person's approach to life. Wise parents know this and intentionally order their lives in ways that will convey the right message to the children. This includes the development of family rituals and traditions which will create "teachable moments." The Jewish community, perhaps more than any other segment of Western society, understands this.

More than three thousand years have elapsed since the inauguration of Passover, when the Israelites were still held as slaves in Egypt. At that time the Lord told Moses, "When you arrive in the land the Lord has promised to give you, you will continue to celebrate this festival" (Exod. 12:25). Passover is still observed in Jewish families on the fourteenth day of the first month (12:6)—Nisan in the Hebrew calendar—and special care is given to explain to the children exactly what is being commemorated. The father of the family is required to answer the questions of his children, which are prompted by the rituals of the Passover meal. In modern Jewish families, the necessary teaching is called the "Haggadah," which is designed to help the father give a correct explanation.

Jesus was careful to observe Passover with his disciples, and it is no accident that Jesus' betrayal, crucifixion, and resurrection took place during the time of annual celebration. This has led Christians to see the Passover as a prefiguration of Christ's death. The Passover lamb was killed and its blood sprinkled on their doorposts in order that the children of Israel might find shelter and thus escape the judgment (Exod. 12:22). Likewise, Christians find shelter through shed blood—the death—of the Lord Jesus as their only hope of salvation and protection from God's judgment. That is why Christians in the West celebrate Easter around the time of Passover.

In light of the traditions, dating back more than three thousand years, that have led to the modern celebration of Easter, it might be worth asking two questions: "How do present day families commemorate the Easter event?" and "How can modern men effectively explain to their children the significance of this great Christian festival?" With appropriate and meaningful family traditions, Easter can be a great teaching moment for the children. There is no doubt that, given the right kind of stimulation, children will ask the right kind of questions. And there should be no question that, given the right kind of opportunity, modern fathers should have the right kind of answers about the deep issues of life. Their children deserve nothing less.

TO READ: *Exodus 12:29-50*

THE MESSAGE
OF DEATH

At midnight the LORD killed all the firstborn sons in the land of Egypt, from the firstborn son of Pharaoh, who sat on the throne, to the firstborn son of the captive in the dungeon. Even the firstborn of their livestock were killed. Pharaoh and his officials and all the people of Egypt woke up during the night, and loud wailing was heard throughout the land of Egypt. There was not a single house where someone had not died.

EXODUS 12:29-30

W hat do Karl Marx, Sigmund Freud, and Albert Einstein have in common? Certainly they all figured prominently in the lists of the most influential people of the twentieth century. Karl Marx's political doctrines lay at the foundation of the Soviet empire, which affected the lives of millions. Sigmund Freud's theories about human personality and behavior have changed the way people are viewed and human problems are addressed throughout the whole western world. Einstein's theory of relativity helped bring the world into the nuclear age, and we have yet to discover the full implications of his work.

But these three men have something else in common: All three of them were Jews. They are thus a reminder of the far-reaching impact that the Jewish people have had during their history. The Jewish people have had a remarkable impact considering their relatively small numbers. It is probably true to say (with apologies to Churchill) that never in the history of human experience have so many been impacted so profoundly by so few!

This people, the Jewish people, were once held as slaves in Egypt for 430 years. They were eventually liberated from their captivity after a desperate show of force on the part of that country's ruler. Despite endless opportunities to let the people go, the Pharaoh of Egypt refused. Eventually he was warned, "This is what the Lord says: About midnight I will pass through Egypt. All the firstborn sons will die in every family in Egypt, from the oldest son of Pharaoh, who sits on the throne, to the oldest son of his lowliest slave. Even the firstborn of the animals will die" (11:4-5). Pharaoh refused to relent, the judgment came, and disaster swept across the land. Every household was affected—"loud wailing was heard throughout the land of Egypt" (12:30).

The change in Pharaoh was startling. When initially approached by Moses and Aaron, he had superciliously declared that he had no knowledge of the Lord and, there-fore, no intention of acceding to the Lord's requests. Then, as the series of disasters struck, he simply tried to emulate them as a show of his own independence and power. But when death finally struck home he not only urged the people to leave—he begged Moses, "give me a blessing as you leave!" (12:32).

Death preaches a powerful message about mortality and human limitations. Sadly, mortality is the only message that some men understand. The greatest Jewish contribution—the life-giving death and resurrection of Jesus—is often overlooked. Jewish history shows that God does intervene in human affairs, that he is concerned about human destiny, and that he will communicate to us in all manner of ways, even through death itself. Death is often bitter, sometimes bloody, but through Christ it has the potential to be blessed.

TO READ: *Psalm 97*

LOVE THE LORD, HATE EVIL

*You who love the LORD, hate evil! He protects the lives of his godly people
and rescues them from the power of the wicked.*

PSALM 97:10

D uring a close reelection campaign, a southern Senator visited a small town in the
hinterland of his state. The issue demanding most attention in this lackluster
election was . . . squirrel hunting. The people were deeply divided over the issue. Some
believed they had the right to hunt the little animals; others thought the practice was
barbaric and should be banned. So the Senator was asked to state his position on the issue.
After careful thought, and probably after checking the polls, he replied, "Some of my
friends are squirrel hunters, and some of my friends think squirrel hunting should be
banned. If you look carefully at my record—and I'm running on my record, don't forget—
you'll know that as a man of principle I stand firmly with my friends."

The story may have value as a satire on modern politics but not as a prescription for
living by principle! On matters of real significance, a man of principle cannot be in favor
of one thing *and* its opposite at the same time! In fact, the extent to which a man shows
his stand for something can often best be determined by the position he takes against the
opposite.

The psalm writer gives us a great example. He wrote, "You who love the Lord, hate
evil!" (Ps. 97:10). There are many ways in which a man shows his love for the Lord. He is
instructed to love the Lord with heart, mind, soul, and strength (Deut. 6:5; Luke 10:27).
Those are positive ways of loving the Lord. But love can be expressed negatively as well.
By hating what God hates, we express love for who God is.

The psalmist says, "Righteousness and justice are the foundation of [God's] throne"
(Ps. 97:2). Obviously, then, unrighteousness and injustice are contrary to his nature and
are, accordingly, evil. The Lord "protects the lives of his godly people and rescues them
from the power of the wicked" (97:10). So concern for the well-being of the godly and
opposition to the wicked exercise of power are good and right, while the converse are evil.

Modern man can detect traces of unrighteousness and injustice in his own treatment
of people, and he can see them in operation in the institutions of his culture. So he has
plenty of opportunities to show that he hates unrighteousness and injustice. When a man
sees the abuse of power and the oppression of the godly, he should be in the forefront of
those who object and endeavor to rectify the situation.

Loving God includes hating what he hates, and that means taking a stand against evil.

TO READ: *John 14:1-14*

SEEING THE INVISIBLE

Jesus replied, "Philip, don't you even yet know who I am, even after all the time I have been with you? Anyone who has seen me has seen the Father! So why are you asking to see him?"

JOHN 14:9

Not many years ago, airliners would often be grounded because of lack of visibility. Now, through satellite technology, it is possible for them not only to know exactly where they are when they are flying blind, but also to be capable of "seeing" an airport shrouded in fog and hidden from view. It isn't quite a case of seeing the invisible, but it is certainly a matter of being able to see what is hidden.

Jesus made many statements about his relationship with the Father. One day, in response to Philip's request to be shown the Father, Jesus stated, "Anyone who has seen me has seen the Father!" (John 14:9). The significance of this statement is seen when we remember that John, in the introduction to his gospel, said, "No one has ever seen God" (1:18).

This was certainly true of Moses, who asked the Lord, "Please let me see your glorious presence" (Exod. 33:18). Moses was told, "You may not look directly at my face, for no one may see me and live" (Exod. 33:20). Ezekiel, in his strange visions of God, never actually saw the Lord, only "a figure whose appearance was like that of a man" (Ezek. 1:26). Even Isaiah, who wrote, "I saw the Lord," gave a limited description of what he saw: "He was sitting on a lofty throne, and the train of his robe filled the Temple" (Isa. 6:1). Even these privileged men were unable to see God face-to-face in a clearly defined and describable way.

Then came Jesus, announcing, "Only I, who was sent from God, have seen him" (John 6:46). Up until that time, God's "invisible qualities," such as his "eternal power and divine nature," had been shown in creation (Rom. 1:20). But now Jesus had arrived to reveal in his own person, using language understandable to humans and in ways decipherable by fallen humanity, what God is really like. For example, Jesus showed humans, who have a limited idea of love, what love really is. Creation could not do that. Jesus did not appear shrouded in mystery, as the Father had appeared to the prophets, giving tantalizing and terrifying glimpses of himself. Instead he carried children in his arms and wept at the tombs of loved ones. In so doing, he showed us that God, whose power is seen in earthquakes and hurricanes, has compassion that can soothe the broken heart. And in going to the cross, Jesus stretched out his arms and welcomed all who will ever come to him. What a sight!

TO READ: *John 15:1-17*

TRUE DISCIPLES

My true disciples produce much fruit. This brings great glory to my Father.

JOHN 15:8

S peakers' Corner in Hyde Park, London, is the place where anybody can get up on a soapbox and say whatever outrageous things come into his or her mind. Some of the speakers speak mainly to themselves, but the more dramatic orators draw a crowd. There is something about human nature that is incorrigibly curious, and curiosity draws a crowd.

This was certainly the case in the Lord's ministry. Jesus had no difficulty attracting an audience, but that did not mean that people readily became his disciples. There were several occasions when the crowds that enjoyed his miracles turned away when Jesus began to make practical applications (see John 6:66).

Jesus knew the hearts of those who crowded around him, and he could easily differentiate between those who were superficially attracted by the drama and those who were true disciples. He said, "My true disciples produce much fruit" (15:8). Physically, fruit is the outward expression of the life hidden inside a tree. Spiritually, the fruit of which Jesus spoke is the practical working out of the life that he puts in the hearts of true disciples.

Discipleship is a matter of believing, but not solely of believing. It is about behaving, too, in a way that Jesus said "brings great glory to my Father" (15:8). True disciples seek to live in such a way that will point people toward God and will demonstrate the power of God at work in human beings.

True disciples glorify God by refusing to live for themselves. There are many ways in which this is borne out practically. Jesus identified one of the most obvious when he said, "I command you to love each other in the same way that I love you. And here is how to measure it—the greatest love is shown when people lay down their lives for their friends" (15:12-13). A loving, sacrificial lifestyle is powerful evidence of true discipleship! To some, this sounds cheerless and unappealing. But Jesus said it leads to a life in which "Your joy will overflow!" (15:11).

What is the secret? Jesus explained, "I am the vine; you are the branches. Those who remain in me, and I in them, will produce much fruit" (15:5). True discipleship is all about having an intimate relationship with the living Lord, a relationship as close and necessary as the relationship between a branch and the vine. Severed branches are fruitless and dead. True disciples are not fruitless, because they're not stupid—they stay attached to the vine! They know that, as Jesus said, "you cannot be fruitful apart from me" (15:4). So they stay close at all times, trusting and obeying God.

Dependence and obedience are the key words of Christian discipleship. Independence and disobedience are the things that ruin the fellowship and destroy the fruitfulness and tarnish the joy. So, check your faith and examine your obedience.

TO READ: *John 16:1–15*

TRANSITION

"I have told you these things so that you won't fall away. . . . Yes, I'm telling you these things now, so that when they happen, you will remember I warned you. I didn't tell you earlier because I was going to be with you for a while longer.

JOHN 16:1, 4

W hen a star player retires, an effective CEO is replaced, or a long-serving pastor dies, the team, the business, or the church faces a potentially critical period of adjustment. Unless the hole in leadership is filled as carefully and promptly as possible, there is always the possibility that the organization or institution will lose momentum and the members will lose heart.

Jesus was well aware of this possibility when he talked to his disciples about his imminent departure. He said, "I have told you these things so that you won't fall away" (John 16:1). But that did not mean a change in his plans, for Jesus reiterated, "Now I am going away to the one who sent me" (16:5). In short, he told them that, though he was going away, there must be no falling away!

There was a distinct possibility that the leaderless disciples would get into serious trouble in their faith. Jesus had given careful thought to the transition his disciples would undergo, and he made sure he prepared them for a successful transition. "You will be expelled from the synagogues," Jesus warned them (16:2). Such a situation would be no big deal for modern people who, on the rare occasions they might be excommunicated, either stop going to church, or go to another, or even start their own! But the prospect of excommunication from the synagogue was a very real threat to first-century disciples. It meant social ostracism, family isolation, and the possibility of closed doors to employment. But there were even more serious possibilities. Hostilities could conceivably intensify to the point where, as Jesus predicted, "Those who kill you will think they are doing God a service" (16:2).

Jesus explained that his leaving was advantageous to them because it opened the door to a whole new dimension of spiritual experience. He promised them, "It is actually best for you that I go away, because if I don't, the Counselor won't come. If I do go away, he will come because I will send him to you" (16:7). He was referring to the Holy Spirit. The Holy Spirit not only would provide comfort and counsel for them in their pain and confusion, but he also would guarantee continuity. Jesus promised, "He will not be presenting his own ideas. . . . He will bring me glory by revealing to you whatever he receives from me" (16:13-14). The disciples need not fear that they would be leaderless, defenseless, or powerless. Neither should they be concerned that the cause to which they were committed would be rudderless. The Holy Spirit would be their guide, their leader, and their power.

Why, then, the change? And where was the advantage in Jesus going? Precisely in this: When the Holy Spirit came, instead of Jesus walking alongside them, they enjoyed the Spirit living within them and working powerfully through them. It was not only a transition—it was a transformation, too.

What could be more exciting and exhilarating for the modern-day disciple than to know that the Christ who walked the shores of Galilee now, through the Spirit, walks with him and resides in him on his way to the office!

TO READ: *John 17:1-26*

THE LORD'S PRAYER

When Jesus had finished saying all these things, he looked up to heaven and said,
"Father, the time has come. Glorify your Son so he can give glory back to you."

JOHN 17:1

J esus told his disciples, "Don't perform when you pray and don't babble when you pray!" They were instructed to go away quietly and unobtrusively to pray (see Matt. 6). He also gave them the model prayer that is commonly called the Lord's Prayer (Matt. 6:9-13). This is surely a misnomer. The Lord himself would never have prayed, "Forgive us our sins" (Matt. 6:12), because he himself never sinned (Heb. 4:15)! It would be better to call Matthew 6:9-13 "The Disciples' Prayer."

The title "The Lord's Prayer" should be reserved for the remarkable and detailed prayer of Jesus recorded in John 17. This passage is a report of Jesus at prayer. Someone has called this the Holy of Holies of Scripture—the most holy sanctuary—because through this intimate conversation of God the Son with God the Father, we can see into the heart of God.

As he prayed, Jesus lifted his eyes to heaven and opened his heart to the Father. First, he prayed for himself: "I brought glory to you here on earth by doing everything you told me to do"—what a statement! Then he asked the Father, "Now, Father, bring me into the glory we shared before the world began" (John 17:4-5). After laying aside his eternal glory and coming to earth to live obediently even to the point of sacrificial death on the cross, the Lord Jesus asked the Father to restore him to glory. This request grants us a tiny insight into the price Jesus paid in leaving heaven for earth. It also shows the anticipation with which he readied himself to return to the Father.

Jesus then prayed for the little group of disciples who were to become the nucleus of the church. One day the church would reach every corner of the world and every ethnic group. Jesus expressed concern for his disciples' well-being in the chosen environment for their evangelistic mission—a hostile world. They would need to be grounded in Scripture, in love, and in unity; otherwise, they would never be able to stand the pressures to which they would be exposed.

Third, and most remarkably, Jesus prayed "for all who will ever believe in me because of their testimony" (17:20). He was talking about those who would come to faith as a result of the apostolic preaching of the gospel. In other words, he was talking about you and me! For us he prayed to his Father, "that just as you are in me and I am in you, so they will be in us, and the world will believe you sent me" (17:21). They will see evidence of lives changed through the transforming power of life in union with God directly attributable to Christ's coming, dying, and rising.

Not only does the Lord's prayer show us the desires of his heart, it shows what he desires our heart desires to be, too—that we may long to share his glory, that we may be upheld on the way to glory, and that in all things we might show forth his glory.

TO READ: *John 18:1-27*

A MAN CALLED PETER

But Jesus said to Peter, "Put your sword back into its sheath.
Shall I not drink from the cup the Father has given me?"

JOHN 18:11

Y ou have to tip your cap to Simon Peter. Standing in a secluded olive grove in the middle of the night, he was suddenly confronted by "the leading priests and Pharisees . . . a battalion of Roman soldiers and Temple guards . . . with blazing torches, lanterns, and weapons" (John 18:3). They had come for Jesus. Undaunted, Peter stepped forward and pulled out his sword. Remember, he was facing a battalion of tough, trained, and armed Roman soldiers. Undeterred by the impossible odds stacked against him, Peter took a swing at the nearest target—an unfortunate servant named Malchus, whose ear he promptly severed. Before he had time to turn his attention to anyone else, and before the startled guard could react, Jesus said, "Put your sword back into its sheath. Shall I not drink from the cup the Father has given me?" (18:11).

Peter had an abundance of raw male courage but a marked lack of spiritual insight. On a scale of 1 to 10, Peter registered a ringing 10 in what passes for real masculinity. No one was going to intimidate him, and no one was going to harm his friend. Sadly, though, he registered a 0 for spiritual insight in this instance.

Peter had been told repeatedly that Jesus would suffer. Only a little while earlier, he had eaten a farewell supper with Jesus during which the Master had carefully explained that he was about to be betrayed (14:18-30). In fact, Jesus had identified the betrayer, Judas Iscariot (13:26). Jesus had also told Peter, "In just a little while I will be gone, and you won't see me anymore. Then, just a little while after that, you will see me again" (16:16). But none of this apparently registered. Peter was more at home swinging a sword against overwhelming odds than unraveling the mysteries of spiritual truth. In our day men say, "No guts, no glory." Peter showed the guts but missed the glory.

Things didn't improve, either. As Jesus was led away, Peter "followed along behind" and found himself in the courtyard of the high priest's house, standing by a fire (18:15-19.) When challenged about his association with the prisoner, he denied it—three times. The man who had faced down a Roman battalion could not stand up to onlookers' questions.

Like many a man, Peter's courage was spotty. He would take a swing at anyone, but taking a stand was more problematic. Sometimes the challenge for the Christian is more in demonstrating moral and spiritual courage than in braving and fighting a physical confrontation.

TO READ: *John 19:28-42*

SECRET DISCIPLES

Afterward Joseph of Arimathea, who had been a secret disciple of Jesus (because he feared the Jewish leaders), asked Pilate for permission to take Jesus' body down. When Pilate gave him permission, he came and took the body away. Nicodemus, the man who had come to Jesus at night, also came, bringing about seventy-five pounds of embalming ointment made from myrrh and aloes.

JOHN 19:38-39

I t's amazing how different men will react to the same situation in totally different ways. For instance, put two men in prison for the same crime. One is deeply remorseful and serves his sentence as a model prisoner and, after his release, lives an exemplary life. The other man becomes hardened, embittered, spends his time in jail perfecting his criminal skills, and, when released, embarks on even more vicious criminal acts.

As soon as it became clear that their leader was being crucified, Peter and other high profile disciples of Jesus went into hiding. Fear and despair gripped them; self-preservation and survival dominated their thinking. They had publicly associated with Jesus for over three years, but now out of fear they disowned him. Meanwhile, Joseph of Arimathea and Nicodemus the Pharisee moved in the opposite direction. Previously in hiding as far as their commitment to Jesus was concerned, they came forward at last after Jesus was so egregiously mistreated.

Nicodemus is carefully identified as "the man who had come to Jesus at night" (John 19:39). When he went to Jesus (John 3), he had apparently been intrigued by Jesus and desirous of knowing more. But he had difficulty understanding, or accepting, what Jesus told him—namely, that "unless you are born again, you can never see the Kingdom of God" (3:3). We don't know if Nicodemus made a definite response to Jesus' message at that time, but we do know that he subsequently took a bold stand in challenging the attempts to arrest Jesus being carried out by the ruling Council, of which Nicodemus was a member (7:50). We have every reason to believe that, by the time Jesus was put to death, Nicodemus was one of his disciples.

Joseph of Arimathea, also a member of the ruling Council, had been "waiting for the Kingdom of God to come" (Luke 23:51). In fact, he "had been a secret disciple of Jesus (because he feared the Jewish leaders)" (19:38). Yet by the time of Jesus' death, he, too, was willing to take a stand—he refused to go along with "the decisions and actions of the other religious leaders" (Luke 23:51).

We know that the ruling Council's hostility against Jesus was fierce and unrelenting and that their power was far-reaching. Anyone who publicly identified with Jesus was in danger of being excommunicated from the synagogue, and thus from Jewish social life—a punishment that few people were prepared to face. Councilmen Nicodemus and Joseph had even more to lose—their position on the Council—by an open stand for Jesus. Not to mention the possibility of being put to death along with Jesus! This accounts for Joseph being a "secret disciple."

At what point these two men of conviction and character came to the point of commitment to Jesus we are not told. It is quite possible that Nicodemus and Joseph had discussed Jesus' startling teaching about the necessity of the new birth as the only entrance to the kingdom. There is evidence that Nicodemus and Joseph gradually came to recognize that their covert belief needed to be expressed in overt action. The dreadful events of Jesus' execution gave them that chance. They took it!

There comes a time when fear must be vanquished by love and trepidation overcome by conviction. Nicodemus and Joseph showed how, while sadly Peter and his friends failed to show up.

TO READ: *Psalm 57*

WAKEN THE DAWN

My heart is confident in you, O God; no wonder I can sing your praises! Wake up, my soul! Wake up, O harp and lyre! I will waken the dawn with my song.

PSALM 57:7-8

After a long, lonely night in a dark, dank cave, nothing lifts the spirits more than the dawning of a new day. Darkness gives way to light, and the sun peers over the horizon, then bursts into blinding sight. Birds strike up their dawn chorus, rejoicing in a new day and a fresh start. Beauty, warmth, brightness, and hope banish the fear and uncertainty of the dark night.

Such an experience inspired David to write this psalm (Ps. 57:TITLE). David's enemy, Saul, and three thousand special troops (see 1 Sam. 24:2) were hunting David like "fierce lions who greedily devour human prey" (Ps. 57:4). In the dim recesses of the cave, David had found cold and comfortless shelter, yet he greeted the dawn with a song (57:8). As he told the Lord, he had learned from long and bitter experience in similar circumstances to "hide beneath the shadow of [God's] wings until this violent storm is passed" (57:1).

When all seemed lost, David focused on "God who will fulfill his purpose for me" (57:2). When Saul's treachery and insane jealousy made David's life one long night of misery, the fugitive psalmist reminded himself, "My God will send forth his unfailing love and faithfulness" (57:3). And when David considered his precarious situation, he stated, "My heart is confident in you, O God; no wonder I can sing your praises!" (57:7).

A thousand years after this psalm was written, David's greatest descendant lay in a dark, dank cave—a tomb, in fact. Jesus had been surrounded by "lions" who had roared for his destruction, whose bitter lies and wicked accusations had torn into his soul "like spears and arrows, and whose tongues cut like swords" (Ps. 57:4). Jesus had suffered the "violent storm" of crucifixion until finally, confidently, he cried out, "Father I entrust my spirit into your hands" (Luke 23:46).

The lions thought they had succeeded in "devouring" Jesus' human flesh. They had succeeded in killing him. But on the Sunday morning after the dark weekend, "as the new day was dawning" (Matt. 28:1), there was a great earthquake, the stone guarding the tomb rolled away, and Jesus rose again from the dead. From that day to this, David's prayer— "May your glory shine over all the earth" (Ps. 57:5, 11)—has been gloriously fulfilled. When Jesus rose again, he banished the darkness of death and flooded our future with the light of hope.

The man who sits shivering in his cave should greet each dawn with a song and a prayer—a song of praise and a prayer that, during this day, the Lord will be "exalted above the highest heavens" (57:5, 11).

TO READ: *Luke 24:1-12*

NO NONSENSE

The women who went to the tomb were Mary Magdalene, Joanna,
Mary the mother of James, and several others. They told the apostles what had
happened, but the story sounded like nonsense, so they didn't believe it.

LUKE 24:10-11

G ladys Aylward was a diminutive servant girl, poorly educated and lacking any marketable skills apart from the ability to do menial work. But she believed God had called her to be a missionary to China. So she made application to a mission board that was looking for potential recruits, was interviewed, and was summarily rejected. The august body who considered her and dismissed her made little attempt to hide their amazement that such an unsuitable young woman should think for a moment that they would be interested in sending her to China as a representative of Christ! Unperturbed, Gladys purchased a train ticket across Russia and Siberia, and after enough adventures to fill a travelogue, she finally arrived in China and embarked on a singularly effective missionary career characterized by untiring service and unbounded courage. The board may have dismissed her, but she was right about her calling!

"Mary Magdalene, Joanna, Mary the mother of James, and several others" (Luke 24:10) would have understood Miss Aylward's experience with the mission board. They, too, stood before an august body, the apostles, and reported what they had seen and been told. They had been to the tomb of Jesus that morning, wondering how they would be able to move the stone guarding the entrance. On arrival, they discovered the stone already moved aside, the tomb empty, and the body gone. Deeply puzzled and distressed, the women were startled by angels, who asked them, "Why are you looking in a tomb for someone who is alive?" (24:5). The angels reminded them that Jesus had repeatedly predicted that he would rise again from the dead, and they informed the women that that was precisely what had taken place.

The women understandably rushed back to "tell his eleven disciples—and everybody else—what had happened" (24:9), only to be unceremoniously rebuffed! To the apostles, their "story sounded like nonsense, so they didn't believe it" (24:11). Never mind that the disciples who had fled the scene were hardly in a position to criticize the women who had shown considerable courage and concern. But the women were right!

There is great danger in dismissing as nonsense what we do not understand. And there is great arrogance in dismissing as irrelevant the sincere testimony of a brother or a sister whose experience differs from our own. It is too easy to dismiss what we will not take the trouble to discover.

Peter, however, quietly slipped out of the room and ran to the tomb to see for himself. Good thing he did, for in seeing the empty tomb he began to rethink his position and, ultimately, he met the risen Lord (24:34).

As Peter discovered, it makes no sense to dismiss as nonsense what doesn't at first make sense. Instead, it makes sense to listen to what others say and see how it could make sense. That's common sense!

TO READ: *1 Thessalonians 4:13–5:11*

AFTER YOU DIE

For since we believe that Jesus died and was raised to life again, we also believe that when Jesus comes, God will bring back with Jesus all the Christians who have died.

1 THESSALONIANS 4:14

There was a man who started exercising regularly when he was in his twenties, stopped smoking in his thirties, regulated his weight in his forties, and died anyway before he was fifty. So goes the tale told by men who don't like to exercise, don't want to stop smoking, and refuse to watch their weight. These men are ignoring well-documented evidence that disciplined living can add to the length of a man's days. But they are right that, whatever precautions are taken, men ultimately "die anyway"!

Given the inevitability of death, it is surprising that men, who normally plan their lives carefully, pay scant attention to their dying and what lies beyond it. Many of them settle for vague hopes or lame jokes regarding the subject. But that is not wise. Men who major on five-, ten-, and fifteen-year plans as a matter of course should not neglect an infinite-year plan—as a matter of prudence.

Apparently, the Christians in Thessalonica were not ignoring the issue of death. In the church in that city, there was a great deal of consternation about death and what lies beyond it. So Paul passed on to them some information he had received "directly from the Lord" (1 Thess. 4:15). With Christ's resurrection as his starting point, Paul told them, "Since we believe that Jesus died and was raised to life again, we also believe that when Jesus comes, God will bring back with Jesus all the Christians who have died" (4:14). Contained in this statement are several powerful truths. One, Jesus rose from the dead. Two, he will return in great glory. Three, Christians go to be with Christ when they die. Four, when Christ returns he will bring with him those have gone to be with him.

These truths are intended to help those who mourn the loss of loved ones, so that they will avoid being "full of sorrow like people who have no hope" (4:13). It is natural for bereaved people to be anxious about their loved ones. Paul assured the Thessalonians that when the Lord returns "with a commanding shout, with the call of the archangel, and with the trumpet call of God" (4:16), he will come *with* the believers who have died, and he will be coming *for* the believers who are still alive on earth. Then they will have a grand reunion with Christ and with each other.

The result of this teaching? "So comfort and encourage each other with these words" (4:18). But remember, this is for those who prepare for eternity.

TO READ: *1 Timothy 6:11–21*

THE ART OF LIVING

But you, Timothy, belong to God; so run from all these evil things, and follow what is
right and good. Pursue a godly life, along with faith, love, perseverance, and
gentleness. Fight the good fight for what we believe. Hold tightly to the eternal life
that God has given you, which you have confessed so well before many witnesses.

1 TIMOTHY 6:11-12

D r. Samuel Johnson, a renowned eighteenth-century writer and witty
conversationalist, spent more than eight years working on a dictionary of the English
language that, when completed, included definitions and examples of forty thousand words.
This son of a bookseller had a lifelong love affair with books and words, and chief among
his books were the Bible and the Book of Common Prayer. At the end of his life, Johnson
stated that the whole point of books is to teach the art of living. So perhaps it would be more
accurate to say he had a lifelong love affair with learning the art of living.

Johnson insisted, "What is new is opposed, because most are unwilling to be taught;
and what is known is rejected, because it is not sufficiently considered that men more
frequently require to be reminded than informed."[23] While the search for new knowledge
is commendable and important, the application of old knowledge is often more fruitful.

No doubt Johnson would have approved of Paul's reminders to Timothy, which
were designed to assist the young man in the art of living. First and foremost, Timothy
needed to be reminded, "You belong to God." To understand this is to grasp four points.
First, if you belong to God you can't belong to yourself—you have handed over the control
of your life to your Creator and Redeemer. Second, the concerns of your life are more
God's concerns than yours. Third, belonging to God inevitably and obviously leads to the
need to "run from . . . evil things, and follow what is right and good." Fourth, this need to
run from evil in turn requires a disciplined approach to "a godly life" made up of "faith,
love, perseverance, and gentleness" (1 Tim. 6:11).

Second, Timothy also needed to be reminded that living as a believer in an unbelieving environment would be a struggle, particularly as he went about fulfilling his calling
to spread the Good News of the gospel. Paul called the struggle a "fight," but it was a
"good fight" (6:12) in which Timothy was expected to participate.

Third, Timothy was reminded that he must never loosen his hold on "the eternal life
that God has given you, which you have confessed so well before many witnesses" (6:12).
Having previously professed faith in Christ and having solemnly testified about salvation
that would lead to life eternal, Timothy must never forget that he had received new life,
nor that he had taken a moral and spiritual stand for Christ.

No doubt there were many things for Timothy to learn that were new, but Paul
decided that he needed to be reminded of the old things more! The apostle knew that
constant reminders about fundamental lessons contribute greatly to the art of living.

[23]*The Rambler*, No. 2.

JUNE

TO READ: *Philippians 3:4-11*

CONVERSION

*Yes, everything else is worthless when compared with the priceless gain of knowing
Christ Jesus my Lord. I have discarded everything else, counting it all as garbage,
so that I may have Christ and become one with him. I no longer count on my own
goodness or my ability to obey God's law, but I trust Christ to save me.
For God's way of making us right with himself depends on faith.*

PHILIPPIANS 3:8-9

D uring the tense and bitter days of the Vietnam War, Cassius Marcellus Clay, the
brash young heavyweight boxing phenomenon, announced that he had joined the
Nation of Islam and had changed his name to Muhammad Ali. He refused to submit to
induction into the Armed Services, claiming exemption on the grounds that he was a
minister of religion. As a result, he was stripped of his boxing titles and was convicted
under the Selective Service Act.

At first, many people thought that Ali's action was just another way of dodging the
draft, that no genuine conversion had taken place. But more than thirty years later, he still
professes allegiance to Islam.

Dramatic as Ali's conversion was, it pales into insignificance beside the conversion
of Saul of Tarsus. He, too, experienced a name change—from Saul to Paul—but that was
the least of the changes he went through. By birth, heritage, and training, Saul of Tarsus
was a proud, brilliant, and intense Jewish Pharisee whose convictions led him to become
the archpersecutor of the fledgling Christian church. In his own words, he said, "I am a
real Jew if ever there was one! . . . I harshly persecuted the church. And I obeyed the Jewish
law so carefully that I was never accused of any fault" (Phil. 3:5-6).

Saul's conversion meant that he completely changed his mind about the most
important things in his life. The main issue in his mind was, what is God's way of "making
us right with himself" (3:9)? Traditionally, he had been taught, and he fervently believed,
that rightness with God was achieved through keeping God's law. This was something that
was dependent on his "own goodness" and "ability to obey God's law" (3:9). That was why
Saul was so fervent as "a member of the Pharisees, who demand the strictest obedience to
the Jewish law" (3:5). But when he grasped that Jesus was the Son of God who had died on
the cross as a sacrifice for sin, he recognized that instead of working to secure his own
salvation (an impossibility!), he should "trust Christ to save [him]" (3:9). He himself
testified, "I once thought all these things were so very important, but now I consider them
worthless because of what Christ has done" (3:7). Salvation, he recognized, was not based
on his own efforts but on Christ's action. Not surprisingly, Saul renounced a religion that
ignored Christ's sacrificial death and resurrection, and he embraced with all his heart the
living Lord Jesus and his cause.

When a man is truly converted to Christ, his life is changed and he changes his
world.

TO READ: *Revelation 1:1–18*

SELF-DISCLOSURE

I am the living one who died. Look, I am alive forever and ever!
And I hold the keys of death and the grave.

REVELATION 1:18

The last book of the Bible, commonly known as "Revelation" (meaning "unveiling" or "disclosure"), should really be called "A Revelation of Jesus Christ" (Rev. 1:1, see NLT footnote). Revelation is all about Jesus letting his people know about himself. It was his intentional self-disclosure!

This important revelation was granted to John in troubled days for the sake of the Christians who lived in the Roman world. John sent it as a letter to seven churches, to encourage them in their faith. The letter was designed to strengthen their resolve and to brace them for the struggles they were facing.

Jesus' self-disclosure was particularly significant to the Christians who first received the letter, because Jesus was reminding them who he is. He was making sure they understood that he is worthy of their trust, committed to their well-being, and certain of his own ultimate victory over the wicked forces so belligerently arrayed against them.

Times have changed, but the message of Jesus' self-disclosure has not—nor has our need to hear it! Jesus has not changed, and Christians are still called to live as Christians—as followers of Christ—in a world that often demonstrates both disregard of Jesus and relentless antipathy toward him. This world is not always a comfortable place for disciples of Jesus.

As John tried to describe the indescribable—a vision of the triumphant Lord—he used the inadequate words available to him, and painted a dramatic picture full of symbols and colorful metaphors. But we are left with only a pale reflection of what he actually saw. When he reported the message Jesus gave him, however, the words were clear and forceful: "Don't be afraid! I am the First and the Last. I am the living one who died. Look, I am alive forever and ever! And I hold the keys of death and the grave" (1:17-18). Jesus wanted the people to know that, as the "First and Last," he was intimately involved in the beginning of all things and in charge until the end of all things. As the "living one," he was distinct from all the dead gods worshiped by other people. But he was not just any "living one"—he had died! He was not just alive, he was alive from the dead, "forever and ever!" Because of his death and resurrection, Jesus had defeated death and was now in charge of both death and the grave. Comforting words, indeed, for Christians facing the possibility of death at the hands of an insane emperor!

Almost two thousand years have elapsed since Jesus revealed himself. They have been centuries of challenge, hardship, triumph, and victory. The little group of apostles has grown to a church of millions throughout the world. And every living member of that church needs to remember what every generation has recognized: simply—who Jesus is! He is the "Alpha" who gives meaning to existence, the Savior who brings salvation to the helpless, and the "living one" who imparts power to the redeemed. And finally, he is the "Omega" who guarantees our eternal destiny.

TO READ: *John 21:1-23*

WHAT ABOUT HIM, LORD?

Peter asked Jesus, "What about him, Lord?" Jesus replied, "If I want him to remain alive until I return, what is that to you? You follow me."

JOHN 21:21-22

S mall boys get upset if they suspect they are not getting the same deal as their siblings and friends. They are quick to shout, "Not fair!" Given time, they grow into big men, but that does not necessarily mean they grow out of the tendency to resent anything they suspect is unequal. So millionaire ballplayers want to renegotiate their contracts if a new recruit reportedly signs a better one. Prisoners write letters of complaint about unequal treatment in their places of confinement. And should a man standing in line at an airport see someone cut into the line, he will voice his displeasure in loud and strident tones.

Peter would have been at home in such company. Jesus had told Peter, rather enigmatically, "When you are old you will stretch out your hands, and others will direct you and take you where you don't want to go" (John 21:18). Peter then noticed John standing nearby and said, "What about him, Lord?" (21:21). Jesus was telling Peter that the future was not going to be pleasant for him, and Peter wanted to know if he was the only one who was going to have a hard time—particularly in comparison to John, who, as everybody knew, had a special relationship with the Lord.

The answer Jesus gave was straight to the point: "If I want him to remain alive until I return, what is that to you?" (21:22). In simple language, that meant that what Jesus decided to do with John was none of Peter's business! John's future was strictly between Jesus and John. In the same way, Peter's future lay in Jesus' hands and was therefore only of concern to Jesus and Peter. What Jesus had told Peter about his own future was all that Peter needed to know.

Jesus added, "You follow me!" (21:22). In light of the future that Peter was being called to live, he could not afford to allow any distractions from the fundamental and all-consuming call to follow Jesus. That was what he had been challenged to do years earlier beside the lake, and his call had not been rescinded or altered.

Trying to understand God's ways of dealing with other people can be confusing. We may become disgruntled, but one thing will help. We should let Jesus do his job, which is to lead, and we should do ours, which is to follow. That will keep us on track.

FOXHOLE FAITH

Now I come to your Temple with burnt offerings to fulfill the vows I made to you—
yes, the sacred vows you heard me make when I was in deep trouble.

PSALM 66:13-14

I t is commonly understood that there are no atheists in foxholes. Men who exhibit little interest in spirituality and eternity are suddenly moved to pray when under fire. Others have been know to experience dramatic conversions under threat of hanging. This phenomenon is similar to the one described by Samuel Johnson, in his famous observation: "When a man knows he is to be hanged in a fortnight, it concentrates his mind wonderfully."[24] In many instances, the promises to God made in the foxhole have been fulfilled when the guns have fallen silent—but not always. And when death sentences have been commuted, some relieved offenders have sadly forgotten the commitments made to God under duress.

The psalm writer, recounting the dire circumstances through which his nation had passed, observed, "We went through fire and flood. But you brought us to a place of great abundance" (Ps. 66:12). This situation offered the chance for the people to express great gratitude in genuine worship, obedience, trust, and service. It also provided the opportunity for shallow promises to be exposed by thoughtless, thankless actions.

The Lord had warned his people of such a possibility when Moses gave them their final instructions shortly before they entered the Promised Land. He told them that their arrival in the "place of great abundance" was "the time to be careful! Beware that in your plenty you do not forget the Lord your God and disobey his commands, regulations, and laws" (Deut. 8:11).

The psalm writer was able to testify, "Now I come . . . to fulfill the vows I made to you—yes, the sacred vows you heard me make when I was in deep trouble" (Ps. 66:13-14). No foxhole faith is in evidence here, only a deep appreciation for mercy extended and grace received. He was deeply aware that the Lord "did not withdraw his unfailing love from [him]" (66:20). The psalmist showed his appreciation first of all in the quality of his response. There is nothing grudging, halfhearted, or coldly formal here. He brought "the best of [his] rams" (66:15), unlike some of his compatriots who were known to "offer animals that [were] crippled and diseased" (Malachi 1:8). His appreciation was shown repeatedly to be real through his desire to share his experience of God's goodness with others—"Come and listen, all you who fear God, and I will tell you what he did for me" (66:16).

What better response can a man have to the Lord's unfailing love than to show unfailing gratitude to the one who has not failed him! Fires, floods, foxholes, and the actions that follow will show the caliber of a man's faith.

---

[24]Samuel Johnson, *Letter to Boswell*, Sept. 19, 1777.

DEDICATED DONKEYS

A firstborn male donkey may be redeemed from the LORD by presenting a lamb in its place. But if you decide not to make the exchange, the donkey must be killed by breaking its neck. However, you must redeem every firstborn son.

EXODUS 13:13

When the Moral Majority, under the leadership of Jerry Falwell, was making headlines, many people suspected that the movement was really an arm of the Republican Party. This meant that committed Democrats were not always enamored of their statements and activities. One such person, fortunately not lacking a sense of humor, wrote to a national magazine asking the editor to inform Jerry Falwell that "if Jesus had wanted us to vote Republican, he would have ridden into Jerusalem on an elephant!" Of course, the donkey is the symbol of the Democrats and the elephant that of the Republicans. Astute readers will remember that Jesus entered Jerusalem on a donkey.

A case can be made that God is looking for dedicated donkeys. The children of Israel were delivered from Pharaoh's tyranny in Egypt only after the angel of the Lord killed the firstborn male of every Egyptian family, while sparing those of the Israelites. In commemoration of this dramatic deliverance, God ordained that all firstborn males in Israel should be dedicated to the Lord. As the Egyptian firstborn males perished during the Exodus, by the same token the firstborn Israelites owed their lives to the Lord's protection and should, out of gratitude, be dedicated to the Lord. The expression "All firstborn sons and firstborn male animals must be presented to the Lord" (Exod. 13:12), meant that they should be slaughtered as a sacrifice of thanksgiving—with two notable exceptions: Firstborn sons and donkeys could be redeemed. That means a substitute animal could be sacrificed for them. The reason for this exception in the case of sons is obvious. In the case of donkeys, it is less so. The donkey was such a "workhorse" that its slaughter would seriously jeopardize the well-being of the people. Therefore, donkeys should be spared. This idea of a substitute sacrifice echoes Paul's words: "I plead with you to give your bodies to God. Let them be a living and holy sacrifice—the kind he will accept" (Rom. 12:1).

Sometimes God calls men to lay down their lives for him and his cause—to make the ultimate sacrifice. More often, the Lord does not ask us to die for him—something that may be accomplished in a moment. Rather, he calls us to live for him—a matter of a lifetime of service. God is looking for dedicated donkeys!

TO READ: *Exodus 13:17–14:4*

DIVINE DETOURS

When Pharaoh finally let the people go, God did not lead them on the road that runs
through Philistine territory, even though that was the shortest way from Egypt
to the Promised Land. God said, "If the people are faced with a battle,
they might change their minds and return to Egypt."

EXODUS 13:17

W hile it is true that the shortest distance between two points is a straight line, it is not always true that a straight line leads to the best route. God's chosen destination for his liberated people was the Promised Land, and "the shortest way from Egypt to the Promised Land" was right up the coast of the Mediterranean from Egypt (Exod. 13:17). But there was one problem with that route—it went straight through Philistine territory, and there was no way that the Philistines would allow the huge crowd of Israelites to pass through their territory unchallenged. Of course, all things are possible for God, but not all things were possible for the Israelites!

In God's opinion, the Israelites were not ready for a fight. So rather than send them on the shortest—and toughest—route, he ordered them on a divine detour. He knew them well enough to know that, glad as they were to escape Egypt and its travails, they would probably have turned tail and headed back to slavery rather than fight for their lives. They would have avoided the short-term problem, which not only would have led to bigger problems but would also have robbed them of a divine destiny. The Israelites probably did not appreciate this at the time—as they began to experience the rigors of wilderness existence, they let it be known that they were less than enthusiastic about their new environment and adventures. What they were led into was far from pleasant. No doubt they were put off by the difficulties and the delays of their route. But perhaps they forgot that what they were saved from was immeasurably worse—and that what they were going toward was immeasurably better!

Detours, disappointments, and delays are rarely pleasant. But if they are truly from God, they are prompted by insights hidden from human view and predicated on divine plans not always understood by man at the time. A man may see his immediate objective and go for it with energy and enthusiasm, only to be stymied and frustrated. What he may not see is the danger that lurks on the way, the disasters that lurk in his path from which he can be delivered only by delay and detour.

TO READ: *Exodus 14:5-31*

STAND STILL
AND GET MOVING

But Moses told the people, "Don't be afraid. Just stand where you are and watch the
LORD rescue you. The Egyptians that you see today will never be seen again.
The LORD himself will fight for you. You won't have to lift a finger in your defense!"
Then the LORD said to Moses, "Why are you crying out to me?
Tell the people to get moving!"

EXODUS 14:13-15

———————————

Its amazing how quickly men forget! Only a few days after begging the Israelites to leave, following the dreadful disaster of the death of the firstborn, Pharaoh and his men regretted the decision. "'What have we done, letting all these slaves get away?' they asked" (Exod. 14:5). So the Egyptians mobilized the army and took off after the escaping slaves. Meanwhile, when the Israelites realized the Egyptian armies were coming after them, they turned on Moses and accused him of leading them into the wilderness against their will, asserting that "Egyptian slavery was far better than dying out here in the wilderness!" (14:12).

With remarkable faith and confidence, Moses told the panicking people, "Don't be afraid. Just stand where you are and watch the Lord rescue you" (14:13). So that is precisely what the people did—probably while paralyzed with fear. But then the Lord commanded Moses, "Tell the people to get moving!" (14:15). So Moses, having just told them to stand still, now told them to get moving!

When Moses told the people to stand still, he was stressing that "the Lord himself will fight for you. You won't have to lift a finger in your defense" (14:14). As things turned out, he was quite right! But at the same time, in order for them to see what God would do, it was necessary for them to move through the opened waters to the other side of the sea.

There are things in life that only God can handle and situations in daily experience for which no man has an answer. But God has the answers. Recognition of this sometimes leads a man to "stand still" and see what God can and will do. It is a matter of trust, of faith. At the same time, while man cannot solve his problems, God may tell him to get moving so that God can solve them. Then it is a matter of obedience.

In fact, all spiritual experience is about faith and obedience. The two are not incompatible. The power to obey becomes available as we trust God to act. Without faith, there will be no obedience, and without obedience there is evidently no faith. So, as the old hymn says, "trust and obey." Or, if you prefer, stand still and get moving.

TO READ: *Exodus 15:19–21*

MIRIAM THE PROPHET

*Then Miriam the prophet, Aaron's sister, took a tambourine
and led all the women in rhythm and dance.*

EXODUS 15:20

When Moses was a baby, his mother took the extraordinary step of floating him in a basket down the Nile River (see Exod. 2:1-10). This was not a case of child endangerment; it was a matter of casting Moses on the mercy of God. However, Moses' mother also exercised prudence by sending Moses' older sister to keep an eye on the baby from the bank of the river. We are not told at this point the name of the sister, but later we find that Moses had a sister named Miriam and a brother named Aaron. So it is reasonable to assume that the sister in this story was Miriam.

Miriam was apparently called and gifted by the Lord to be a prophet. Aaron fulfilled a similar role. When Moses complained that his speaking abilities were limited and that he would rather not go to Pharaoh with God's message, the Lord said, "Aaron will be your spokesman to the people, and you will be as God to him, telling him what to say" (4:16). Later, the Lord amplified his calling of Aaron and said to Moses, "Your brother, Aaron, will be your prophet; he will speak for you. Tell Aaron everything I say to you and have him announce it to Pharaoh" (7:1-2). There is no doubt that Miriam saw herself in the same light because with Aaron she stated, "Has the Lord spoken only through Moses? Hasn't he spoken through us, too?" (Numbers 12:2). There is every reason to believe, therefore, that Miriam's ministry involved attending upon the Lord, hearing his word, and announcing it to the people.

After the enormous victory over the Egyptian army, Moses led the people in a "song to the Lord" (Exod. 15:1). Unfortunately, while we have the triumphant words of the song, we do not have the music. But we do know that it had rhythm! So much rhythm that Miriam grabbed a tambourine and "led all the women in rhythm and dance" while singing the chorus of the hymn (15:20).

It does not take a lot of imagination to recognize that if Miriam were to reappear and act in this manner in some segments of the church today, she would cause quite a stir! In others, she would be quite a hero. She would quickly become the center of controversy, because she engaged in a prophetic ministry, she used percussion in worship, and she felt it was appropriate to dance before the Lord!

Those of us who question such activities today would do well to consider Miriam, while those who would use her as a role model should remember that even prophets have faults, and gifted speakers sometimes get things wrong (see Numbers 12:1-16).

TO READ: *Exodus 16:1-36*

DAILY BREAD

*And the LORD said to Moses, "I have heard the people's complaints. Now tell them,
'In the evening you will have meat to eat, and in the morning you will be filled
with bread. Then you will know that I am the LORD your God.'"*

EXODUS 16:11-12

T here can be few sights more pitiful than that of starving children with distended bellies held in the arms of emaciated mothers whose sores are filled with flies. Through the medium of television, most people are familiar with such images, even if they have never traveled in famine regions.

It should not be difficult to imagine the fear that gripped the hearts of the Israelites as, one month into their wilderness march, they realized that they had no visible source of food. Famine stared them in the face. Understandably, they turned on Moses and told him, "Oh, that we were back in Egypt. . . . It would have been better if the Lord had killed us there! At least there we had plenty to eat" (Exod. 16:3).

Moses, quite rightly, was able to point out that it was not his fault that they were in such a perilous predicament. He had not wanted the job of bringing them into the wilderness—it was God's idea, so if anyone should be blamed it was the Lord! But at the same time, if God had brought them out of Egypt, presumably he had plans to care for them in the wilderness. This was the case, and the Lord said, "Look, I am going to rain down food from heaven for you" (16:4). He gave the people details about the daily supply, including specific instructions about gathering and storing the strange food. The Israelites called the food "manna," which means "what is it?" Even forty years later they still didn't know what it was!

The Lord intended to supply what they needed on a daily basis. So they should trust him to do that by collecting only one day's food at a time and trusting him to provide double the amount on the eve of Sabbath, so they would not need to collect any on the day of rest. "But, of course, some of them didn't listen" (16:20). They thought they knew better, and they missed the opportunity to trust God.

When Jesus taught his disciples to pray, he included in the list of legitimate petitions, "Give us our food for today" (Matt. 6:11). Jesus reminded his disciples that God can be trusted to give us what we need when we need it. He does not guarantee to meet our wants. He meets our needs! He does not promise a stocked fridge—just today's food. Daily we learn to trust and we discover contentment. Sadly, if, like the Israelites, we don't listen, our manna may turn to maggots (16:20).

TO READ: *Exodus 17:1–7*

LEARNING
FROM HISTORY

*Moses named the place Massah—"the place of testing"—and Meribah—"the place of
arguing"—because the people of Israel argued with Moses and tested the LORD
by saying, "Is the LORD going to take care of us or not?"*

EXODUS 17:7

Young people are rarely interested in history. Their past holds little of interest, and
their future beckons alluringly. Older people show more interest in the subject.
Their beckoning future is shorter than their fading past, so their interest in history is
easily explained. But young people should realize that the lessons of history are designed
to save them from mistakes in the future. As George Santayana stated, "Those who
cannot remember the past are condemned to repeat it."[25]

This is certainly true from a biblical perspective. Take, for instance, the incident at
Massah and Meribah. Water was in short supply, so the Israelites understandably were
panicking. As usual, they vented their frustration on long-suffering Moses, who, once
again, turned to the Lord for a solution, which the Lord immediately provided through
a miraculous intervention. The Lord told Moses, "Strike the rock, and water will come
pouring out" (Exod. 17:6). He did, and it did!

But by this time the Lord's patience was wearing thin. The redeemed people were
"testing the Lord" (17:2). As a result of their habitual grumbling, distrusting, arguing, and
defying the Lord, they eventually forfeited the right to enter the Land of Promise. Instead
of enjoying the life they were intended to enjoy because of the Lord's bounty, they died in
despair in the wilderness.

David, the psalm writer, using this incident from Israel's history, found it necessary
to remind his contemporaries, "Don't harden your hearts as Israel did at Meribah, as they
did at Massah in the wilderness" (Ps. 95:8). Without apology, he drew a profound lesson
from Israel's past. He explained that in the same way the wilderness travelers rebelled
against the Lord and perished in the wilderness, the people of his day were "hardening
their hearts"and facing the same consequences. So he exhorted them, with anguish, "Oh,
that you would listen to his voice today!" (Ps. 95:7). More than a thousand years later, the
writer to the Hebrews picked up on the incident, applied David's exhortation, and warned
first-century Christians, "Be careful then, dear brothers and sisters. Make sure that your
own hearts are not evil and unbelieving, turning you away from the living God" (Heb.
3:12).

The lesson from history is simply this: Don't take God for granted. Don't abuse his
grace. Don't test his patience. Those who do so may discover his wrath. And that would
mean, as the Lord said, "they will never enter my place of rest" (Heb. 3:11). A relevant
statement, whether or not you are interested in history! For if there is one thing people
hope for, it is that they will eventually rest in peace.

[25]George Santayana, *The Life of Reason*, vol. 1.

TO READ: *Psalm 34*

THE SHADOW
OF SHAME

Those who look to him for help will be radiant with joy;
no shadow of shame will darken their faces.

PSALM 34:5

W. H. Auden, in one of his poems, talked about the "faces along the bar" and how they reflected the lives of their owners, "who have never been happy or good."[26] Auden's insights were accurate. While some eyes dance with intelligence, more seem weary with looking. While smiles lurk perpetually at the corner of some lips, potential snarls curl downward on others. And the brows of many are permanently creased with furrows of worry, rather than displaying the relaxed muscles of a contented life.

David, the psalm writer, recognized that faces, including his own, tell a story. He talked about "those who look to [the Lord] for help will be radiant with joy" (Ps. 34:5). He believed that looking to the Lord changes the way you look! Paul outlined a similar idea when he said, "We can be mirrors that brightly reflect the glory of the Lord. And as the Spirit of the Lord works within us, we become more and more like him and reflect his glory even more" (2 Cor. 3:18).

Throughout his life David had been exposed to dangers and sorrows that had driven him deeper into a life of trust and dependence on the Lord. As a result, David was able to say, "I prayed to the Lord, and he answered me, freeing me from all my fears" (Ps. 34:4). There was a definite connection between looking to the Lord in prayer and the radiant joy on David's face when delivered from the fears that had gripped him. Facial muscles long accustomed to being knotted with tension were relaxed by joy, and David became radiant!

In the past, fear had contorted David's features, and shame had darkened his face. The burden of unforgiven sin had shown with the heaviness of unrelieved shame. But as he had looked to the Lord for forgiveness, he had been relieved of guilt and released from shame. And he promised others that if they, too, looked to the Lord, "no shadow of shame [would] darken their faces" (34:5). The furtive look that fears exposure would flee, and the worried frown that dreads discovery would disappear.

When all has been exposed and forgiven, there is nothing to fear. Release and relief are free to relax the face, and smiles are born.

The faces along the bar of life belong to people looking for solace in their pain, longing for friendship in their loneliness, hoping for joy in the midst of their disappointments. They need a smile, a touch, a message of encouragement. Who better to bring it than the man who can say with conviction, "Taste and see that the Lord is good" (34:8).

[26]W. H. Auden, "September 1, 1939.

TO READ: *Hebrews 6:1-12*

SPIRITUAL PROGRESS

So let us stop going over the basics of Christianity again and again.
Let us go on instead and become mature in our understanding. . . .
God willing, we will move forward to further understanding.

HEBREWS 6:1, 3

After a young mother had safely tucked her small child into bed, said prayers, taken him his drink of water, and finally returned downstairs for a few quiet moments on her own, she heard a thump on the floor above. She rushed into her child's bedroom and found him lying dazed on the floor. Picking him up she asked, "What happened?" He replied, "I fell out of the bed because I stayed too near where I got in."

The recipients of the letter to the Hebrews were in similar danger, as far as their newfound faith in Christ was concerned. They had been introduced to "the basics of Christianity"—such things as "turning away from evil deeds," placing "faith in God," "instruction about baptisms, the laying on of hands, the resurrection of the dead, and eternal judgment." Now it was time for them to "become mature in [their] under-standing" (Heb. 6:1-2). Not for a moment was it suggested that these matters were insignificant. In fact, they were (and are) of prime importance for the life of faith. But there is more, much more, to be discovered and experienced. Not to press on is to stay too near where one got in!

The writer of the letter went on to outline the dire consequences of spiritual indifference and carelessness. Such an attitude can harden one into outright apostasy. The things that once were held dear are denied, and love of Christ, which once motivated and mobilized a life of trust and obedience, degenerates into anger, antipathy, and hostility toward Christ and his cause.

The issues raised here address the condition of those who intentionally reject what they previously embraced and deny what they formerly affirmed. Should they reject Christ's love, "nailing the Son of God to the cross again" (6:6), there is no other basis for their forgiveness. Should they deny the gracious work of the Spirit, there is no other dynamic to draw them back to the Savior.

There is no suggestion here that those who genuinely love the Lord and who seek, however inadequately, to serve him, and who are all too aware of their lack of faith and worry about their inconsistent life, should live in dread of slipping out of grace. "God is not unfair" (6:10). He knows our fallenness and understands our struggles.

The man who determines not to stay too close to where he got in need never fear he will lapse into apostasy. God will hold him fast.

TO READ: *Hebrews 6:13-20*

ANCHOR FOR THE SOUL

God has given us both his promise and his oath. These two things are unchangeable
because it is impossible for God to lie. Therefore, we who have fled to him for refuge
can take new courage, for we can hold on to his promise with confidence.
This confidence is like a strong and trustworthy anchor for our souls.
It leads us through the curtain of heaven into God's inner sanctuary.

HEBREWS 6:18-19

A symbol points beyond itself to something significant. For instance, the flag of the United States symbolizes the fifty current states with stars and the thirteen original states with bars. The most common symbol of the Christian faith is the cross, which points unerringly to the central doctrine of Christianity—that the Lord Jesus died and rose again for our redemption. But in the early days of the Christian church, other important symbols were commonly used. In the catacombs of Rome, where large numbers of Christians were buried, the murals painted there often depicted a dove, a fish, and an anchor. The dove symbolizes the Holy Spirit, the Greek word for fish is an acrostic of the Greek words for "Jesus Christ God's Son Savior," and the anchor depicts security in the storms of life.

The writer of Hebrews chose the symbol of the anchor to speak about the truthfulness of God's Word, the certainty of his promises, and the integrity of his person. Abraham proved a great example. When the Lord reiterated to the patriarch that he planned to give him many descendants, he said, "Because you have obeyed me and have not withheld even your beloved son, I swear by my own self that I will bless you richly" (Gen. 22:16-17). God not only promised; he underlined the promise by swearing an oath by himself—for no greater oath was possible—that he would do as he promised. And eventually he did!

This example, and many others down through history, should suffice to convince even the most skeptical heart that what God says, he means; what he promises, he does; and what he commits to do, he is perfectly willing and able to accomplish.

Recognizing this does something for a man's confidence. If he has "fled to [the Lord] for refuge, [he] can take new courage, for [he] can hold on to his promise with confidence" (Heb. 6:18). No matter how lacking he might be in confidence in his own abilities, such a man has no grounds for doubting God's capabilities. Regardless of how untrustworthy he has found men to be, he knows in his heart the Lord's integrity. So he faces life with hope and confronts challenges with confidence. He knows that, as he relies on who the Lord is and counts on what the Lord has promised, his anchor will hold. The storms may blow, his anchor holds. Life may drag, his anchor won't!

TO READ: *Hebrews 7:1-14*

A MAN CALLED MELCHIZEDEK

Consider then how great this Melchizedek was. Even Abraham,
the great patriarch of Israel, recognized how great Melchizedek was
by giving him a tenth of what he had taken in battle.

HEBREWS 7:4

The relationship between the Old Testament and the New Testament has been described as follows: "The New is in the Old concealed, the Old is in the New revealed." There are good grounds for believing this is an accurate assessment of the relationship, as can readily be seen from the way Jesus "quoted passages from the writings of Moses and all the prophets, explaining what all the Scriptures said about himself" (Luke 24:27), and from the way Old Testament passages were interpreted in the New Testament to show that they held messages that would only be understood in New Testament times.

An example of the Old Testament being revealed in the New is found in the interpretation of the story of Melchizedek. This rather enigmatic figure appeared briefly in the biblical record when he encountered Abraham after Abraham's famous victory over five kings (Genesis 14:17-20). Melchizedek was "king of the city of Salem and also a priest of God Most High" (Heb. 7:1). He blessed Abraham for what he had done. Abraham, in turn, gave Melchizedek 10 percent of his spoils. There is no record of Melchizedek's parentage or progeny, and his name means "king of justice." "Salem," the name of the city over which he reigned, means "peace."

Those are the details, spoken and unspoken, which the writer of Hebrews applies to Christ. Because Melchizedek received tithes from Abraham and gave a blessing to Abraham, he was seen as superior to Abraham. And because there is no record of his parentage or progeny, he is seen typologically as living on. In addition, because Levi, the father of the Jewish priesthood, was, as it were, "in Abraham's loins" (7:10), Levi's priesthood was inferior to the priesthood of Melchizedek, precisely because Abraham was inferior to Melchizedek!

It must be admitted that this interpretation is hard for Westerners to grasp. The application of this story by the writer of Hebrews uses typology, a method of interpreting Scripture that is not commonly used today, even though the method was common in the early days of the church. The point of all this in Hebrews was to show that the Jewish (Levitical) priesthood was incapable of offering the salvation which only the eternal priesthood of Jesus (Melchizedek) could provide. Therefore, the Jewish people who had been attracted to Christ but were in danger of drifting away from him should recognize that only Christ can offer salvation. Should they turn away from him, they would find hope in no other system. This is something that Jesus himself underlined when he insisted, "I am the way, the truth, and the life. No one can come to the Father except through me" (John 14:6).

TO READ: *Hebrews 7:15-28*

JESUS, THE HIGH PRIEST

Jesus remains a priest forever; his priesthood will never end. Therefore he is able,
once and forever, to save everyone who comes to God through him.
He lives forever to plead with God on their behalf.

HEBREWS 7:24-25

I f people only attend church at Christmas and Easter, it is quite possible that they will never get further than thinking about Jesus as a baby who was born in a stable and cradled in a manger, who grew up, was crucified and rose again, and more or less disappeared from the scene, leaving some very good teachings that should not be taken too seriously.

But many people who attend church on a regular basis—not just at Christmas and Easter—often miss out on another important dimension of the Savior's ministry—that which is celebrated on Ascension Day. The full significance of the birth, death, and resurrection of Jesus cannot be grasped without a solid understanding of the continuing ministry of the risen Lord. His work did not end when he rose again from the dead. He returned to heaven where he continues his ministry to this day—and forever.

Drawing from the rich history of the Jewish people, the writer of Hebrews compared the work of the risen Lord with that of a human priest. One of the obvious disadvantages of a human priest is that he is susceptible to death, and when he succumbs, his priestly ministry is terminated. Jesus, however, is "a priest forever" (Heb. 7:17). His continuing priesthood is exercised in "the power of a life that cannot be destroyed" (7:16), and "his priesthood will never end" (7:24). In practical terms this means that he can save people "once and forever" (7:25), because his priesthood knows no end or interruption.

Those who have come to faith in the Lord Jesus can say with assurance that they have been saved. They know this as a past experience. But they need more than that. They must face life on a daily basis, and they will continually come up against things that will rob them of their joy and hinder them in their growth. They need to know what it is to be saved on an ongoing basis. They need not just a salvation in the past, but also an experience of spiritual deliverance in the present. To make this possible, Jesus "lives forever to plead with God on their behalf" (7:25), in order to apply the benefits of his death on a daily basis to those who believe in him.

Being aware that the Lord Jesus is, at any given moment, praying for him will alert a Christian man to the supply of divine resources available to him in response to Jesus' intercession. Secure in this knowledge, he will be better equipped to live wisely and well on a daily basis. And he'll enjoy the benefits of Christmas and Easter daily, not just annually.

TO READ: *Hebrews 8:1–13*

WHEN GOD SAYS "I WILL"

"But this is the new covenant I will make with the people of Israel on that day,
says the Lord: I will put my laws in their minds so they will understand them,
and I will write them on their hearts so they will obey them.
I will be their God, and they will be my people."

HEBREWS 8:10

In the traditional marriage service, the minister asks the groom, "Will you take this woman to be your lawfully wedded wife?" To this question the groom is required to answer, "I will." Similar questions are then addressed to the bride. Following the answer "I will" and the saying of vows, the couple are declared man and wife. The marriage covenant has been established. If both of them keep their promises, they stand to live a life of mutual enrichment, delight, and support. But sadly, the "I will" often turns into "I won't." The covenant is broken, the marriage is dissolved, and the family disintegrates.

Israel had repeatedly broken the covenant that God had entered into with them, but God had not given up on his recalcitrant people. He proposed a "new covenant" in which he made many "I will" promises. These promises need to be understood and embraced.

"I will make a new covenant" (Heb. 8:8) meant that God would take an initiative that only he could take. Fallen man could not initiate a new relationship with an offended deity, but God could initiate a new relationship with his fallen creatures—and he did. It was a covenant of his design and his making.

"I will put my laws in their minds" (8:10) promised to imprint the truth of God's promises on the inner recesses of the minds of God's people. Instead of looking at laws etched in stone, as in the old covenant, God's people would always have available to them insight into the truth.

"I will write them on their hearts" (8:10) promised not only insight into what God was saying and requiring but it also guaranteed that God's people would be able to respond in trusting obedience. Laws written in stone that are beyond a man's ability to obey produce only frustration. Truth written in the mind and engraved on the heart promises insight and ability and the possibility of glad fulfillment.

"I will be their God" (8:10) was not a new promise, but it needed to be reiterated. God's people must often have wondered about their status, given their rebellion and antipathy toward him.

"I will forgive their wrongdoings" (8:12) spoke a merciful word to troubled hearts. To this day, God offers freedom from guilt and release from shame so that the forgiven may live in newness of life.

"I will never again remember their sins" (8:12) offered something that no human can offer. We can promise to forgive, but we cannot promise to forget! God promises both!

Blessed is the bride whose groom keeps his "I wills." More blessed is the man who knows the covenant God, whose "I will" will never be changed to "I won't."

TO READ: *Hebrews 9:1-14*

BEHIND THE CURTAIN

So Christ has now become the High Priest over all the good things that have come.
He has entered that great, perfect sanctuary in heaven, not made by human hands
and not part of this created world. Once for all time he took blood into that
Most Holy Place, but not the blood of goats and calves. He took his own blood,
and with it he secured our salvation forever.

HEBREWS 9:11-12

When God delivered the Israelites from their slavery in Egypt, he had more in mind than redressing heinous social injustice. God's intention was that the liberated people should enter the Promised Land and that they would be established there as a unique people. Their lifestyles would demonstrate to the neighboring people that the Israelites were specifically and specially set apart for God.

God wasted no time in teaching the people what this meant in the early days of the wilderness journeys. He handed down to Moses minute details concerning a special portable structure called the tabernacle, which the people had built and which would occupy a dominant position in the camp, whenever they were stationary, and in the ranks, when they marched toward their destiny. God said, "I want the people of Israel to build me a sacred residence where I can live among them. You must make this Tabernacle and its furnishings exactly according to the plans I will show you" (Exod. 25:8-9).

The details given to Moses about the architecture, materials, and furnishings seem at first glance to be both extravagant and unnecessary, in light of the fact that the escaping slaves were heading for the Promised Land. But as time would show, the details of the Tabernacle were specifically designed to model spiritual principles. The people could hardly fail to see and appreciate these principles as the tabernacle was built and as it stood prominently in their midst.

The tabernacle was divided into two sections that were separated by a thick curtain. The priests went in and out of the first section daily, but no priest was allowed to enter behind the curtain in the daily liturgy. Only the high priest could go behind the curtain, and that only on one day per year, the Day of Atonement, and then only under the strictest circumstances. The inescapable lesson for the Israelites was that the presence of God could not be entered glibly and casually. The sins of the people were offensive to a holy God, and as a result, man was separated from God and could only approach God as God himself ordained and allowed.

This dramatic ritual not only portrayed the holiness of God to the children of Israel, it prefigured the wonderful work of Christ on the cross. For when Jesus died and rose again, he entered into the unmediated presence of God as our High Priest. In so doing, he went behind the curtain into the holiest place and "secured our salvation for ever" (Heb. 9:12). Only Jesus could offer "himself to God as a perfect sacrifice for our sins" (9:14). Therefore, only Jesus could enter the presence of God and make it possible for forgiven men to do so, too. Jesus drew back the curtain and invited forgiven men to meet God. God is no longer hidden and remote. So now, men once estranged from God by sin can enjoy through Christ an intimacy with him that satisfies their deepest longings and meets their profoundest needs.

TO READ: *Psalm 36*

RIVERS OF DELIGHT

How precious is your unfailing love, O God! All humanity finds shelter in the shadow of your wings. You feed them from the abundance of your own house, letting them drink from your rivers of delight. For you are the fountain of life, the light by which we see.

PSALM 36:7-9

The differences between men and women have been well documented—and exaggerated! We are told, with some justification, that men are from Mars and women are from Venus. It should be pointed out that not all men and women fit neatly into these stellar stereotypes. Men have been sighted caring for infants and women now play rugby!

In the frontier days of America, men used to stand outside the doors of churches, purportedly to guard the worshiping women from marauding Indians. At least, that is what they claimed! Perhaps it was an effort to explain their traditional masculine disdain for religion and their assumption that spiritual activity was for women. "Men go to bars, women sit in pews!"—or so the thinking went.

This kind of spiritual stereotyping is not uncommon to this day. Many men today would have difficulty imagining what David was talking about when he said of the Lord, "All humanity finds shelter in the shadow of your wings. You feed them from the abundance of your own house, letting them drink from your rivers of delight" (Ps. 36:7-8). Talk of "shadow of your wings" and "rivers of delight" has too much of a feminine ring for testosterone-driven males.

And yet it was David, who was not lacking in traditional masculinity, who penned these words. He spoke of the Lord in contrast to his observations of men. His was a rugged life, which had included close encounters with "blind conceit," the "sinful plots," and the "crooked and deceitful" activities of men (36:2-4). He knew enough about the way "sin whispers to the wicked, deep within their hearts" and the inability of the godless to "see how wicked they really are" (36:1-2) to recognize that men, for all their posturing, are not the masterful creatures they fondly imagine themselves to be.

There are qualities of character and experiences of life that men would do well to explore and discover. Qualities like unfailing love, faithfulness, righteousness, and justice (36:5-6), which enrich the life and ennoble the soul. But for this to happen, men need "honest hearts" (36:10)—hearts honest enough to admit need and deficiency and to confess sin and unrighteousness, and humble enough to forsake postures of self-sufficiency, and realistic enough to admit the need to take "shelter in the shadow of [his] wings" (36:7). Men need hearts that confess to spiritual thirst and unabashedly turn to the one who is "the fountain of life, the light by which we see" (36:9). To do this is not to deny masculine uniqueness. It is to discover divine fullness.

TO READ: *Exodus 25:1-22*

THE ARK

Place inside the Ark the stone tablets inscribed with the terms of the covenant,
which I will give to you. Then put the atonement cover on top of the Ark.
I will meet with you there and talk to you from above the atonement cover
between the gold cherubim that hover over the Ark of the Covenant.
From there I will give you my commands for the people of Israel.

EXODUS 25:21-22

The ark that was popularized in the movie *Raiders of the Lost Ark* was a small acacia wood chest approximately 3'9" long, 2'3" wide, and 2'3" high, and it was overlaid with gold. When the Jerusalem temple was destroyed by the Romans in A.D. 70, the ark disappeared. Nothing is known of its whereabouts, but a lot is known about its significance. At least Hollywood got the part about its being lost correct!

The divinely-designed ark was created to symbolize the Lord's royal and holy presence, first in the tabernacle in the wilderness and later in the Jerusalem temple. God had specifically stated "I want the children of Israel to build me a sacred residence where I can live among them" (Exod. 25:8). The Lord was expressing his desire to make his presence known among his people during their earthly pilgrimage. The transcendent God, who created and upholds the universe, who dwells in brilliant and awesome glory, removed from sin and separate from sinners, desires to be known intimately and to assure his people by his presence of his love and concern for them. This is a truth that every generation should revere.

Despite the Lord's expressed desire for intimacy with his people, there was to be no thought of flippancy or casualness on their part. He was among them, but he was still holy. The ark was to be placed in the Most Holy Place, where only the high priest was allowed to enter, and that only once a year at the stipulated time and in the appropriate manner. The appropriate manner included the sprinkling of the place of meeting with the blood of an innocent sacrifice intended to wash away the sins of the people. The lid of the ark, which incorporated two hammered gold "cherubim," was known as the "atonement cover" (25:20), the place of divine enthronement, about which God promised, "I will meet with you there" (25:22). Under the lid were the "stone tablets inscribed with the terms of the covenant" (25:21)—the sole basis upon which men could meet with God!

Sinful man cannot enter the divine presence on his own terms whenever and however he wishes. He may do so only on the terms outlined by the Holy One. From the ark we learn that a holy God desires intimacy with his sinful people, but only because he chose to reach out to them and only when they come confessing their sin and seeking his forgiveness on the basis of a substitutionary sacrifice.

The ark may be lost, but its symbolism and significance should never be lost on us, for Christ is the substance of which the ark was the shadow.

TO READ: *Exodus 28:1-30*

ALL DRESSED UP

> *"Your brother, Aaron, and his sons, Nadab, Abihu, Eleazar, and Ithamar,*
> *will be set apart from the common people. They will be my priests and will minister*
> *to me. Make special clothing for Aaron to show his separation to God—*
> *beautiful garments that will lend dignity to his work."*
>
> **EXODUS 28:1-2**

A ll dressed up and nowhere to go" was William Allen White's sardonic comment on the demise of the Progressive Party when, in 1916, Theodore Roosevelt withdrew from the presidential campaign. Cinderella, of course, had the opposite problem—all ready to go and nothing to wear.

The high priest of Israel had neither problem, because he was given strict and detailed instructions about the clothing he was required to wear whenever he went about his priestly duties. The priests were "set apart from the common people" and their task was to minister to the Lord (Exod. 28:1). The "special clothing" made for Aaron, the high priest, was designed "to show his separation to God—beautiful garments that will lend dignity to his work" (28:2). There was to be no mistake about Aaron's identity or the dignity of his office. He was God's man, and his appearance and deportment were to reflect his unique status as the one who represented man to God and God to man. The common man, on seeing the resplendent high priest, would immediately recognize something of the grandeur of the Lord he served.

The ephod (28:6) and the chestpiece (28:15) both bore precious gemstones on which were engraved the names of the twelve tribes of Israel. As the high priest, specially dressed for the occasion, entered the presence of the Lord in the Most Holy Place, the Lord was "reminded" (28:29) of his people. Inside the chestpiece were placed two mysterious objects called Urim and Thummim that were "used to determine the Lord's will for his people" (28:30).

In actuality, the Lord did not need to be reminded of the needs of his people—he was present among them as they traveled through the wilderness—but the ornamental stones served as a reminder to Aaron, as he dressed, that the Lord was not forgetful of his people. And as Aaron appeared before the Lord, symbolically bearing the weight of the people on his shoulders and over his heart, he was taking this burden to the Lord. As the Urim and Thummim were brought into play, there was a powerful statement of dependency upon the Lord and desire to know and do his will.

Aaron was all dressed up and he had somewhere to go—and something special to do! So do all modern people who profess the name of Christ. They represent him by their deportment and behavior. They bring before the Lord the names of those in need and they constantly seek his guidance as they minister to others. Such activities will serve to "lend dignity to their work" (28:1).

TO READ: *Exodus 32:1-14*

FICKLE FAITH

When Moses failed to come back down the mountain right away,
the people went to Aaron. "Look," they said, "make us some gods who can lead us.
This man Moses, who brought us here from Egypt, has disappeared.
We don't know what has happened to him."

EXODUS 32:1

W hen the boss is out of town, the office staff often proves the old adage, "When the cat's away, the mice will play." Nevertheless, good leadership is often sorely missed, and the boss's return is usually welcomed.

For the children of Israel, Moses was the boss. He was a visible reminder of the presence of the Lord in their midst, a tangible expression of God's leading in their lives. So even though they at times threatened to reject his leadership and return to Egypt, they became very nervous when he went away to meet with the Lord on Mount Sinai. They said, "This man Moses, who brought us here from Egypt, has disappeared. We don't know what has happened to him" (Exod. 32:1). Their consternation was understandable. They had been deposited leaderless in the middle of a vast wilderness.

Their course of action was understandable, too, though not acceptable. They panicked and decided to take matters into their own hands. They approached Aaron. "'Look,' they said, 'make us some gods who can lead us'" (32:1). Their plan was to go back to the kind of idol worship they had left behind in Egypt.

Amazingly, Aaron acquiesced. He instructed the men, "Tell your wives and sons and daughters to take off their gold earrings, and then bring them to me" (32:2). The people did as Aaron directed, and the donated gold was made into a golden calf. Incredibly, the people declared this statue to be "the gods" that had brought them out of Egypt! Aaron promptly built an altar and announced, "Tomorrow there will be a festival to the Lord" (32:5). But the situation became completely unmanageable when the "festival to the Lord" quickly turned into unabashed "pagan revelry" (32:6). The Lord was incensed, Moses was appalled, Aaron was rebuked, the calf was ground to powder, and many of the people were killed as a result of their own fickleness.

When people panic, they resort to desperate measures. They turn to what they fondly imagine will prove to be an immediate solution, however illogical or even immoral. They abandon their principles, they deny their commitments, and they make decisions in haste that they are then required to repent of at leisure.

What is most needed at such a time is a cool head and clear conviction. Imagine how the situation would have changed if the people had come to Aaron and said, "Aaron, we are frightened, we are unsure, we don't know which way to turn. Moses has disappeared; what shall we do?" Aaron could have said, "I don't have the answers to your questions. I understand your fears, and I, too, am afraid. But this one thing I know. The Lord brought us this far and he will not abandon us. He has proved faithful in the past, he will be faithful in the future. So we will trust and not be afraid."

Fickle faith founders, but firm faith flourishes.

TO READ: *Exodus 32:15-35*

ACCEPTING
RESPONSIBILITY

After that, he turned to Aaron. "What did the people do to you?" he demanded.
"How did they ever make you bring such terrible sin upon them?" "Don't get upset,
sir," Aaron replied. "You yourself know these people and what a wicked bunch they
are. . . . So I told them, 'Bring me your gold earrings.' When they brought them
to me, I threw them into the fire—and out came this calf!"

EXODUS 32:21-22, 24

E ven presidents have been known to avail themselves of the chance to duck responsibility. President Nixon left office insisting, "I am not a crook." President Clinton responded to his accusers by saying, on one hand, "It depends on what the meaning of 'is' is," and, on the other hand, making a vague admission of guilt—"Mistakes were made." Both men could reasonably have stood up and said, "I did it. I was wrong. I'm sorry. I accept full responsibility for my actions." Sadly, if men insist that they are not responsible for their actions, they often fail to see that they are making themselves nothing more than helpless victims in a cruel world. Not a very manly posture!

Aaron and Moses present us with a stark contrast in this regard. When confronted concerning his behavior in the golden calf episode, Aaron responded, "Don't get upset, sir. . . . You yourself know these people and what a wicked bunch they are" (Exod. 32:22). In other words, while Aaron didn't quite say, "The devil made me do it," he effectively said, "The people pushed me into it!" It was not Aaron's fault; it was the fault of that "wicked bunch"! But his ingenuousness took a leap forward when he added, "So I told them, 'Bring me your gold earrings.' When they brought them to me, I threw them into the fire—and out came this calf!" (32:24). Out came this calf, indeed! So it was the fire's fault!

Surely Aaron must have known that he had folded under pressure when he owed the people leadership. And surely he knew better than to expect anyone to believe that a fire produces, unaided, a golden calf. Unless, of course, he wanted to suggest that the calf made itself! Aaron's dissimulation simply compounded his failure, when a simple acknowledgment of culpability and acceptance of responsibility would have paved the way for healing and restoration.

Moses went to the opposite extreme! He returned to the Lord to plead the case of the people. He did not minimize the depth of their sin, and he did not deny the need for judgment. But he said to the Lord, "Please forgive their sin—and if not, then blot me out of the record you are keeping" (32:32). Was Moses tacitly suggesting that he believed he bore some responsibility for the failure of the people and should therefore shoulder some of the blame? We don't know, but we can certainly see the difference between a man who will not admit his own failure and one who will go the extreme of taking the failure of others upon himself. We have no difficulty recognizing the real man!

TO READ: *Exodus 33:1-23*

UNDERSTANDING GOD

Inside the Tent of Meeting, the LORD would speak to Moses face to face, as a man speaks to his friend. Afterward Moses would return to the camp, but the young man who assisted him, Joshua son of Nun, stayed behind in the Tent of Meeting.

EXODUS 33:11

The universe of which we are a part is full of vast mysteries. We don't know its age, we can only guess at its size, and speculation is rife concerning the details of its generation. Having said that, there is no doubt that in recent years our knowledge of the universe has increased dramatically. Gone are the days when Galileo struggled with the church over the issues of the earth's place in the solar system, and no longer do mariners dread the Straits of Gibraltar for fear they might be approaching the edge of a flat earth. We know the earth revolves around the sun and not vice versa; we know the earth is a globe. But while our knowledge of the universe has grown exponentially, our knowledge of God has not.

Who can say that modern man knows the eternal God more intimately than Moses? Moses regularly met with the Lord "face to face, as a man speaks to his friend" (Exod. 33:11.) And which modern man would dare claim to know the risen Christ better than Paul the apostle, who met Christ on the Damascus road?

There may be two reasons for this. Firstly, modern man may not be as eager to know and understand God as his forebears were. While the advances of science have increased our knowledge of how the world works, and the wonders of technology have greatly enriched our lives materially, the result has been a tendency to worship the creation at the expense of the Creator, to love the material rather than the Maker. Secondly, God has traditionally and historically set limits on his own self-revelation. To Moses, whom he called "friend" (33:17), God said, "You may not look directly at my face, for no one may see me and live" (33:20). Moses' request for a greater vision of the Lord in order that he might be better equipped to serve the Lord was completely understandable. The Lord's response was a reminder that, however intimate a man may become with God, man is limited in his capacity to know God.

The full revelation of divine majesty and glory must wait until man is glorified in God's eternal presence. In the interim, modern man should combat a minimal knowledge of the Lord by seeking to know him better, while recognizing that a hunger to know God is indicative of a longing for eternity and a desire for the ultimate which will never be satisfied in time and space. In this life, the best we may hope for is to see God "from behind" (33:23). In eternity, we will see him face-to-face.

TO READ: *Exodus 34:1-35*

GOD'S AUTOBIOGRAPHY

*He passed in front of Moses and said, "I am the LORD, I am the LORD, the merciful
and gracious God. I am slow to anger and rich in unfailing love and faithfulness.
I show this unfailing love to many thousands by forgiving every kind of sin and
rebellion. Even so I do not leave sin unpunished, but I punish the children
for the sins of their parents to the third and fourth generations."*

EXODUS 34:6-7

A mother and her small son on vacation in a national park suddenly confronted a huge
bear on a narrow trail. The mother had recently been influenced by the teachings of a
sect that believed that if you exercised enough faith no harm could come to you. So, looking
at the bear she told her son, "Now you realize that the bear can't hurt us, don't you?" The
small boy replied dutifully, "Yes Mother, I know the bear can't hurt us and you know the
bear can't hurt us. But what does the bear know?" In such a situation the opinions of mother
and child were irrelevant—only the bear's opinion mattered! (I'm sure you'd like to know
what happened, but I've never heard the rest of the story!)

Many people today have well-formed opinions of God. They share them with their
friends and workmates and take great comfort in finding agreement. But there is a problem:
What really matters is not what I think about God or what my friends think about God.
The crucial question is what does God think about God? Everything else is fundamentally
irrelevant. Fortunately, we are not left merely to speculate on this matter.

One day God published a very brief autobiography to Moses on the mountain. First,
he repeated "I am the Lord" (Exod. 34:6). This was a reminder that his name is descriptive
of who he is. The title, "Lord," which means "I am," communicates his eternal being and
his self-sufficiency. As God's personal name, it also communicates his desire to have a
relationship with his people.

If the title "Lord" conveys his grandeur and awesomeness, the description of him as
"merciful and gracious" reminds us that he is approachable and compassionate, deeply
concerned with our well-being and more than ready to reach out to us.

"Slow to anger" describes God's justice, mercy, and grace in a fine balance. His
justice demands that every infringement of his will and every rejection of his character
merit his indignation and divine disapproval. His decision to make humans responsible
beings requires that their actions bear consequences. But the "slow" demonstration of his
righteous anger is a constant reminder that he gives people ample opportunity to repent
and be forgiven.

"Rich in unfailing love and faithfulness" speaks volumes about God's total commitment to his purposes, his unchanging character, and his total reliability.

God's love, which transcends every human idea of love, does not mean that he will "leave
sin unpunished." In fact, God states that sin will have repercussions for generations (34:7).

Plenty of people will attempt to write God's biography. Too few will read his
autobiography. But it is written plainly, and it is easy to understand how good and how
gracious the Lord is.

TO READ: *Psalm 116:1–19*

HOW TO SAY "THANK YOU"

What can I offer the LORD for all he has done for me? I will lift up a cup symbolizing his salvation; I will praise the LORD's name for saving me. I will keep my promises to the LORD in the presence of all his people.

PSALM 116:12-14

T here are times when life is so rich that even surly men smile and the most ungrateful are thankful. Feelings of well-being that well up in the soul demand to be expressed. Such times are difficult times for the atheist, because he has no one to thank. For the believer there is no such problem—he knows whom to thank. But he often wonders what he can do to express his gratitude adequately.

The psalm writer asked the question, "What can I offer the Lord for all he has done for me?" (Ps. 116:12). In other words, "What can you give a God who has everything?"

Fortunately, the psalm writer was able to answer his own question. First of all, he "will lift up a cup symbolizing [God's] salvation" (116:13). This refers to the psalmist's commitment to participate in regular formal worship where actions such as lifting high a cup of wine symbolically demonstrated in visual and dramatic ways the deep experiences of the heart. He will say "thank you" by making regular worship in the community of believers a priority. A modern man does a similar thing when he passes up Sunday morning golf in order to attend Sunday morning worship at church with his family, and when he takes Communion there as an outward expression of the inward knowledge that his sins have been forgiven through the sacrifice of the Lord Jesus on the cross.

Second, the psalm writer adds, "I will praise the Lord's name for saving me" (116:13). He has already stated, "I love the Lord because he hears and answers my prayers" (116:1). Love demands opportunities for expression, and formal praise affords such opportunities. While the psalmist has no difficulty articulating his own love, many men are not so gifted. So they should know how important it is for them to be in attendance when the people of God lift their voices in praise as they sing anthems and songs that express their joy.

Third, the psalmist states, "I will keep my promises to the Lord in the presence of all his people" (116:14). He knows that men make great promises at times of extreme danger or delight but tend to forget them when the grand moment passes away. But not the psalmist—he will keep his promises, and he will do it in such a way that men know he is a man of integrity and devotion.

You can play golf on your own—but it is better played with friends. You can worship on your own—but it is better shared with God's people. It is how you say "thank you" to the God who saved you.

TO READ: *Hebrews 11:1-40*

WHAT IS FAITH?

What is faith? It is the confident assurance that what we hope for is going to happen.
It is the evidence of things we cannot yet see.

HEBREWS 11:1

E verybody believes something. Everyday life is not possible without the exercise of belief, trust, and dependence. An activity as mundane as driving along a road requires belief that the signs are truthful, confidence that other drivers are trustworthy, and trust that when you have a green light the opposite direction will have a red—and that those coming toward the red will stop! Faith at the level of ordinary living is commonplace. But faith is also exercised at a much higher level.

After the early generations of Christians "first learned about Christ," their faith was strengthened so they could remain "faithful even though it meant terrible suffering" (Heb. 10:32). Their faith showed itself "in confident trust in the Lord" (10:35). Their whole lives could be summed up in the ancient statement, "a righteous person will live by faith"—a "faith that assures [one's] salvation" (10:38-39).

The significance of faith cannot be overestimated and must never be underestimated. But what is faith?

Faith is believing that something you have been told is true. The conviction that it is true is based on the source of the information being trustworthy. Trust is placed in that which is believed to be true, to such a degree that the believer begins to look forward to the actualization of that which is believed. In this way faith becomes "the confident assurance that what is hope for is going to happen" (11:1). This confident assurance begins to captivate the thinking of the believer so that even when the consequences of their believing become a challenge, and even a threat, to their physical well-being, they do not waver—they remain faithful. For those who are full of faith are, by definition, faithful!

Should we be tempted to embrace the common philosophy that "seeing is believing," we should remember that in fact, much of our "seeing" is determined by our "believing." When Jesus walked on the water to the disciples, they did not believe in people walking on water (and who could blame them?!)—but they did believe in ghosts. So what they believed determined what they saw! Believing was seeing. For faith "is the evidence of things we cannot yet see" (11:1).

No human was present at the beginning of creation—no one saw what happened. So speculation and scientific exploration continue unabated to this day. But the believer accepts that it is "by faith we understand that the entire universe was formed at God's command" (11:3). The believer's life is all about believing in every dimension. The big issue is, who and what do you believe!

TO READ: *Hebrews 12:1-13*

THE STRUGGLE AGAINST SIN

You have not yet given your lives in your struggle against sin.

HEBREWS 12:4

E very four years, the Olympic Games provide unprecedented opportunities for world-class athletes from every corner of the earth to compete against each other for ultimate athletic prizes. So great are the stakes that many have been tempted to cheat—and some have even succumbed to temptation. Even the venerable Games Committee has been caught in unseemly, if not illegal, practices.

Originally, in ancient Greece, only men were allowed to compete, and only after they were able to show that they had adhered to strict, mandatory training and dietary rules and had prepared themselves thoroughly for the honor of competing. Not only were the games reserved for male athletes, but they also were limited exclusively to male spectators. In addition, the athletes were required to compete naked! They were literally required to "strip off every weight" that would hinder their ability to "run with endurance the race" set before them (Heb. 12:1).

The writer of Hebrews used this analogy with great effect as he compared the Christian experience to a race to be run before "a huge crowd of witnesses" (Heb. 12:1). The "witnesses" referred to were probably the "martyrs"—(the Greek word for "witness" being *martys*) who had already laid down their lives for the cause of Christ.

The weight we need to lay aside includes "the sin that so easily hinders our progress." Sin can and should be stripped off because it hinders spiritual growth very "easily." It must be dealt with severely. The Christian is being advised to identify his spiritual Achilles' heel—a vulnerable area in his life that needs careful and constant attention.

In addition, believers need to be reminded about the "struggle against sin" (12:4). This struggle can become so intense that it leads to their giving up their lives. When believers resist sin, sometimes those around them who are sinning become violent in their opposition.

Sin will hinder a man while running the race—"the life of faith" (12:1)—and can only be dealt with by "keeping our eyes on Jesus." Jesus suffered, too. He died for our sins, and it is for him and his cause that we are running the race! He is the final umpire, and he alone will keep us on track.

TO READ: *Hebrews 12:14-29*

A BITTER ROOT

Look after each other so that none of you will miss out on the special favor of God.
Watch out that no bitter root of unbelief rises up among you,
for whenever it springs up, many are corrupted by its poison.

HEBREWS 12:15

S ibling rivalry is one thing. Ongoing, unrelenting, bitter antagonism between brothers is entirely different. The healthy challenges of brothers vying for attention, relishing competition, and comparing skills serve to develop a young man's maturity in relationships. But misunderstandings can occur even in the best relationships between brothers. Even the best relationships can quickly sour if rivalry is allowed to fester and settle into noxious bitterness.

Such was the case between Esau and his brother, Jacob. Jacob was no paragon of virtue, but he had spiritual sensitivity that his elder brother lacked. Esau was an "immoral" and "godless" man. He was immoral in that he insisted on taking two foreign wives who "made life miserable [the word means "bitter"] for Isaac and Rebekah" (Gen. 26:35)—so much so that his mother said, "I'm sick and tired of these local Hittite women. I'd rather die than see Jacob marry one of them" (Gen. 27:46). Esau was godless in that "he traded his birthright as the oldest son for a single meal" (Heb. 12:16), an action which might not seem particularly significant in our day and age but in his time was a monumental rejection of spiritual heritage and privilege.

Esau, of course, was free to live whatever life he wanted to live, but he was not free to choose the consequences of his lifestyle. So when he realized what he had lost—"his father's blessing"—and went after it with "bitter tears" (Heb. 12:17), he became deeply embittered. While he subjected his parents to situations which were bitter for them, he became embittered when the things that he had brought on himself came full circle.

His "repentance," however, was unavailing. What had been done was done and could not be undone. Life is like that! Sin has consequences, and they can be bitter. Moreover, it appears that Esau's "bitter tears" were not tears of repentance for sin but of sorrow about consequences. This is not at all uncommon. Men are often very sorry that they have to bear the bitter consequences of their actions without being willing to call their sin what it is—sin—and turn from it with a deep desire "to live a clean and holy life" (Heb. 12:14).

An embittered, unrepentant Esau can become "a bitter root of unbelief" which can leave many "corrupted by its poison" (12:15). A bitter root is a disaster because it spreads its bitterness, affecting the perceptions of others, destroying relationships, sowing disharmony, and creating rancor.

The warning here is "watch out" (12:15), because the bitter root may be you!

MONEY, SEX, AND POWER

Give honor to marriage, and remain faithful to one another in marriage.
God will surely judge people who are immoral and those who commit adultery.
Stay away from the love of money; be satisfied with what you have. For God has said,
"I will never fail you. I will never forsake you." . . . Remember your leaders who first
taught you the word of God. Think of all the good that has come from their lives,
and trust the Lord as they do.

HEBREWS 13:4-5, 7

I n the early days of the Christian church, it was not uncommon for believers to suffer intense hardships, even martyrdom, for their faith. Roman emperors such as Diocletian, became incensed with the burgeoning church and inflicted great pain, harm, cruelty, and death on the defenseless followers of Jesus. But then, in A.D. 312, Constantine became emperor and embraced Christianity. Very soon, Christians, instead of being a persecuted minority, became a decidedly mixed-bag majority. Dedication to Christ became watered-down, and the church became corrupt. The answer for many was to flee into the desert, where they became not only separated from the world but also from the worldliness of the church. They took three vows—poverty, chastity, and obedience. They saw the abuse of money, sex, and power as the root problems in the church.

It has been said that time marches on but things never change. And to some extent that is true. It is certainly a fact that problems in the modern church are usually related to the abuse of money, sex, and power—the same problems that appeared in the early days of the ascetics. But we should note that these were the problems confronting the writers of the New Testament as well!

"Give honor to marriage, and remain faithful to one another in marriage. God will surely judge people who are immoral and those who commit adultery" (Heb. 13:4). This is a statement about the divinely ordained sanctity of marriage and the sinfulness of sexual activity—whether heterosexual or homosexual—outside marriage.

"Stay away from the love of money; be satisfied with what you have" (13:5). This is a warning against getting so absorbed with money and all that it can provide that you fall in love with getting it and spending it, hoarding it and wasting it.

"Remember your leaders who first taught you the word of God. Think of all the good that has come from their lives, and trust the Lord as they do" (13:7). This is not only an admonition to those who follow but also a challenge to those who exercise the power of leadership. They are to remember that the privilege of leadership is not to be abused but must be applied to provide direction and encouragement to others, so that they will grow in godliness through teaching by word and example.

As long as there are men, there will be money, sex, and power. As long as there are Christian men, there will be those who know how to use—not abuse—all three. It is our calling to do so.

TO READ: *Hebrews 13:8-16*

JESUS CHRIST IS THE SAME

Jesus Christ is the same yesterday, today, and forever.

HEBREWS 13:8

L ife can take alarming twists and turns in a matter of moments. An automobile accident takes a life, a doctor's appointment identifies a critical sickness, a call to the manager's office heralds a dismissal, a downturn in the stock market signals financial ruin, a phone call announces an arrest. Suddenly and without warning, life is turned irrevocably upside down.

There is a special charm in the terse but powerful statement, "Jesus Christ is the same yesterday, today, and forever" (Heb. 13:8). Of course, while the statement is complete in itself, it also should be seen in its context. "Yesterday," Jesus Christ was the one whom the leaders of the church in its infancy trusted. The writer of Hebrews insisted, "Think of all the good that has come from their lives, and trust the Lord as they do" (13:7). As the readers remembered the early church leaders and their godly lives, they could see something of the faithfulness of Jesus as he had proved himself trustworthy throughout their experience. So in their present trials, the writer said, Christians should recognize that Jesus would be everything to them that he had been to the previous generation of their leaders.

As a result, they must "Today" avoid being "attracted by strange, new ideas" (13:8). If Jesus was all that was necessary for powerful living in a bygone time, nothing had changed. He would be adequate for the present day, too. So the "new ideas" that were being propagated were not only unnecessary, but they also were unacceptable if they in any way diminished the sufficiency of the Lord Jesus in the lives of believers. Moreover, this situation would never change. "Forever," Jesus would be the same.

Life is made up of uncertainties. In the midst of uncertainty, there is one who is certain, unshakable, immovable, solid as a rock, reliable, constant, and totally trustworthy. Henry Francis Lyte probably had Hebrews 13:8 in mind when he wrote in his famous hymn, "Abide with Me":

Change and decay in all around I see,
Oh Thou who changest not, abide with me.

There is always a certain fascination with new ideas. For many people, novelty is an antidote to boredom. That which has become predictable and permanent loses its charm, and people look to be excited, invigorated, and freshened by something new. What they need is to be excited and renewed daily in the knowledge that the all-sufficient Christ is with them. This way, when change comes, Christ will be front and center—unchanging. And in a changing scene, they will be found trusting and thriving—unchanged.

JULY

TO READ: *Hebrews 13:17-25*

SPIRITUAL LEADERSHIP

Obey your spiritual leaders and do what they say. Their work is to watch over your souls, and they know they are accountable to God. Give them reason to do this joyfully and not with sorrow. That would certainly not be for your benefit.

HEBREWS 13:17

There are many dimensions to leadership, but one of the most obvious is that leadership requires "follow-ship." If no one is following, then it is clear that no one is leading. The key, then, to all leadership is relationship—between those who exercise leadership that others want to follow and those who are eager to follow such leaders. It is a relationship where the leader generates in others a desire to follow, and the followers gladly and willingly respond to the leader's initiatives.

The task of "spiritual leaders" is to "watch over . . . souls" and to model a lifestyle that produces much good and which others will wish to emulate (Heb. 13:17). The care of souls requires a heart filled with compassion and concern, a servant spirit, an ability to teach by both precept and example, and a willingness to tell people what they do not want to hear and to direct them where they do not wish to go when necessary. All this comes out of a genuine desire to see people nourished and nurtured in their walk of faith. Or as the author of Hebrews explained it: "May the God of peace, who brought again from the dead our Lord Jesus, equip you with all you need for doing his will" (Heb. 13:20-21). This should be the objective of the spiritual leader.

The spiritual well-being of spiritual leaders is, of course, extremely important. It springs first from their personal relationship of "trust" in the "Lord" (13:7). Second, it arises from the fact that "they know they are accountable to God" (13:17). Leaders who are so self-confident that they sense no need to trust the Lord in order to accomplish their work are bound to fail. The care of souls requires integrity, insight, discernment, and the spiritual dynamic necessary to effect change. And leaders who forget that those they minister to belong to the Lord—they are his sheep—may begin to abuse them or to use them for their own ends. Moreover, leaders who ignore their own ultimate accountability to the Lord may lapse into carelessness, callousness, or carnality.

Followers need to be reminded, "Obey your spiritual leaders and do what they say" (13:17). Obedience does not come easily for many people. They prefer independence to obedience. They resent anything that demands something. And should they claim to follow with that attitude, they make leadership a nightmare if not an impossibility. But willing followers give leaders reason to lead "joyfully and not with sorrow" (13:17). And this is to everyone's advantage.

GOD BLESS US!

May God be merciful and bless us. May his face shine with favor upon us.

PSALM 67:1

According to Jewish custom, Psalm 67 is recited at the termination of the Sabbath, the day set aside each week specifically for rest, reflection, worship, and thanksgiving. At the end of this time, the people pray, "May God be merciful and bless us. May his face shine with favor upon us" (Ps. 67:1).

The request of the psalm writer and those who, to this day, recite this psalm is clearly based on the ancient blessing pronounced by Aaron and repeated down through the centuries: "May the Lord bless you and protect you. May the Lord smile on you and be gracious to you. May the Lord show you his favor and give you his peace" (Numbers 6:24-26). The exact nature of the requested blessing was spelled out by Moses in detail. God would bless their "towns" and "country," "children" and "fields," "herds" and "flocks," "baskets" and "kneading bowls." In fact, God would bless everything associated with their "coming and going" (Deut. 28:3-6). All these blessings were physical, but spiritual blessings were promised, too. It was as the Israelites contemplated their physical blessings that they recognized the spiritual dimensions of their blessedness at the hand of a merciful and gracious God. In the material blessings given to them they could see the way in which the Lord was making "his face shine with favor upon" them (Ps. 67:1).

But the prayer of the worshipers went far beyond a concern for personal blessings. Beyond the boundaries of their own lives lay "people" and "nations" who also needed the blessing of God on their lives. So, having sought their own blessing, the worshipers then added, "May your ways be known throughout the earth, your saving power among people everywhere" (67:2). Those who know the blessings of God upon their lives should never become so enamored of their blessed condition that they ignore a world outside that lacks what they enjoy in abundance.

What enlarges the vision of the recipient of divine blessing? It is the recognition that the Lord "direct[s] the actions of the whole world" (67:4). Ingrained selfishness precludes a vision that stretches beyond the borders of one's self. But the reminder that "the whole world" is precious to the Lord serves to redress such imbalance. Those who taste God's blessings begin to feel his heartbeat, and their heart cry becomes, "May the nations praise you, O God" (67:5).

There is no better way to end a day of worship and blessing than to seek the blessing of the world that lacks it! And what blessing there is in being a blessing!

TO READ: *Deuteronomy 8:1–20*

THE PERILS OF PLENTY

When you have eaten your fill, praise the LORD your God for the good land he has given you. But that is the time to be careful! Beware that in your plenty you do not forget the LORD your God and disobey his commands, regulations, and laws.

DEUTERONOMY 8:10-11

T here's an old saying: "I've been poor, and I've been rich. Rich is better." Those who have experienced both poverty and plenty would probably agree, and those who have only experienced poverty certainly believe that plenty is much more appealing. But there are perils in plenty. This was fully understood by the writer of Proverbs, who said, "Give me neither poverty nor riches! Give me just enough to satisfy my needs. For if I grow rich, I may deny you and say, 'Who is the Lord?' And if I am too poor, I may steal and thus insult God's holy name" (Prov. 30:8-9). A remarkably mature—and rare—attitude!

The Lord told Moses to warn the children of Israel about the unique perils they were facing as they prepared to enter a land filled with promise and plenty. In their wilderness journeys, they had been severely tested by the Lord in order to "teach [them] that people need more than bread for their life; real life comes by feeding on every word of the Lord" (Deut 8:3). "Feeding on every word of the Lord" means, among other things, trusting his promises and obeying his commands. Because of the people's extremity in the barren wilderness, they had no alternative but to trust the Lord—he alone provided food for them—and they had been forced into obedience because of the strict discipline imposed upon them on their journey. But once they entered the Promised Land, life would be different. Moses told them, "It is a land where food is plentiful and nothing is lacking" (8:9). So they were told, "When you have eaten your fill, praise the Lord your God for the good land he has given you" (8:10). They were also warned, "That is the time to be careful! Beware that in your plenty you do not forget the Lord your God and disobey his commands, regulations, and laws" (8:11). After the years of poverty when they had learned obedience and dependence, they were now being introduced to plenty when they were to respond in praise and thanksgiving. But sometimes plenty provokes pride rather than praise. The people of Israel were forewarned against thinking that it was their "own strength and energy that made [them] wealthy," because the Lord gives "power to become rich" (8:17-18).

The more successful men become, the more self-sufficient they tend to be. The wiser men become, the more thankful they are to the Lord who gave them success.

TO READ: *Deuteronomy 11:1–17*

HABITS OF THE HEART

If you carefully obey all the commands I am giving you today, and if you love the
LORD your God with all your heart and soul, and if you worship him,
then he will send the rains in their proper seasons so you can harvest crops of grain,
grapes for wine, and olives for oil.

DEUTERONOMY 11:13-14

On May 11, 1831, a French sociologist named Alexis de Tocqueville arrived in New York for an eight-month visit to the fascinating young United States of America. On his return home, he wrote *Democracy in America*, which first appeared in French in four volumes. He was greatly impressed with much that he saw in the United States, although he worried about "individualism"—a new word in those days. He was particularly interested in what he called the "habits of the heart" of the American people. By this he meant the opinions and ideas that "shape mental habits," and form the "moral and intellectual dispositions of men."[27]

Moses didn't use the same terms, but he was clearly concerned about the "habits of the heart" among the Israelites. He told them, "If you carefully obey all the commands I am giving you today, and if you love the Lord your God with all your heart and soul, and if you worship him" (Deut. 11:13), then the result would be a blessed experience in the Promised Land. On the other hand, he warned, "But do not let your heart turn away from the Lord to worship other gods" (11:16). The consequences of letting their hearts turn away from the Lord would be severe.

Habits of the heart are formed as the mind embraces certain principles, the emotions respond to these principles, and decisions are made based on them. So in the case of the Israelites, it was necessary for them to acknowledge what they knew of God from his dealings with them. They needed to respond appropriately to his gracious provision and care for them, and they had to enter into a covenant of trust and obedience with him. As time went on, these understandings, feelings, and decisions would become habitual, and their lifestyles would reflect their heartfelt love for God and would be demonstrated in wholehearted worship. Conversely, if they allowed opinions and desires based on the religions that honored other gods to formulate in their hearts, their habits and their lifestyles would become incompatible with their professed allegiance to the Lord. In other words, everything was related to the habits of their hearts.

Modern believers need to be conscious of the habits of their own hearts. We should take the time to explore the sources of our opinions and to evaluate the nature of our own desires. We should be willing to ask hard questions about the reasons for our decisions and check carefully the outcomes of our actions. The habits of a man's heart profoundly affect the world he inhabits and the inhabitants thereof.

---

[27] Alexis de Tocqueville, *Democracy in America*. Discussed in Robert Bellah, et al., *Habits of the Heart*.

TO READ: *Deuteronomy 11:16-32*

EDUCATING CHILDREN

*Commit yourselves completely to these words of mine. Tie them to your hands
as a reminder, and wear them on your forehead. Teach them to your children . . .
so that as long as the sky remains above the earth, you and your children
may flourish in the land the LORD swore to give your ancestors.*

DEUTERONOMY 11:18-19, 21

P arents have often expressed concern about public schools. In their complaints they
point to violence, unruly behavior, the availability of drugs, declining standards of
discipline and teaching, the absence of spiritual principles, and the overt communication
of material that they believe is either inappropriate or just plain wrong. Many parents have
responded by withdrawing their children and teaching them at home. Home-schooling
has grown remarkably in popularity during the late years of the twentieth and early years
of the twenty-first centuries. Critics of this approach were surprised, therefore, when the
first three places in the 2000 National Spelling Bee were won by home-schooled
children—one of whom had placed second in the National Geography Competition the
previous week.

Spiritually-minded parents who home-school their children like to point out that
when Moses instructed the children of Israel about life in the Promised Land he told
parents not only to "commit yourselves completely to these words of mine" but also to
"teach them to your children" (Deut. 11:18-19). Moses was referring, of course, to the
things that the Lord had told him to tell the people. Not everybody applies these instructions in the same way that home-schooling parents do, but *every* responsible parent
should be making serious application of them.

Moses' point was that, in order for the children of Israel to live well in the Promised
Land, they must honor the Lord with lives characterized by loving, trusting obedience.
They were told to write out the Lord's instructions (11:20) and "Tie them to your hands as
a reminder, and wear them on your forehead" (11:18). This was a highly visual reminder
that their thoughts and actions were to be in accordance with the Lord's wishes and
expectations.

The Lord did not leave anything to chance as far as the teaching of divine principles
to children was concerned. He told parents, "Talk about them when you are at home and
when you are away on a journey, when you are lying down and when you are getting up
again" (11:19). The Lord was pointing out to them that the disciplines of morning and
evening instruction—at breakfast and at bedtime, for example—are invaluable, and that
life is full of teaching moments.

Whether at home or on a journey, wise parents should by word and example take
the opportunity to answer children's questions, to provoke their curiosity, and to correct
their misunderstandings. And the purpose of this kind of education? "So that as long as
the sky remains above the earth, you and your children may flourish" (11:21). That should
be incentive enough!

TO READ: *Daniel 7:1-14*

THE WINNER

*As my vision continued that night, I saw someone who looked like a man coming
with the clouds of heaven. He approached the Ancient One and was led into his
presence. He was given authority, honor, and royal power over all the nations of the
world, so that people of every race and nation and language would obey him.
His rule is eternal—it will never end. His kingdom will never be destroyed.*

DANIEL 7:13-14

The Middle East is littered with the ruins of great civilizations. It is still possible,
millennia later, to gain some idea of their long-lost magnificence. More recently, the
twentieth century saw the rise and fall of the mighty Third Reich, and the tyrannical Soviet
empire under Stalin collapsed in ruins. The lesson we learn from the ruins is this: Great
empires pass away. Even the most fearsome human powers have their day and pass away.

Daniel, in one of his remarkable visions, saw the overthrow of four powerful,
fearsome beasts representing four mighty empires. While this was going on, he "watched
as thrones were put in place and the Ancient One sat down to judge" (Dan. 7:9). In
contrast to the rulers whose empires pass away and who inevitably leave the scene of their
triumphs, the "fiery throne" was occupied by an "Ancient One" from whose presence
flowed "a river of fire" (7:9-10). Surely this is a symbolic representation of God himself—
eternal, powerful, overwhelmingly magnificent, in control of everything, and ready to
exercise judgment on the nations and the empires.

Possibly, Daniel wondered who would occupy the throne set up alongside the "fiery
throne." If he did, he was not left in the dark for long. He "saw someone who looked like a
man coming with the clouds of heaven. He approached the Ancient One and was led into
his presence" (7:13). Daniel did not say specifically that this person, "who looked like a
man," actually occupied a throne alongside the Ancient One. But he did say that the
person "was given authority, honor, and royal power over all the nations of the world"
(7:14). So it is not unreasonable to assume the throne was set for him.

But who was the person received into the presence of the Lord, who on the one
hand displayed the attributes of deity, in that he came "with the clouds of heaven" (7:13),
and yet at the same time "looked like a man" (7:13)? What was the identity of the one
who, having entered the divine presence, was granted a "kingdom" whose "rule is
eternal—it will never end" (7:14)? Surely none other than the ascended Lord Jesus, who,
having completed his earthly work of redemption, returned to the Father and was given
the placed of highest honor!

Daniel teaches us that even in earth's darkest hour, the "Ancient One" and his
partner on the throne are in control, quietly building the eternal "kingdom that will never
be destroyed" (7:14). We know who wins in the end!

TO READ: *Micah 4:1-13*

WHEN WARS WILL STOP

*The LORD will settle international disputes. All the nations will beat their swords
into plowshares and their spears into pruning hooks. All wars will stop,
and military training will come to an end.*

MICAH 4:3

In 1919, at the end of the First World War, the League of Nations was formed with a view toward preventing further hostilities. Sadly, the project failed to stop the outbreak of World War II in 1939—and the League collapsed. At the end of World War II, the United Nations was created, with much the same purpose—"to save succeeding generations from the scourge of war, which twice in our lifetime has brought untold sorrow to mankind."[28] While the United Nations still exists and has done much good work, it, too, has failed to achieve its stated goal. When the Soviet regime collapsed—an event which President George Bush said heralded "a new world order"—it was only a matter of months before Saddam Hussein invaded Kuwait and the Gulf War broke out. Human history shows that even with the best intentions and the strongest will in the world, it has been impossible for man to stop war.

In light of this, the words of the prophet Micah take on special poignancy: "All wars will stop, and military training will come to an end" (Micah 4:3). Micah was pointing to a time of unprecedented peace, which would take place after God's people had suffered a time of desperate suffering and shame in exile. He was speaking about the restoration of a despised remnant, the rebuilding of the destroyed city of Jerusalem, and the establishment of a new kingdom.

In the time of Jesus the people of Israel were still looking forward to this restoration. Before Jesus' crucifixion, his disciples were confident that Jesus would go about fulfilling Micah's prophecy by ridding Israel of the Roman occupation and bringing them peace and prosperity. But their hopes were dashed when he died. However, after his resurrection from the dead, the disciples quickly resorted to their earlier hopes and asked Jesus, "Lord, are you going to free Israel now and restore our kingdom?" (Acts 1:6). Jesus made it clear in his response that his kingdom was not that kind of kingdom. Instead, he indicated that Micah's prophecy would be fulfilled when his eternal kingdom, populated by the redeemed, is established.

This is the kingdom for which Christians pray repeatedly, "May your kingdom come soon" (Matt. 6:10) and about which Jesus said, "My Kingdom is not of this world" (John 18:36). Wars will cease one day, but only when Christ's eternal kingdom comes. Until then, Paul's words speak loudly: "Do your part to live in peace with everybody, as much as possible" (Rom. 12:18). We may not be able to stop wars. But by God's grace we can obey this command and, "as much as possible," live in peace with others.

[28]From the Preamble to the United Nations Charter.

TO READ: *Genesis 49:1-28*

WHAT IS GOING TO HAPPEN

The scepter will not depart from Judah, nor the ruler's staff from his descendants,
until the coming of the one to whom it belongs, the one whom all nations will obey.

GENESIS 49:10

F armers would be delighted if they could accurately predict the weather. Investors would give anything to know in advance exactly how the market will behave. And leaders in all sectors, both public and private, do not hesitate to employ "futurists" to foresee the megatrends of the future so that they can plan accordingly. Knowing the future can be decidedly advantageous.

The Old Testament patriarchs were, on occasion, blessed with this unusual ability. And they used it to pass on blessings to their sons that, among other things, conveyed information concerning the future. A classic example of this occurred when "Jacob called together all his sons and said, 'Gather around me, and I will tell you what is going to happen to you in the days to come'" (Gen. 49:1). We can only imagine the mixed emotions with which Jacob's sons gathered to hear their father's words—if their future was anything like their past, it was going to be a very mixed bag of experiences. One by one, in birth order, Jacob spoke to each of them in the hearing of all the brothers.

Jacob's words to Judah are particularly significant for us today. He started out by praising Judah's obvious leadership abilities, which his brothers also recognized, and which succeeding generations would acknowledge. "Your brothers will praise you. . . . All your relatives will bow before you" (49:8). Judah's no-nonsense leadership style would be strong and "like a lioness—who will dare to rouse him?" (49:9). Then, looking much further into the future, Jacob foretold, "The scepter will not depart from Judah . . . until the coming of the one to whom it belongs" (49:10).

Matthew's Gospel opens with a genealogical table that shows clearly that the great king David, who reigned over Israel at its peak, was a descendant of Judah (see Matt. 1:3-6). Given the subsequent history of the tribe of Judah, there can be little doubt that Jacob in his prophetic vision was "seeing" the reign of David when he said "the ruler's staff [will not depart] from his descendants" (Gen. 49:10). But the words he added concerning the one to whom the scepter belongs—"the one whom all nations will obey"—pointed far beyond David to his most famous descendant, Jesus (see Matt. 1:3-16).

Jacob's vision foresaw a day yet to come—when "great David's greater son" will reign eternally.[29] Jacob knew this three millennia ago! Wise men still know it today—they've seen the future as revealed in Scripture concerning the ultimate triumph of the Lord Jesus and have committed their eternal well-being to Him. They have taken appropriate action—like a smart farmer or a savvy investor!

---

[29]James Montgomery, "Hail to the Lord's Anointed," 1821.

TO READ: *Psalm 24*

ANCIENT GATES

Open up, ancient gates! Open up, ancient doors, and let the King of glory enter.
Who is the King of glory? The LORD, strong and mighty,
the LORD, invincible in battle.

PSALM 24:7-8

T he arch over the gates of the infamous Nazi concentration camp Auschwitz to this
day bears the slogan "ARBEIT MACHTS FREI"—"Work makes one free." In that the
intended fate of the unfortunate people who were herded into the camp was to be worked
to death, the slogan is a sick joke about freedom through death, which exacerbates the
horror of the scene. It's hard to imagine a more hopeless entrance anywhere in the world.
It reminds us of the entrance to hell in Dante's *Divine Comedy*. According to Dante, the
gates of hell carry the sign, "Abandon hope, all ye who enter here." Both thoughts—of
people being herded into Auschwitz to their death and of the unrepentant being swept
into the hopelessness of hell—are chilling in the extreme.

These pictures of hopelessness stand in marked contrast to the tone of Psalm 24,
which speaks about the gates to the "mountain of the Lord" (24:3), the doors to the
presence of God. The psalm was probably written to celebrate the day when David brought
the ark of the covenant onto Mount Moriah, the eventual site of the temple (see 2 Sam.
6:12-19). Even as far back as the wilderness journey from Egypt to the Promised Land, the
children of Israel marched behind the ark, which they believed guaranteed them victory
over their enemies (see Num. 10:33-36). The children of Israel thought of the Lord as the
"King of glory . . . the Lord, strong and mighty, the Lord, invincible in battle" (Ps. 24:8).
The entering of the ark into the temple signified God's entering. It was, therefore, a great
cause for rejoicing. These gates were welcoming "the King of glory"!

Mount Moriah had been set apart for the worship of the Lord to whom "the earth"
and "everything in it" rightfully belongs. (Ps. 24:1). Recognizing God's sovereign rule
required that men should come before him in worship. The question then became, "Who
may climb the mountain of the Lord? Who may stand in his holy place?" (24:3). Such a
glorious, mighty Creator and Redeemer could not be approached casually or flippantly.
The would-be worshipers were told, "Only those whose hands and hearts are pure, who
do not worship idols and never tell lies" (24:4).

In other words, only those who know their impurities and deviousness and have
sought and found forgiveness can enter through the gate and worship as they ought. Those
who do so are promised that they will find "the Lord's blessing and have right standing
with God their savior" (24:5).

A vision of the majesty of the Lord and a humble approach to him as "Savior"
qualifies a man to enter and "worship the God of Israel" (24:5-6). Those who enter
through this gate do not abandon hope—they discover glory!

A NEW SONG

They sang a new song with these words: "You are worthy to take the scroll and break
its seals and open it. For you were killed, and your blood has ransomed people for
God from every tribe and language and people and nation. And you have caused
them to become God's Kingdom and his priests. And they will reign on the earth."

REVELATION 5:9-10

Throughout the long history of the Christian church, many things have changed, but none has changed more than musical styles in worship. Each succeeding generation and each differing culture has looked for styles of worship that are relevant and pleasing both to the worshipers and to the Lord. As a result, new songs have found their way into the ecclesiastical repertoire alongside old favorites. This is something that is clearly indicated in the standard Anglican hymnbook, which is called simply *Hymns, Ancient and Modern.*

In John's dramatic vision of heaven, "the twenty four elders . . . sang a new song with these words: 'You are worthy to take the scroll and break its seals and open it. For you were killed, and your blood has ransomed people for God' (Rev. 5:9-10). In biblical parlance, "a new song" heralded a new insight or a new discovery of truth, and this was no exception. The elders' praise was augmented almost immediately with "the singing of thousands and millions of angels around the throne" (5:11). The reason for all this singing and praising was that, finally, a man had stepped forward to break the seals and open the scroll "in the right hand of the one who was sitting on the throne" (5:1). This securely sealed scroll, which was "sealed with seven seals" (5:1), contained the story of human history. It had remained sealed—not understood—until this man stepped forward to open it and make known the eternal purposes of the Lord, who was seated on the throne. This was cause for great praise, thanksgiving, and jubilation! It was a new experience, meriting a new song.

The only man "worthy to take the scroll and break its seals and open it" was identified as "the Lion of the tribe of Judah, the heir to David's throne" (5:5). This is the same one foreseen by Judah's father Jacob as he pronounced blessings on Judah shortly before dying (Gen. 49:9-10). The description of the "Lion" is unusual—as a "Lamb that had been killed but was now standing," possessing "seven horns and seven eyes, which are the seven spirits of God" (5:6). Yet this description is deeply and richly symbolic of Jesus, who laid down his life as a willing sacrifice, and who is now risen from the dead and invested with the sevenfold (symbolizing "perfect" and "complete") authority of God and the sevenfold wisdom and insight of the Spirit. He is, in other words, the central figure of human history and the only one who can make sense of it.

New songs of worship should reflect fresh insights into the wonder of God's purposes and should be expressions of worship to him. Style is not unimportant, but substance is vital.

197

TO READ: *Revelation 11:1–19*

JUDGMENT
AND REWARD

"The nations were angry with you, but now the time of your wrath has come. It is time to judge the dead and reward your servants. You will reward your prophets and your holy people, all who fear your name, from the least to the greatest. And you will destroy all who have caused destruction on the earth."

REVELATION 11:18

Viewed from space, planet Earth looks small and fragile. An infinitesimal fragment in the vastness, it is apparently an idyllic planet, the scene of peace and tranquility. But we know that its history is one of unending tension and hostility, fragmentation and conflict, both petty and cataclysmic. How could something so small and beautiful be so full of ugly dissension and huge heartbreak? And where will it all end? Will the fragile planet itself become a victim of its inhabitants' unruliness?

Speculation on such questions has gone on down through the centuries. But in more recent times, as man's penchant for self-destructive behavior has been matched by his technological expertise, predictions of the planet's demise at man's intentional or inadvertent hand have grown in volume and intensity. But while speculations say one thing, revelation says another.

The book of Revelation, John's vision of heaven, included insights into the future. At one point he describes "loud voices shouting in heaven, 'The whole world has now become the Kingdom of our Lord and of his Christ, and he will reign forever and ever'" (Rev. 11:15). The Lord is further identified as "the Lord God Almighty, the one who is and who always was" (11:17). This designation, which speaks of God's almightiness and his eternalness, suggests that during the unruly history of planet Earth, the all-powerful Lord has not been exercising his power and authority as he might have—otherwise, he would have put down all insurrection and banished all dissension and fragmentation. But things are not always as they appear. John sees into heaven and into the future, where it is said of the Lord, "Now you have assumed your great power and have begun to reign" (11:17). God's people have prayed for centuries, "May your kingdom come soon" (Matt. 6:10). This grand universal kingdom will come, and "He will reign forever and ever."

But what of the unruly powers that be? John says, "The nations were angry with you, but now the time of your wrath has come" (Rev. 11:18). The Lord God Almighty will execute judgment and "will destroy all who have caused destruction on the earth." But the message for God's people is positive and encouraging: "Lord God Almighty, . . . you will reward your prophets and your holy people, all who fear your name, from the least to the greatest" (11:18).

God is in control. While at times that does not seem to be the case, he truly is the "Lord God Almighty." When he is ready, he will assume his great power and bring judgment and reward. Be sure you know which will be in your future.

TO READ: *Revelation 19:1-21*

THE WHITE HORSE

Then I saw heaven opened, and a white horse was standing there. And the one sitting
on the horse was named Faithful and True. For he judges fairly and then goes to war.
. . . He was clothed with a robe dipped in blood, and his title was the Word of God.
. . . On his robe and thigh was written this title: King of kings and Lord of lords.

REVELATION 19:11, 13, 16

C ountless armies have marched through the land of Israel down through the centuries. But not all armies have come to fight. When Palestine was a British protectorate, before the modern state of Israel was founded in 1948, British troops were stationed there to maintain law and order. General Gordon, their commanding officer, was also a committed Christian. On the day that he led his troops into Jerusalem, on reaching the gate of the ancient city, he dismounted from the white horse he was riding and walked through the gate leading the horse. He explained to his troops, "The only person entitled to enter Jerusalem riding a white horse is 'the King of kings and the Lord of lords.'"

General Gordon was referring to today's passage in Revelation 19. In John's symbolic language, the rider on the white horse was "named Faithful and True," "his title was the Word of God," and "on his robe and thigh was written this title: King of kings and Lord of lords" (Rev. 19:11, 13, 16). These descriptions may seem strange to modern ears, but these titles and names express symbolically the following truths: his power and authority surpass all the powers of the rulers of this world; his status as the one who makes known the purposes and plans of God himself is overwhelming; and his character, unlike that of the kings and lords of this world, is totally reliable, without deviousness or chicanery. "He judges fairly and then goes to war" (19:11).

But who is this awesome, mysterious figure? John identified "the Word" as Jesus when he wrote, "In the beginning the Word already existed. He was with God and he was God . . . and we have seen his glory" (John 1:1, 14). Then in his vision of the "Son of Man," John noted that "a sharp two-edged sword came from his mouth" (Rev. 1:16). He is Jesus, the risen, triumphant Lord, whose kingdom will not pass away. John sees him in the role of a warrior-king about to exercise judgment on his enemies—something that will take place at the end of time. This is a dimension of Christ's ministry that is often overlooked, ignored, or even rejected. But it should be remembered that his judgment will be just—"He judges fairly." Moreover, he is "clothed with a robe dipped in blood" (19:13)—a vivid reminder that he who will ultimately judge came first to be our Savior. Judgment will be reserved for those who reject his saving grace and repudiate his righteous rule. He rides an awesome white horse, but for the humbly repentant he will graciously dismount.

TO READ: *Revelation 21:1-8*

ALL THINGS NEW

"He will remove all of their sorrows, and there will be no more death or sorrow or crying or pain. For the old world and its evils are gone forever." And the one sitting on the throne said, "Look, I am making all things new!" And then he said to me, "Write this down, for what I tell you is trustworthy and true."

REVELATION 21:4-5

Modern politicians often end their speeches with a rhetorical flourish that promises a better world "for our children and grandchildren." Such sentiments strike a chord in most hearts—who does not wish for a better world for the rising generations? Politicians may commit to banishing poverty, providing quality education, putting an end to war, or starting health insurance for all. Noble sentiments all, but desperately difficult to achieve.

It is interesting to note that "the one sitting on the throne" did not promise to make this a better world, he announced a new one! He said, "Look, I am making all things new!" (Rev. 21:5). That is precisely what John saw. He records, "Then I saw a new heaven and a new earth, for the old heaven and the old earth had disappeared" (21:1). The reason for this drastic action—the disappearance of the old and the creation of the new—is explained: "The old world and its evils are gone forever" (21:4). The evils that pervade this old fallen world can never be eradicated by the best government or the most enlightened politicians. Evil is too deeply ingrained. This world will not ultimately be perfected as evil is incrementally abolished. This world as we know it will be abolished, and a new one established in its place. This is the message of John's vision of the end.

But who can accomplish such a feat and produce an environment where "there will be no more death or sorrow or crying or pain" (21:4)? The answer is "the one sitting on the throne" whose self-description is "I am the Alpha and the Omega—the Beginning and the End" (21:6). It stands to reason that the only one who can legitimately bring about this world's demise is the one who brought it into being, and the only one who can deal with the problem of evil, which is responsible for all that is wrong with this world, is the one who is intrinsically holy, righteous, and just—the Alpha and the Omega! And he will.

This vision of the ultimate conquest of evil and the establishment of a new heaven and a new earth has led some to assume that nothing needs to be done about this world's ills. But compassion and love insist that even if we cannot eradicate evil, we can certainly alleviate it. And we must never forget that when political promises of a better world disappoint, the divine assurance of a new world helps us hope in the midst of death, sorrow, crying, and pain.

TO READ: *Revelation 21:9-27*

MIXED METAPHORS

Then one of the seven angels who held the seven bowls containing the seven last plagues came and said to me, "Come with me! I will show you the bride, the wife of the Lamb." So he took me in spirit to a great, high mountain, and he showed me the holy city, Jerusalem, descending out of heaven from God.

REVELATION 21:9-10

A British parliamentarian once said, "I smell a rat, I see it floating in the air, and I'll nip it in the bud." What he meant was that he suspected something was not quite right, and he intended to find out what was wrong and put an end to it. But he unwittingly bequeathed to literature a superb example of mixed metaphor. What he said made up in color what it lacked in clarity—something that metaphors, both mixed and unmixed, tend to do. But if clarity suffers, the point may be missed.

John recorded a fine mixed metaphor when he wrote about an angel saying to him, "Come with me! I will show you the bride, the wife of the Lamb" (Rev. 21:9). We have no way of knowing what John expected to see, but the angel, he tells us, "showed me the holy city, Jerusalem, descending out of heaven from God" (21:10). So the bride was a well-known city situated in a historic geographical location, and yet it was descending out of heaven. John's description certainly was not lacking in color!

The dimensions of the city show quite clearly that this was no literal Jerusalem: "It was in the form of a cube, for its length and width and height were each 1,400 miles" (21:16). The twelve gates bore "the names of the twelve tribes of Israel," and "the wall of the city had twelve foundation stones, and on them were written the names of the twelve apostles of the Lamb" (21:12, 14). So the "city" in some symbolic way was built upon the historic people of Israel and the apostolic work of the early church's leadership. The link with the apostles' city gives a clue that the city is related to the church—something that becomes very clear when we remember that the church is described in Scripture as "the bride of Christ" (Eph. 5:25-27)—which is just how the city was described!

So John saw a vision of the future glory of the people of God, the bride of Christ. This glory is something that can only come from God, because only he can make those who by nature were estranged from him into his own people. God was telling us that despite the turmoil of this world's struggles, the church will survive and triumph. It will be a glorious church, as suggested by the proliferation of jewels in its description. It will also be a global church, for "the nations of the earth will walk in its light" (21:24). And it will be a grateful church made up entirely of "those whose names are written in the Lamb's Book of Life" (21:27). And there are no mixed messages about that!

TO READ: *Revelation 22:1-21*

HERO WORSHIP

I, John, am the one who saw and heard all these things. And when I saw and heard
these things, I fell down to worship the angel who showed them to me. But again he
said, "No, don't worship me. I am a servant of God, just like you and your brothers
the prophets, as well as all who obey what is written in this scroll. Worship God!"

REVELATION 22:8-9

D espairing parents, on noting their sons' behavior, have been known to say, with a
note of resignation in their voice, "Boys will be boys." Others have pointed out,
"Boys will be boys, but if you're patient, boys will be men." Even so, most men would
admit to there being a little boy lurking somewhere in their mature masculinity.

Take hero worship, for example. It is understandable when boys wear the sportswear
popularized by their favorite superstars, but it is rather surprising when a middle-aged
stockbroker wears similar clothes on weekends. Perhaps men never really grow out of hero
worship. It may be that men see in those whose lives are larger than life something attractive
to which they aspire, something appealing that they admire.

This may very well be harmless enough, but John's worship of the angel who guided
him through the intricacies and mysteries of his vision was unacceptable. John records,
"When I saw and heard these things, I fell down to worship the angel who showed them
to me" (Rev. 22:8). A clear case of hero worship of the highest order! But the angel said to
him, "No, don't worship me. I am a servant of God, just like you and your brothers the
prophets, as well as all who obey what is written in this scroll. Worship God!" (22:9).
John's hero worship elicited two responses. First, he must not worship an angel. Second,
he must worship God only.

Many modern sports heroes would never be confused with angels, so the adulation
that is all too often heaped upon them is misplaced—particularly if those who indulge in
hero worship fail to recognize that worship is reserved exclusively for God, to whom it
rightfully belongs. "Worship God!" was the angel's brief but unambiguous order. It is a
brief and unambiguous word for modern men, too.

It is interesting to note throughout the book of Revelation how often worship is
associated with "falling down" (see Rev. 4:10; 5:8; 7:11; 19:10; 22:8). This suggests that
when a man rightly understands who God is, he will be awestruck by the discovery. When
a man recognizes what it means to worship, he will humbly and joyfully prostrate himself
at the master's feet in a posture of willing submission and service.

The angel connected two vital themes in his instructions about worship. He
explained how true worship issues from an obedient heart. When former hero-worshipers
become true worshipers, they, in turn, become the real heroes their youngsters need to
emulate as they learn to worship the one truly worth worshiping.

TO READ: *Psalm 135*

ONE GENERATION
AT A TIME

The LORD has chosen Jacob for himself, Israel for his own special treasure.

PSALM 135:4

I t is hardly a coincidence that some of today's great baseball players are the children of former baseball legends, that many top stock car drivers are the sons and granddaughters of the original stock car pioneers, that the sons of former heavyweight boxing champions are now earning a living in the ring, or even that some of our best preachers are preachers' kids. It is beyond question that one generation can pass on interest and passion, knowledge and discipline, to the next generation. The choices of each generation can have a lasting and profound impact.

What is true in the natural world is certainly true of the spiritual realm. There is a certain expectation in Scripture that spiritual heritage will be treasured by each generation and transmitted to the next. The psalm writer said, "Let each generation tell its children of your mighty acts" (Ps. 145:4). This injunction states an expectation that each generation will be conversant with the stories about God's dealings with the human race and that they will treasure these stories enough to pass them on. There is also the assumption that each generation will be interested enough in the well-being of the rising generation to take time to nurture them in the things of the Spirit.

Each generation should recognize the importance of communication from the older to the younger if there is to be any continuity of principles, priorities, and lifestyle values in any given society. Sadly, in contemporary culture many young people have minimal contact with their elders but have maximum interaction with their peers. The result is a subculture with little or no sense of history or heritage, of transcendent values or spiritual realities.

It has been said that the Christian faith is never more than one generation away from extinction. This may be an alarmist statement, but there is an element of truth in it. There are cultures in the western world at the present time that have seen a progressive decline in spiritual nurture over three generations to such an extent that these cultures, which were previously strongholds of the faith, are now post-Christian societies, mission fields as dark as any primitive society.

The answer to such a threat is simple—every man who brings a child into the world should accept the privilege and responsibility of seeing that his child is given a working knowledge of the Lord, his dealings with mankind, his offer of salvation, and the joys of living in vital communion with him. No one can guarantee the next generation will come to faith, but everyone can make sure they have the chance.

TO READ: *1 Corinthians 3:5-17*

GOD'S BUILDING

The one who plants and the one who waters work as a team with the same purpose.
. . . We work together as partners who belong to God. You are God's field,
God's building—not ours. Because of God's special favor to me,
I have laid the foundation like an expert builder.

1 CORINTHIANS 3:8-10

Three men working on a building site were doing the same kind of work. One day, they were asked to describe their work. One said, "I shovel dirt into a wheelbarrow, push it across the site, and empty it." The second said, "I come to work to make a living, to put food on the table and a roof over my kids' heads. Then I go home." The third said, "I'm privileged to be building a cathedral." The first saw work as drudgery; the second as a means to an end. The third, however, had a sense of grandeur and purpose in what he was doing.

When Paul talked about his work and that of his fellow workers, he said, "[We] work as a team with the same purpose." That purpose was to build "God's building" (1 Cor. 3:8-9). He could have described his work as getting on a ship, sailing to a new city, preaching, getting beaten up and thrown in jail, and then moving on. But he saw the grand picture—he was building "God's building"—the church.

Paul wanted the Corinthians to recognize and revere the church. He told them, "Don't you realize that all of you together are the temple of God and that the Spirit of God lives in you?" (3:16).

But he and his fellow apostles were not in this work alone. He claimed, "I have laid the foundation. . . . Now others are building on it" (3:10). And he had stern words for those who were involved in continuing the work of building "the temple of God." They "must be very careful." Great care had to be exercised to ensure that they built on the proper foundation, the only legitimate foundation for the church—"Jesus Christ" (3:11). Obviously, any building erected without an adequate foundation cannot stand. In the same way, any church that gets away from loving, worshiping, and serving the Lord Jesus cannot claim to be a genuine church.

Paul was well aware of the dangers of apostasy. But he also worried about the way churches would go about being the church and the kind of church work they would do! He said some work is like "gold, silver, [or] jewels." When tested in fire, it survives. Other work resembles "wood, hay, or straw" (3:10). It cannot survive a blazing inferno. Paul's point? "Everyone's work will be put through the fire to see whether or not it keeps its value" (3:13).

Church life is neither mundane nor routine—it is God's work. We're building God's building, and he expects quality workmanship.

TO READ: *1 Corinthians 12:1-13*

SPECIAL ABILITIES

I will write about the special abilities the Holy Spirit gives to each of us. . . .
It is the one and only Holy Spirit who distributes these gifts.
He alone decides which gift each person should have.

1 CORINTHIANS 12:1, 11

Most things slip away into the mists of history, remembered at most by only a few people—if any. Some special things endure, though. The works of Leonardo da Vinci, Mozart, and William Shakespeare are greatly valued today, long after the men themselves have passed on. These men had special abilities that gave their work special value and secured for them a special place in the world of achievement.

One of the most remarkable realities of human history is the survival and growth of the Christian church. The church was founded by Jesus, who spent his life in a limited sphere of influence. It was entrusted to a small group of men who had initially failed miserably to further his cause. The church has subsequently spread to the four corners of the world, touching billions and transforming society wherever its influence has spread. From a human point of view, this is a remarkable achievement. There's something special about the church.

But what is special about it may be a surprise to many people. It is not necessarily that the church is made up of remarkable people. On the contrary, Paul tells us that it is intentionally made up of few who are "wise in the world's eyes, or powerful, or wealthy" (1 Cor. 1:26). The question that must then be asked is, "How could the church become so remarkable, so unique, so special when made up of people who are quite ordinary?"

The answer is found in Paul's statement "about the special abilities the Holy Spirit gives to each of us" (12:1). The church is special because she is comprised of ordinary people who have been granted "special abilities" by the Holy Spirit.

The effectiveness of the church is directly related to the church's grasp of the significance of this special gifting by the Holy Spirit. It should be noted that the "special abilities" are given to "each of us." The vast numbers of people who make up the worldwide church are impressive, but what is infinitely more impressive is the truth that these vast numbers of people have all been given special abilities by the Holy Spirit. That means there is a vast amount of special ability latent in the church.

These abilities vary in much the same way that the members of the human body differ from each other. It is the Holy Spirit "alone [who] decides which gift each person should have" (12:11).

Each man should be aware of his special abilities and be exercising them. And when a church full of people do this—it is special!

TO READ: *1 Corinthians 2:1-16*

SECRET WISDOM

I do speak with words of wisdom, but not the kind of wisdom that belongs to this world, and not the kind that appeals to the rulers of this world, who are being brought to nothing. No, the wisdom we speak of is the secret wisdom of God.

1 CORINTHIANS 2:6-7

There's a kind of wisdom known as "street smarts." It is the wisdom of the street child who is deprived of home and family and learns how to survive in a vicious, hostile environment without love and by his wits. In his netherworld, he prospers.

Then there's the wisdom of the philosophy major in an elite college. He studies the discussions of Socrates, learns the findings of Plato, and becomes acquainted with classical thought and its application to the modern world. The street child, smart beyond imagination in his concrete jungle, would be as lost in the classroom as the student would be in the cities' ghettos. They both have accumulated wisdom, but each has a wisdom irrelevant to the other's world.

When Paul preached the gospel in Corinth, he was well-acquainted with the wisdom of the classical philosophers, but he avoided using their language and he chose not to use their arguments. He did this for a very good reason. He was speaking of a wisdom that was as foreign to the Greeks of Corinth as the "wisdom" of the street child and the philosophy major are foreign to each other. Paul was not speaking unwisely. On the contrary, he said, "I do speak with words of wisdom, but not the kind of wisdom that belongs to this world, and not the kind that appeals to the rulers of this world, who are being brought to nothing" (1 Cor. 2:6). Instead, "The wisdom we speak of is the secret wisdom of God" (2:7).

The great Greek philosophers who had used their considerable intellectual abilities to ponder the great themes of human existence had, at best, been able only to speculate on answers. They had tried to unlock "the secret wisdom of God," which only God could unlock. These speculations caused massive problems to the classical thinkers. The secret wisdom of God centered around Jesus dying on a cross for the sins of the world. This concept was so appalling to the Greek Corinthians that many of them rejected it as nonsense. Their problem was that they were relying solely on human rationality and ignoring the mysterious work of the Holy Spirit. But, as Paul said, "Only those who have the Spirit can understand what the Spirit means" (2:14). And only those who have God's Spirit can understand what God in his wisdom is saying.

Street smarts don't work in the Ivy League, and classical thought is useless on the streets of the ghetto. But the secret wisdom of God is relevant in both places, and it change lives wherever and whenever it is embraced.

TO READ: *Galatians 5:16-25*

LIVING A NEW LIFE

So I advise you to live according to your new life in the Holy Spirit. Then you won't be doing what your sinful nature craves. . . . Those who belong to Christ Jesus have nailed the passions and desires of their sinful nature to his cross and crucified them there.

GALATIANS 5:16, 24

When a man gets married, he embarks on a new life. Later, when he retires, he starts another new life. Should he eventually lose his wife, he begins all over again. Life is all about changes, challenges, and choices.

The more drastic changes in life, such as marriage, retirement, or bereavement call for far-reaching adjustments. But none is so far-reaching as the change that takes place when a man commits his life to Christ. Paul describes this as "new life in the Holy Spirit" and calls the believer to live accordingly (Gal. 5:16). The fundamental difference in such a new life is described as no longer "doing what your sinful nature craves," but living now by the Holy Spirit (5:16). This involves following "the Holy Spirit's leading in every part of our lives" (5:25). Two options are clearly presented—either following a "sinful nature [that] loves to do evil" (5:17), or living in such a way that "the Holy Spirit controls our lives" (5:22).

New believers are often surprised to discover, after the initial joy of committing their lives to Christ has worn down a little, that they struggle to live a new life. They expected that everything would be fresh, new, and wonderful and that they would somehow be transported into a new kind of stratospheric spirituality—free from pain, struggle, worry, or defeat. They need to learn that even though they are now in Christ, the "two forces"— the sinful nature and the Holy Spirit—"are constantly fighting each other, and your choices are never free from this conflict" (5:17).

This may seem to be rather discouraging information, but it needs to be seen that the believer is not impotent in the midst of this struggle. He has the freedom and the power to choose whether he will be dominated by the sinful nature or be led by the Spirit of God. In fact, he is required to make this choice—or more accurately, a continual series of choices.

To choose to "follow the Holy Spirit's leading" includes recognizing that in saying yes to Christ, the believer said no to the sins for which Christ died. He has "nailed the passions and desires of [the] sinful nature" to the cross, and he continues to say no to them (5:24). At the same time, he says yes to the gracious working of the indwelling Holy Spirit. As he does this, he finds he's living a new life—a rich life, a full life, a life that honors God and blesses people.

TO READ: *2 Corinthians 3:1–18*

A LETTER FROM CHRIST

Clearly, you are a letter from Christ prepared by us. It is written not with pen and ink, but with the Spirit of the living God. It is carved not on stone, but on human hearts.

2 CORINTHIANS 3:3

P residents of the United States, after their terms of office, often establish a presidential library where their correspondence is archived for posterity. For similar reasons, the letters of literary figures are often published posthumously, and the devotees of notable people will pay large amounts of money just to possess one of their letters.

It would be a waste of time speculating on the possible market value of one of Jesus' letters, because there are none in existence. That is, there are none written with ink on parchment.

However, Paul said of the Corinthian Christians, "Clearly, you are a letter from Christ prepared by us. It is written not with pen and ink, but with the Spirit of the living God. It is carved not on stone, but on human hearts" (2 Cor. 3:3). This is an extraordinary statement! The reason Paul wrote it was that Paul's authenticity was being challenged in the Corinthian church. Some people, not believing that he was really an apostle, were demanding that he show his credentials. His response was that the changed lives of the Corinthians were his credentials. They themselves were evidence of God's work through Paul in Corinthian hearts. He didn't need letters of commendation when the whole congregation was made up of living letters written by Christ himself!

To press home his point, Paul reminded his readers of what happened when God had carved a letter "of written laws . . . etched in stone" (3:6-7). Paul was referring, of course, to the law given to Moses. This law had served to condemn the people, because they had constantly broken it. But now God has established a "new covenant" through Christ. Instead of bringing condemnation and death, the new covenant "makes us right with God" (3:9). It is the people who have been made right with God who are Christ's letters that can be read by other people.

But what do other people read in these human letters? First, Paul notes, "Since this new covenant gives us such confidence, we can be very bold" (3:12). Others see a confidence that is not arrogant self-confidence but joyful confidence in the promise of God, that God will accept all who come to him through his Son. Others also read about the freedom enjoyed by God's people—"wherever the Spirit of the Lord is, he gives freedom" (3:17). This is not the freedom to do what people want, but the freedom to do what they ought. Most importantly, when others read these letters from Christ, they learn about Christ and gain a vision of him—"as the Spirit of the Lord works within us, we become more and more like him and reflect his glory even more" (3:18).

These letters are not for archives, where they will gather dust. They are for public reading, where they will transform their readers. We who believe are letters from Christ that are signed, sealed, and delivered with love.

TO READ: *2 Timothy 1:1-14*

FAN THE FLAMES

This is why I remind you to fan into flames the spiritual gift God gave you when
I laid my hands on you. For God has not given us a spirit of fear and timidity,
but of power, love, and self-discipline. So you must never be ashamed to tell others
about our Lord. . . . With the strength God gives you, be ready to suffer
with me for the proclamation of the Good News.

2 TIMOTHY 1:6-8

There's a tendency among believers to place the heroes of the faith on pedestals that they, the heroes, would never have mounted. This is especially true of the heroes of the faith whose lives are recorded in the Bible. While we incline to think of these biblical heroes as always on top of their game, the Scriptures go to great lengths to show that, in actuality, they suffered from the same kinds of discouragement, disappointment, disillusionment, and dysfunction as we. The value of these men and women to us is not to be found in their exemption from the ills that trouble us, but rather in seeing the ways in which they handled them and lived well through them.

Take Timothy, for example. Timothy was a protégé of the great apostle Paul, who spoke in the most affectionate terms about the young man. But that did not stop the apostle from identifying potential problems in Timothy's life—and speaking about them firmly and lovingly. So he wrote in his letter to Timothy, "I remind you to fan into flames the spiritual gift God gave you when I laid my hands on you" (2 Tim. 1:6). Apparently, even Timothy was capable of allowing his divine calling and enabling to lapse into a smoldering rather than a blazing condition. Paul added, "God has not given us a spirit of fear and timidity, but of power, love, and self-discipline" (1:7). Timothy lived in tough times, and Paul expected that they would get worse (and he was right!). So it was understandable if Timothy, like most normal people, experienced pangs of trepidation when he considered his calling and the environment in which he was to live it out. Perhaps Timothy's timidity was most obvious in his apparent reluctance to speak openly about Christ. So Paul reminded him, "You must never be ashamed to tell others about our Lord" (1:8).

It is important to note that Paul was not simply giving Timothy a rah-rah pep talk. He also was reminding him of fundamental spiritual principles that Timothy needed to apply in order to live well in his natural difficulties. He was reminding Timothy of "the spiritual gift God gave [him]," of "the faith and love that [he had] in Christ Jesus," and particularly of "the help of the Holy Spirit who lives within us" (1:13-14).

This biblical hero, Timothy, was not a hero because he was immune to fear and oblivious to danger. He was a hero because he suffered as normal men suffer and through the power of divine enabling in the Holy Spirit he was able "to hold on" and ultimately triumph. We all can do that.

TO READ: *Psalm 33:1-22*

COSMONAUTS AND ASTRONAUTS

Let everyone in the world fear the LORD, and let everyone stand in awe of him.
For when he spoke, the world began! It appeared at his command.

PSALM 33:8-9

I n the early days of the space race, much more was at stake than technological bragging rights. The USSR and the USA, with their competing and contradictory ideologies, were squaring off with each other in a great struggle for the hearts and minds of the human race. When the Soviet cosmonauts returned from their spell in space, they dutifully reported that they had seen no sign of God and therefore had concluded that he was not there. But when a group of American astronauts circling the globe read portions of the Psalms extolling the wonders of creation and its Creator in the hearing of millions, a powerful statement was broadcast concerning God's presence and power. It is impossible to say whether or not anybody's views on the existence of God were changed by these opposing statements. The fact remains that, when some look into creation, they see the Creator, while others view the same data and see only creation.

The psalm writer was firmly in the camp of the astronauts, rather than that of the cosmonauts. He said, "Let everyone in the world fear the Lord, and let everyone stand in awe of him. For when he spoke, the world began! It appeared at his command" (Ps. 33:8-9).

The psalmist went even further. He did not believe in a Creator who, having created the world, went into retirement and left creation to its own devices. Instead, he said, "The Lord looks down from heaven and sees the whole human race. From his throne he observes all who live on the earth. He made their hearts, so he understands everything they do" (33:13-15). The thought of an actively observant Lord was precious to the psalmist. Even though the behavior of the human race is so often beyond comprehension, the Lord understands everything they do! Surely it is advisable for men to be acquainted, at least minimally, with what the Scriptures say about God's perception of humanity. Men who are thus acquainted can take great comfort and find grounds for hope in God's nearness and understanding.

Men can also take comfort in knowing God's intentions for humanity. These intentions are hinted at by the psalm writer when he says, "The Lord watches over those who fear him, those who rely on his unfailing love" (33:18). He intends to love them unfailingly, and to watch over them ceaselessly—those who "depend on the Lord," that is!

The Soviet cosmonauts saw nothing but a mechanical universe, while the astronauts saw a creation that mirrored its Creator. With whom would you rather fly?

TO READ: *Numbers 16:1-15*

POWER PLAY

One day Korah son of Izhar, a descendant of Kohath son of Levi, conspired with
Dathan and Abiram, the sons of Eliab, and On son of Peleth, from the tribe of
Reuben. They incited a rebellion against Moses, involving 250 other prominent
leaders, all members of the assembly. They went to Moses and Aaron and said,
"You have gone too far! Everyone in Israel has been set apart by the LORD,
and he is with all of us. What right do you have to act as though you are
greater than anyone else among all these people of the LORD?"

NUMBERS 16:1-3

C huck Colson, the former White House aide, says, "Power, privilege, position, prestige, and parties—these are the perks of politics." No doubt there are many men who enter politics with a deep desire to further the well-being of their society. But for others, it is the "perks" that woo them into political life. The opportunity to exercise power and to gain prestige brings its own rewards. Of course, those who hold the power do not relinquish it readily, and those who crave it don't always use the most benign methods to gain it. The results are often power plays—and they can be ugly (the 2000 Presidential election being a case in point).

Korah is a fine example of power-play politics. Korah was a Levite who had special responsibilities and privileges. But this was not enough for him. He resented Moses' authority, claiming that everybody was equal and, accordingly, Moses had no right to exercise leadership over anyone else. Korah said, "You have gone too far! Everyone in Israel has been set apart by the Lord, and he is with all of us. What right do you have to act as though you are greater than anyone else among all these people of the Lord?" (Num. 16:3). To reinforce his point, Korah "incited a rebellion against Moses, involving 250 . . . members of the assembly" (16:2).

As is often the case in matters of contention, there was a germ of truth in what the disaffected were saying. The people of Israel had all been set apart by the Lord for himself, and the Lord was certainly with all of them. In that the contenders were perfectly correct.

But Korah and his friends were still the ones who had "gone too far" (16:7). While they were all set apart for the Lord in one sense, there was another sense in which each one had his allotted place in the divine economy. But they were not willing to acknowledge this—they wanted to rise above their own allotted place and deny Moses his. Korah was a Levite; he was not a priest. Moses was the leader of Israel; he was not subservient to Korah and his 250 rebels. And it was the Lord who had determined these roles. As Moses pointed out to Korah & Company, "The one you are really revolting against is the Lord!" (16:11). Korah and his collaborators were attempting a power play. In response, the Lord made Moses' leadership abundantly clear. Unfortunately, not every power play is as quickly remedied.

Ultimate authority resides with the Lord—he delegates as he chooses. So embrace what he grants you and avoid grasping for what isn't yours. Otherwise, you might be fighting God. And you could get burned!

TO READ: *Numbers 16:16-50*

BETWEEN THE LIVING AND THE DEAD

Aaron did as Moses told him and ran out among the people. The plague indeed had already begun, but Aaron burned the incense and made atonement for them. He stood between the living and the dead until the plague was stopped.

NUMBERS 16:47-48

When President Reagan narrowly survived an assassination attempt on March 30, 1981, he was rushed to a Washington D.C. hospital, critically wounded. When his wife, Nancy, arrived, Reagan quipped, with rare humor, "Honey, I forgot to duck." People who are fired upon at such short range usually don't get a chance to duck. In fact, they rarely manage to dodge a bullet at all. If they are fortunate enough to do so, they take extra care in the future.

The children of Israel dodged a major bullet, figuratively, when Korah and his rebel followers challenged the leadership of Moses and Aaron—or, more accurately, the Lord's leadership. When Moses and Aaron realized the depth of the Lord's anger against the people of Israel, they "fell face down on the ground. 'O, God, the God and source of all life,' they pleaded. 'Must you be angry with all the people when only one man sins?'" (Num. 16:22). The Lord responded to their intercession by warning the people to steer clear of Korah and his fellow conspirators. When the earth opened up and swallowed them, the people "dodged the bullet."

Amazingly, however, "the very next morning the whole community began muttering again against Moses and Aaron, saying, 'You two have killed the Lord's people!'" (16:41). Some people never learn! If Moses and Aaron at this point had thrown up their hands and resigned, it would have been perfectly understandable! They had been falsely accused of abusing their powers in the first place. They had responded by opening themselves up to public scrutiny in which they had been thoroughly vindicated. They had graciously intervened on behalf of the people and saved them from a terrible fate. And they had been instrumental in allowing the people to see that the Lord really was at work in their midst. In return, they were accused of killing the Lord's people!

But they did not quit. Instead, "Moses said to Aaron, 'Quick, take an incense burner and place burning coals on it from the altar. Lay incense on it and carry it quickly among the people to make atonement for them'" (16:46). With the plague already raging, Aaron "stood between the living and the dead until the plague was stopped" (16:48).

The leadership of Moses and Aaron was questioned by lesser men, but their behavior in the midst of disaster and their performance of a thankless task among unthankful people were exemplary. They literally stood between the living and the dead and didn't duck—or even flinch! You don't criticize such leadership—you follow it.

TO READ: *Numbers 17:1–13*

GOD AND AUTHORITY

"Put these staffs in the Tabernacle in front of the Ark of the Covenant, where I meet with you. Buds will sprout on the staff belonging to the man I choose. Then I will finally put an end to this murmuring and complaining against you."

NUMBERS 17:4-5

We love to grumble about the government, but there is one thing worse than government—having no government at all. A state of anarchy has existed from time to time in countries like Sudan, Rwanda, Burundi, and Indonesia, where law and order collapsed and fear, violence, carnage, and destruction took over. Although we may not like those in authority, we need them to keep the peace.

There came a time in Israel's history when there was such a breakdown in law and order that "the people did whatever seemed right in their own eyes" (Judges 21:25). Those who resented being told what they could or could not do no doubt enjoyed the freedom to live without restrictions and enthusiastically indulge themselves in unrestrained living. This was not a new state of affairs. The Israelites had, throughout their history, shown a marked preference for the freedom to do what they wanted and a definite distaste for authority in any form. Even in the early days, after their remarkable deliverance from slavery of Egypt, when one would have thought they would be ecstatic about divine leadership and direction, they showed a constitutional aversion to God's leadership through Moses and Aaron.

The issue was of such magnitude to God that he explained to Moses how to "put an end to their complaints against me and prevent any further deaths" (Num. 17:10). It is important to note that the people's complaints against Moses and Aaron were, in God's view, complaints against him. Moses and Aaron were not self-appointed or democratically elected; they were divinely ordained. So to question them was to question God, and to rebel against them was to rebel against the Holy One of Israel.

The Israelites were reluctant to accept God's authority through Moses and Aaron, so God determined that a showdown was necessary. He instructed Moses to collect "wooden staffs, one from each of Israel's ancestral tribes" (17:2). These staffs represented the leader of each tribe. Then Moses stored them in the tabernacle, per the Lord's instructions. On returning the next morning, the staff belonging to Aaron and the tribe of Levi "had sprouted, blossomed, and produced almonds!" (17:8). Of all the leaders of Israel, when it came down to the priesthood, Aaron was God's man—the main man. It wasn't that Aaron's rod was special. Aaron was special because God had appointed him—and the miraculous rod was God's way of showing it to the people beyond doubt.

In our times, men still resent authority and much prefer the absence of restrictions. They fondly imagine that this leads to freedom and fullness of life. Granted, authority can be abused, and oppression can result. But rightly understood and appropriately applied, authority is divinely delegated for man's good. Man may not like it—but God insists on it. A man may think that doing what seems right in his own eyes is the way to go. Sadly, he doesn't see it is the way to go downhill—rapidly!

TO READ: *Numbers 20:1-13*

MIRACLE AT MERIBAH

Then [Moses] and Aaron summoned the people to come and gather at the rock.
"Listen, you rebels!" he shouted. "Must we bring you water from this rock?" . . .
But the LORD said to Moses and Aaron, "Because you did not trust me enough
to demonstrate my holiness to the people of Israel, you will not lead them
into the land I am giving them!"

NUMBERS 20:10, 12

That a great miracle occurred at Meribah cannot be disputed. The vast crowd of Israelites traveling through the barren wilderness had come to the end of their tethers—and their water supply. So they did what came naturally. They blamed Moses and Aaron and delivered yet another litany of woes and complaints. They stated, rather obviously, "This land has no grain, figs, grapes, or pomegranates. And there is no water to drink!" (Num. 20:5). We cannot, of course, minimize the seriousness of their predicament—no water in a barren wilderness spells disaster. Moses and Aaron did not dismiss the complaints. They went immediately to the tabernacle and prostrated themselves in prayer before the Lord. What else could they do?

The Lord instructed them to assemble the people and "command the rock over there to pour out its water. You will get enough water from the rock to satisfy all the people and their livestock" (20:8). The rock poured forth its water as promised, the people and their livestock were satisfied as predicted, and every one went home happy! Right? Wrong!

While the great miracle took place, something else of great significance happened, too. Moses and Aaron, after forty long years leading the people through the wilderness, were banned from entering the Promised Land. This surprising turn of events happened because, as the Lord explained to Moses and Aaron, "You did not trust me enough to demonstrate my holiness to the people of Israel" (20:12). The problem was a lack of trust which in some way detracted from the wonder of God's action on behalf of his people. But what exactly was this lack of trust? It was betrayed by what Moses said, perhaps in a fit of frustration and temper: "'Listen, you rebels!' he shouted. 'Must we bring you water out of this rock?'" (20:10). Now, preachers are not supposed to talk to their people like that, but Moses' intemperate language was not the problem. The issue was that Moses was implying that bringing water out of rocks was *his* specialty—not God's.

At this point God had had enough of Moses. God's whole purpose in allowing the people to come to the point of desperation in the water shortage was to show his "holiness"—his uniqueness. Moses had spoiled that by implying that he was doing the job.

It is sad that the miracle of rushing water was ruined by what gushed out of Moses' mouth. Men who speak rashly and react impulsively run the risk of, like Moses, missing out on God's best!

RELATIVE VALUES

But the king of Edom said, "Stay out of my land or I will meet you with an army!"
. . . Because Edom refused to allow Israel to pass through their country,
Israel was forced to turn around.

NUMBERS 20:18, 21

W e can choose our friends, even if we do not have a similar freedom of choice with our relatives. In many instances, our closest friends are also our nearest relatives, but experience shows that it is not uncommon for tensions to exist between those who share a common heritage and genetics! In an extended family, quite often the origins of the tensions are long past, but succeeding generations keep the tensions alive by recounting, and even exaggerating, slights and insults. In extreme instances, bloody conflict has resulted.

Strong tensions existed between the Israelites and the Edomites. They were "relatives" (20:14), having descended from the brothers Jacob and Esau. But Esau's unresolved enmity toward Jacob became Edom's bitter grudge against Jacob's descendants. If Edom and Israel could have stayed out of each other's way, all would have been well. But in the long march from Egypt to the Promised Land, the land of Edom offered a convenient route. So Moses "sent ambassadors to the king of Edom" (20:14), courteously asking permission for the Israelites to travel through Edomite territory. He reminded them of their blood relationship, he recounted Israel's hardships and the blessings of divine intervention, and he promised that no harm would come to either the economy or the infrastructure of the land. The king of Edom not only rejected the request but threatened military action if Moses and his people trespassed. Faced with a fight, the Israelites, deciding in this instance that "discretion is the better part of valor," turned around and embarked on yet another wearisome detour.

While it was understandable that the king of Edom was nervous about allowing this vast crowd of people, along with their flocks and herds, to traverse his land, the extent and manner of his reaction speaks volumes about his state of mind. Deep antagonisms were at work. Otherwise, he would have mixed his natural trepidation with concern for the well-being of his relatives, and would have made some attempt to help them even if he couldn't allow them to go through the territory.

Perhaps the Edomites were still smarting over the way that Esau, their forefather, had been mistreated by his brother Jacob, the forefather of the Israelites, years before, and they had not been willing to "let bygones be bygones." In such cases someone needs to decide enough is enough, and instead of prolonging the estrangement, take steps to resolve the tension.

It may not always be possible to make your relatives your best friends, but it is surely worth working hard to ensure they aren't your worst enemies.

TO READ: *Numbers 21:1-20*

SERPENT ON A POLE

Then the LORD told him, "Make a replica of a poisonous snake and attach it to the top of a pole. Those who are bitten will live if they simply look at it!" So Moses made a snake out of bronze and attached it to the top of a pole. Whenever those who were bitten looked at the bronze snake, they recovered!

NUMBERS 21:8-9

To the modern mind, serpents hardly seem to be appropriate symbols of healing. And yet to this day, a serpent on a pole is a symbol of the medical profession. Greek mythology tells the story of Aesculapius, a revered healer, who used snakes in his healing practice. Statues of this mythological character show him holding a staff entwined with a serpent. A serpent cult was one of the most common cults in the whole of the Middle East in ancient times. What connection there is between the cult, mythology, and the biblical story of Moses and the serpents is not clear. As we shall see, however, Jesus took the story seriously, and so should we.

The Israelites had once again been disappointed and frustrated, so they reverted to blaming Moses, who himself had just been dealt the shattering blow that he would not be allowed into the Promised Land. The people complained about everything, including the food that God miraculously provided for them on a daily basis. So they were exposed to the snakes, many were bitten, and not a few died.

The people recognized that their sinfulness had contributed to their predicament, so they repented and begged Moses to pray for them, which he did. Moses received word from the Lord: "Make a replica of a poisonous snake and attach it to the top of a pole. Those who are bitten will live if they simply look at it!" (Num. 21:8). The result was astounding. "Whenever those who were bitten looked at the bronze snake, they recovered!" (21:9). Those who looked at the pole in obedience to God's word and in dependence upon God's promise were healed.

Apparently, Moses' snake on a pole was preserved for future generations. In the time of Hezekiah, it became an object of idolatrous worship (2 Kings 18:4). The people had succumbed to the age-old problem of substituting an aid to worship in place of the one to be worshiped. They were venerating a bronze snake on a wooden pole instead of trusting the eternal God on the heavenly throne.

Centuries later, Jesus told Nicodemus, "As Moses lifted up the bronze snake on a pole in the wilderness, so I, the Son of Man, must be lifted up on a pole, so that everyone who believes in me will have eternal life" (John 3:14-15). Jesus was repeating the age-old principle of blessing. It is God who heals both body and soul in response to faith and obedience, in the context of his eternal plan. And he regularly uses both modern medicine and old fashioned preaching to do it!

ONE DAY
IN THE SANCTUARY

*Then one day I went into your sanctuary, O God, and I thought about the destiny of
the wicked. Truly, you put them on a slippery path and send them sliding over the
cliff to destruction. . . . Their present life is only a dream that is gone when they
awake. When you arise, O Lord, you will make them vanish from this life.*

PSALM 73:17-18, 20

D o you remember Idi Amin, the infamous butcher of Uganda? The last I heard, he
was sitting by a pool in Saudi Arabia, watching satellite television. How about
Papa Doc, the ousted Haitian dictator? He settled down in a nice villa in the south of
France. Some people sure land on their feet!

Wherever Asaph the psalm writer looked, he saw that "the proud . . . prosper despite
their wickedness" (Ps. 73:3). They seem to be immune from pain, they enjoy good health,
they appear to be trouble-free, they make money effortlessly, they have "everything their
hearts could ever wish for" (73:7), and all the time they "scoff and speak only evil . . . they
boast against the very heavens, and their words strut throughout the earth" (73:9). In stark
contrast, Asaph, who had tried to live rightly before the Lord, testified, "All I get is trouble
all day long; every morning brings me pain" (73:14). He had to admit, "I envied the proud
when I saw them prosper despite their wickedness" (73:3). It was a great mystery to him
that the lives of the godless were trouble-free, while the lives of the godly were trouble-
filled. This mystery so perplexed Asaph that he found himself being dragged down with
envy, even questioning, "Was it for nothing that I kept my heart pure and kept myself from
doing wrong?" (73:13). Like the godly people around him, he was "dismayed and
confused," asking, "Does God realize what is going on?" (73:10-11).

"Then one day," Asaph wrote," I went into your sanctuary, O God, and I thought
about the destiny of the wicked" (73:17). Going into the place of worship and into God's
presence removed Asaph from a purely materialistic, secular environment, which had deeply
permeated his thinking, and refocused his attention on such spiritual issues as "destiny" and
the meaning of this "present life" (73:17, 20). When material benefits and secular pleasures
dominated his thinking and became the criteria by which he evaluated the "good life," he
knew nothing but despair and disillusionment. But when he remembered that life is more
than "things," he recognized that those who have it so good really are not having such a
good time after all—"their present life is only a dream that is gone when they awake" (73:20).

But Asaph still needed reassurance that the godly life is the right life. He began to
think realistically: "My health may fail, and my spirit may grow weak" (73:26). He should
have said "will fail" and "will grow weak." That led him to think about "heaven" and
generated a triumphant exclamation, "Whom have I in heaven but you? I desire you more
than anything on earth" (73:25).

With heaven in his thoughts, Asaph was back on track—sadder and wiser, stronger
and settled, calm and collected, contented and confident. And no longer envying the
godless—more likely, he was pitying them. A visit to God's sanctuary can do that!

TO READ: *Luke 2:25-40*

OLD, BOLD PROPHETS

"I have seen the Savior you have given to all people. He is a light to reveal God to the nations, and he is the glory of your people Israel!"

LUKE 2:30-32

In the fraternity of fliers they say, "There are old pilots, and there are bold pilots. But there are no old, bold pilots." Those who choose to fly by the seat of their pants run the risk of being prematurely laid to their rest.

The same is not necessarily true of prophets. There are old, bold prophets. Simeon is a great example. He had been around a long time and had earned a reputation for righteousness and devotion. "He was filled with the Holy Spirit, and he eagerly expected the Messiah to come and rescue Israel" (Luke 2:25). Although he was advanced in years, he did not spend his time reminiscing about "the good old days." Instead, he "eagerly expected" Messiah's coming and the glory days that would follow. This did not mean he was living an illusion about his days being numbered—he was fully convinced that "he would not die until he had seen the Lord's Messiah" (2:26). As soon as he had seen Jesus, Simeon calmly prayed, "Lord, now I can die in peace!" (2:29). In other words, here was an old man growing old gracefully.

But Simeon was a bold man, too. Referring to the baby Jesus in his arms, he prayed to the Lord in front of Mary and Joseph, with insight born of the Spirit, "He is a light to reveal God to the nations, and he is the glory of your people Israel" (2:32). Bold words, indeed. This baby, according to the bold old man, was none other than the Messiah. In addition to being the glory of Israel, he was about to bring light to the world—to Israel and to lands far beyond Israel. No wonder Joseph and Mary were amazed.

But there was more. Simeon went on, "This child will be rejected by many in Israel, and it will be their undoing" (2:34). Simeon was daring to suggest not only that Messiah was not the exclusive preserve of an elite Judaism, but he was audacious enough to say that sections of Judaism would reject him and Messiah would be their undoing! And, speaking the truth in love, he did not hide from Mary the sobering news, even on this happiest of days, that "a sword will pierce your very soul" (2:35).

Old, bold men speak truth with love in the Spirit out of rich experience. They are national treasures. We need more of them!

AUGUST

TO READ: *Luke 2:41–52*

RAISING AN ADOLESCENT

[Jesus'] parents didn't know what to think. "Son!" his mother said to him. "Why have you done this to us? Your father and I have been frantic, searching for you everywhere." "But why did you need to search?" he asked. "You should have known that I would be in my Father's house." But they didn't understand what he meant.

LUKE 2:48-50

James Dobson, a highly-regarded Christian psychologist and best-selling author on family matters, says, "I used to have four theories and no children. Now I have four children and no theories." Many people have benefited greatly from Dr. Dobson's advice on child rearing. But realistically speaking, raising adolescents is not like drawing a picture by joining the numbers—it is a matter of molding a person, of assisting in the development of a person of eternal worth. And every person is different.

We have very little information about the adolescent years of Jesus. But we do have the account of one telling incident that took place, which is full of great value to modern parents. The twelve-year-old Jesus had traveled from Galilee to Jerusalem for the Passover festival. At the conclusion of the festival, the great crowd of Galileans set out for home through the wilderness of Judea, down to Jericho, and up the Jordan valley. During the first day's journey, Jesus' parents assumed that he was with other friends or relatives among the travelers. It was only at the end of the day that they realized that he was not there. He was missing. So they retraced their steps to Jerusalem (a full day's journey), hunted for him for three days, and eventually came across the boy. He was unperturbed, engaged in theological discussions with the teachers of the law. When they remonstrated with him, he calmly responded, "You should have known that I would be in my Father's house" (Luke 2:49).

Not for the first time was it recorded that a pair of parents talking to their son "didn't understand what he meant" (2:50)! The root of the problem was that the parents did not understand their son and the son had little perception of what was in the parents' hearts. And that is at the root of many problems in raising adolescents.

They all returned to Nazareth, where "he . . . was obedient to them," and Mary "stored all these things in her heart" (2:51). (We don't know what Joseph did, though!) The boy was responsive to parental concerns, while the parent was reflective about the boy's development.

The boy's development took place in a balanced and God-honoring way. He "grew both in height and in wisdom, and he was loved by God and by all who knew him" (2:52). In other words, he developed physically, intellectually, spiritually, and socially. And no parent could ask for more than that.

It is without doubt that this should be the parents' goal. How it is achieved will vary from child to child. But in every case, children need to be responsive, and parents need to be reflective. Imperfect parents never raise perfect kids. But mature parents give their children monumental advantages.

TO READ: *Luke 3:1-20*

THE ETHICS
OF BELIEVING

Prove by the way you live that you have really turned from your sins and turned to God. Don't just say, "We're safe—we're the descendants of Abraham." That proves nothing. God can change these stones here into children of Abraham. Even now the ax of God's judgment is poised, ready to sever your roots. Yes, every tree that does not produce good fruit will be chopped down and thrown into the fire.

LUKE 3:8-9

A small boy was playing on the floor near the radio, which was broadcasting a religious service. As the voice of the minister intoned the words of the Apostles' Creed—"I believe in God . . ."—the small boy, without looking up or even pausing in his play, added, "So do I," and carried on—as if nothing had happened. Obviously familiar with the ritual and at ease with the concept of God, the boy had no difficulty stating his belief. But his statement, which was no doubt true, was strangely empty—it was more reflexive than reflective.

Such an approach to belief in God is perfectly understandable for a small boy. But similar attitudes are as troublesome as they are common in grown people. Many profess to believe in God, but some say it in such a way that it appears to have little impact on the way they live their lives. Their attention is not deviated from the their toys for a fraction of a second. Surely to believe in God should at least give cause for thought and prompt a pause for reflection.

This was one of the concerns of John the Baptist. He spoke out fiercely against the "nominalism" of the religion of his day. His contemporaries not only believed in God, they believed they were God's favorites. "We're safe—we're the descendants of Abraham," they claimed. In a sense they were right; God had made a special covenant with Abraham, and they were indeed Abraham's descendants. But as John pointed out to them, "That proves nothing. God can change these stones here into children of Abraham" (Luke 3:8). Merely to claim a special relationship with God, giving no evidence by living a life of humble submission to God and trust in him is to qualify for divine judgment. John warned them ominously, "Every tree that does not produce good fruit will be chopped down and thrown into the fire" (3:9).

This got the attention of John's hearers! When they asked what they should do (3:10), John explained that they should *demonstrate* that they had "turned from their sins and turned to God to be forgiven" (3:3). They would demonstrate that they were changed by changing the way they treated other people (3:11-14).

Truly forgiven sinners are thoroughly repentant and deeply changed people. They do not continue callously in their sin, nor do they embrace carelessly their forgiveness. Instead, they learn to hate the sin they loved, and they start to love the people they despised. The wealthy become generous, the corrupt become honest, the powerful become gentle, the discontented become satisfied, and the merciless become merciful. All this because they truly believe. To paraphrase John, "Let those whose belief does not behave beware!"

TO READ: *Luke 4:1-13*

RESISTING TEMPTATION

Then Jesus, full of the Holy Spirit, left the Jordan River. He was led by the Spirit
to go out into the wilderness, where the Devil tempted him for forty days.
He ate nothing all that time and was very hungry.

LUKE 4:1-2

The comedian Flip Wilson used to impersonate a lady called Geraldine, who explained that nothing was really her fault because, she said, "The devil made me do it!" In more sophisticated terms, the brilliant and tragic Irishman, Oscar Wilde, wrote in *Lady Windermere's Fan*, "I couldn't help it. I can resist everything except temptation." Wilde and Wilson had little in common, but they did share one thing: an apparent belief that temptation is something that happens to people, against which they are defenseless, and for which they cannot be held accountable.

Scripture flatly disagrees. Temptation is real, but must not be casually dismissed as inevitable or helplessly yielded to as invincible. Temptation is an integral part of life, intentionally permitted by God, designed to present men with an opportunity to decide between doing what is right and choosing to go wrong. Temptation overcome is a test passed with flying colors, while being overcome by temptation is a craven capitulation to evil and a resounding defeat for good.

Jesus showed the way to triumph over temptation. Hungry, tired, and lonely after forty days and nights fasting in the wilderness, he was offered the chance to break his fast by changing a stone into a loaf of bread. It was a not-so-subtle temptation to take matters into his own hands rather than to trust the one into whose hands he was committed. His response—"People need more than bread for their life" (Luke 4:4)—showed he was not about to desert God for bread. Jesus 1, Satan 0.

Next, Jesus was offered power and status in return for believing a lie and perpetrating fraudulent worship. His response—"You must worship the Lord your God; serve only him" (4:8)—rebuffed the devil and reaffirmed his commitment to truth and his disdain for the abuse of power and prestige. Jesus 2, Satan 0.

Finally, Jesus was offered the chance to "prove" his faith by an act of sheer irresponsibility. Standing on the "highest point of the Temple" he was encouraged to "jump off" (4:9)—an act purportedly legitimized by a doubtful application of Psalm 91. He responded, "Do not test the Lord your God" (4:12). Jesus 3, Satan 0. So the Devil retreated—for a while.

It may be objected that we are not Jesus, so we cannot be expected to stand against Satan. It can legitimately be said in response that we don't face Satan as he did, either. But more significantly, we do have the Spirit and we do have God's Word. Jesus overcame by "the Holy Spirit's power" (4:14) and deft use of "the Scriptures." By God's grace, we can do that!

TO READ: *Luke 4:14-30*

FAITHFUL AND FICKLE

[Jesus] taught in their synagogues and was praised by everyone. . . .
When they heard [what he said], the people in the synagogue were furious.
Jumping up, they mobbed him and took him to the edge of the hill on which
the city was built. They intended to push him over the cliff.

LUKE 4:15, 28-29

The ballplayer who scores the winning goal in one game and makes a fatal mistake in the next game goes from hero to goat in a hurry. The problem does not so much lie with him. He is doing his best both when he scores the winning goal and when he inadvertently makes an error. When he scores he is not Superman, and when he errs he is only human. The problem lies with the crowd. They praise him to the heights one minute and consign him to the depths the next. When they like what he does, they're faithful to him; but when things go wrong, their fickleness shows.

No one knew the fickleness of the crowds better than Jesus. On returning from his encounter with the evil one in the wilderness, he soon became very well-known and well-liked in the region of Galilee. "He taught in their synagogues and was praised by everyone" (Luke 4:15). When Jesus revisited his boyhood home, Nazareth, he was asked to read the Scriptures in the synagogue and he startled everyone by making a direct application of Isaiah's words to himself. At the end of the reading from Isaiah 61:1-2, he said, "This Scripture has come true today before your very eyes!" (4:21). The people in his hometown synagogue reacted with appreciation for the "gracious words that fell from his lips" (4:22) and with incredulity, for they knew his background and could not understand how he could say what he was saying. But nevertheless, "All who were there spoke well of him" (4:22).

Jesus, however, began to challenge them in ways that they did not appreciate. He made it clear to them that in the same way that Elijah and Elisha had not performed their ministries in Israel, so he had not performed his miracles in his hometown, because "no prophet is accepted in his hometown" (4:24). By this he meant—and the people knew it— that just as Israel was unprepared to respond to Elijah and Elisha, so also Jesus' neighbors in Nazareth were unwilling to respond to his message. On hearing this, they "were furious. Jumping up, they mobbed him and took him to the edge of the hill on which the city was built. They intended to push him over the cliff" (4:28-29). Talk about a fickle crowd!

It is unlikely that you will be pushed off a cliff today, but it is possible that you will tell a friend the truth and have him go off the deep end! Both fans and friends can be fickle when faced with facts.

TO READ: *Luke 4:31–41*

AUTHORITY
AND POWER

Jesus cut him short. "Be silent!" he told the demon. "Come out of the man!" The demon threw the man to the floor as the crowd watched; then it left him without hurting him further. Amazed, the people exclaimed, "What authority and power this man's words possess! Even evil spirits obey him and flee at his command!"

LUKE 4:35-36

What's the difference between an ineffective teacher and a school yard bully? The former has authority without power, while the latter has power without authority. The teacher, by virtue of his position, can rightly expect to be treated with respect and courtesy. Should this courtesy not be forthcoming, he has the power to enforce his wishes on recalcitrant pupils. Should he, however, be intimidated by his pupils, or lack the support of his superiors, he may be unwilling or unable to enforce his authority. So, clothed with authority, he is stripped of power.

On the other hand, the bully knows how to throw his weight around and to get people to do what he wishes them to do. He has no right to do this, but what he lacks in authority he more than makes up in power. Our world is full of ineffective authorities and highly effective bullies.

When Jesus went to Capernaum, he taught the people and they remarked that "he spoke with authority" (Luke 4:32). This was clearly illustrated in the way he dealt with "a man possessed by a demon" (4:33). Jesus ordered the confrontational demon, "Be silent! . . . Come out of the man!" (4:35). And the demon did. The response of the crowd was, "What authority and power this man's words possess!" (4:36). Jesus was neither an ineffective teacher nor an unrestrained tyrant. He possessed all the authority of heaven, and through the Spirit he had all the power to go with it.

Modern-day disciples need to be fully versed in the subject of their authority and power. Once they take upon themselves the name of Christ by responding to his call, they receive the blessed Holy Spirit. At once they possess both power and authority. As they speak Christ's word and take their stand in his name, they are invested with his authority. To the extent that they rightly represent the words that Christ spoke, they speak his authoritative word. As they rightly represent him and his cause, it is in his name that they function. They lack nothing in authority. They must believe it and live in the good of it! But in order to show the reality of their claim to the authority of Christ, they must also demonstrate the power of Christ's Spirit in their lives. The Spirit indwells them to empower them. So, conscious of their calling and empowering, modern-day disciples go about their lives. They do not live like intimidated teachers or schoolyard bullies, but as followers of him of whom it was said, "What authority and power this man's words possess!" Their power and authority belong to Christ, in whose name they go forth.

THE SURROUNDING LORD

Just as the mountains surround and protect Jerusalem, so the LORD surrounds and protects his people, both now and forever.

PSALM 125:2

A nyone who has served in the military and has endured a route march knows that it helps to sing as you go. Drill instructors are well aware of this, and they encourage the men to sing—usually songs with inappropriate lyrics.

The pilgrims making their way up the rugged hills of Judea to the city of Jerusalem also knew that singing helped them along their way. But the songs they sang were in a nobler vein. They focused on the purpose of the march. The pilgrims were heading to the holy city, to house of the Lord, to worship. The songs they sang were called "songs for the ascent," because they were written to be sung on the way up through the mountains to Jerusalem to celebrate one of the festivals. Psalm 125 is one of these songs.

As the worshipers made their way toward Jerusalem, it would not escape their attention that the city was ringed by mountains. From a military point of view, Jerusalem was strategically placed in a position that was readily defensible. This led the pilgrim-worshipers to sing, "Those who trust in the Lord are as secure as Mount Zion" (Ps. 125:1). Living in days when they were never far from invading armies or marauding bands of robbers, the pilgrims to Jerusalem were extremely conscious of their security while traveling. Mount Zion was as secure as you could get in those days, but living in the Lord was far more secure. So they sang, "Just as the mountains surround and protect Jerusalem, so the Lord surrounds and protects his people, both now and forever" (Ps. 125:2). The reason for this triumphant attitude, mirrored in their joyful singing, was simply that they knew that "the wicked will not rule the godly, for then the godly might be forced to do wrong" (Ps. 125:3). By this they did not mean that the godly were immune to trouble and exempt from the blows and batterings of evil men. Far from it. But it did mean that the Lord who encircled them was presiding over them even in their troubles and would not leave them defenseless. As requested, the Lord could be trusted to hear the prayer, "Do good to those who are good, whose hearts are in tune with you" (125:4). And he could be trusted to respond positively.

Those who preferred to "turn to crooked ways" (125:5) were free to do so, for the Lord does not force himself on anyone. But the crooked must expect eventually to be banished from the Lord's presence. Not so those who "trust in the Lord" (125:1). They will have "quietness and peace" (125:5)—they will relax in the special knowledge that they are secure in the Lord.

So, even if today you are going uphill—try singing as you go.

TO READ: *Joshua 1:1–18*

SELF-INTEREST

Then Joshua called together the tribes of Reuben, Gad, and the half-tribe of Manasseh. He told them, . . . "Your wives, children, and cattle may remain here on the east side of the Jordan River, but your warriors, fully armed, must lead the other tribes across the Jordan to help them conquer their territory."

JOSHUA 1:12, 14

S ome people think that God gave Israel two commandments when he told them to love their neighbors as they loved themselves. Command number one—love yourself. Command number two—love your neighbors. The argument goes that, as some people have a low self-image, they need to learn how to love themselves before they can love anybody else. But apart from the fact that Scripture says nothing of the sort, common sense tells us that everybody, however low his or her self-image, is governed to a certain extent by self-interest and instincts for self-preservation. The reality is that self-interest is behind much that makes the world go round.

Self-interest was a reality in the ancient world, too. On their way to the Promised Land, the children of Israel passed through and conquered territory that lay on the eastern shores of the Jordan river. Some of the men involved in the fighting decided that they would prefer to stay there rather than go ahead with the rest of the people, crossing the Jordan and starting the slow and painful task of occupying the land God had given them. After all, they had large flocks and herds, it was good land, and it was there for the taking! So they asked to be excused from the occupation of Canaan and to be allowed to settle down, secure their families, and get on with the business of living their lives. Self-interest was ruling supreme!

Moses was not at all pleased when he heard their request, and he told them in no uncertain terms that they were just like the people who had turned back from entering the land forty years earlier. He called them "a brood of sinners, doing exactly the same thing" (Num. 32:14). Moses also said, "Do you mean you want to stay back here while your brothers go across and do all the fighting?" (Num. 32:6). He obviously suspected self-interest was at work! But the tribesmen replied, "We simply want to build sheepfolds for our flocks and fortified cities for our wives and children. Then we will arm ourselves and lead our fellow Israelites into battle until we have brought them safely to their inheritance" (Num. 32:16-17). Since they were willing to bear their share of the burden of fighting, Moses agreed to their proposal. Joshua reminded them, the tribesmen kept their promise, and self-interest was subsumed by the Lord's interest in his work and by the interests of others. And this is how they loved the Lord and their neighbors as they loved themselves.

The instinct for self-preservation is fine. Self-interest is here to stay. But self-absorption has to be seen for what it is—immaturity run rampant. Caring for and loving others sacrificially is the only way to grow.

TO READ: *Joshua 3:1-17*

TRIAL BY WATER

Now it was the harvest season, and the Jordan was overflowing its banks. But as soon as the feet of the priests who were carrying the Ark touched the water at the river's edge, the water began piling up at a town upstream called Adam, which is near Zarethan. And the water below that point flowed on to the Dead Sea until the riverbed was dry. Then all the people crossed over near the city of Jericho.

JOSHUA 3:15-16

I n Western courts of law, the adversarial system is supposed to establish the innocence or guilt of the accused. The prosecution presents its case, the defense challenges it and presents its own version of events, and then the judge or jury evaluates the evidence and arrives at a verdict. There have been too many examples of the innocent being condemned and the guilty being released for one to place total confidence in the system as it stands, but it is much to be preferred to the methods used in the ancient Near East. The courts in those days determined the guilt or innocence of the accused by simply throwing him into a river. If the accused drowned, he was guilty; if he didn't, he was innocent! It was called trial by water.

Joshua told the children of Israel as they were approaching the Jordan River at flood tide, "Today you will know that the living God is among you"(Josh. 3:10). Joshua was referring to a trial by water that the Lord himself would pass through. The priests were ordered to make ready "the Ark of the Covenant, which belongs to the Lord of the whole earth" (3:11) and carry it into the middle of the Jordan. The symbolism was powerful—the Lord himself was taking his stand in the water. It was his trial by water. "As soon as the feet of the priests who were carrying the Ark touched the water at the river's edge, the water began piling up at a town upstream called Adam. . . . And the water below that point flowed on to the Dead Sea until the riverbed was dry" (3:15-16). The people passed over and the ark was delivered to dry land. Most significantly, the Lord was shown to be "the living God," not only to Israel but also to the terrified inhabitants of the neighborhood whose last hope of stopping the encroaching Israelite army—the Jordan River—had not only failed to stop them but had provided evidence of the uniqueness of the Lord and his people.

The people of Israel had heard from their forefathers about the crossing of the Red Sea, but that was their parents' story. The new generation needed their own demonstration of the Lord's power and sovereignty—and the Lord gave it to them.

Each generation needs to learn the lessons of history—the story of God's dealing with his people through the ages—but it also needs to see in its own time, in its own way, the evidence that the Lord is still "the living God" who stands against all opposition and proves he is Lord. And God provides it!

227

TO READ: *Joshua 4:1-24*

MEMORIALS

"We will use these stones to build a memorial. In the future, your children will ask,
'What do these stones mean to you?' Then you can tell them, 'They remind us that
the Jordan River stopped flowing when the Ark of the Lord's covenant went across.'
These stones will stand as a permanent memorial among the people of Israel."

JOSHUA 4:6-7

T he Vietnam Memorial and the Tomb of the Unknown Soldier in Washington remind people of the men and women who lost their lives in the service of their country. In the same way, the Cenotaph in Whitehall, London, brings to remembrance those whose lives were summarily cut short in the cause of protecting and serving their homeland. Sculptures in lands around the world are designed to help people remember the heroes of the past. But it is all too easy for succeeding generations to become so familiar with the memorials that their significance is lost. In most people's minds, Memorial Day in America has nothing to do with foreign wars and everything to do with the beginning of summer! But in forgetting our history, we not only overlook the great cost of the benefits we enjoy, but we also may repeat the mistakes of the past which we failed to learn. Memorials have a major purpose.

God told his ancient people to build memorials at significant times. He wanted them to be able to recall significant events. Few events were more significant to the Israelites than the crossing of Jordan. It marked the end of forty desperately sad years and the beginning of a new era—life in the land of ancient promise. So the Lord told Joshua to organize twelve men representing the twelve tribes, who would each take a stone from the middle of Jordan and "use these stones to build a memorial" (Josh. 4:6). The memorial was built to be a reminder: "In the future, your children will ask, 'What do these stones mean to you?' Then you can tell them, 'They remind us that the Jordan River stopped flowing when the Ark of the Lord's covenant went across'" (4:7). The Lord insisted that succeeding generations not be left in the dark about his dealings with his people.

Good parents not only learn the meaning of memorials and pass the meaning on, but they also know the value of creating memories in their own families so that children will not grow up ignorant of their heritage. Good parents go out of their way to stimulate the curiosity of their children in the direction of things the children need to learn. And nothing is more important than children growing up to know the Lord! So good parents thank God for divinely-ordained memorials, like Sunday (the Lord's day to begin each week), and the simple memorial of bread and wine that commemorates the greatest of events. And they pass on the memories to those who, one day, will pass them on again.

TO READ: *Joshua 2:1-21; 6:15-25*

THE VALUE OF ONE

*"The city and everything in it must be completely destroyed as an offering to the
LORD. Only Rahab the prostitute and the others in her house will be spared, for she
protected our spies." . . . So Joshua spared Rahab the prostitute and her relatives who
were with her in the house, because she had hidden the spies Joshua sent to Jericho.
And she lives among the Israelites to this day.*

JOSHUA 6:17, 25

T he award-winning movie *Saving Private Ryan* depicts a courageous attempt to save
the life of an individual soldier in the heat of a great battle. Complete with dramatic
effects and searing portrayals of modern warfare, the movie packs a powerful emotional
punch. It has also garnered its critics, who point out that it is highly unlikely that, in the
heat of modern warfare, a squad of soldiers would be put at risk to save the life of an
individual.

That may be so, but the story of Rahab of Jericho shows that, in God's eyes, the
value of one is immense. When Joshua's spies entered Jericho in order to plan the invasion
and capture of the city, they stayed in the home of Rahab, who then saved their lives. At
great personal risk, she stood between the spies and those who wanted to do them harm.

Rahab's motivation was clear. She told the spies, "the Lord your God is the supreme
God of the heavens above and the earth below" (2:11). She admitted that the people of
Jericho were living in mortal dread of the advancing Israelites, and her actions could have
been construed as nothing more than a "convenient conversion" to save her own skin. But
the spies believed her and promised that she and her family would be saved when the city
was taken, provided she identified her home clearly by leaving a "scarlet rope hanging
from the window" (2:18).

Rahab did what she was instructed and the Israelites did what they had promised. In
the dreadful battle that ensued, as the invaders "charged straight into the city from every
side and captured it" and then set about completely destroying it (6:20-21), Rahab and her
family were neither forgotten nor overlooked. Somebody was given the task of finding her
home in the chaos of battle, fighting through to her side, and physically taking her out of
harm's way. Why? Precisely because the men of Israel were men of their word and she was
valuable in the Lord's eyes.

How valuable was she? Incredibly, Rahab appears in the genealogy of the Lord Jesus
(see Matt. 1:5). Despite her troubled past, both the writer of Hebrews (Heb. 11:31) and
James (James 2:25) speak of her as an example of faith at work.

In the heat of battle, individuals are often expendable. In the warm heart of God,
though, individuals are never expendable. Each of us is of infinite worth to him. And in
the clashing strife of modern life, God never loses sight of those who belong to him.

TO READ: *Joshua 14:1–15*

HALFHEARTED OR WHOLEHEARTED

"But my brothers who went with me frightened the people and discouraged them
from entering the Promised Land. For my part, I followed the LORD my God
completely. So that day Moses promised me, 'The land of Canaan on which you were
just walking will be your special possession and that of your descendants forever,
because you wholeheartedly followed the LORD my God.'"

JOSHUA 14:8-9

A s an athletic contest approaches its closing stages and the contestants are neck-and-neck, it is often a matter of who wants it most, of who is the hungriest! If there is nothing to choose between the physical abilities, the conditioning, and the skills of the athletes, the winning edge frequently comes down to a matter of heart—where desire and determination dwell, where commitment and courage reside.

If heart makes the difference in athletic contests, then it makes a world of difference in spiritual experience. Take Caleb, a man who "wholeheartedly followed the Lord [his] God" (Josh. 14:9). At the age of eighty-five, he was still recognized and respected for his commitment. Born in the land of Egypt of parents living in servitude, Caleb had at some point in his life determined to be a wholehearted follower of the Lord. He had plenty of examples of halfhearted followers around him. No doubt a recognition of their ambivalence, married to his convictions about the Lord, had determined for him that nothing less than a complete commitment of life to the Lord was acceptable.

The kind of commitment Caleb had in mind meant that he remained committed in bad times as well as good. It sustained him through the short-term and in the long haul. When others backed off out of fear, he pressed on out of faith. Obstacles that deterred others spurred him on. Promises by God were to be claimed to the full. He did not ask for help to rid the enemies in his land; he simply asked for a chance to take them on and "drive them out . . . just as the Lord said" (14:12). And when difficulties arose, he was not to be found in the pack but out front, saying his piece and leading his men (see Num. 14:5-9, 24).

It has often been pointed out that there are at least three kinds of men: Those who make things happen; those who watch things happening; and those who ask, "What happened?" No prizes need be awarded for recognizing to which group Caleb belonged!

Can a constitutionally halfhearted person become a wholehearted follower of the Lord? If so, what does it take? The answer is this: If God is who he says he is and can be trusted to do what he had promised, then he is worthy of our loving, trusting obedience. That is the stuff from which wholeheartedness is made.

TO READ: *Joshua 23:1-16*

THE DANGER
OF SUCCESS

*"The LORD has driven out great and powerful nations for you, and no one has yet
been able to defeat you. Each one of you will put to flight a thousand of the enemy,
for the LORD your God fights for you, just as he has promised.
So be very careful to love the LORD your God."*

JOSHUA 23:9-11

Yesterday's victories do not guarantee tomorrow's triumphs. Napoleon's string of victories was stopped at Waterloo, and Hitler's relentless eastward march came to an end in the ruins of Stalingrad. The champions of any sport know that all winning streaks come to an end, and even the most successful salesman knows that one day he will not be able to close the deal.

Sometimes the heady atmosphere of continual victory contributes to the factors that lead to eventual defeat. Appropriate confidence degenerates into unseemly cockiness, healthy respect for the opposition hardens into unhealthy disparagement, and careful preparation gives way to careless attitudes and a casual approach.

Joshua, the seasoned general, knew this. His fighting forces had tasted the thrills of victory over an extended period. So toward the end of his life, Joshua reminded the leadership of Israel, "The Lord has driven out great and powerful nations for you, and no one has yet been able to defeat you" (Josh. 23:9). The emphasis was on the Lord, so he added, "The Lord your God fights for you, just as he has promised" (23:10). It seems unthinkable that the Israelites, whose victories had been so spectacular that they were unmistakably the work of the Lord, would ever overlook their complete dependence on divine intervention in their affairs. But victorious armies do grow careless, and winning teams do get away from the things that brought them success. Israel was no exception. So, Joshua insisted, "Be very careful to love the Lord your God" (23:11). Winning the war is one thing, maintaining the peace quite another. But the same principle of trusting, obeying, and loving the Lord applies to both.

Joshua had the foresight to recognize that victorious Israel could fall on its face. He recognized that there were still undefeated enemies in their midst who would dearly love to bring Israel's winning streak to an end. So he posited the unthinkable possibility that the day might dawn when the Lord would "no longer drive [the enemies] out," and he warned that they could become "a snare and a trap to you, a pain in your side and a thorn in your eyes, and you will be wiped out from this good land the Lord your God has given you" (23:13).

Joshua did not envision that the triumphant Israelite army would suddenly become incompetent, or that their experienced leaders would mysteriously lose their strategic skills. It was more serious than that. He saw a day when the armies might discount the Lord and become so sure of themselves that they would no longer love him and honor him, when they would slide into compromise and lapse into disobedience and head for disaster. That's the way to guarantee that yesterday's victories turn into tomorrow's defeats. It is a way of snatching defeat from the jaws of victory!

TO READ: *Psalm 27*

CONVERSATIONS WITH THE LORD

Listen to my pleading, O LORD. Be merciful and answer me! My heart has heard you say, "Come and talk with me." And my heart responds, "LORD, I am coming."

PSALM 27:7-8

When Billy Graham was a young evangelist, he was invited to meet with Winston Churchill during the Harringay Crusade in London, the great British wartime leader. He was no doubt surprised and gratified to receive such an invitation. Although he has maintained strict confidentiality concerning the details of his meeting with the Prime Minister, Dr. Graham has spoken about his feelings as he was ushered into the Prime Minister's residence at 10 Downing Street. In the presence of eminence, the young Graham felt uncertain, perhaps even inadequate.

King David, too, received an invitation one day that delighted him, but which no doubt caused him to feel some uncertainty, too. David records, "My heart has heard you say, 'Come and talk with me.' And my heart responds, 'Lord, I am coming'" (Ps. 27:8). An invitation to "come and talk with" the Lord! David was totally aware of the eminence and majesty of the Lord, and he needed no one to remind him of his humble origins as a shepherd boy outside Bethlehem. He doubtless had overwhelming feelings of inadequacy as he made his way into the sanctuary to have his talk with the Lord.

But David remembered, "The Lord is my light and my salvation—so why should I be afraid? The Lord protects me from danger—so why should I tremble?" (27:1). David was invited to converse with the one who had repeatedly shown that he was firmly on David's side. So he could approach the meeting, not casually or flippantly, but not fearfully or in trepidation either. Quietly and confidently, he could come before the Lord and say what was on his mind.

And what was on his mind? David wanted more than anything else to learn the secret of living in the conscious enjoyment of the Lord's presence. "The one thing I ask of the Lord—the thing I seek most—is to live in the house of the Lord all the days of my life, delighting in the Lord's perfections and meditating in his Temple" (27:4). This is an unusual request for a king, a warrior, an active man, a man of the people. But it is a genuine and heartfelt expression of deep spiritual longing for a closer walk with the Lord! David wanted to talk to the Lord about the uncertainties of his life and to seek assurance of the Lord's continued direction, oversight, and protection in his life. "Do not hide yourself from me," he asked. "Teach me how to live, O Lord" (27:9, 11).

Every man has an open invitation to have a conversation with God. It is an invitation to open his heart to the Lord and to say what is on his mind! It is a strange man who passes on such an invitation.

TO READ: *Ruth 1:14-22*

BITTERNESS AND GRACE

But Ruth replied, "Don't ask me to leave you and turn back. I will go wherever you go and live wherever you live. Your people will be my people, and your God will be my God. . . ." [Naomi told them,] "Don't call me Naomi. Instead, call me Mara, for the Almighty has made life very bitter for me."

RUTH 1:16, 20

F amiliarity with spiritual issues over many years can breed disregard for them. The disciplines of spiritual life can become mundane. Then they are neglected and eventually fall into a state of serious disuse. Prayer is forgotten, worship loses its attraction, and service is burdensome. Estrangement from God's people results. Sometimes a believer of long standing becomes weary of the things of the Lord and wearisome to all around him. By contrast, the new believer is so freshly alive to spiritual reality and so deeply grateful for grace received that he lives joyfully. Prayer is a delight, worship is a joy, service is a privilege, and fellowship is a treat.

What happens when the long-term believer living a joyless and disconsolate life meets a young believer living in the joy of salvation? This seems to have been the situation in the remarkable relationship between Naomi and Ruth. The older woman, a native of Bethlehem, had left with her family during a severe famine. The family had arrived in the land of Moab (traditionally an inhospitable place for people from Judah) and had apparently settled down there for a period of ten years. During this time, her sons had married Moabite women—not the sort of thing that was expected of God's people. Then tragedy struck three times: Naomi not only lost her husband but both her sons as well. Deciding that she had nothing left to live for in Moab, and hearing that times were better in Judah, Naomi determined to return to her hometown.

One of Naomi's daughters-in-law stayed in Moab. The other, Ruth, accompanied her mother-in-law back to Bethelehem. Ruth was utterly committed to her mother-in-law's well-being. She even insisted, "Your people will be my people, and your God will be my God. May the Lord punish me severely if I allow anything but death to separate us!" (Ruth 1:16-17). Ruth had become a devoted follower of Jehovah! She had intentionally turned from the worship of Moabite gods and had turned to the Lord for salvation. Commitment and compassion flowed from her heart—no doubt as a result of her newfound faith.

On arriving in Bethlehem, Naomi refused to answer to her name (which means "pleasant") because, she said, "the Almighty has made life very bitter for me" (1:20). She demanded that henceforth she should be called "Mara" (which means "bitter"). In essence, Naomi was saying, "How can you call my life pleasant? It's been very bitter." The old-time believer had become sadly embittered by life, while the new believer grew sweeter.

In the community of believers, the ones who have traveled the road longest are supposed to show the way to the new arrivals. Sometimes, though, it works the other way around!

TO READ: *Matthew 1:1-17*

FAMILY TREE

Salmon was the father of Boaz (his mother was Rahab). Boaz was the father of Obed (his mother was Ruth). Obed was the father of Jesse.

MATTHEW 1:5

N ot long ago it was customary for families to record their family's history in a special family Bible. Births, deaths, marriages, and other notable events were noted, and this information served as a great and accurate resource for establishing a family tree. Unfortunately, with the demise of family devotions in many homes, old family Bibles have gone the way of the dinosaurs. So genealogies are harder to research and preserve.

In ancient times, however, the maintenance of genealogical records was a matter of great importance. This becomes obvious when we read the biblical records. For instance, Ezra the scribe was identified as "son of Seraiah, son of Azariah," with no less than fourteen other "son of" statements linking him to the first high priest, Aaron (Ezra 7:1-5). There was to be no doubt in anyone's mind that Ezra was a valid member of the priestly fraternity. Similarly, the genealogies of Jesus found in the Gospels are the most important in the Bible—and in some ways the most surprising. Matthew traced Jesus' earthly family all the way back to Abraham and David, while Luke traced the Savior's human origins all the way to Adam. Matthew was anxious to show that Jesus belonged to the royal line of David, while Luke, with his emphasis of Jesus being a descendant of "Adam [who] was the son of God" (Luke 3:38) is much more universal in outlook. But perhaps the most striking thing about either genealogy is Matthew's inclusion of women. Women rarely appeared in Jewish genealogies, yet Matthew included four of them! Not only that, the four women he included were probably considered Gentiles in their day, and each of them had characteristics that made them less than desirable to traditional Jews. Both Tamar and Rahab were prostitutes, Bathsheba was an adulteress, and Ruth was a Moabitess.

We can only speculate why these four women were included. Perhaps Matthew wanted to demonstrate that God uses the most unlikely people to work out his plans. Remarkable! As Paul explained to the Corinthians, God "chose things despised by the world, things counted as nothing at all, and used them to bring to nothing what the world considers important" (1 Cor. 1:28). In the case of Ruth, while she may have come from a despised race and may have been disregarded by many people in her day, she demonstrated a nobility of character that was extraordinary and a faithfulness and a selflessness that were exemplary.

Surely what God looks for is a person whose heart is right before him, regardless of race, class, or even one's past!

MIRACLES

Then the dead boy sat up and began to talk to those around him! And Jesus gave him back to his mother. Great fear swept the crowd, and they praised God, saying, "A mighty prophet has risen among us," and "We have seen the hand of God at work today."

LUKE 7:15-16

M atthew Arnold concluded the preface to the 1883 edition of his monumental work *Literature and Dogma* with the bold statement, "Miracles do not happen." Those more interested in sports than either literature or dogma disagree. They insist that the age of miracles continued to 1969, when the New York Mets won the National League pennant and then went on to win the World Series! Arnold, of course, was serious. The sporting crowd was simply being facetious.

But what are *we* to say about miracles? Miracles are those events for which, according to Western patterns of thinking, there is no immediate natural explanation. Reverent people do not hesitate to attribute them to divine intervention. They reason that God, who made the world and who upholds it, is perfectly free and able to intervene in its affairs and workings whenever and however he wishes, in order to further his own purposes. Those who, like Arnold, have determined that a miracle is not about to happen—for whatever reason—have either dismissed God as reality or banished him to a position of irrelevance as far as this world and its affairs are concerned.

Scripture speaks regularly of miracles, including some of the most dramatic performed by Jesus, himself. They were certainly acts of compassion—as was clearly the case in the raising of the bereft widow's only son from the dead (Luke 7:11-17). But there were many bereft widows with dead sons and an abundance of destitute beggars in Christ's time. And he did not raise or heal them all. He was not selective in his compassion, so apparently he was selective in his demonstrations of power.

Those who are at the opposite end of the scale from Matthew Arnold think that miracles should be normative, that God should be performing them all the time. Miracles by definition are not normative—they are extraordinary! Neither are they promised by the Lord to all people whenever they desire or require one. Furthermore, there is no guarantee that those who see a miracle will be led to live in devotion to the Wonder-worker. Many of the people who witnessed the miracles of Jesus demanded to see more but declined to stand by his side at the time of his rejection.

To say that miracles don't happen is to be dogmatic without warrant. To insist that they should be normative is to be expectant without wisdom. To believe that they serve God's purposes in his time is to be reverent and worshipful. Miracles do happen—even after the 1969 Word Series.

TO READ: *Luke 7:18-35*

DOUBT

John's two disciples found Jesus and said to him, "John the Baptist sent us to ask, 'Are you the Messiah we've been expecting, or should we keep looking for someone else?'"

LUKE 7:20

E ach year, *Time* magazine identifies a "Person of the Year," usually to a mixed reaction from their readers. For instance, in the year 2000, *Time* chose George W. Bush, the winner of the controversial and hotly contended 2000 presidential contest. But at the end of 1999, they picked a "Person of the Century": Albert Einstein, the great theoretical physicist whose theory of relativity changed the way we think about the world. Here again the choice did not elicit universal approval, because there was no agreement on the criteria used to make the judgment.

One day, Jesus picked his "man of the millennium." Jesus said, "I tell you, of all who have ever lived, none is greater than John" (Luke 7:28). He was speaking of John the Baptist. His point was not to shower accolades on John, but rather to show that "even the most insignificant person in the Kingdom of God is greater than he is" (7:28). Jesus' point was that, superb as John was, he lacked the basic experience of the most humble person who had discovered the reality of God's kingdom through faith in Christ.

All this could not, however, detract from the significance of John's stature as a man of outstanding ability and integrity. It is interesting to note, therefore, that Jesus' comment came in the context of something in John's life which indicated that even he had an Achilles' heel. John had just sent a message to Jesus by way of two disciples, asking, "Are you the Messiah we've been expecting, or should we keep looking for someone else?" (7:19). John was the one who had pointed to Jesus and boldly declared, "Look! There is the Lamb of God!" (John 1:36). But now he was having doubts. His Achilles' heel was showing!

Perhaps the reason for John's doubts was to be found in his personal experience. He knew that one of the evidences of Messiah's arrival would be that he would "proclaim that captives will be released" (Luke 4:18). But John was languishing in a prison cell—from which he was never released! Jesus' response was that there was plenty of evidence that he was fulfilling Isaiah's Messianic prophecy (Luke 7:22; see Isaiah 61:1-2). Jesus had referred to this prophecy at the beginning of his ministry (Luke 4:18-19). But even though he specifically told John about his miracles—"the blind see, the lame walk, the lepers are cured, the deaf hear, the dead are raised to life, and the Good News is being preached to the poor" (7:22), in keeping with John's predicament he made no mention of the captives being released!

Jesus had no easy answers for John's personal hardship, just enough evidence for John's faith to be strong. But even though it wasn't strong at that time, Jesus still thought he was the greatest! Even great men are allowed their weaknesses—including having doubts!

LOGIC AND LOVE

"I tell you, her sins—and they are many—have been forgiven, so she has shown me much love. But a person who is forgiven little shows only little love."

LUKE 7:47

Love can be quite illogical. It has its own set of rules that are more emotional than rational. And logic can be decidedly unloving. Built on major and minor premises and arriving at incontrovertible conclusions, logic can easily lose sight of human beings and their needs.

Take as an example the dinner party at Simon the Pharisee's house where Jesus was the guest of honor. A woman of unsavory reputation (an "immoral woman," Luke 7:37), unwelcome in such company, joined the party (as custom allowed) and embarrassed the guests by weeping over Jesus' feet as he reclined at the table, anointing his feet with expensive perfume, and kissing and drying them with her hair.

This was where Simon's logic took over.

Major premise—Real prophets have nothing to do with sinful women.
Minor premise— Jesus is allowing this woman to touch—and caress!—him.
Conclusion—"This proves that Jesus is no prophet" (7:39).

The obvious passion in the woman's behavior, her unrestrained expression of adoration and respect, and her heartfelt tears of sorrow and joy—all these left Simon the Pharisee cold. Logic triumphed over love in his heart.

Jesus, with the benefit of laser insight, read Simon's mind and "answered his thoughts" (7:40)—much to Simon's chagrin. Subtly and masterfully, Jesus got Simon to agree that, in a case where one person is forgiven much and another little, it is not unusual to find that the one forgiven most is most appreciative. Simon's logical mind could handle that with ease! But what he couldn't handle was the application Jesus made. Jesus pointed out to Simon that the woman's behavior, which Simon found so distasteful, was in fact much more appropriate than the cold, heartless "welcome"—lacking even common courtesies—that Jesus had received from Simon (7:43-46).

But Jesus was not commenting on social graces—or even on their lack. He was speaking about the issue of love. Jesus saw the difference between Simon's behavior and the woman's as a matter of love, and a special kind of love at that! It is the love that comes from the knowledge of forgiveness. Simon knew nothing of this—because he recognized nothing of his own need. His logic no doubt kept him insulated from guilt and, therefore, isolated from grace. But the woman, who was neither insulated from guilt nor isolated from grace, relied only on her experience of forgiveness. Overwhelmed with gratitude, she showed her love. Extravagantly, beautifully, and illogically!

Men don't need to "get in touch with their feminine side" to experience and express Christ's love. They just need to think logically about Jesus and his grace and let their reciprocal love show. To their surprise, they might find their expressions of love defying their masculine logic!

TO READ: *Luke 8:1–15*

PRODUCTIVE LISTENING

[Jesus'] disciples asked him what the story meant. He replied, "You have been permitted to understand the secrets of the Kingdom of God. But I am using these stories to conceal everything about it from outsiders, so that the Scriptures might be fulfilled: 'They see what I do, but they don't really see; they hear what I say, but they don't understand.'"

LUKE 8:9-10

A preacher once told a group of students that he had so much to tell them that he didn't know where to begin. In saying so, he committed a fundamental error! This became apparent when a smart young listener suggested, "Well, begin near the end." People need no encouragement to score points off preachers! It is all too easy to charge preachers with going on too long, or with curing people's insomnia. And some of the good-humored teasing is sometimes not too far from the truth!

But what about listeners who don't play their part in the communication exercise? Effective communication requires hearing as well as speaking, apprehending as well as articulating.

Jesus addressed this issue forthrightly. He explained that he had decided to teach in parables—simple stories with profound meanings—precisely because of the different ways listeners respond to what is being said (Luke 8:9-10). A parable can be heard at a very superficial level, without any moral or spiritual significance being discerned or applied. A parable can also have a life-transforming impact on the hearer if the lesson is taken seriously. So the issue becomes not the effectiveness of the speaker, but the attentiveness of the hearer!

The illustration of the sower sowing seed was masterful. All Jesus' hearers were familiar with the process of scattering seed because they were farmers. In Jesus' story, some of the seed fell on the path, some into shallow soil, some among thorns, and some in rich soil. This certainly matched the listeners' own experience of sowing. They all knew that some of the seed would respond in a very superficial, shallow manner and amount to nothing, while some of it would bear a rich, fruitful harvest. But Jesus' real point was lost on some of them. His point was that the same is true of his hearers! "Good soil," he told his disciples privately, "represents honest, good-hearted people who hear God's message, cling to it, and steadily produce a huge harvest" (8:15).

Productive hearing requires two things. First, it requires the right heart attitude: a positive approach and a serious intent to apply the truth honestly. Second, it requires a willingness to work for the long haul on what is being said, not just for a moment or two. There's an element of "clinging" to the truth of the message, and there must be a "steady" or consistent application of what is heard. This way, huge harvests of blessing abound in the hearts of hearers.

Much has been written on the subject of effective speaking, but little is said on the role of attentive hearing. No doubt preachers in pulpits need to sharpen their skills. But people in pews need to focus their concentration, too.

TO READ: *Psalm 91*

SHADOW
OF THE ALMIGHTY

Those who live in the shelter of the Most High will find rest in the shadow of the Almighty.

PSALM 91:1

I n two of her books, *Through Gates of Splendor* and *The Shadow of the Almighty,* Elisabeth Elliot tells the story of five American missionaries, including her husband, Jim, who were martyred in the jungles of Equador in 1956. The title of the second book was clearly taken from Psalm 91, which the five young men took very seriously as they embarked on the hazardous task of making contact with the primitive Auca people. After a number of promising contacts with the Indians through an ingenious method of lowering buckets of gifts from a plane tightly circling over the village, the men landed on a strip of sand on a jungle riverbank and awaited the arrival of their new "friends." But the missionaries were cruelly murdered and their bodies left in the muddy waters of the river.

Whatever natural fears the young men may have had, they were undoubtedly allayed by the words, "Do not be afraid of the terrors of the night, nor fear the dangers of the day, nor dread the plague that stalks in darkness, nor the disaster that strikes at midday" (Ps. 91:5-6). Whatever reservations they may have entertained, they presumably took great comfort in the words "If you make the Lord your refuge, and you make the Most High your shelter, no evil will conquer you" (91:9-10). And yet the reality is that these trusting young men were speared to death within days of their arrival in Auca territory.

We don't know how much warning—if any—the missionaries had of the impending attack, but they had hung their hearts over the words, "The Lord says, 'I will rescue those who love me. I will protect those who trust in my name. When they call on me, I will answer; I will be with them in trouble. I will rescue them and honor them'" (91:14-15). The obvious question on the minds of many at the time of the tragedy—and in succeeding years—was, "What went wrong?" Did God's promises not stand up under the weight of trust put in him? Did God renege on his commitment to the safety of his young servants? Had they misread or misinterpreted the Scriptures? And the answer, although hard to find, is surely that the Lord did "rescue them" from their earthly pain and "honor them" in his immediate presence. Ever since their deaths, they've enjoyed his promise to "satisfy them with a long life"—as long as eternity—"and give them [his] salvation" (91:15-16). Truly they found "rest in the shadow of the Almighty" (91:1).

Faith takes the long view—God's shadow is a long shadow.

TO READ: *Judges 7:1-22*

VALUABLE BUT EXPENDABLE

It was just after midnight, after the changing of the guard, when Gideon and the one hundred men with him reached the outer edge of the Midianite camp. Suddenly, they blew the horns and broke their clay jars. Then all three groups blew their horns and broke their jars. They held the blazing torches in their left hands and the horns in their right hands and shouted, "A sword for the LORD and for Gideon!"

JUDGES 7:19-20

C hristianity is full of paradoxes. We die to live, we are humbled to be exalted, the first shall be last, and the expendable are the valuable. Paradoxes!

Gideon and his men must have been the biggest underdogs in military history when they set out to do battle with the Midianites. Overwhelmingly outnumbered and under-armed, they had been whittled down to three hundred men, and their arsenal consisted of pots holding torches and a sword apiece. Thus equipped, they surrounded the camp of the Midianites in the dead of night. On command they smashed the clay jars to the ground. The silence was shattered; the night sky was flooded with light. The Midianites in panic began attacking one another, and when the survivors fled, Gideon's army finished them off with their swords.

The apostle Paul was apparently referring to this event when he explained his approach to his work as an apostle. He explained that, God had commanded light to shine at Creation, just as he had shone the knowledge of Christ into Paul's heart. "But," he said, "this precious treasure—this light and power that now shine within us—is held in perishable containers, that is, in our weak bodies" (2 Cor. 4:7). As long as the clay jar of his physical body was intact, the light would not shine out. But if the jar cracks and breaks, then the light shines through. Paul saw himself as expendable in the service of the Master. He was not interested in painting the outside of his life or even fixing the cracks. His interest was in letting the glory of God shine through his humble life. If the way he handled affliction glorified God, he would welcome afflictions. If the way he responded to pressures demonstrated the power of God, then let the pressures continue.

Brave words indeed! It is the man who regards himself as expendable who is ultimately valuable. A man who will not stoop to care for a dirty child keeps his pride intact and his soul impoverished. But the man who spends his vacation money on the support of an orphan, or invests his television time at a rescue mission, or passes up a promotion so he can be involved in his church, may find some wear and tear on his finances and his leisure time. But he will know fullness of joy in his heart. It's the broken pots that let the light shine—the intact ones simply sit prettily in their own darkness.

TO READ: *Judges 9:1-21*

LUST FOR POWER

"Then all the trees finally turned to the thornbush and said, 'Come, you be our king!'
And the thornbush replied, 'If you truly want to make me your king,
come and take shelter in my shade. If not, let fire come out from me
and devour the cedars of Lebanon.'"

JUDGES 9:14-15

A wise man once said, "Power corrupts, and absolute power corrupts absolutely." But the power that corrupts has an appeal. Men still seek it, because they feel they can enjoy the freedom that power brings without suffering the corrupting bondage it imposes.

God tried to warn his people of this danger. They listened with tin ears. Israel was called to be a theocracy—they were to live under divine rule. But for a theocracy to work, the people must honor the Lord and walk in his ways. The children of Israel had no intention of living this way. They looked longingly at the surrounding monarchies and longed for a similar system. So they asked their hero, Gideon, to accept the role of king, but he declined and said, "I will not rule over you, nor will my son. The Lord will rule over you" (8:23).

When Gideon died, his son Abimelech had no such compunctions. He wanted to rule, so he set about establishing his power base. First he went to Shechem, the home of his mother, Gideon's concubine. There he played the ethnic card, telling his relatives that, because he was their "flesh and blood," they could expect a better deal from him than from any of his seventy half-brothers, who he implied were looking for a chance to take over. The result was that he won their support, collected their money, and hired some mercenaries. Then he murdered all his half-brothers. Nice guy! Thus he dealt with any possible opposition—or so he thought. But one brother, Jotham, escaped. Jotham courageously appeared on a rock overlooking Shechem and loudly proclaimed a parable about a useless bramble becoming king. The message was abundantly clear: Jotham's useless half-brother was offering what he could not give, but he would stop at nothing to get power!

The desire for a degree of power over our own lives is understandable. But power over other people is often involved, because if others control us we are not in control. This is where the problems arise. In the human heart, a legitimate desire for freedom from oppression can quickly become a lust for power over others. Then anything goes. The depths to which the human soul can then plunge are unfathomable. The noble themes of the French Revolution—"liberté, égalité, fraternité"—quickly degenerated into a bloodbath. Those who were freed from oppression mercilessly oppressed the opposition. There's only one sure way to handle the lust for power, and Gideon said it: "The Lord will rule over you!"

TO READ: *Judges 13:1-14*

PARENTAL LIMITS

"You will become pregnant and give birth to a son, and his hair must never be cut.
For he will be dedicated to God as a Nazirite from birth.
He will rescue Israel from the Philistines."

JUDGES 13:5

W omen in developed countries who become pregnant know that the health and well-being of their unborn children is directly related to the care they take with their own diets and lifestyles. In fact, expectant mothers can be charged with serious offenses if they jeopardize the well-being of their unborn child.

In Old Testament days, this kind of information about diet and lifestyle was not readily available. However, there were situations in which expectant mothers were told to take special precautions in their diet because of the special nature of their child.

Such was the case for the wife of "Manoah from the tribe of Dan" (Judges 13:2). She had been unable to bear a child. Then she was visited by an angelic messenger, who not only gave her the good news of her impending pregnancy but also announced that her son would be a Nazirite, a man dedicated to the Lord for special service. Manoah's wife was instructed, "You must not drink wine or any other alcoholic drink or eat any forbidden food" (13:4). As an evidence of his special status and responsibilities, her son would never be allowed to have those things, and it had to start while he was in the womb. In addition, his hair was never to be cut. As a result, he would readily be identified as a man dedicated to God. Manoah and his wife duly carried out their instructions and the boy, Samson, was born. No doubt he was told about the unique circumstances of his birth and his privileges and responsibilities as a Nazirite.

The day would come, of course, when the young man would develop a mind of his own, and the ability of his parents to control him would be limited. He would begin making his own decisions. If he chose to shave his head and take to alcoholic beverages, there would be little that they could do about it.

Godly parents in all generations have been faced with similar issues. In good faith they dedicate their children to the Lord (though they rarely encourage the unrestrained growth of hair!), and they earnestly set about the task of raising their children in the knowledge and acknowledgment of the Lord. And so they should. But there comes a time when their role is limited and the responsibility shifts to the young person. At this point, great care is called for. Authoritative statements will rarely produce positive results, and a parent's frustration at the young person's failure to live up to expectations will rarely turn things around. But consistent example and winsome concern, coupled with prevailing prayer, work wonders. That's because you can't manufacture dedicated servants. But you can help grow them!

TO READ: *Judges 14:1-20; 16:1-4*

CALLING AND CHARACTER

One day . . . [Samson] noticed a certain Philistine woman. . . . "I want to marry
a young Philistine woman I saw in Timnah." . . . One day Samson went to the
Philistine city of Gaza and spent the night with a prostitute. . . . Later Samson fell
in love with a woman named Delilah, who lived in the valley of Sorek.

JUDGES 14:1-2; 16:1, 4

When President William Jefferson Clinton was impeached, the United States was anything but united in its attitude toward what was happening. Apart from the obvious political maneuvers that were taking place, a great debate was going on regarding the nature of leadership. There were those who insisted that the president was clearly doing a fine job and his personal life was of no concern to anyone else. On the other hand, others argued that a major aspect of the president's job description is to provide moral leadership to the nation, and this he had manifestly failed to do. Underlying this debate was a bigger question—what role does moral character play in the life of a leader?

The question could certainly have been asked of Samson, the gifted strong man of ancient Israel. God had called Samson to be a Nazirite, a man dedicated to God's service from the womb. Samson's mission was to overpower the enemies of God's people. In order to fulfill his calling, he had been specially endowed with supernatural strength. The most obvious outward evidence of Samson's Nazirite calling was his uncut hair. Because his supernatural gifting (his *charisma*) was directly related to his calling, his strength remained undiminished as long as his hair remained uncut. So there was no question about his calling or his *charisma*. But sadly, there were major questions about his moral character.

In particular, Samson's relations with the fairer sex left much to be desired. His unsuccessful marriage to a Philistine woman (14:1-20), his dalliance with a Philistine prostitute (16:1-3), and his ill-fated love affair with Delilah, yet another Philistine (16:4-22), speak volumes about his character. The one thing more important than anything else in Samson's life was the maintenance of his Nazirite vow. But as soon as he "fell in love" with Delilah (16:4), he disregarded the fact that her unusual interest in the secret of his strength was directly related to a Philistine plot to destroy him, and he recklessly played with her and his vow until he was defeated. Samson was careless about his character, he was casual about his calling, and inevitably, he was stripped of his *charisma*.

Whatever politicians and the public decide about the place of character in the life of a president, there is no question about its significance in the life of a spiritual leader. The words of Dr. Peter Kuzmic, the gifted and powerful Christian leader in the former Yugoslavia, should be heeded. He told a reporter at the height of the Bosnian crisis, "Charisma without character equals chaos." Too bad Samson never met Peter Kuzmic!

TO READ: *Judges 16:4-22*

RESTORATION— IN TIME?

*Delilah lulled Samson to sleep with his head in her lap, and she called in a man
to shave off his hair, making his capture certain. And his strength left him. . . .
So the Philistines captured him and gouged out his eyes. They took him to Gaza,
where he was bound with bronze chains and made to grind grain in the prison.
But before long his hair began to grow back.*

JUDGES 16:19, 21-22

In the 1980s, a number of highly visible and influential televangelists experienced
high-visibility moral failures. The effects of this tragic demise of spiritual leadership
will reverberate well into the next century. When a Christian leader experiences moral
failure, the fallout is immeasurable. The leader is shamed, his family is dismayed, his
followers are confused, his enemies are delighted, and (most importantly) the cause of
Christ is set back. So great are the ramifications that the credibility of the Christian cause
is called into question. Accordingly, great care is needed if the offending parties are to be
treated appropriately.

Herein lies an apparent problem. Some people, quoting Paul, say, "If another
Christian is overcome by some sin, you who are godly should gently and humbly help
that person back onto the right path. And be careful not to fall into the same temptation
yourself" (Gal. 6:1). From that point of view, the fallen leader should promptly be restored
to leadership, shouldn't he? The issue Paul is talking about here, however, is fellowship,
not leadership. Certainly a fallen brother should be helped to come to terms with his sin,
repent, and seek restoration. It is a completely different question, however, whether or not
the fallen leader should be restored to leadership. If the impression is given that the leader
"got away with it," what does this say to the confused followers who have been deceived
and disillusioned? How can onlookers take the moral pronouncements of the church
seriously if leaders who defy them are treated with kid gloves when discovered? A safe rule
of thumb should be this: It is always appropriate to take steps to restore a fallen brother to
fellowship, but it does not follow that a disqualified leader should be restored to *leadership*.

The balance can probably be found in the story of Samson. After his crushing defeat
and fall, Samson was blinded, imprisoned, chained, and humiliated. No doubt he was
given ample opportunity to contemplate his actions, to evaluate his behavior, and to come
to conclusions about the ways in which he had abused his calling and failed in his God
appointed task. We are not told about his heart-attitude at this time, but subsequent events
hint that he probably came to a point of repentance and desired to be restored to his
former power and glory. But it would take time.

There is a subtle but powerful statement in the story. We are told, "Before long his
hair began to grow back" (Judges 16:22). He was being given a chance to show, by
allowing his hair to grow, that he was renewing his vows. It takes time for a Nazirite's hair
to grow. And the restoration of a fallen leader is not the work of a moment. But handled
properly, a fallen brother can be restored. In some instances a failed leader can even be
reinstated—but not quickly. It takes time.

TO READ: *Judges 16:23-31*

STRENGTH
IN WEAKNESS

*Then Samson prayed to the LORD, "Sovereign LORD, remember me again.
O God, please strengthen me one more time so that I may pay back
the Philistines for the loss of my eyes."*

JUDGES 16:28

H aving been captured by Israel's traditional enemies—the Philistines—as a result of his own ill-discipline and carelessness, Samson was blinded and put to work in a mill. The Philistines interpreted Samson's downfall as a triumph for their national deity, Dagon. So they organized a huge celebration to honor him. "They praised their god saying, 'Our god has delivered our enemy to us!'" (Judges 16:24). Religious fervor, fueled by alcohol, stirred up the crowd until they demanded that Samson be brought out and further humiliated. So the pitiful, blinded, former strong man was led by the hand into the midst of the jeering crowd, where they proceeded to make sport of him.

Samson was born with the express intention that he should "rescue Israel from the Philistines" (13:5). This was his *raison d'être*, his reason for being. But his present circumstances were a brutal reminder of his ignominious failure. Far from delivering Israel from the Philistines, Israel's mighty man was held by them, bound and blind, his life blighted. So not only was Samson an object of ridicule, but he had also dragged Israel down to the status of laughingstock. Even worse, he had given the followers of Dagon the opportunity to believe that their man-made idol was stronger than and superior to the Creator God, Jehovah.

As Samson stood in the midst of the crowd, unseeing but aware, he prayed! "Sovereign Lord, remember me again. O God, please strengthen me one more time so that I may pay back the Philistines for the loss of my eyes" (16:28). Apparently, even at this juncture, Samson had vengeance in mind, rather than the fulfillment of his divinely-ordained task—to deliver Israel from the Philistines. But he acknowledged that the Lord was the source of his strength and that his failure had left him estranged from his God. And he now wanted to be strengthened again.

God granted his request. While Samson was concerned about revenge for his eyes, God was interested in displaying his own majesty and superiority to man-made idols. So, in one awesome display of power, Samson pushed on the main supports of the building. Both he and the jeering crowd were then ushered into eternity amid screams of terror and a monumental architectural collapse.

Questions naturally come to mind. For example, was God aiding a vengeful man or assisting a suicide? But these questions overlook the main point of the story: God is willing to use imperfect people to further his ends—so long as they acknowledge their dependence on him. It was true of Samson, and it is true of you and me.

TO READ: *Psalm 62*

TRYING TO GET RICH

Don't try to get rich by extortion or robbery. And if your wealth increases,
don't make it the center of your life.

PSALM 62:10

For the first time ever, more than 50 percent of American households invest in the stock market. Given the opportunities for online trading and the lure of get-rich-quick investments, some young families are selling family heirlooms to invest the proceeds in the market. Some even take out second mortgages on their homes with a view toward quickly doubling their money on Wall Street. Others make plans to make enough money to enable them to retire by fifty years of age at the latest. Such is the state of financial frenzy in which many live during prosperous times and bull markets!

King David lived in very different days. There was no stock market, and even charging interest was looked upon with disfavor. But David recognized that "try[ing] to get rich" (Ps. 62:10) was on the minds of at least some of his contemporaries. He warned them about trying to get rich by "extortion or robbery." For those who had no intention of engaging in fiscal illegalities, David added, "And if your wealth increases, don't make it the center of your life." In saying this, the great king put his finger firmly on a sensitive spot.

Wealth has its own fascinating allure. It holds out the promise of the "best of everything"—the best seat in the stadium, the best table in the restaurant, the best car in the lot, the best school in the suburbs. It beckons with offers of untold delights, it suggests it can cure all ills and satisfy all desires, it whispers that it can open doors otherwise closed, and it boasts that it can solve intractable problems. Is it any surprise that people look to wealth as their savior and make it the center of their lives?

There is nothing intrinsically wrong with wealth. How can there be when God is the one who gives people the ability to get wealth (see Deut. 8:18). It is the prominence that wealth is afforded in the heart that is often wrong. Wealth—or the search for it, or the control of it, or the expenditure of it—does not belong in the center; it is at best peripheral.

Powerful as wealth is—and who can deny its power?—wealth can do nothing about a fundamental aspect of human existence. Human beings are extremely fragile. "If you weight them on the scales they are lighter than a puff of air"(Ps. 62:9). Not only is wealth incapable of solving this "unbearable lightness of being," but when a man for whom wealth is central is wafted into eternity, he goes minus his center. He is hollow. And standing before the one who is *the* center to all life, he sees his error—but too late.

STATUS

Then there was an argument among them as to which of them would be the greatest.

LUKE 9:46

W hen men get together, they love to talk—about themselves! They tell war stories from the battlefield or (more likely) the football field. They talk about the fish they caught (and the one that got away), the deal they closed, the raise they negotiated, the car they drive, or the promotion they're expecting. The issue is not so much competence as competition. They're not necessarily trying to show that they are great—just that they're greater. The competitive instinct seems to come with the testosterone.

When Jesus' disciples got together, it was no different. Luke tells us that the disciples had a difficult time understanding why Jesus, at the height of his popularity and success, told them that he would be betrayed. In their minds, he stood on the brink of triumph. In his mind, he was staring at a cross. Jesus was trying to convey to his students that he was about to take the lowest possible place (Luke 9:44). They responded by getting into "an argument . . . as to which of them would be the greatest" (9:46). So sure were the disciples that Jesus would banish the Romans and restore Israel's independence and glory, with Jesus himself as the supreme ruler, that the only significant thing remaining to be discussed was the role that each of them would play in the new administration. And that made the competitive juices flow.

But Jesus, who "knew their thoughts" (9:47—presumably when they saw him coming they abruptly changed the subject), chose not to discuss who would be greatest. Instead, at a much more elementary and necessary level, he illustrated what it means to be "great." Placing a little child before them (in that culture a child had practically no social or legal status), Jesus told them that a great person is one who reaches out to people whom, like the child, society regards as insignificant. In ministering to the "insignificant" there is a sense in which we minister to the Lord himself.

Jesus was not deifying the poor or the helpless. He was reiterating the worth of all of God's creatures. That being the case, the great man is not driven to compete and compare. He is much more inclined to reach out to the lowly than to be grasping for the top. Should he ever worry that his masculinity is slipping, he looks again at the one who was—and is— the greatest!

TO READ: *Luke 9:49-62*

THE COST
OF DISCIPLESHIP

Jesus told him, "Anyone who puts a hand to the plow and then looks back is not fit for the Kingdom of God."

LUKE 9:62

D ietrich Bonhoeffer, the brilliant young German theologian, was executed by the Nazis in the concentration camp at Flossenburg on April 9, 1945. This modern martyr had thought and written much about the cost of discipleship, not least because of the perilous times in which he lived. He was convinced that the gospel that Jesus preached to his disciples was not without challenge—but not without its own special comfort, too. Bonhoeffer said, "The command of Jesus is hard, unutterably hard, for those who try to resist it. But for those who willingly submit, the yoke is easy, and the burden is light."[30]

He was right. Jesus was not at all reluctant to rebuke his wayward followers. When they tried to stop an exorcist who was not in their group, they were told, "Don't stop him! Anyone who is not against you is for you" (Luke 9:50). When they wanted to exterminate some Samaritans, they were rebuked by the Lord for suggesting such a thing (9:51-55). And those who gave halfhearted responses to his call, like the man who indicated he would follow Jesus if it didn't interfere with his family life, were told, "Anyone who puts a hand to the plow and then looks back is not fit for the Kingdom of God" (9:62).

The problem with plowing and looking back at the same time is not so much a stiff neck as a crooked furrow. And the end product of the Christian that halfheartedly follows Christ is a crooked life. A halfhearted Christian commits part of his life to Christ and manages the rest personally.

There is something in a man's heart that is resistant to a wholesale commitment to the lordship and leadership of Christ. It is hard for the man as he resists, because a battle of wills is in progress. It is a battle the man cannot win, but he insists on fighting to his own dismay and discomfort. It would be far better to accept the rebuke of the Lord. It is infinitely better to see things his way. And it is wonderfully liberating to exchange the harsh shackles of selfishness for the benign restraints of Christ's call, wherever it leads.

Bonhoeffer went to his death, which he called the "solemnest feast on the road to eternal freedom."[31] He was convinced that this, the ultimate cost of discipleship, was a price well worth paying. This is an approach to discipleship that bears the stamp of authenticity.

[30]Dietrich Bonhoeffer, *The Cost of Discipleship*.
[31]Dietrich Bonhoeffer, "Stations on the Road to Freedom."

THE LAMBS VERSUS THE WOLVES

"Go now, and remember that I am sending you out as lambs among wolves."

LUKE 10:3

In the professional sports world we have the Bears, the Lions, the Jaguars, the Rams—but never the Squirrels or the Lambs. There is something muscular, aggressive, and intimidating about the former—those names command respect. But a sports team named the Squirrels or the Lambs would generate pity and concern and laughter.

The people of Jesus' time weren't into professional sports, but they still had an aggressive side and did not hesitate to impose their wills, like bears and lions, on others. This, however, did not concern Jesus. He frankly said that, as far as his men were concerned, they were about to be commissioned "as lambs among wolves" (Luke 10:3). His team of witnesses was not called the Capernaum Cheetahs or the Jerusalem Jaguars. They were the Lambs, and their opponents in the first round were the Wolves. "No contest," you say. "If it was a prize fight, the referees would stop it in the first round!"

But Jesus knew better. Lambs they were to be, and wolves their opponents certainly were. But the difference was found in the statement, "I am sending you" (10:3). The secret of effective Christian ministry is not found in the extraordinary abilities of those who are sent, but rather in the sovereign authority of the one who sends. Without his sending, the seventy-two would never have ventured forth. And without the assurance, "I have given you authority over all the power of the enemy" (10:19), the Lambs would never have taken the field. But they did! And what was the final score? Lambs 72, Wolves 0.

Jesus was the one who "chose" the seventy-two (10:1). He himself is the "Lord who is in charge of the harvest" (10:2). He is the one to whom the disciples should "pray" (10:2). He, and he alone, can adequately "send" people where they need to go to do what they must do. He is the one who gives instructions on the behavior of disciples, on ministry techniques, on the solemnity of the occasion, and on the urgency of the hour. It is to him that tired but excited disciples return, and it is from him that they hear the words, "Don't rejoice just because evil spirits obey you; rejoice because your names are registered as citizens of heaven" (10:20).

What, then, is the role of those who are sent out by Jesus? It is to be willing to be *propelled* into the action—against all odds, sometimes against better judgment, and occasionally against concerted advice. Then their job is to *proclaim*—to let people know about Jesus and his kingdom. Their role is also to *pray* for reinforcements! Finally, they are to *persevere*. This way, the Lambs will rout the Wolves every time!

TO READ: *Luke 10:25-37*

GOOD SAMARITANS

"Now which of these three would you say was a neighbor to the man who was attacked by bandits?" Jesus asked. The man replied, "The one who showed him mercy." Then Jesus said, "Yes, now go and do the same."

LUKE 10:36-37

Generally speaking, the typical man in the street dislikes those who come across as "holier-than-thou." He has little time for "do-gooders," but he usually has a warm place in his heart for a "good Samaritan." He likes the idea of Boy Scout-style behavior that helps old ladies across the road and runs errands for shut-ins. But is this really what Jesus had in mind when he told what is arguably his most famous story, the parable of the Good Samaritan? Hardly!

The context of the story is critical. "An expert in religious law stood up to test Jesus by asking him this question: 'Teacher, what must I do to receive eternal life?'" (Luke 10:25.) The Good Samaritan story was prompted by a question about eternal destiny and life in the hereafter, about eternal communion with or separation from God. Jesus responded by asking the expert for his understanding of Moses' instructions to "love the Lord your God with all your heart, all your soul, all your strength, and all your mind" and "Love your neighbor as yourself" (10:27, see also Deut. 6:5; Lev. 19:18). The clear implication was that the way to eternal life is through absolutely meticulous and perfect fulfillment of the law. The legal expert retorted, because he wanted "to justify his actions, . . . 'And who is my neighbor?'" (10:29). In response, Jesus told his story about the Good Samaritan. Jesus made it clear that the Samaritan was the model of neighborliness.

The "expert" in the law had, no doubt, tuned in to rabbinical teaching that conveniently limited the definition of "neighbor" and "neighborliness" to a select group of associates. Jesus widened the definition to show that anyone can be a neighbor, and that neighborliness should be shown to everyone. Bleeding victims in the ditch are neighbors, and so are despised and ostracized Samaritans.

More significantly, Jesus pointed out that human efforts—at neighborliness or anything else prescribed by the law—fall far short of meriting eternal life. Understanding this, a man is driven to grace—his only hope of life eternal. Jesus insisted, in his run-ins with the legalists, that he had not "come to call the righteous but sinners to repentance" (Luke 5:31).

There is a pervasive idea in Western culture that a "good life" in the here and now merits eternal life in the hereafter. But the parable about the Good Samaritan contradicts this dangerous misunderstanding. A clear word from the apostle Paul puts the matter beyond doubt: "The wages of sin is death, but the *free gift of God* is eternal life through Christ Jesus our Lord" (Rom. 6:23, emphasis added). Eternal life is about a free gift, not about a good life. But those who receive the gift will have a deep desire to live a good life. Just like the Samaritan!

SEPTEMBER

TO READ: *Luke 10:38–11:13*

THE BARRENNESS
OF BUSYNESS

*The Lord said to her, "My dear Martha, you are so upset over all these details!
There is really only one thing worth being concerned about. Mary has discovered it—
and I won't take it away from her."*

LUKE 10:41-42

There's danger in being idle. As Isaac Watts wrote:

*For Satan finds some mischief still
For idle hands to do.*[32]

Good honest work, quite apart from exercising muscles and putting food on the table, also acts as a deterrent against the temptations that cluster around an idle life. But if busyness is the antidote to idleness, we should be aware that there's a sting in the tail of busyness, too.

Martha, the friend of Jesus, is a great example. No one can fault the lady for being busy when she found that Jesus and his hungry disciples had arrived for lunch. And her frustration with her sister who sat around talking when she could have been doing kitchen duty is perfectly understandable. But when Martha remonstrated with Jesus and suggested that he "tell her to come and help" (Luke 10:40), he replied that Mary had grasped something that Martha had overlooked. But what was it?

Martha is the patron saint of all those who are so busy that they don't have time to care for the nourishment of their own souls. What they are doing is necessary, important, helpful—but ultimately destructive! As they expend physical and emotional energy, they neglect the infusion of spiritual power.

Mary knew better than to let this happen with her. She took an opportunity that was all too scarce for women in those days: to sit "at the Lord's feet, listening to what he taught" (10:39).

Put in the simplest of terms, busyness leads to barrenness. Busyness keeps us away from taking the time to read, mark, learn, and inwardly digest God's Word. Being nourished by God's Word is like a conversation between two friends who listen and respond to each other and are encouraged by the encounter. Spiritual nourishment flows to the life of the man who regularly takes time to listen to the Lord in his Word and then responds in prayer to what the Lord has said.

Of course, prayer that is based on God's Word is more likely to be close to the mind of the Lord than prayer that comes purely from the self-interest of the one praying. This is clear from the prayer Jesus taught his disciples (11:1-4). This prayer is concerned first that the Lord's "name be honored," then that his "Kingdom come soon." Then, and only then, prayer turns to legitimate matters of personal concern—such as "our food day by day," relationships where we sin and others sin "against us," and spiritual issues such as "temptation."

It is true that the cure for idleness is busyness. But beware the barrenness of busyness that ignores the secret of blessedness.

---

[32] Isaac Watts, *Divine Songs*.

TO READ: *Luke 11:14-28*

MISSING THE POINT

"You say I am empowered by the prince of demons. But if Satan is fighting against himself by empowering me to cast out his demons, how can his kingdom survive? . . . But if I am casting out demons by the power of God, then the Kingdom of God has arrived among you."

LUKE 11:18, 20

Ever since the Supreme Court passed down its decision in the case of *Roe v. Wade*, legalizing abortion in the United States, the subject has been one of an intense debate that shows no sign of abating. Those who favor the decision like to classify the sides in the argument as those who are "pro-choice" versus those who are "anti-abortion." Their descriptive choices clearly indicate their biases! Why not describe the sides as those who are "pro-life" versus those who are "anti-babies"?

The supporters of abortion frame the argument as a matter of freedom of choice on the part of women and a refusal to allow government to interfere in the most intimate areas of a person's (the woman's) life. In endeavoring to counter those arguments, one salient point is all too often overlooked—or ignored. In the USA for three decades now, up to 1.5 million babies annually have had their lives ended and have been denied the right to live before they were even born! In other words, the argument for "freedom of choice" totally misses the point that 1.5 million people per year are being denied the freedom to choose!

Sometimes we become so wrapped up in a relatively minor aspect of an issue—in this case, a woman's right to choose—that we become blinded to a monumental aspect of the issue—in this case, the extermination of millions of babies. But there's nothing new about this strange human aberration. For example, Jesus performed miracles. Modern men tend to dismiss the accounts of the miracles, either by saying, "Miracles don't happen," or by saying, "The primitive people of Jesus' day didn't understand what we understand and they characterized as miracles what we now know were perfectly normal events which can be readily explained." But no such argument took place among the eyewitnesses! They didn't doubt for a moment that Jesus performed miracles—they only debated how he did it. Some said, "No wonder he can cast out demons. He gets his power from Satan, the prince of demons!" (Luke 11:15). Others, not so sure, played it safe and "asked for a miraculous sign from heaven" (11:16).

Jesus quickly exposed the fallacies in the arguments of those who saw him as an ambassador of Satan by asking the question, "If Satan is fighting against himself by empowering me to cast out his demons, how can his kingdom survive?" (11:18.) Good point! Why would Satan, the prince of demons, spend his time and energy destroying demons? As Jesus said, "A kingdom at war with itself is doomed" (11:17).

Those who thought Jesus was being empowered by Satan were missing the point! The point was simply this—while they were arguing about how he performed the miracles, they were overlooking the fact that the miracles were demonstrating unambiguously that "the Kingdom of God [had] arrived" (11:20).

It is tragic to be arguing about freedom of choice and government intervention—both legitimate concerns—while missing the point that babies are dying. And it is disastrous to argue about miracles and miss the coming of the kingdom!

TO READ: *Psalm 85*

HISTORY AND HIS STORY

I listen carefully to what God the LORD is saying, for he speaks peace to his people, his faithful ones. But let them not return to their foolish ways.

PSALM 85:8

The pessimist says, "If history teaches us anything, it teaches us that it doesn't teach us anything!" Depending on your point of view, this could be a statement condemning history to the garbage can and to all those who teach it to redundancy. Or it could be a sad statement concerning human obduracy and stupidity. Whichever way we interpret the aphorism, we need to reject its conclusion, because history rightly taught and properly learned is a repository of great truth that has immense value. For example, the person who believes that God is active in the affairs of men sees history as "his story" and learns through it valuable lessons from him. History is all about the ways that the great Creator and Redeemer has acted, intervened, worked out his purposes, and revealed his true nature as years have succeeded years and centuries have rolled by into millennia.

It is certainly the case in God's historic dealings with Israel that there are lessons to be learned. Those who have "eyes to see" can clearly discern the ways in which God was in control, even in the dark days of Israel's history. As a result, students of Israel's history, having looked back and pondered God's activities in the past, have been equipped to look forward and anticipate his activity in the future. The psalmist, for example, wrote joyfully about God's historic dealings: "You have poured out amazing blessings on your land! You have restored the fortunes of Israel. You have forgiven the guilt of your people—yes, you have covered all their sins" (Ps. 85:1-2). This was not wishful thinking and idle speculation on the part of the psalm writer. It was historically verifiable fact. God really had done all those things. Of this they could be sure—and they were!

Because the psalm writer was clear about the past, he was confident of the future. So he sang, "Now turn to us again, O God of our salvation. . . . Won't you revive us again, so your people can rejoice in you?" (Ps. 85:4, 6). How could he possible ask this of the Lord? Because God had done it before! What God had been he would continue to be, and what he had done he would continue to do.

The psalmist had learned an important lesson: The God of history is the God of today—and of tomorrow. So confident was the psalm writer that his prayers would be answered that he began to speak of them as if they had already been fulfilled. "Unfailing love and truth have met together. Righteousness and peace have kissed!" (85:10). With great confidence he added, "Our land will yield its bountiful crops" (85:12). He had learned God's ways from history, and he could see what was coming.

History is not an endless succession of meaningless events, nor is it a continuous cycle of empty repetition. It is the story of the God of heaven at work on earth! And it is a treasure trove of wisdom for those who learn its lessons.

TO READ: *1 Samuel 1:1-28*

PROMISE KEEPING

"I asked the Lord *to give me this child, and he has given me my request.*
Now I am giving him to the Lord, *and he will belong to the* Lord *his whole life."*
And they worshiped the Lord *there.*

1 SAMUEL 1:27-28

P romises made in times of intense anguish sometimes fade from the memory once the anguish has been assuaged. *God,* a man might pray, *if you'll only bring my wife back home, I promise I'll never abuse her again.* Or, *Lord, if you help me find a job, I promise I'll never touch a drop of liquor again.* Or, *Father, if you'll only get this plane down safely, I'll devote the rest of my life to being a missionary or a monk or something. Just so long as we land safely.* We've all heard prayers like this—or prayed them ourselves!

The problem with promises like these is that they are rarely born of conviction— they tend more to be matters of convenience. As we don't like to be inconvenienced, we resort to various techniques to avoid it, even to the point of striking an empty bargain with the Almighty. But paying the dues, or fulfilling our part of the "bargain," can become another source of inconvenience. So payment is often rationalized into oblivion. Granted, there are exceptions. Martin Luther, having survived an encounter with lightning, followed through on his promise and did become a monk! But such men are the exception rather than the rule.

Hannah was another great exception. In her deep desire to bear a child, she prayed earnestly and promised, "O Lord Almighty, if you will look down upon my sorrow and answer my prayer and give me a son, then I will give him back to you. He will be yours for his entire lifetime" (1 Sam. 1:11). In her case, the dedication of her boy to the Lord would be more than a brief ritual. He would leave home and be placed in the care of an old priest whose own family was a dysfunctional disaster (2:12-17). Hannah could have found many good arguments for reneging on her promise, but she faithfully followed through. So as soon as he was weaned, Samuel left home and took up residence in the temple.

Elkanah, Hannah's husband, was not the most sensitive human being (1:8). But he showed appropriate concern for his wife and her monumental decision to keep her promise when he told her, "May the Lord help you keep your promise" (1:23). That was the key. If the promise was made to the Lord and the Lord had done what was requested, then the Lord would enable her to do her part of the arrangement. As she was faithful, he, too, would be faithful.

Making a deal with God under duress may be a questionable deed. But making a solemn vow, as Hannah did, is not. What is questionable is the attitude that regards a promise made to the Lord as nonbinding. Better not to promise than to promise and renege, and better still to promise and perform.

TO READ: I Samuel 2:12-26

THE LORD'S HELPER

Now Samuel, though only a boy, was the Lord's helper. He wore a linen tunic just like that of a priest. . . . And the LORD gave Hannah three sons and two daughters. Meanwhile, Samuel grew up in the presence of the LORD.

1 SAMUEL 2:18, 21

An old storekeeper once said, "Give me the help of a boy, and I'll have the help of a boy. Give me the help of two boys, and I'll have the help of half a boy. Give me three boys, and I'll have no help at all." The storekeeper spoke with the voice of experience! Boys and helpfulness don't always go together.

It is surprising, therefore, to read that "Samuel, though only a boy, was the Lord's helper" (1 Sam. 2:18). It is surprising that the boy proved so helpful, but it is more surprising that the Lord accepted help from a boy! After all, he is almighty God. Why does he need a boy for help?

There is no suggestion here of any deficiency or shortfall in God. He is perfectly capable of running the world he created, and he has no problem managing the universe he upholds by his mighty power. But he does allow human beings to cooperate with him in his purposes. Even more than that, he delegates tasks to human beings that he specifically designed them to undertake.

So Samuel in early days learned that his young life counted for something important. While he missed out on some aspects of home life because of his unusual life in the temple (visits from the family occurred only annually), he experienced the priceless privilege of growing up "in the presence of the Lord" (2:21). In one sense, since God is omnipresent, we all grow up in his presence. But it is one thing to grow up in his presence and another to recognize it and relate to him. Many men and boys grow up without the conscious knowledge that they live under divine protection, are nurtured by divine provision, and are only a prayer away from divine empowerment. But not Samuel, the Lord's helper. Even though he was separated from his family and was raised in such abnormal circumstances, he experienced no harm at all—as he "grew taller, he also continued to gain favor with the Lord and with the people" (2:26). A thoroughly balanced kid and the Lord's helper to boot!

There can be no greater privilege in life than to recognize that one is cooperating with God as he works out his eternal purposes. Nothing can invest the mundane with a sense of magnificence quite like understanding that one is functioning as the Lord's helper! That being the case, what better time for a man to learn this than when he is young? Lessons embraced in formative years become deeply embedded in the human soul and never leave, even though they may for a time be ignored. What more could you wish for your kids?

TO READ: *1 Samuel 3:1–21*

HEARING VOICES

So [Eli] said to Samuel, "Go and lie down again, and if someone calls again, say,
'Yes, LORD, your servant is listening.'" So Samuel went back to bed.
And the LORD came and called as before, "Samuel! Samuel!"
And Samuel replied, "Yes, your servant is listening."

1 SAMUEL 3:9-10

P eople who claim to hear voices in our time are usually regarded with suspicion— understandably so, because many of them use the voices to "explain" actions that were bizarre or even criminal. People who say they have seen a vision are generally given more of the benefit of the doubt, but what they claim to have seen is often treated with scant regard. Of course, the problem with claiming either to hear voices or to see visions is that it is usually impossible for a third party to verify the claim's validity.

When young Samuel heard a voice in the middle of the night, he did not suspect anything out of the ordinary. He assumed it was blind, old Eli calling for help. Only after three visits from Samuel did it dawn on the priest that the voice was the Lord's. "In those days messages from the Lord were very rare, and visions were quite uncommon" (1 Sam. 3:1). So rare and uncommon were visions and messages from the Lord, apparently, that even Eli, the custodian of the Lord's temple, was not expecting to hear from him! Fortunately, when Eli eventually recognized that the Lord had broken his silence and was trying to attract Samuel's attention, he gave the right advice: "Go and lie down again, and if someone calls again, say, 'Yes, Lord, your servant is listening'" (1 Sam. 3:9).

The question that modern men may ask on reading this story is, "Does God speak to people today?" Different answers will come from different sources. Some will reject the idea out of hand. Others will claim to hear God speaking to them in a voice as clear as a man's voice. Still others will be more guarded and claim that, while they have never heard an audible voice, they believe God has communicated with them through the Scriptures or through a friend or even in a dream.

Those who claim that God does not speak to men today have no grounds for their unbelief. They cannot conclusively say, "He cannot speak"; they have no reason to say, "He would not speak"; and they are not in a position to say, "He does not speak." By the same token, those who claim to hear God speak to them need to beware of attributing to God their own impressions. They should test what they believe they have heard against what they know God has revealed in the Scriptures.

The key to proper listening is a right attitude. Like Samuel, the good listener realizes he is nothing more nor less than the Lord's servant and is ready to say, "Yes, Lord," to what he hears.

TO READ: *1 Samuel 4:1-11*

THE LOST ARK

*After the battle was over, the army of Israel retreated to their camp, and their leaders
asked, "Why did the LORD allow us to be defeated by the Philistines?"
Then they said, "Let's bring the Ark of the Covenant of the LORD from Shiloh.
If we carry it into battle with us, it will save us from our enemies." . . .
So the Philistines fought desperately, and Israel was defeated again.*

1 SAMUEL 4:3, 10

H ophni" and "Phinehas" are not the kind of names that mothers today give to
their sons. They are not particularly attractive names, and the men who bore the
names were singularly unattractive men. Along with their father, the elderly Eli, Hophni and
Phinehas were priests of the Lord in the tabernacle at Shiloh. They abused their privileged
position by seducing the women worshipers who came to the tabernacle—actions that in the
modern world would have sent them to prison for a long time. Their father, Eli, was perfectly
aware of what was going on, and he rebuked them verbally, but he took no further action.
He was weak, and they were disrespectful, so he did nothing.

When the Israelites were defeated by the Philistines in another of their petty wars,
Israel's military leaders determined that it was the Lord who had allowed the defeat
(1 Sam. 4:3). So they determined to turn that around by removing the ark of the covenant
from its sanctuary and carrying it to the battle field. The two notorious young priests not
only granted the ignominious request, but they personally assisted in transporting the ark
to the place of battle. The assumption on the part of Israel was that, since the Lord had
clearly been absent, so through the ark he was now present, and thus victory was assured.

The ark belonged in the Most Holy Place, not on the field of battle, and the priests had
no business taking it there. But its arrival had a partial beneficial effect. The Philistines,
whose knowledge of Israelite religion left much to be desired, still understood that the ark
represented the presence of God, and historically, when God had been present among his
people, they had been a formidable force. But strangely, instead of folding in terror before
the presence of the Lord, the Philistines fought harder, and they won! Not only did they
defeat Israel, but the ark was captured. The unthinkable had happened! God had been
hijacked by pagans.

Right from the beginning, the Israelites had recognized that their problem was not
primarily military—it was spiritual. But their solution was all wrong. They assumed that if
they went through a religious act, if they featured a religious symbol, that would solve the
problem. But the ark contained the Ten Commandments. These were not symbols to be
carried but laws to be obeyed. Even the priests carrying the ark were contravening these
laws with impunity. Israel was rotten to the core. That was why they had lost the battle.

Religious symbolism has never cured spiritual corruption. Only repentance and a
work of God's grace does that.

ICHABOD

She named the child Ichabod—"Where is the glory?"—murmuring, "Israel's glory is gone." She named him this because the Ark of God had been captured and because her husband and her father-in-law were dead. Then she said, "The glory has departed from Israel, for the Ark of God has been captured."

1 SAMUEL 4:21-22

D uring the great Welsh Revival of 1904, the churches and chapels of Wales were crowded with worshipers seeking to "get right with God." Miners covered with coal dust went straight from the pits to the church, and the valleys rang with the grand sound of Welsh voices singing the great hymns of the faith. An American tourist who was familiar with the stories of the revival was anxious to visit the towns and villages where the Spirit of God had moved. He found an old Welshman who took him around to some of the chapels and churches, where he reminisced about the great preaching and singing of bygone days. But then, with a tremor in his voice, he said, "The glory has departed. You could write across the front of the church in great big letters the word 'Knickerbocker.'" Unfortunately, the word he meant was "Ichabod."

But give the old Welshman some credit. Even if he was a little confused, at least he knew about a Bible story that most people have not encountered! It is the story of what happened when a messenger brought word back to Shiloh of Israel's defeat in battle and the capture of the ark. When poor old Eli—the fat, blind priest—heard about the ark and the deaths of his sons (he seemed more concerned about the former than the latter), he fell off his bench, broke his neck, and died. Eli's daughter-in-law, the wife of Phinehas, the philandering priest, gave premature birth to a son and died in childbirth. But before she died, she murmured, "Israel's glory is gone," and she named her son "Ichabod," which means, "Where is the glory?" (1 Sam. 4:21).

The Middle East is littered with the magnificent ruins of formerly great cities whose glory has long departed. Many of those cities are the ancient sites of first- and second-century churches that are now nowhere to be seen. Now there is no church, no Christian witness. The glory has gone. In the great cathedrals of Europe, where vast crowds once gathered for worship, now only tourists with cameras flood the ancient aisles, clambering unthinkingly and unknowingly over the graves of the great men and women of God who once stood tall and strong for the Lord in that place. The glory has gone.

The church is never more than one generation away from extinction. In some places, it happens through violent persecution. In others, through slow moral erosion. That erosion takes place in the hearts of individuals who, like Hophni and Phinehas, go through religious motions with hearts estranged from God. When that happens *en masse*, Ichabod! The glory departs.

TO READ: *1 Samuel 8:1–21*

TRUSTING YOUR OWN INSTINCTS

*"Do as they say," the L*ORD* replied, "for it is me they are rejecting, not you.
They don't want me to be their king any longer."*

1 SAMUEL 8:7

W e humans have a great capacity for trusting our own instincts more than God's principles. We are adept at blocking out divine warnings and no amount of divine prompting will divert the intent soul from the path that most appeals. So God allows his children to go ahead and waits for them to face the reality that he has spoken and that they have ignored.

Toward the end of Samuel's life, God's people felt that they were missing out on something good by doing things God's way. They saw that their neighbors' religions were much laxer than the worship of Yahweh, and they appreciated the political power and military muscle exercised by neighboring kings. By comparison, the religious and political structures that God had ordained for Israel seemed too demanding on one hand and not secure enough on the other. It was easy to have gods who mirrored all the worst attributes of fallen humanity and encouraged similar behavior from their adherents, as was the case in many of the surrounding nations, but it was challenging and serious to worship the Lord, who called people to holiness of life. It was hard to trust God when the enemies arrived on the doorstep, while it seemed much easier to turn to a human king who could rally a fighting force and rout the enemy.

So Israel indicated that they would like a change. Samuel was upset, because he understood the implications: Israel was turning away from faith in the Lord and choosing self-reliance. "It is me they are rejecting, not you," the Lord explained (8:7). The Lord allowed Israel to have what they wanted, but warned them of the consequences. Samuel passed on the message, but to no avail. They wanted what they wanted—a human rather than a divine king. And they did not want to be told divine truths about human kings.

Human instincts are not always wrong, but God's principles are always right. If our instincts flatly contradict divine instructions, our instincts must be jettisoned. The key is to submit our instincts to his scrutiny rather than to impose our intentions over his sovereignty. If we trust him to be our King, we may not always have something visible in which to put our confidence, but we will always have something much better: the eternal, almighty God, who always works for our good.

WORSHIP THE LORD

*Give honor to the LORD, you angels; give honor to the LORD for his glory
and strength. Give honor to the LORD for the glory of his name.
Worship the LORD in the splendor of his holiness.*

PSALM 29:1-2

H istorically, worshipers have expressed their praise, raised their petitions, communicated their message, and encouraged their hearts with music. But musical styles
change, so music as worship has taken many forms. Accordingly, music has often been the
center of controversy. This was true even at the time of the Reformation—the Reformers,
who agreed on many things, did not arrive at a consensus on the subject of music. And at
the present time, the struggle over what constitutes worshipful music is so severe in some
quarters that people talk about "worship wars"!

In the nineteenth century, William Booth burst on the church scene in England. In
response to the economic and spiritual degradation rampant in his homeland, he founded
the Salvation Army, a vibrant, aggressive, avant-garde ministry that reached out to the
poorest of the poor with a holistic message of salvation through the Lord Jesus. Booth was
no stranger to controversy. Among other things, he adapted secular tunes to evangelistic
and worship uses. To those who questioned him, he proclaimed, "Why should the devil
have all the best tunes?"

Surprisingly, there are reasons to believe that David expressed similar sentiments
when he composed Psalm 29. Scholars tell us that this psalm bears evidence of having
been used originally in the worship of Baal, a false god in ancient Palestine. Should that be
true, King David and General William Booth had more in common than we had realized!

What can be said with confidence is that the Baal worshipers attributed to Baal
attributes that David knew belonged exclusively to the Lord. The Lord was God of creation
and Baal was not. Therefore, David exhorted worshipers to recognize that "the voice of the
Lord echoes above the sea. The God of glory thunders" (Ps. 29:3). These words pointed
out that in nature, particularly in the violent storms common to Palestine, there is a
reminder that "the voice of the Lord is powerful: the voice of the Lord is full of majesty"
(29:4).

Reverent souls recognize that the Lord's hand is to be seen in all his handiwork,
and his voice is to be heard in the mighty and subtle sounds of nature. Such souls have
no difficulty turning their hearts to worship. In David's case, he encouraged the angels to
join him in giving "honor to the Lord for his glory and strength," and he called on both
angels and mortal beings to "worship the Lord in the splendor of his holiness" (29:2).

We need more men who, resenting "other gods" being honored with the honor due
only to the Lord, will unabashedly give him glory and will insist that others join in the
worship. Why should the devil have all the best tunes—and why should false gods get all
the glory?

TO READ: *Matthew 10:16-42*

ROSES HAVE THORNS

"A student is not greater than the teacher. A servant is not greater than the master."

MATTHEW 10:24

Public figures and advertisers often make their pronouncements in such a way that negatives are obscured by positives. We are well aware of this, and we greet much of what we are told with skepticism. We inquire, "Where's the catch?"

The pronouncements of Jesus were refreshingly different. There was no small print, no obscuring of the downside. He made it clear that anyone who became his disciple could expect the same kind of treatment that was being meted out to him. He warned, "A student is not greater than the teacher. A servant is not greater than the master" (10:24). Not only would his disciples be subjected to harassment and persecution, but much of it would come from those nearest and dearest to them (10:21-22, 34-36).

Despite the costs, millions through the centuries have chosen to follow Jesus. They have discovered a cause to live for in a world that lacks meaning and significance. They have believed that Christ is the world's only hope, and to be identified with him and his cause is to be part of the only lasting solution to human ills. They have taken seriously his words, "Don't be afraid of those who want to kill you. They can only kill your body; they cannot touch your soul" (10:28). They have discovered that the downside Jesus predicted is manageable because he also promised the empowering of the indwelling Spirit. They have taken great comfort in the fact that God, who keeps inventory on sparrows and records hair loss on men (10:29-30), will not let any eventuality escape his attention. And when it is all over they anticipate a promised reward of eternal proportions!

Sometimes life doesn't treat us as kindly as we fondly imagine it should. We are often told, "Nobody said life would be a rose garden." But in a very real sense Jesus *did* say this! Rose gardens are full of both roses and thorns. Roses and thorns are what he predicted, and that is exactly what his followers experience. He gives us the roses of his love and grace, but we also experience the thorns of adversity and opposition. You can't have the former without the latter.

When you feel the sharpness of adversity's thorns, remember that Jesus felt the pain of the cross to purchase for you the sweet fragrance of his salvation. He regarded his thorns as necessary and worthwhile in order for the roses to bloom. So should we. So smell the roses and look out for the thorns! He promised you both.

TO READ: *Matthew 10:28-42*

HAIR LOSS

"Don't be afraid of those who want to kill you. They can only kill your body; they cannot touch your soul. Fear only God, who can destroy both soul and body in hell. . . . The very hairs on your head are all numbered. So don't be afraid."

MATTHEW 10:28, 30-31

I f we are to believe television advertisements, hair loss is a matter of grave concern for men. When bald spots appear and hair lines recede, men spend anxious moments peering into their mirrors, anxiously monitoring hirsute progress (or regress!), worrying about lost youth, and trying desperately to shore up their flagging spirits and their depreciating self-worth. But advertisements tell us that, given the right kind of treatment, their hair can grow again, youth and vigor will be restored, and with luxuriant locks in place they can face the world again, confident and carefree.

If men are concerned about their hairstyles, God is even more so. Jesus indicated that heaven shows surprising interest in a man's hair. He said, "The very hairs on your head are all numbered" (Matt. 10:30). The significance of what Jesus was saying cannot be overemphasized. He wanted men to know that they are so precious in God's sight that their lives are divinely monitored. What this means is they should be able to approach life's vicissitudes with confidence, not so much because their hairline is in place, but because their hairs are numbered, meaning the minute details of their lives are known to God—and he cares about them. How much does he care? Changing the picture slightly, Jesus said, "Not even a sparrow, worth only half a penny, can fall to the ground without your Father knowing it. . . . So don't be afraid; you are more valuable to him than a whole flock of sparrows" (10:29, 31). As the old spiritual says,

His eye is on the sparrow.
And I know he watches me![33]

Life can be unnerving, and circumstances can be disconcerting. But the worries of life must be placed in their proper context. Losing your head matters a whole lot more than losing your hair! But even more important than losing your head is losing your soul. Jesus' comment on this is noteworthy: "Don't be afraid of those who want to kill you. They can only kill your body; they cannot touch your soul. Fear only God, who can destroy both soul and body in hell" (Matt. 10:28).

So, next time you look in the mirror to monitor your hairline, remember that every hair is inventoried in heaven, because every detail of your life is infinitely precious to God. And don't forget that one day your hairline won't matter—the only thing that will matter is heaven or hell!

[33] Civilla Martin, "His Eye Is on the Sparrow.

TO READ: *Matthew 13:1-23*

THE SEED AND THE SOILS

My job was to plant the seed in your hearts, and Apollos watered it,
but it was God, not we, who made it grow.

1 CORINTHIANS 3:6

The Church's mission is to spread the gospel. This has been done with varying degrees of effectiveness through the centuries, but recently more attention has been given to communicating the Good News to different kinds of people in ways that they will understand and embrace. Jesus had something to say on this subject.

Middle Eastern farmers of the first century sowed their seed as they walked up and down their land with a basket of seed on their hips, scattering seed in a sweeping arc. The seed would fall on all kinds of soil. Some would flourish, and the rest would never produce at all. Jesus used this common occurrence as an illustration of what happens when the Good News of the kingdom is spread abroad by his disciples.

God's word is like seed. When it is presented to men and women, it meets with a variety of responses. Some hearers are so well prepared that they eagerly respond. They receive the message, believe it, and embrace it, and new life begins to show (13:23). But sadly, other hearers are so hardened—perhaps disinterested or antagonistic—that the truth is quickly lost on them (13:19). Some hearers respond shallowly with intellectual assent and even a glad acknowledgment of the truth that hides an unchanged heart (13:20-21). Others fail to recognize the unique significance of the message, its importance lost among all the other things that clutter their lives (13:22).

What does this mean for the disciple who is eager to propagate the Good News? First, he should have confidence in the power of God's word, just as the farmer has confidence in the ability of his seed to produce. Second, the disciple must recognize that he is responsible to communicate the truth, but he cannot control the response. The farmer is responsible to sow the seed, but he cannot ensure a good harvest, no matter how much preparation he makes. Third, the disciple will meet people who want to evaluate the message, while in fact it is "evaluating" them! The soil doesn't "evaluate" the seed—it's vice versa! Fourth, the disciple must remember that people by nature are spiritually blind and deaf—they need God's miraculous intervention in their lives (13:12, 15).

Paul got it right when he said, "My job was to plant the seed in your hearts, and Apollos watered it, but it was God, not we, who made it grow" (1 Cor. 3:6). We are responsible for the sowing, but God is responsible for the growing.

THE SIGN OF JONAH

As the crowd pressed in on Jesus, he said, "These are evil times, and this evil
generation keeps asking me to show them a miraculous sign. But the only sign
I will give them is the sign of the prophet Jonah."

LUKE 11:29

P eople who struggle with faith sometimes say that, if they could have actually seen
Jesus at work and heard him with their own ears, they would not have any problems
believing. As understandable as this may be, it is probably not true. Some of the people
who saw Jesus at work and who heard him speak still struggled with believing! They
argued with him over what he had said, they were dissatisfied with the miracles he
performed, and they kept asking him for more miraculous signs.

Jesus' response to their lack of belief is enlightening. He saw their attitude not so much
as a struggle to believe, but as a symptom of "evil times" and an "evil generation" (Luke
11:29). He was convinced that his contemporaries had been given more than enough
evidence that he was who he claimed to be. Their unbelief was not an unfortunate or
unavoidable lack of faith—it was an outright act of wickedness. They chose not to believe
and demanded further signs.

One day, Jesus said that there would be no more signs except one—"the sign of the
prophet Jonah" (11:29). Jesus' listeners were familiar with the story of the prophet. When
God commissioned Jonah to head in an easterly direction to preach to the city of Nineveh,
Jonah intentionally headed west to Tarshish. But not for long! God hurled a storm at the
ship, and Jonah was hurled overboard by the reluctant crew when they discovered he was
responsible for their plight and when rowing and praying hadn't worked for them. Then a
large fish swallowed him and regurgitated him three days later. When God again told Jonah
to go to Nineveh, there were no arguments! Jonah arrived in Nineveh and preached as he
had been told. He made quite a stir—revival swept the city.

Perhaps some of Jesus' listeners understood what Jesus meant by the "sign of the
prophet Jonah," but many of them certainly did not. So to give them another hint, Jesus
added, "Someone greater than Jonah is here" (11:32). He was referring to himself. And the
sign that he would bring—the sign to end all signs—would be like what happened to Jonah.
Jesus would go down into death (rather than into the sea), would be buried for three days
(in a tomb rather than in a fish), and on the third day would rise from the dead (by his own
power rather than by being spit out). Thereafter he would show himself openly and preach
the Good News of the kingdom. That was the final sign, which in Jesus' opinion is more
than adequate as a basis of faith for all men at all times.

The issue for men today becomes, "How do I respond to Jesus' resurrection from the
dead?" Christianity stands or falls on this tenet of the faith. If Christ is risen, he is all he
said he was—the Messiah, the Son of God, the eternal king. If he isn't risen, he's dead—
and irrelevant. Either way, we don't need more signs. We need to choose to believe what
the evidence clearly shows. To refuse to believe is simply wickedness.

TO READ: *Luke 12:1–12*

PUBLIC LIFE,
PRIVATE LIFE

Jesus turned first to his disciples and warned them, "Beware of the yeast of the Pharisees—beware of their hypocrisy. The time is coming when everything will be revealed; all that is secret will be made public."

LUKE 12:1-2

C haracter and reputation should never be confused. A man's reputation is what people think he is. His character is what God knows he is. Living as we do in an image-conscious society, great emphasis is placed on how we appear in public. So business men are told how to dress for success and are encouraged to wear the right kind of power suits and ties. Politicians listen to focus groups and watch polls carefully to monitor any changes necessary in their "image." Even teenagers, ever conscious of peer pressure and acceptance, insist on the right kind of gear in order to be the right kind of cool. Image, public persona, reputation—these are what really matter to our culture. What a man is in private, what he is in the eyes of God—his character—is not given as much attention. In fact, we are told repeatedly that private life is of no concern to anyone other than the individual. So public image is of concern to the masses, but private life is of concern only to one. Right? Wrong!

Jesus knew full well that public image can be a projection of what is palpably false. In fact, he had in front of him a clear example of this. So he warned, "Beware of the yeast of the Pharisees—beware of their hypocrisy" (Luke 12:1). The Pharisees were masters of image; they were practiced at projecting a piety that was not a reflection of inner reality. Jesus had a name for it: He called it hypocrisy. Their lives were an act, a charade, a travesty.

Jesus went on, "The time is coming when everything will be revealed; all that is secret will be made public" (12:2). The barrier between private and public will be breached. The gap between what people think we are and what God knows we are will be bridged. There will be no difference between private and public life—everything private will be made public. We will be known as fully as God knows us.

So how should a man respond? He should be more concerned about how he appears to God than about how he is viewed by people. What he is in private—his character—should take priority over how he appears in public—his reputation. Reputation is not insignificant, but it can be inaccurate. Good people are sometimes given a bad name, while rogues are often praised to the skies. But it will not be so in heaven. What the world needs is men of sound character who earn a solid reputation. Their character pleases God, and their reputation blesses humanity.

TO READ: *Luke 14:25-35*

COUNTING THE COST

So no one can become my disciple without giving up everything for me.

LUKE 14:33

Telling it like it is is generally regarded as a rugged masculine trait. No beating about the bush, just straight talk, man to man. That is what men say they want to hear, and that is exactly what Jesus gave them. But when push came to shove, not everybody wanted to listen!

Jesus undoubtedly had mass appeal. There was something magnetic about his personality, his teaching, and particularly his miracles. His popularity served to get his message out to vast numbers of people, and his presence among the people promised blessing previously unknown. But the pathway to blessing led through the valley of submission to his lordship, and the people didn't all want to follow it. As Jesus spelled out the ramifications of his lordship, the people began to realize the far-reaching consequences of following him.

Jesus used no slick sales techniques that promised the earth at bargain prices. Instead he offered abundant life on the basis of acknowledging that he is the Lord and Savior. "No one can become my disciple without giving up everything for me" (14:33). In response to Jesus' love, which knows no bounds, his people should love him unequivocally. And if he, in his capacity as Lord of their lives, requires his people to release what had been exclusively their own, they should gladly relinquish their rights and acknowledge his right to direct what is in fact *his* own.

It is precisely because Jesus' words are so uncompromising that some people feel uncomfortable actually telling people what Jesus said. Our culture specializes in the "soft sell," the presentation that minimizes the product's drawbacks. The soft sell trumpets words like, "free," "no obligation," "return if for any reason it does not meet your needs," and "no payment until 2010." Such techniques are the norm, so some people believe that no one would respond to the Master's tough-love approach. But in this they are quite wrong. There are innumerable people who rejoice in a challenge and thrill to the possibility that they could actually be different and make a difference. Jesus was not only interested in saving people from a wasted eternity—he was committed to making their wasted lives count. He had come to change the world, and the words he spoke would resonate with potential world changers.

Salty talk, this! But Jesus knew that sugarcoated talk never made salty saints.

TO READ: *Psalm 10*

GOD AND THE RAT RACE

Why do the wicked get away with cursing God? How can they think,
"God will never call us to account"?

PSALM 10:13

L ife is a rat race—and the rats are winning!" Many of our contemporaries think this way, and sometimes it seems they are right. The psalmist would probably not have thought of his world as a rat race, nor would he have called its inhabitants rats. But that description would certainly fit his perception of what was going on around him.

Functional atheists are the rats who populate the rat race. Functional atheists are not theoretical atheists—people who argue philosophically that God does not exist. Rather, they are people who live and function as though God does not exist (10:4, 11-13). He is for them a nonfactor, a total irrelevance. Functional atheists disdain utterly any concept that there is a God who rules the universe, who determines the way we should live, and who holds us accountable. They casually trample underfoot any thought of divine rule, divine order, or divine retribution. And they seem to get away with it! Life for them is sweet.

For the psalmist, life was bitter. While the rats were coming up roses, the psalmist was picking thistles. It was seeing that the rats seemed to be winning that stuck in the psalmist's craw. It was bad enough that they lived as if God were dead, or at least incapacitated. But it was infinitely worse that God seemed to be assisting their conclusions by being conspicuously absent. Glibly they said, "Nothing bad will ever happen to us! We will be free of trouble forever!" (10:6). Happily they insisted, "God isn't watching! He will never notice!" (10:11). And God seemed to be letting them get away with it. It seemed the rats were winning and the referee wasn't even watching!

But the psalmist clung to two things. He believed with all his heart that "The Lord is king forever and ever!" (10:16) and that the Lord "will bring justice" (10:18). If those things are true, there is hope that righteousness will ultimately triumph. We may not see it in our lifetime because the Lord operates in the forever and ever. We may not experience it the way we want, but we can bear in mind that the Lord knows "the hopes of the helpless" and "will listen to their cries and comfort them" (10:17). He will make sure that justice is ultimately done (see Luke 16:19-31).

We can face the rat race and know that God wins—not the rats! We can run the race God's way, not theirs. And we can concentrate on the God standing at the finishing line rather than on the rats nipping our heels.

TO READ: *Genesis 4:1–16*

CHOICES AND CONSEQUENCES

"You will be accepted if you respond in the right way. But if you refuse to respond
correctly, then watch out! Sin is waiting to attack and destroy you,
and you must subdue it."

GENESIS 4:7

M an would like very much to be free to make his own choices and to be exempt
from the consequences of his decisions. For instance, he likes sexual freedom but
dislikes sexually transmitted diseases. So he seeks ways to engineer "safe sex." Man wants
freedom without consequences.

Adam, the first man, was free to obey or disobey God, but he was not free from the
consequences of his decision. God had given him a lot of freedom in the garden—Adam
could eat from any tree at all except for one. And he had been told that if he disobeyed, he
would surely die (2:17). Instead of listening to God and staying within the limits of his
God-given freedom, Adam listened to the voice of evil, embraced sin, and went ahead in
disobeying God. Perhaps he assumed that God would not do what he said he would do.
Or, maybe he thought that enjoying his "freedom" would be worth whatever sanctions
came. He was wrong, though, because the consequence of his decision was death—
spiritual death in his relationship with God and the death of his body. But the
consequences did not end there.

In the next generation Adam's son Cain also became alienated from God. He, too,
ignored God's warning, listened to the voice of evil, and embraced sin. Then he complained,
"You have banished me from my land and from your presence; you have made me a
wandering fugitive" (4:14). But why was he in this state and why was he complaining?
Simply because he, too, had rebelled against God's command and had chosen the pathway
of "freedom." Cain had been informed by God, "You will be accepted if you respond in the
right way. But if you refuse to respond correctly, then watch out! Sin is waiting to attack and
destroy you, and you must subdue it" (4:7). He chose not to "watch out" but rather to
plunge ahead. Committed as he was to his freedom of choice, Cain still had difficulty
accepting that his sin had consequences. His complaint shows that he wanted not only the
right to sin freely, but also the right to be free from responsibility and exempt from the
fallout.

Man's freedom to choose his actions is one side of the equation, and God's freedom
to choose the consequences is the other. We may be free to choose, but we are not free
from the consequences. The sin may be over in a moment, but the consequences may last
a lifetime—or even forever.

TO READ: *Genesis 17:1-14*

WHAT'S IN A NAME?

When Abram was ninety-nine years old, the LORD appeared to him and said,
"I am God Almighty; serve me faithfully and live a blameless life. . . .
What's more, I am changing your name. It will no longer be Abram;
now you will be known as Abraham, for you will be the father of many nations."

GENESIS 17:1, 5

A bram was ninety-nine years old when the Lord appeared to him and introduced himself as "God Almighty"—*El Shaddai* in Hebrew. That God disclosed himself by name meant not only that he wanted Abram to know who he is, but also that he was inviting Abram to experience intimacy with him. In effect, God was saying, "You can call me El Shaddai, Abram." Abram discovered that God Almighty was eager to be known on an intimate basis.

When El Shaddai, God Almighty, invited Abram into an intimate covenant relationship, he gave him a new name—a name that contained God's covenant promise in its meaning. El Shaddai wanted his new friend to understand what was going to happen in the future. He had decided that Abram should be the means whereby all the nations of the world would be blessed, with a family numbering in the millions from among his descendants. To reinforce the message, Abram underwent a name change from *Abram*, meaning "exalted father," to *Abraham*, meaning "father of many."

Along with a new name, God Almighty gave Abraham and his family a new identity as a people set apart for relationship with him. The token of this relationship was that Abraham and his descendants would be circumcised. The name and the token both indicated the same identity as God's people.

God may not give us a new name now, but he does give a new name in heaven to everyone who has a covenant relationship with him (Rev. 2:17). That name represents the new identity of a person changed by Christ. And a changed man who engages in careful study of God's word gains a deeper knowledge of the Lord and a clearer understanding of himself. (It is only as we see ourselves as God sees us and know ourselves in relation to God that our self-understanding is accurate.) This deepening of insight and excitement of discovery in turn create a freshness of message and a sharpening of focus, and the man who lives in the power of El Shaddai becomes like a father to many.

Names matter. They express who we are and whose we are. So when it comes to naming our own children, it's a good idea to give them names that will remind them of our aspirations for them. Their names can help them understand their identity. A lot can be expressed in a name.

GOD'S PRESENCE

Then Jacob woke up and said, "Surely the LORD is in this place, and I wasn't even
aware of it." He was afraid and said, "What an awesome place this is!
It is none other than the house of God—the gateway to heaven!"

GENESIS 28:16-17

J acob, on the run from his brother, alone in inhospitable territory, settled down for the
night with a rock for a pillow—hardly the most comfortable set of circumstances! But
he had brought this situation on himself. We have no knowledge of his thoughts as he
settled down for the night, but we do know that he could not have anticipated what
happened. In a dream he was given a pictorial reminder that God and his angels are
actively involved in the affairs of men on earth. The Lord told him in that dream that he
could count on the Lord's presence at all times and that the Lord had great plans for him
that he was committed to bringing to pass.

On waking, Jacob exclaimed, "Surely the Lord is in this place, and I wasn't even aware
of it" (28:16). It is not surprising that he was unaware of the Lord's presence, because no
doubt he was absorbed with his own schemes and anxieties. It took a dramatic dream when
he was all alone to arrest his attention and focus his mind on the presence of God.

Amazing, isn't it, that we men who think we know so much don't even know the
presence of the Lord at times? In our world there are so many distractions—far more than in
Jacob's day. The man who spends all his time amid the tensions and clamors of life may not
be conscious of the Lord's presence, particularly if he is carrying the cares and consequences
of past actions. The man whose conscience is weighed down with his actions and whose life
is burdened with the consequences is not usually super conscious of the Lord. But the Lord is
present nevertheless.

We men need to find a quiet place where the Lord can speak the truth to us in love.
If the only time he can arrest our attention is while we are sleeping, then we are probably
too busy and our minds are too full of "the cares and riches and pleasures of this life"
(Luke 8:14). But if he does arrest our attention, we will be struck with the awesomeness of
the Lord. And then no doubt we will, like Jacob, respond with a refreshed commitment of
service and allegiance to the God who was there all the time but we didn't know it.

TO READ: *Genesis 39:1-23*

SECRETS
OF JOSEPH'S SUCCESS

The LORD was with Joseph and blessed him greatly as he served in the home of his Egyptian master. Potiphar noticed this and realized that the LORD was with Joseph, giving him success in everything he did.

GENESIS 39:2-3

J oseph's early life could be described as, "From the pedestal to the pit to the penthouse to the prison." Talk about a roller-coaster ride! After being sold into slavery by his brothers, he arrived in the household of a man of influence. Instead of bemoaning his fate, Joseph set to work utilizing the obvious gifts God had entrusted to him. The result was recognition and advancement. Unfortunately, the recognition factor worked in more than one direction. The boss's wife noticed Joseph and made advances to him, which Joseph rebuffed rather than dishonor his master and sin against his God. As we know, "hell hath no fury like a woman scorned," so Joseph ended up in prison, guilty of being honorable. But even there he conducted himself with great integrity and industry. Very soon Joseph was not only running the prison, he was also counseling some of Pharaoh's out-of-favor men.

There are a number of principles of success to be learned from Joseph's success story. First of all, as he languished in prison he embraced the moment. Second, he never allowed the vision of success to cloud his vision of what was ethically right. Third, he adapted himself to his changing situations rather than exerting his energies in fighting them. Fourth, he saw in every problem a possibility. Fifth, he knew how to snatch victory from the jaws of defeat. Sixth, he knew there was no substitute for hard work. And seventh, long before Paul told the slaves of his day, "Work hard and cheerfully at whatever you do, as though you were working for the Lord rather than for people" (Col. 3:23), Joseph did it.

All of Joseph's "secrets of success" were rooted in his relationship to the Lord. It was the Lord who was with him in the pit, and it was the Lord who was the source of all his gifts. It was the Lord who said what was right, it was the Lord who was working out his eternal purposes, and it was the Lord to whom Joseph would one day give an account. When life is lived with God as the Lord, the location is of secondary importance—whether it be the pedestal or the pit, the prison or the penthouse. What really matters is that life is lived in and through, and before and because of, the Lord. That is the way to success. For it takes the Lord to make a man successful, wherever he may be.

TO READ: *Exodus 6:1-8*

THE I AM

"Therefore, say to the Israelites: 'I am the LORD, and I will free you from your slavery in Egypt. I will redeem you with mighty power and great acts of judgment. I will make you my own special people, and I will be your God. And you will know that I am the LORD your God who has rescued you from your slavery in Egypt."

EXODUS 6:6-7

I n Africa, parents name their children after events that coincide with the birth of the child. In America, parents sometimes name their children after their favorite celebrities. In my native England, parents usually name their children after another family member. But in ancient times, names held special significance. They often described the personality and significance of the one bearing the name. So, for instance, Jacob needed a new name when God turned his life around, and he became Israel; and Jesus was given his name precisely because Jesus means "God is the Savior."

Moses and Aaron had just confronted Pharaoh and demanded that he let Israel go and worship God in the wilderness. Pharaoh responded by increasing the burden of their slavery. The leaders of Israel blamed Moses and Aaron for their woes. What a predicament they were in! But as always, Moses looked to the Lord for help.

In response, God reminded Moses, "I am the LORD" (Exod. 6:6). The Hebrew word translated "LORD" is *Yahweh* or *Jehovah*—a name so sacred to the devout Jew that he will not even pronounce it. The name is related to the verb *to be*, which is significant when we remember that God had also told Moses that his name is "I AM THE ONE WHO ALWAYS IS" (3:14). Moses needed to know that the Lord is the unchanging one, the one who always is, without beginning, without end, totally self-contained and self-sufficient, not dependent, not contingent, lacking nothing, complete and entire in himself.

"What's in a name?" asked Shakespeare. *Everything,* if it is the name of the great I AM. God's name is a revelation of who he is. We failing, fragile creatures need to be constantly reassured that the Lord is the One Who Always Is. When we get this straight, it does not matter that things change, that the future is obscure, that fears assail us, or that doubts beset us. *He* does not change, and in him we find our security and our confidence. Remember, Jesus' final words to his disciples were, "I am with you always, even to the end of the age" (Matt. 28:20). Because he is with us, we can have complete confidence in him.

TO READ: *Exodus 23:1-13*

HAVES AND HAVE-NOTS

"Do not twist justice against people simply because they are poor. . . . Do not oppress the foreigners living among you. You know what it is like to be a foreigner. Remember your own experience in the land of Egypt."

EXODUS 23:6, 9

An underclass seems to emerge in every culture. Social scientists theorize about the reasons for this sociological phenomenon, but the ancient Scriptures spend less time theorizing and more time giving instructions to the privileged regarding their responsibilities to the underprivileged.

The children of Israel had been in the underprivileged category for many years during their Egyptian slavery. But once they were freed from bondage and were headed for the land of promise, it was time for them to remember their social obligations to those not so fortunate as they. These people—the poor, the widows, the orphans, and the foreigners—were extremely vulnerable to the exploiter and had to be protected from those who would callously make their sad situation worse. These vulnerable people were in dire straits for a variety of reasons, but in each case they were to be treated with justice and love, because they, too, were people with dignity, made in God's image.

The principles outlined here, forbidding exploitation and mandating justice, apply to our situation today—even if the specific instructions do not apply. The ban on charging interest on loans, for instance, was designed to ensure that the poor were given a chance to escape their poverty; it probably did not refer to commercial loans. The restriction on keeping a man's cloak overnight simply meant that even interest-free loans required collateral, but if the only collateral available was a poor man's "poncho" he should not be deprived of it during the long, cold night. Even hard-nosed business should have a smiling face.

Our concern for the vulnerable and needy does not stem from political ideology, as we in the modern world might be tempted to assume, but from a profound theological conviction that all people, made in God's image, must be treated with respect, biblical love, and compassion. The application of these ancient laws for modern-day business is that the powerful are not to exploit the powerless; the "haves" are to be concerned for the "have-nots"; and business must not be driven solely by the profit motive. Sound business practice must embrace justice, compassion, and generosity. It's a sobering thought that with God the bottom line is not necessarily the top priority.

PRAISING GOD

*May the words of my mouth and the thoughts of my heart be pleasing to you,
O LORD, my rock and my redeemer.*

PSALM 19:14

T here are lots of things wrong with our world. But there are lots of things right about it, too! The things that are wrong point to the cataclysmic Fall, where arrogant man thought he knew better than God and plunged the world into chaos. The things that are right remind us that the world, tarnished though it is, still bears witness to its superb Creator.

Silently the heavens speak. Without uttering a sound or a word they proclaim mightily the wonders of their Creator. Morning by morning the glorious sun rises and speaks of the relentless faithfulness of a totally reliable God. Evening by evening the stars shine brightly and remind us of his brilliant vastness. To those who have ears to hear and eyes to see, "the heavens tell of the glory of God" (19:1).

But to many the message is indistinct. Silent speaking does not register with them, and wordless messages convey little. So God gave his word. It supplements creation's revelation and glorification of God. It speaks where creation is silent; it communicates to those to whom the sun says little about God and the stars say nothing about deity. It is "sweeter than honey" (19:10) to those who dip into its riches. There they find truth that revives and encourages, warnings that protect and preserve, instructions that command and direct, and promises that gladden and delight. Scripture speaks, and its very words bring glory to God.

But black print on white paper says little to some, since they are too busy to read, too disinterested to inquire. That's where you and I come in. God must be glorified and his truth must be broadcast, whether by silent sun and sparkling star, by written word, or by truth spoken and lived out. Humans can do what the word and the creation cannot do— we alone can take the truth and explain it in glowing, vibrant terms that help men to see, and nothing in the world can articulate God's praise like man.

That is why God equips us to proclaim him in worship, and that is why he commissions us to spread his truth in witness. That is why we must pray, like the psalmist, "May the words of my mouth and the thoughts of my heart be pleasing to you, O Lord, my rock and my redeemer" (19:14). We are his unique mouthpieces, like nothing else on earth!

CRAFTSMANSHIP

I have filled him with the Spirit of God, giving him great wisdom,
intelligence, and skill in all kinds of crafts.

EXODUS 31:3

An unusually humble poet once wrote, "Poems are made by fools like me, but only God can make a tree." He was not a fool, because he recognized his limitations. But he was right about only God making trees. Yet God has passed on some of his creative ability to men. God creates and man crafts.

It all started with a man called Jubal. He was "the inventor of the harp and flute" (Gen. 4:21). God gave him a gift. He could hear the sound of the wind in the trees and the song of the birds on the branches, and perhaps he thought, *that's beautiful,* and something in his heart longed to reproduce the sound. So with dexterous fingers and divinely imparted originality he fashioned a flute. Then maybe he listened to the rippling sound of a brook on pebbles. With great ingenuity he duplicated the lovely sound on a harp. His half brother Tubal-cain was different. He was more artisan than artist, but he fashioned beautiful things, too, as "he was the first to work with metal, forging instruments of bronze and iron" (Gen. 4:22).

Then along came Bezalel, a Spirit-filled man whose divinely imparted skills spanned all manner of craftsmanship. He was equally at home working in metals, wood, or gems. He made things that were essentially practical but unfailingly beautiful. For him it was not enough to make things that worked. His craftsmanship reflected something of his delight in the things God had made. His handiwork was an expression of praise and appreciation—a piece of work that was in itself an act of worship.

Unfortunately, music can get ugly, and bronze and iron can be fashioned into instruments of torture. But it need not be so. There is beauty all around in God's handiwork. The man who serves God will see it, appreciate it, and with God-given talent reproduce it to God's glory and man's delight. There's too much ugliness and sordidness in the world for which men are responsible. We need more Jubals, Tubal-cains, and Bezalels, producers of beauty and purveyors of delight. We need more men for whom creation is such a delight that they want to preserve it, to portray it, and to pick its bountiful richness. We need more men who see that God is the ultimate Creator who has called them to be consummate craftsmen. Many men have a tendency to destroy. More men are needed who will beautify our world and glorify their Lord.

TO READ: *Exodus 39:32-43*

FAITHFULNESS
IN THE DETAILS

So the people of Israel followed all of the Lord's instructions to Moses.
Moses inspected all their work and blessed them because it had been done
as the LORD had commanded him.

EXODUS 39:42-43

Y ou've probably heard it said that "the devil is in the details." What you may not have
heard is that the Lord is interested in the details! He expects those who take their
spiritual lives seriously to show their faithfulness not only in the major issues but in the
minor details, too.

God Almighty made it clear that he intended to dwell among the people of Israel,
whom he had chosen. Even in their wilderness travels he had indicated that his presence in
their midst was vital to their identity and survival. Accordingly, God ordered his people to
build a structure that would be appropriate to their environment—a tent in a desert. More
important, it was a structure worthy of his presence. God conveyed minute details concerning size, structure, materials, and decorations to Moses.

Given the difficult circumstances under which these people worked, it is noteworthy
that they took no shortcuts, used no inferior materials, and took pains to finish the work
as stipulated. The people building the tabernacle in the desert were doing their work as
unto the Lord, and for them a job well done was the least their God deserved. The quality
of their work was testimony to their faithful commitment to him. On inspection of the
finished work, Moses noted that the "people of Israel followed all of the Lord's instructions," and he called together the workmen and "blessed them because it had been done
as the Lord had commanded him" (39:42-43).

Modern workmen are not always as assiduous. They call in sick when they are not,
they cut corners if no one is watching, they contract for one commodity and slip in
another. Employees rip off management, and managers abuse employees. Many people
feel the workplace is a rat race and the rats are winning. What a place for the man of God
to show he marches to a different drummer!

We are called to live out our discipleship by being faithful to God in the details of
our lives. The Lord deserves to be well served; those who do so in their daily lives are
simply being faithful. Faithfulness comes in many shapes and sizes, but it never includes
shortcuts, shoddy materials, and half measures. Faithfulness, even and especially in the
details of our lives, is what God desires.

TO READ: *Leviticus 4:22-35*

SACRIFICIAL FORGIVENESS

"If any of the citizens of Israel do something forbidden by the LORD,
they will be guilty even if they sinned unintentionally."

LEVITICUS 4:27

S ome men seem surprised when they do something wrong—as if they think they are incapable of engaging in such an act. But usually they recover quite quickly and either forget about it or, if the matter lingers in their memory, they are encouraged to "forgive themselves"! Now that concept is as odd as it is common. Think about it. How can a man forgive himself? If some wrong has been done, and someone has been wronged, then only the person who has been wronged can forgive the wrongdoer. The wrongdoer can't forgive himself, and neither can a third party forgive him. If you punch me on my nose, only I can forgive you—you can't exonerate yourself, and even your doting mother can't forgive you.

Here's the point about man's sin. While it is true that most sin negatively affects others and we are responsible for the harm done to them, the person who has really been wronged is God. Sin is a denial of the authority of God, a repudiation of God's right to determine what is right and what is wrong, a rejection of his gracious direction of our behavior. So sin is primarily against God, and if he is the one wronged, then he alone is the one who can forgive.

This leads to two monumental questions. First, if God alone can forgive sin, will he? The answer to this is YES! He will! He has proved that by forgiving the Israelites through their sacrifices, and he has proved that to us by forgiving us through Christ. Second, what price does God demand in order for forgiveness to be made available? More than the sum total of what human effort can ever pay. We can never pay for our own sins, so God paid for them.

The New Testament discusses the issue of sacrifice as follows: "Under the old covenant, the priest stands before the altar day after day, offering sacrifices that can never take away sins. But our High Priest offered himself to God as one sacrifice for sins, good for all time. Then he sat down at the place of highest honor at God's right hand" (Heb. 10:11-12). Don't assume you can forgive yourself—you can't! Let God do the forgiving—he can! And he will.

TO READ: *Leviticus 16:1-22, 29-34*

YOM KIPPUR

*On this day, atonement will be made for you, and you will be cleansed
from all your sins in the Lord's presence.*

LEVITICUS 16:30

G od decided to go and live with his people in the wilderness. The tabernacle—the house he had them build for him—was a masterpiece. Meticulously designed down to the last detail, it symbolized his holy presence in their midst. The people were invited to visit the house, and the high priest was allowed to enter the Most Holy Place, but, sinful as they were, their presence served to defile God's dwelling place. As a result, on the Day of Atonement ceremonial cleansing of both place, priest, and people was required.

On that day, celebrated now as Yom Kippur, the high priest was required to wash thoroughly, then to sacrifice a bull for his own sins and his family's sins. Then two goats were presented to the freshly cleansed high priest. The first was sacrificed to cleanse the tabernacle, the place of worship. Then, after ceremonially laying the confessed sins of the people on the head of the second goat, the priest sent it off into the wilderness.

As bizarre as these rituals may seem to us today, the symbolism was unmistakable to the people of Israel: God's judgment for sin was being meted out on an innocent substitute, and the sins of the people were being removed from sight and memory. No Israelite observing these solemn procedures could ever assume that the Holy God takes sin lightly. By the same token, he could easily have seen that this same God, while appalled at his people's sinfulness, nevertheless takes great pains to make reconciliation and forgiveness available.

The elaborate systems of tabernacle and temple have served their purpose and passed away. They pointed to Christ, and he has fulfilled all that they promised. No longer is there a need for goats to be offered and for blood to be shed. Christ has done it all. By his death a final sacrifice has been made. Through his death God's dwelling place, the church, has been cleansed and made holy, and through his death sins are forgiven, banished from God's sight and memory. The day that Christ died is our permanent and lasting Day of Atonement, so we no longer need this yearly ritual. But behind the ancient Israelite ritual we can see the reality of Christ, and we can respond with reverent rejoicing.

TO READ: *Leviticus 19:1-19*

HOLINESS AND PICKING GRAPES

"When you harvest your crops, do not harvest the grain along the edges of your fields,
and do not pick up what the harvesters drop. It is the same with your grape crop—
do not strip every last bunch of grapes from the vines, and do not pick up the
grapes that fall to the ground. Leave them for the poor and the foreigners
who live among you, for I, the LORD, am your God."

LEVITICUS 19:9-10

Linking the holiness of God and picking grapes may be something of a stretch; but God did it, so we need to be stretched.

The holiness of God refers not only to his sinlessness, but more fundamentally to his "otherness." God declared such things as the ground, special pans, and special days to be holy, not because they were sinless (how could a pan be "sinless"?), but because they were separate, set apart, "special." So God, being utterly other and set apart, calls his people to be holy. This does not mean he expects them to be sinless (he knows better!), but he does require them to be "other," separate, distinct. This includes not engaging in the sinful lifestyles of their neighbors. But what does this holiness look like?

Holiness is essentially practical. It shows itself in family relationships, in work and rest habits, in neighborliness, and in matters of compassion and justice. This brings us to the grapes. When the Israelites finally arrived in the Promised Land and enjoyed the vineyards that were already there, they might have gotten so carried away with harvesting their crops that they would overlook the poor people who were either looking longingly at the abundance or working hard in the vineyards for less than adequate wages. God, who consistently embraces the cause of the underprivileged, stated that some grapes were to be left unpicked specifically for these people, and some crops were to be deliberately left for the benefit of those who had no harvest of their own. To do so was a matter of holiness, because it showed how different God's people would be from the surrounding nations, who often showed no mercy to the poor. So you see, there is a very definite link between being holy and picking grapes!

There is also a link between holiness and opening doors for old people, picking up beer cans left in the countryside, caring for AIDS patients, reviewing the way you pay your employees, treating a baggage handler with courtesy, and showing respect to a waiter. In some ways holiness is not easy. But in our culture so many people behave so badly that it is not very difficult to stand out, to be separate, to be holy—simply by treating people properly!

TO READ: *Leviticus 23:1-22*

HANGING TOGETHER

"You may work for six days each week, but on the seventh day all work must come to a complete stop. It is the Lord's Sabbath day of complete rest, a holy day to assemble for worship. It must be observed wherever you live."

LEVITICUS 23:3

God loves celebrations, and he encourages his people to enjoy them too! When God completed his work of creation, he rested. Thereafter, his people were told that they, too, should rest on the seventh day, the Sabbath. Some of their pagan neighbors did a similar thing, but they did it because they believed that the seventh day was unlucky. The Israelites believed it was holy—special. A special holy day set apart for rest, worship, and celebration. Rest alone was not the purpose of the Sabbath. On the rest day, and on other special occasions, God's people were called to celebrate "a holy day to assemble for worship" (23:3).

It is important for us to note the role that regular rest, regular worship, and community celebration played in Israel's lifestyle. Great emphasis was placed on the people as a whole ceasing work and coming together at certain times so that they could collectively acknowledge the Lord. Communal celebration served to bind the people together with a sense of common roots, aspirations, objectives, and orientation, all focused on the Lord himself. Down through the years, as the Sabbaths were observed, the children of Israel were strong in the Lord and victorious against their enemies in a hostile world. But when common celebration took a backseat, friction, fracturing, and fragmentation became common.

There's a lesson here for modern man. It is now a well-established fact that regular rest is in man's best interests, but not enough attention is paid to the need for worship and community celebration. Our culture, unlike that of Israel, is pluralistic. We lack commonality, and the fissures and divisions are plain to see and alarming to observe. Communities without commonality are a contradiction in terms. But if little commonality exists, we need to create more by establishing events that bring people together, giving them time to see each other relax, presenting opportunities to learn different customs and observe different traditions. This is not only true in secular society but also in the believing community. Some Christians see little significance in belonging to a community of believers, and many Christian communities show little or no interest in joining together in common praise and service. The framers of the Declaration of Independence knew the value of community. Benjamin Franklin, who was one of them, said, "We must indeed hang together, or, most assuredly, we shall all hang separately." Their concern was personal survival; our concern should be corporate cohesion and well-being of our community.

OCTOBER

WAITING PATIENTLY

I waited patiently for the LORD to help me, and he turned to me and heard my cry.

PSALM 40:1

I t isn't just people who try our patience. Situations do it too. We find ourselves in places we don't want to be, doing things we have no desire to do, in circumstances we don't want to embrace, and there's little or nothing we can do about it. So we fume and fester, and our frustrations intensify.

David knew all about this. He was God's man, but he spent far too much time on the run from his enemies. The throne was his by right, but the wilderness was where he spent many a night (see 1 Sam. 16:13; 18:1–24:22). He said, "Troubles surround me—too many to count! They pile up so high I can't see my way out. They are more numerous than the hairs on my head. I have lost all my courage. Please, Lord, rescue me! Come quickly, Lord, and help me" (Ps. 40:12-13). It is not surprising that he turned to the Lord for help, and it is perfectly understandable that he wanted it "quickly." Men usually want solutions to be delivered at once, if not sooner. But note how David began this Psalm. "I waited patiently for the Lord" (40:1). His natural desire for quick solutions had been tempered by long experience of the way God works. David's natural desire for a quick answer was tempered by a willingness to "wait patiently." He knew from previous experience that it was only a matter of time before he could once again testify, "He lifted me out of the pit of despair, out of the mud and the mire. He set my feet on solid ground and steadied me as I walked along" (40:2).

God is not the God of the quick fix. Neither is he the Lord of the instant. He takes his time growing an oak from an acorn and allows the long winter to prepare the earth for the warmth of spring. But it is precisely the promise of spring that makes the winter more palatable, and it is the certainty that an oak lies hidden within the acorn that makes it bearable to wait for the tree to grow.

Why, we wonder, does God take his time? No doubt his reasons are many and profound, but perhaps it is because we can only appreciate how solid is the rock he provides when we have thoroughly experienced the mud and the mire.

TO READ: *Numbers 5:11-31*

SUSPICION

*"This is the ritual law for dealing with jealousy. If a woman defiles herself by being
unfaithful to her husband, or if a man is overcome with jealousy and suspicion
that his wife has been unfaithful, the husband must present his wife before the LORD,
and the priest will apply this entire ritual law to her."*

NUMBERS 5:29-30

I n our culture, sexual morality is regarded as a purely personal matter. How you live is
viewed as your own business, and issues of adultery and unfaithfulness are settled
privately between a man and his wife. But for Israel, marital faithfulness and sexual morality
were community concerns. From the beginning of Creation, God had ordained that a man
and a woman should establish a family and that the family should become the foundational
building block of society. Anything, therefore, that would jeopardize the well-being of
marriages and families was much more than a private matter. It was seen as a threat to the
fabric of society and, accordingly, was a concern for the community as a whole.

So how did the community intervene when a husband suspected his wife of
unfaithfulness? If a husband was suspicious that his wife was being unfaithful, he was
required to bring his wife before the priest, who would then engage in a complicated
procedure to ascertain her guilt or innocence. This procedure was designed to protect the
powerless wife. The husband was not free simply to pass judgment by his own initiative.
Instead, the issue had to be handled "before the Lord" in the Holy Place, with full
knowledge of the community and under the guidance of the religious leaders. Actually,
Israel's procedure was very merciful for the woman. In neighboring states, a woman in
similar circumstances would have been required to throw herself in the river. If she
survived she was innocent, if she drowned she was guilty—and dead!

Matters of suspicion between husband and wife are to be dealt with honestly and
openly with each other before the Lord. This requires a willingness to talk with each other
about deep personal matters and a readiness to pray together about their spiritual and
moral well-being. Of course, couples should start by learning to talk and pray openly
about lesser issues. Then, when problems arise, they will have a more solid basis for
finding a solution.

Sexual morality is critical for the well-being of a society, and so it is not a purely
personal affair. Stable cultures require stable families, and stable families are built by
stable marriages. Stable marriages thrive on marital faithfulness, and marital faithfulness
is nurtured by marital openness. So start with open, honest, and truthful communication
with each other.

TO READ: *Numbers 6:22–27*

GOD'S PEACE

May the LORD show you his favor and give you his peace.

NUMBERS 6:26

G od blesses his people. We receive great benefits from our association with him. These benefits are designed to enrich our lives, and this enrichment becomes evident to those who live within the sphere of our influence. So God blesses people in order that they might be a blessing!

It was customary for the Israelites to be "blessed" by the high priest. The Israelites had been called by God to be his unique people, and this blessing would designate them as such. As the surrounding people groups observed the conditions under which God's people lived and the special ways in which they conducted their lives, it would become apparent that they were no ordinary people and their God was no ordinary god. The people would exhibit the divine favor by demonstrating that God had given them "his peace." The word *peace* means literally "wholeness" or "well-being," and it was no ordinary sense of well-being that they would enjoy. It was the well-being that comes only from God himself—his peace!

Paul talked about "God's peace which is far more wonderful than the human mind can understand" (Phil. 4:7). God's peace, which is the "peace of God," should not be confused with "peace with God." The "peace of God" is the inner state of well-being that is the birthright of those who have responded to God's offer of forgiveness and have been brought into a position called "peace with God." The peace *of* God is a result of having peace *with* God. The former is a result of the latter.

This inner sense of wholeness is something that cannot be explained in purely human terms. Anyone can seem to be at peace when he has eradicated all stress and negotiated the end of all hostility. But the peace of God is that which we enjoy while the stress continues unabated and the hostility persists. How can this be? It works when we realize that when we have committed ourselves to the Captain of our salvation in ongoing, trusting obedience, he will make our well-being his personal responsibility. So we can rest assured in his benevolence and competence in the midst of the storms of life. We can live with an equanimity that defies description and surpasses belief.

TO READ: *Numbers 11:1-15*

WHINING ABOUT DINING

Then the foreign rabble who were traveling with the Israelites began to crave the good things of Egypt, and the people of Israel also began to complain. "Oh, for some meat!" they exclaimed. "We remember all the fish we used to eat for free in Egypt. And we had all the cucumbers, melons, leeks, onions, and garlic that we wanted."

NUMBERS 11:4-5

Foreign travel can be a challenge. The food is often below par, the accommodations can leave much to be desired, the travel arrangements are usually haywire, and there is no air conditioning. A sure and certain recipe for complaints!

As the children of Israel set out on their foreign travel, they certainly complained. The novelty and excitement of being delivered from slavery in Egypt began to wear off once they embarked on their second year of freedom. The wilderness was no easy place to live even when they were settled in camp, but it only took three days on the march before the people began to complain to the Lord about their hardships. Some of the "foreign rabble" in the party became quite outspoken about their preference for Egyptian cuisine, and the Israelites joined in complaining about their steady diet of manna. I suspect many of us who are used to our comfortable lifestyle would have joined in the complaining of the wilderness travelers!

We may be surprised at how severely God responded to his people's complaints, but we must remember that God had a grand plan for his people. This plan included redeeming them from Egypt (which he had miraculously accomplished), supporting tens of thousands of people in an inhospitable wilderness, taking them into the Promised Land, and enabling them to overthrow the resident population. For this plan to be accomplished, the Lord required his people's unwavering obedience and unfaltering trust. He was, and is, looking for those who would cooperate rather than complain, who would count their blessings rather than chorus their gripes. But neither was forthcoming from them. While God was focusing on the monumental issues, God's people were whining about dining.

In the long run, the wisest policy is to get on board with what God is doing, whether or not it makes us comfortable. The best way to get on board with him is to trust that he knows what he is doing, to obey what he tells us to do, and to have a thankful attitude for everything he has given us. If we don't, he might become angry with such ungrateful, uncooperative children. He might give us what we want, and then we may discover we don't want it. If we *do* get on board with God, we will arrive in the Promised Land, and that's better than leeks, onions, and garlic.

TO READ: *Numbers 14:1-25*

PATIENCE IS A VIRTUE

*"Please, Lord, prove that your power is as great as you have claimed it to be.
For you said, 'The LORD is slow to anger and rich in unfailing love, forgiving every
kind of sin and rebellion. Even so he does not leave sin unpunished, but he punishes
the children for the sins of their parents to the third and fourth generations.'
Please pardon the sins of this people because of your magnificent, unfailing love,
just as you have forgiven them ever since they left Egypt."*

NUMBERS 14:17-19

W hen we think of masculine virtues, patience does not come immediately to mind. Perhaps this is because men like to fix things and to do it quickly. We like to be in control—to make things happen. But there are times in the divine plan when there are things that we cannot fix or situations that do not respond to our solutions. What then? The natural reaction is to try harder and increase the blood pressure. But not in the divine economy. With God, patience is the word!

Surely the greatest example of patience is found in the Lord's dealings with his creatures. During the long history of the chosen people, God had countless opportunities to demonstrate his patience with them. He had declared that he is "slow to get angry" (Ps. 103:8). Even at the point of considering whether to wipe them out and start again with Joshua and Caleb, God stood by his rebellious people and gave them yet another chance. Such patience! This did not mean that he turned a blind eye toward their rebellion. On the contrary, God insisted on punishing evil, but always in the context of patience and long-suffering.

God's need for patience was not exhausted when he got his people into the land he had given them. He is still subjected to provocation when people say, "Jesus promised to come back, did he? Then where is he? Why, as far back as anyone can remember, everything has remained exactly the same since the world was first created" (2 Pet. 3:4). Now, God is certainly capable of fixing that situation by sending his Son immediately, and there is no doubt that he could deal expeditiously with the scoffers. But he chooses not to. Why? Peter says, "The Lord isn't really being slow about his promise to return, as some people think. No, he is being patient for your sake. He does not want anyone to perish, so he is giving more time for everyone to repent" (2 Pet. 3:9). Instead of reacting to provocation, God chooses to bide his time. He knows what he is planning to do, and he will work when he is good and ready.

We can learn from this. Not everything can be fixed the way we think it should be, but that does not mean that good cannot come out of the situation. If God, who can fix anything whenever he wants, chooses to live with things that are less than ideal while he works out his purposes, so can we. God's patience is certainly good for us—where would we be without it? And being patient is good for us, too. There's no telling where we'll be without it.

TO READ: *Numbers 22:4-41*

HIDDEN AGENDAS

"Why did you beat your donkey those three times?" the angel of the LORD demanded.
"I have come to block your way because you are stubbornly resisting me."

NUMBERS 22:32

W hat you see is what you get" is not always true, particularly in the business world.
Take Balaam, for example. He is one of the Bible's most perplexing characters.
When King Balak of Moab saw the children of Israel approaching the Promised
Land—through his backyard!—he sent for Balaam to pronounce a curse on them and
thereby halt their progress. Balaam consulted the Lord and was told not to accede to the
king's request, even though financially the offer was very attractive. King Balak, on hearing
of Balaam's refusal, increased the offer. In response, Balaam sought and was given permission by the Lord to go—on the condition that he only say what the Lord told him to say.
Then, when Balaam set out, the Lord was upset that Balaam was going, even though the
Lord had said he could! Either the Lord was being incredibly fickle, or Balaam was hiding
something and the Lord knew it. The latter solution is most in keeping with what we know
of God's character.

After being rebuked by his donkey and the Lord for "stubbornly resisting" the Lord,
Balaam finally came through and did what was right. It would appear that he continued to
struggle with whether to obey or disobey the Lord; otherwise, there would have been no
reason for him to respond repeatedly to Balak's requests that he curse the people. Also,
even though Balaam blessed Israel verbally, he was later responsible for causing them to
rebel against the Lord (31:16; see 25:1-3; Rev. 2:14). On the outside, Balaam was claiming
to do what was right, but on the inside he was flirting with a desire to do what was wrong
(see 2 Pet. 2:15-16). The pressure point in this case was money, and the motive was greed.

There's nothing new about that. When money enters the equation, principles come
under pressure. The natural tendency is to opt for that which is comfortable, profitable,
and popular. Sometimes the choice is between what is comfortable and what is right, what
is popular and what is true, or what is profitable and what is good. The right choice is to
opt for what is good and right and true. Men in business must constantly scrutinize their
inner motives and make these tough decisions. A torn heart may beat under a well-cut suit,
but God knows the heart and examines the motives, and he is the one who passes
judgment. Better to be poor and right than wrong and rich.

TO READ: *Numbers 32:1-42*

WHOLEHEARTEDNESS

"The LORD was furious with Israel and made them wander in the wilderness for forty years until the whole generation that sinned against him had died. But here you are, a brood of sinners, doing exactly the same thing! You are making the LORD even angrier with Israel. If you turn away from him like this and he abandons them again in the wilderness, you will be responsible for destroying this entire nation!"

NUMBERS 32:13-15

There comes a time in life when we are called to "fish or cut bait," when we are required to "put up or shut up." Such a time had arrived for God's wilderness-weary people. With their wilderness wanderings at last behind them, the children of Israel were rapidly approaching the time when they would enter the Promised Land. The time had come to show that they believed God and were committed to his purposes. They would cross the Jordan, overcome the inhabitants, and divide up the land as it was apportioned to them. Then they would receive their inheritance. This was no time for vacillation or spinelessness. It was time for wholehearted commitment!

We can, therefore, understand Moses' disappointment and disgust when the tribes of Reuben and Gad asked if they might be allowed to settle east of Jordan, since they preferred the land there to the land that lay on the other side. Moses' reaction was violent! He raged at them for their apparent lack of commitment; he paralleled their attitude to that of the previous generation, which had chosen not to cross the Jordan, thus resulting in forty years in the wilderness; and he accused them of destroying the morale of the people and jeopardizing the whole venture. Then he pointedly remarked that, of the whole previous generation, only Joshua and Caleb would enter the land, because "they have wholeheartedly followed the Lord" (32:12).

After Moses had cooled off a little, the delegation was able to assure him that they were not opting out of their responsibilities to the rest of the people. They would fulfill all their military obligations and only then return to their homes. So Moses granted them their request on this basis.

Moses was surely right in recognizing the potential dangers inherent in halfheartedness. He knew that divided loyalties make for halfhearted commitments, which in turn produce shallow convictions and eventually can lead to compromise and defeat. They were entering an era when men made of sterner material were needed.

Our days are similar, and our needs are the same. This is the time for modern-day Calebs and Joshuas to step forward and show the way to the wavering, to strengthen the knees of the feeble, and to lead the uncertain away from the broad paths of compromise into the narrow lanes of commitment. This is the time for wholehearted commitment.

TO READ: *Psalm 51*

GUILT, SHAME, AND CONFESSION

Wash me clean from my guilt. Purify me from my sin.
For I recognize my shameful deeds—they haunt me day and night.

PSALM 51:2-3

Not everyone who is guilty feels shame. It is possible to chloroform the conscience, so false innocence is not uncommon. Still, not everyone who feels shame is guilty—false guilt can be imposed by the ignorant or the abuser. But when we do what God forbids and are guilty before God, feeling guilty and ashamed is an appropriate response. When a man has done wrong, he should never be ashamed of being ashamed. The real shame is shamelessness that denies wrongdoing and thus neither seeks nor receives forgiveness.

King David had done what God forbids. For many months after David's adultery, his complicity in murder, and his constant efforts to hide the truth and dodge responsibility, David did nothing to set matters right with his Lord (see 2 Sam. 11). Then the intrepid Nathan came on the scene and confronted him (2 Sam. 12:1-14). David must have fondly imagined that the things he had done were lost in the mists of time, forgotten by God and unknown to man. But they weren't! The things he had done were written in bold, red ink on an open page in God's book, which God read aloud to Nathan, his prophet. But David, when confronted, bravely and humbly faced up to what he had done. Then he pleaded with the Lord, "Wash me clean from my guilt. Purify me from my sin. For I recognize my shameful deeds—they haunt me day and night" (51:2-3). Once David faced his guilt, the appropriate vocabulary flowed from his lips. Guilt, evil, sin, shame. David called on the Lord's mercy, love, and compassion. There was not a word of excuse, not a suggestion of alibi.

David was guilty, ashamed, and miserable, but he wanted a fresh start. And he got it! The broken bones of his shattered life were healed, his willing spirit was reestablished, the old vigor was restored, the joy came surging back, and the forgiven man went on his way rejoicing and serving. (Not that he escaped the consequences—see 2 Samuel 12:10.)

Men should never be ashamed to admit their guilt, and they should never be guilty of denying their shameful actions. Men have difficulty saying, "I was wrong, and I'm sorry. Please help me!" Perhaps it has to do with the male ego. We apparently have a deep need to project an image of confidence, competence, and control. But we need to realize that real men don't hide behind fragile egos—they come clean about their shortcomings, and they grow strong through admitting their failures.

TO READ: *Deuteronomy 1:19-33*

THE WAY FORWARD

*"I said to you, 'You have now reached the land that the LORD our God is giving us.
Look! He has placed it in front of you. Go and occupy it as the LORD, the God
of your ancestors, has promised you. Don't be afraid! Don't be discouraged!' "*

DEUTERONOMY 1:20-21

I f we don't learn from history, we'll probably repeat it. Perhaps that is why Moses was careful to remind the children of Israel that their forefathers had experienced a failure of both nerve and faith, and as a result they had wasted forty years in the wilderness. If the people did not learn from that experience, but repeated the failure of nerve and the lack of faith, there was no telling where they might end up. Moses had no interest in returning to the wilderness in another holding pattern. For the people of Israel, the way forward was the way of faith.

Forty years earlier, confronted with the awesome task of moving into enemy-held territory, the people had sent scouts in to spy out the land. The scouting report brought them into a dilemma. On the one hand, the land was full of promise—as promised! On the other hand, it was full of giants, both real and imaginary. The sons of Anak were very big and very real. But the Israelites' inordinate fears were without substance, and their imagined problems lacked reality. They failed to imagine how big and real their all-powerful God is. As a result, they fell back rather than pressing forward.

A careful recounting of God's actions in the past should lead a trusting person to have confidence in his saving power in the future. But some of us are more cautious than others, some more calculating than the rest. Some of us can recognize opportunities in every difficulty, while others see difficulties in every opportunity. We're all wired up differently. But there is a factor that should loom larger than personality or temperament: the God factor! When we recognize who God is and what he has promised, we should have no problem trusting him to carry through in the future.

Who God is, what he has done, and what he has promised to do have been fully documented. So we are faced with the challenge of deciding whether he is worthy of ongoing trust and whether we will choose to trust him. Notice the word *choose*. It comes down to a matter of choice in the end. The earlier generation of Israelites "refused to trust the Lord [their] God" (1:32). Now the later generation were being given their chance to choose or refuse. We have the same opportunity every day of our lives. We either choose to trust or we refuse to trust. And the result? Living in the land of promise or wandering in the wilderness.

TO READ: *Deuteronomy 4:1-14*

SPIRITUAL LAWS
OF GRAVITY

"But watch out! Be very careful never to forget what you have seen the LORD *do for you. Do not let these things escape from your mind as long as you live! And be sure to pass them on to your children and grandchildren. Tell them especially about the day when you stood before the* LORD *your God at Mount Sinai, where he told me, 'Summon the people before me, and I will instruct them. That way, they will learn to fear me as long as they live, and they will be able to teach my laws to their children.' "*

DEUTERONOMY 4:9-10

O beying laws does not come naturally—or easily! Sometimes we feel that the laws are bad laws or that they are unfair, or we don't like the government that passed them! So we find ways around them rather than submitting to them. But what about God's laws? Why would we have a problem with them? Perhaps it's because we don't recognize that they are for our benefit.

When Moses reminded the children of Israel of the importance of obeying God's laws, he said, "Obey them so that you may live, so you may enter and occupy the land the Lord . . . is giving you" (4:1). The pathway for God's people to enjoy all that the Lord had provided for them was, and is, to obey God's laws.

Take God's laws for the physical universe. If we "obey" the laws of thermodynamics, we stay warm. If we "disobey" them, we get burned or frozen. If we "submit" to the law of gravity, we stay stable and secure, but if we attempt to defy this law, we may put ourselves or others in danger.

It is the same with the moral and social laws that God has created for human well-being. Try to imagine a neighborhood in which neighbors actually treat each other with love and respect! Think of the difference it would make if nobody stole or killed or lied! Our relationships would be transformed. Yet this is what would happen if people obeyed God's laws!

Left to themselves, people fall into ignorance of God's laws and reap the awful results of living out of step with the Creator. Constant referral to God's laws is necessary. Even a casual glance at the Old Testament shows that God repeatedly sent his servants to help his people remember the value of his laws.

If an entire generation raises its children without God's laws, a society will live in ignorance of the truth, leading to societal collapse and individual disaster. This is exactly what we see today. So the call to teach our children to obey God needs to be heard very urgently. Teaching God's laws to children may not be fashionable, but it is smart! Moses himself said those who teach their children God's laws display "wisdom and intelligence." How's that for powerful motivation?

TO READ: *Deuteronomy 9:1–21*

HUMBLING REALITY

I will say it again: The LORD your God is not giving you this good land because
you are righteous, for you are not—you are a stubborn people.

DEUTERONOMY 9:6

T he man who walks with his nose in the air is liable to land in trouble. Or if you prefer, "Pride goes before destruction" (Prov. 16:18). By contrast, the humble man walks with his nose down and his eyes fixed on the road, because he knows his propensity for going wrong, his capacity for missteps.

It would not have been surprising if the children of Israel had assumed that they merited God's extraordinarily generous treatment of them. God had delivered them from their bondage in Egypt, had taken the initiative to make a unique covenant with them, and had fed them and protected them for forty hair-raising years in a desolate wilderness. And finally he was giving them the land that had previously belonged to other people. They must have been righteous!

The reality is, the Israelites were anything but righteous. So Moses took steps to bring them face-to-face with reality, which would lead to appropriate humility. He told them, "Don't say to yourselves, 'The Lord has given us this land because we are so righteous!' . . . The Lord your God is not giving you this good land because you are righteous, for you are not—you are a stubborn people" (Deut. 9:4-6). Then he embarked on a long recital of events that showed unequivocally that they were remarkably undeserving of the blessings bestowed upon them. For them to think they were blessed because they deserved it would have been rank fantasy.

God was not being unkind in reminding Israel of their unworthiness. He knew that the more self-satisfied they became, the more they were in danger of spiritual pride and eventual downfall. On the other hand, the more they recognized God's grace and mercy, the more their hearts would be gripped by his love, moved by his grace, and touched by his mercy. Hearts so affected become loving, obedient hearts. That's where true blessing is found, and that is what God wanted for his people.

It's hard for men today to be humble, since they are so smart and have accomplished so much. But a few reflective moments will help us realize that humility is necessary and anything else would be grossly inappropriate. The thoughtful man knows that unless God provides him air to breathe, food to eat, and raw materials with which to work, he cannot produce. And the insightful man sees that unless God gives him blessings that are completely undeserved, he cannot even exist! Reality is humbling, but those who humble themselves make God proud.

TO READ: *Deuteronomy 15:1-18*

GENEROSITY MEANS BUSINESS

Give freely without begrudging it,
and the LORD your God will bless you in everything you do.

DEUTERONOMY 15:10

M odern businesses state that they exist "to make a profit" and "to provide a service." Some even add "to care for the well-being" of their workforce. But often this concern is more pragmatic than anything else—a happy worker is a more productive worker! It is more a concern for the bottom line than for the worker on the assembly line.

The Lord handed down to Israel a unique set of principles for doing business. Take, for instance, the law of release. Every seventh year the land had to be left uncultivated in order that it might have a Sabbath rest, so that it might be more productive. The law of release stated that, when the Sabbath year came, people laboring under debt were granted release from their debt. Whether the release was a permanent cancellation or a temporary reprieve has been debated. Either way, sharp businessmen, knowing that the year of release was coming, would not wish to make a loan where repayment would be delayed—or even cancelled! But God instructed them not to be "mean-spirited" and to make the loan anyway! A similar provision related to the situation of those in a state of bankruptcy who had no option but to sell themselves—their only remaining asset—into slavery. The law of release stipulated that, when the Sabbath year arrived, such slaves should be allowed to go free. Understandably, some businessmen were reluctant to let go of free labor. But God told them not only to let them go but to give them "a generous farewell gift."

What should be the attitude of the Christian businessperson? If he doesn't provide a product or service he'll be out of business, and if he doesn't turn a profit he'll go bankrupt. So those two objectives are "givens." But what should be his attitude to the people he works with or who work for him? To answer this question, we need to remember that the Christian man in business is a Christian first and a businessman second. His business activities provide the environment in which his Christian convictions shine through. Nowhere will this be more evident than in the way he treats people. But how should he treat them? He should remember that he is not dealing solely with a human machine but with a person—a person whom God made and for whom Christ died, and whose well-being is one of God's concerns. So the Christian businessman's major concern should be how to treat people, who have eternal worth, in a way that pleases God. For God, generosity is a given, and with God, a generous approach means business!

TO READ: *Deuteronomy 24:10-22*

BUSINESS INTEGRITY

*"Never take advantage of poor laborers, whether fellow Israelites or foreigners living
in your towns. Pay them their wages each day before sunset because they are poor
and are counting on it. Otherwise they might cry out to the LORD against you,
and it would be counted against you as sin."*

DEUTERONOMY 24:14-15

I ntegrity results when things are integrated—when such things as belief and behavior fit together and coincide. For instance, business integrity means that the businessman delivers on what he promises and stands by what he says. Promise and performance match each other.

The moral integrity of God's people was clearly a major concern for Moses as he gave final instructions concerning life in the Promised Land. He explained that the legislation was designed to "cleanse the evil" from among them, and that the Lord would "count it as a righteous act" if they followed these precepts. In other words, there was a profound spiritual dimension to the way the Israelites conducted their daily lives. It was not just a matter of being good for goodness' sake or of being kind because their neighbors were nice people. It was more important than that! It was a matter of living according to divine dictates so that evil might be banished and so that the Lord would be honored among them.

From our modern perspective, these laws appear to be remarkably detailed, but the underlying factor in most of them was relational integrity. The evil that had to be banished was the evil of wrong relationships, and righteousness was the way they treated other people rightly. This was to be applied particularly in the area of business dealings. Great emphasis was placed on treating the underprivileged rightly, and great censure was placed on those who failed to do so.

Integrity in business is of paramount importance because it helps save society from moral pollution, it helps ensure proper care for the downtrodden, and it helps protect the powerful from spiritual degeneration through the wrongful exercise of their power. By treating people rightly, the "haves" are protected from debilitating greed and the "have nots" are delivered from cancerous envy. Then the workplace is a better place to be, and the changed attitudes find their way home, where the family benefits, too.

In disputes about working conditions or remuneration in our culture, remedies are usually sought through unions, strikes, and arbitration. In many instances, equitable solutions are discovered. But in ancient Israel there was another powerful factor. A disgruntled worker could always "cry out to the Lord against you," and if you were in the wrong, "it would be counted against you as sin." That way of looking at things is most appropriate even today. Heaven keeps books on our business dealings, too.

TO READ: *Deuteronomy 28:1-24*

DELIGHTFUL OBEDIENCE

"If you obey the commands of the LORD your God and walk in his ways,
the LORD will establish you as his holy people as he solemnly promised to do.
Then all the nations of the world will see that you are a people claimed by the LORD,
and they will stand in awe of you."

DEUTERONOMY 28:9-10

T here's no such thing as a free lunch." That is the strong conviction of many men: "If you want anything you've got to earn it!" It would appear that the Lord was saying this to his people, that the best way to get what they wanted was to be good, and then God would reward them. After all, he did say, "You will experience all these blessings if you obey the Lord your God" (28:2). This way of looking at things falls neatly into line with the all-too-common perception that "there's no such thing as a free lunch," the perception that God's blessing has to be earned. But that is not the meaning of this Scripture.

All Scripture must be read in context and in harmony with other Scriptures. The context of all the Mosaic legislation was the covenant. The covenant was a divine initiative by which God freely offered to undeserving people blessings they could never merit and most certainly never earn. He did this out of pure love and sovereign grace. Israel was required to respond to God's "amazing grace" in humble trust and then out of gratitude to live a life of loving obedience. Grace would lead to faith demonstrated in obedience.

The same principle applies to us today and is clearly spelled out in the New Testament. Paul told the Ephesians, "God saved you by his special favor when you believed. . . . Salvation is not a reward for the good things we have done. . . . He has created us anew in Christ Jesus, so that we can do the good things he planned for us long ago" (Eph. 2:8-10). Obedience, both for the ancient Israelites and for us, is not the means whereby we merit blessing. It is the evidence that we are grateful for blessings received.

Obedience motivated by gratitude is warm, ungrudging, wholehearted. Obedience born of necessity is often reluctant, truculent, and calculating. Sadly, even the recipients of grace can slip into the attitude of those who are strangers to such mercy. They then become candidates for discipline and censure. But the goal is always that they rediscover the undeserved benefits of grace and the unlimited blessings of obedience.

There is no joy for God, or us, in an attitude that says, "I'll do it if I must," or "I'll do this if you will do that." But there is joy in saying, "I'll do this, Lord, because you have done so much for me. I'm grateful, and I know this brings you delight. Thank you. I love you." Many men find obedience a drag, but godly men find doing what God asks a delight.

PRAYER FOR A DARK LAND

O God, why have you rejected us forever? Why is your anger so intense against the sheep of your own pasture? Remember that we are the people you chose in ancient times, the tribe you redeemed as your own special possession! And remember Jerusalem, your home here on earth.

PSALM 74:1-2

The Promised Land, once so full of promise, was now "full of darkness and violence" (74:20). The temple so beautifully designed and exquisitely crafted was no more, and the walls of the city lay in ruins, the gates chopped down like so much firewood (74:3-8). The people of the land languished far away in exile, bemoaning their fate, weeping bitter tears of regret, and praying deep prayers full of longing. All that they had hoped for had failed, and they had only themselves to blame.

But one thing bothered the exiled of Israel (74:1): Had God finally abandoned them permanently? There were no miracles to suggest the Lord was still interested, no powerful prophets presenting words from God's throne (74:9). The heavens were silent and the earth was desolate. Had God finally and irrevocably abandoned them?

The question is valid. Does there come a point in a nation's history where the Lord says, "Enough is enough! I'm through with those people"? The history of God's people, which the psalmist mentions, strongly suggests that God is willing to forgive and restore a nation in response to the prayers of his people (see also 2 Chron. 7:14).

The writer of this psalm reminded the Lord that the Lord had a great history of deliverance (74:2), that his holy name was being abused (74:7, 10), that his people were in dire straits (74:19), that his enemies were having a field day (74:18), and that he had made certain promises that he must not forget to fulfill (74:20).

So what of the nations of the world? Are there dark places where light should be shining? Does violence prevail where people should be living in peace? Of course! And what should God's people be doing? They should be calling on the Lord, reviewing the history of God's workings, counting the promises of his grace, and rebuking his enemies. Like humble doves among predators, God's people should be living wisely and winsomely in his power, ready not only to pray but also to play an active part in the answers to their own prayers. It is the "poor and needy ones" who will eventually give praise, it is the weak and foolish ones through whom God works (1 Cor. 1:26-29), and it is those who call on his name who become the agents of his working (see Neh. 1:11).

When God moves in a dark and violent land, he begins with his people and works through them. So instead of cursing the darkness, let us call on the Lord and gear up for action—for him!

TO READ: *Deuteronomy 30:1-20*

CHOOSE LIFE

"Today I have given you the choice between life and death, between blessings and curses. I call on heaven and earth to witness the choice you make. Oh, that you would choose life, that you and your descendants might live! Choose to love the LORD your God and to obey him and commit yourself to him, for he is your life. Then you will live long in the land the LORD swore to give your ancestors Abraham, Isaac, and Jacob."

DEUTERONOMY 30:19-20

L ife is full of choices. Some are made for you, the rest you make. You cannot choose to be born, but you can choose how to live. You are not free to select your DNA, but you can choose to pursue an MBA. The choices you make shape the life you will live.

Before the children of Israel entered the Promised Land, Moses required them to choose how they would respond to God and to face what would happen as a result—choices and consequences. He also explained that if they strayed from God's path and were disciplined by him, they should return to him and be reconciled to him. But whether sooner or later, the choice between life and death was clear: loving God meant life, while turning away from him meant death.

We today still need to confront courageously the choice between life and death, blessing and cursing. Blessing is not automatic. It does not flow unbidden into a man's life. Blessing comes when we respond affirmatively to the Lord's call to live obediently. Echoing Moses, Jesus said, "You must love the Lord your God with all your heart, all your soul, and all your mind" (Matt. 22:37), and he commanded potential disciples, "Follow me." In words similar to Moses', Jesus warned people, "You can enter God's Kingdom only through the narrow gate. The highway to hell is broad, and its gate is wide for the many who choose the easy way. But the gateway to life is small, and the road is narrow, and only a few ever find it" (Matt. 7:13-14). God still lays before us the options of trusting obedience and willful disobedience, and he outlines the results of the options: Life eternal on the one hand, perishing on the other.

God bestows upon man the ultimate privilege of choosing freely which way he will go. Of course, there would be no choice to make if God had not first chosen to reach out to us. So man's freedom to choose is a gift of grace. God chose to offer us life, then he chose to let us choose. Now the choice is ours! God offers the gift of eternal life to anyone who will repent and believe. God calls us to respond. If we obey his call, if we choose to go his way, we receive the gift. And it's the biggest gift ever offered to those who face the biggest choice ever made.

TO READ: *Judges 4:1-24*

VISIONARY LEADERSHIP

Barak told her, "I will go, but only if you go with me!" "Very well," she replied,
"I will go with you. But since you have made this choice, you will receive no honor.
For the Lord's victory over Sisera will be at the hands of a woman."
So Deborah went with Barak to Kedesh.

JUDGES 4:8-9

L eadership comes in many styles, and leaders come in various shapes and sizes. Not all leaders are big, bold, brassy, and bossy. Some are quiet, humble, gentle, and caring. Some leaders develop in old age, while others appear to be gifted leaders from adolescence. God plays no favorites when it comes to leadership. In fact, sometimes he seems to delight in raising up the unexpected and appointing the unlikely. Like Deborah!

King Jabin had been a thorn in Israel's side for twenty years. During this time, Deborah rose to a position of prominence as judge and prophet. Then the children of Israel cried out to the Lord in their distress. In response, God spoke through Deborah and commanded Barak to fight King Jabin's army. God even promised to give Barak victory. But Barak did not want to go alone. He said he would only go into battle if Deborah went with him. This she did, the battle was won, King Jabin was overthrown, and Israel lived peacefully for forty years.

This incident says much about leadership. The Lord had clearly imparted gifts of discernment and communication to Deborah. As she exercised these gifts, she was confirmed as judge and prophet. From her remarks to Barak, it seems clear that it was unusual for a woman to be in her position in that culture. Some say she was only in this position because Barak was such a weak man, but she was a judge long before Barak came on the scene. It would seem more appropriate to say that God sovereignly raised up a woman as a leader because he wanted this woman to lead!

On the other hand, Barak is often portrayed as weak and ineffectual, but he did rally ten thousand men who followed him when he led them into battle, and he did win! So much for weakness and ineffectiveness! It would seem more appropriate to say that he put more "confidence in human effort" (Phil. 3:3) than in the Spirit of God. His eyes of faith were perhaps a bit clouded, while Deborah's vision was strong and clear. As a result, Deborah warned him that the honor of victory would accrue to a woman rather than to him, and that is precisely what occurred.

From this we can see that leadership is more about vision than gender. Godly leaders are willing to walk by faith rather than by sight. They can plunge into the unknown trusting God's word. People will follow such leaders, and as leadership is all about "followship," this is critical. If they aren't following, you aren't leading.

TO READ: *1 Samuel 13:1-14*

DOING RIGHT UNDER PRESSURE

Saul waited there seven days for Samuel, as Samuel had instructed him earlier,
but Samuel still didn't come. Saul realized that his troops were rapidly slipping away.
So he demanded, "Bring me the burnt offering and the peace offerings!"
And Saul sacrificed the burnt offering himself.

1 SAMUEL 13:8-9

Many a good man has failed under pressure. His cash flow depleted with critical bills due, he "borrows" his boss's funds with the intention of returning them in a couple of days. Or with his job on the line and productivity down, he "bends" the rules, alters the facts, and saves the day—or so it seems, until he is found out.

King Saul is a great example. He had been instructed by Samuel, his spiritual mentor, to go to Gilgal and wait seven days for Samuel to come and bless the troops and lead them in worship before they went into battle (10:8). Gilgal was remote, a safe haven from their mortal enemies, the Philistines, so the time could be spent in careful, unhindered preparation. But the Philistines gathered a huge army and went after Saul. They came and camped at Micmash, which is just a stone's throw from Gilgal. So Saul's troops became restive and began to desert. As Saul saw his combat force dissipating, he panicked. In direct contravention of his instructions from the Lord, Saul went ahead with the spiritual exercises, which were not his domain. Just as he was concluding them, Samuel arrived, roundly rebuked Saul for his action, and advised him that his days as king were numbered.

The pressure revealed the faults. Saul had a tendency to panic and not trust, and a proclivity to take things into his own hands rather than to believe that the Lord had things under control. He bypassed obedience when the end seemed to justify the means. Saul's lack of faith led to direct disobedience of God, a sure recipe for disaster for the leader of God's chosen people. He had to go.

Saul's fatal flaws were neither unusual nor uncommon. Similar faults appear regularly in men under pressure. In times of stress, substituting personal agendas and human effort for trusting obedience and obedient faith is like a skydiver dispensing with a parachute and substituting flapping his arms. Both will make a brave show, but neither will achieve the desired objective. Both are a free-fall to disaster. Much better to keep the parachute of faith open.

TO READ: *1 Samuel 17:32–51*

THE FIGHT OF FAITH

David shouted in reply, "You come to me with sword, spear, and javelin,
but I come to you in the name of the LORD Almighty—
the God of the armies of Israel, whom you have defied."

1 SAMUEL 17:45

T he life of faith is a battle. Jesus warned his disciples that the world in which they were living had rejected and persecuted him, so they should expect to be rejected and persecuted themselves. In addition, a believer recognizes that his motives are not always lily-white, and his desires all too easily degenerate into lusts that he has to counter. Added to that, the evil one, whose objective is to subvert the purposes of God, hates those who have become obstacles to his plans by allying themselves with Christ. So our typical enemies—the world, the flesh, and the devil—ensure that the life of faith is a battle.

But how is the fight of faith to be fought? The account of David's battle with Goliath holds many clues. There is no doubt about the immensity of the task that confronted David—otherwise, Saul would have settled the issue long before the precocious David arrived on the field of battle. But Saul and his men were thoroughly impressed with the power of the giant, and so they were terrified. David, for his part, was fearless. He wasn't concerned about the giant's strength, because he saw God's power as greater. He also saw Goliath's bravado as direct defiance of God's armies, and thus of God himself. David could not accept this as the status quo, so he decided to act. Undeterred by the naysayers' efforts to dissuade him from taking on Goliath, David reminded them of his own experience—that the Lord is able to save—and he was calmly convinced that the Lord would act in this situation, too. Then, rejecting the trappings that Saul tried to lay on him, David carefully selected five smooth stones for his sling. Armed with this minimal arsenal, he approached the giant "in the name of the Lord Almighty" (17:45). It is important to note that he did not just stand there waiting for the Lord Almighty to smite the giant. He took what he had in hand, utilized the skills he had acquired on the lonely hillsides of Bethlehem, and slung his shot. The result was stunning! He then borrowed the stunned giant's sword and finished him off.

The enemies of our soul are real and not to be underestimated, they are to be engaged and not avoided, and they are to be countered using the five smooth stones of Scripture, prayer, fellowship, worship, and discipline. Like David, we must develop our skills in handling our own smooth stones in the power of the Lord. The results will be stunning.

TO READ: *1 Samuel 20:1-15*

HELPING THOSE IN TROUBLE

"And may you treat me with the faithful love of the LORD *as long as I live.*
But if I die, treat my family with this faithful love,
even when the LORD *destroys all your enemies."*

1 SAMUEL 20:14-15

Helping people in trouble can be challenging, uncomfortable, time-consuming, dangerous, and expensive. But it is also right and good, rewarding and God-honoring.

David had more than his share of trouble, not the least of which was his relationship with Saul. King Saul was a veritable museum of emotional diseases. Given to fits of melancholia that plunged him into murderous rages, he lived an acutely paranoid existence. Unfortunately for David, the king's hatred and jealousy were mainly directed at him. This made for a decidedly uncomfortable experience for David, who found himself persona non grata at court and deemed it necessary to head for the wilderness in search of a little safety.

Fortunately for David, young prince Jonathan gladly helped his troubled friend. Jonathan was aware of the immense popularity of David, and no doubt he recognized a potential rival for the throne in the young charismatic hero. In fact, from a purely political point of view, having David dead would have been much more attractive for Jonathan than having David alive! When Jonathan protested that David's reading of the situation was terribly wrong, perhaps David wondered momentarily if Jonathan secretly wanted him out of the way.

But the two young men, whose status and situations were so different, had important things in common. They both valued their strong friendship. They both took seriously their commitment to the Lord, whom they knew to be the God of "faithful love" (20:14), and they recognized that the followers of the Lord needed to treat others with this "faithful love" also (20:15). This was not just a matter of personal friendship, which was certainly very strong; it was all about treating people rightly and recognizing that the Lord himself was watching and caring.

We serve a Lord who distinguished himself by the way he helped a helpless race in deep trouble. Like Jonathan, he saw our lost condition, was moved with compassion, and made a commitment to us. Christ did not hesitate to pay the extreme sacrifice. Reaching us in our troubled state, he drew us back to himself and granted us a place in his royal family. So next time you don't feel like helping, remember the One who helped you!

CONSULTING THE LORD

So David asked the LORD, "Should I go out to fight the Philistines?
Will you hand them over to me?" The LORD replied,
"Yes, go ahead. I will certainly give you the victory."

2 SAMUEL 5:19

A consultant is usually someone who has proved, through long experience, that he knows what to do, and who is willing, for a fee, to share his insights with those who seek his help. More experienced and insightful than any human consultant is the Lord. The Lord's credentials are impeccable, he is anxious to be consulted, and he offers his insights free of charge. Sadly, he is not always consulted, nor is his advice always sought out.

David was too smart to make such a serious mistake. The Philistines, on hearing of David's accession to the throne of Israel, decided that they needed to get control of him in a hurry, so they sent their hordes to capture him. This presented the new king with an immediate crisis. David was no stranger to military action, and he had proven many times that he was not lacking in strategic know-how or sheer courage. And he had with him many experienced veterans of foreign wars. So he had no shortage of military intelligence available. But David was smart enough to know he needed more than that—he needed divine guidance. With wisdom befitting a king, he asked the Lord what he should do.

Many men have stumbled at this point. Some are too self-confident and do not wish to consult the Lord, while others do not know how to consult him. They trust their own instincts and expertise rather than the Lord and then make decisions that lead to problems. They do not realize that the Lord knows what is best for them and is eager to work in their lives.

So the key is to consult the Lord. But how? David's methods are not stipulated. Either he received a message from the Urim and Thummim (a means of communication of which we know very little), or a gifted seer or prophet told him a word from the Lord. We may not know David's methods, but we can certainly follow his example, because we are talking about the same God! We can bring our choices to the Lord in prayer, study the word of God for guiding principles, listen to the counsel of wise people in our lives, and, using our God-given reasoning capabilities, arrive at the direction we will take, all the time asking the Lord to stop us if we are making a wrong decision. There is nothing more comforting than knowing that we can bring our decisions to the Lord in this way and then go ahead, knowing that he is in charge and is leading us through his Holy Spirit.

TO READ: *Psalm 78:11–57*

GOD'S BROKEN HEART

*Oh, how often they rebelled against him in the desert and grieved his heart
in the wilderness. Again and again they tested God's patience and
frustrated the Holy One of Israel.*

PSALM 78:40-41

H ave you ever wondered how God feels about human behavior? We know that we
get upset when people hurt us, and if we cause pain we feel bad about it. But what
about the impact of our behavior on God?

In the time of Noah, we are told, "The Lord observed the extent of the people's
wickedness, and he saw that all their thoughts were consistently and totally evil. So the
Lord was sorry he had ever made them. It broke his heart" (Gen. 6:5-6). Human sin
apparently broke the divine heart.

After the Flood things did not improve appreciably. In the long and tortuous history
of the children of Israel, God suffered constant heartache. The cycle of sin, repentance,
recommitment, restoration, apathy, decline, oppression, repentance, and recommitment
continued in relentless fashion. This revealed the obduracy of man and the patience of
God, as man's behavior subjected the Lord to ongoing heartbreak.

Psalm 78 catalogues for all time the many sins of ancient Israel and the many
gracious acts of God. No matter how much good God sent to his people, or how much
chastisement, "They did not keep God's covenant, and they refused to live by his law"
(78:10; see 78:11-16, 31-33). Sometimes they did repent and return to God, but their zeal
was short-lived and often insincere (78:36-37). The writer of this psalm summarized the
situation by saying, "Oh, how often they rebelled against him in the desert and grieved his
heart in the wilderness. Again and again they tested God's patience and frustrated the Holy
One of Israel" (78:40-41).

We do well to consider the impact of human behavior on the heart of God. Human
sin is an affront to God. It is a denial of his sovereignty. It is a statement by one created
from dust that he is taking control from the Creator. That breaks God's heart. When sinful
actions predominate in our lives, they demonstrate the extent of human fallenness. When
a man's heart is corrupt, his humanity is polluted. Understandably, God is indignant
about man's condition and actions, so he disciplines his erring children. But even his
discipline stems from his brokenhearted love.

A vision of God's heart may soften and break the most hardened human heart. And
that can lead to our hearts being molded into that for which he created and redeemed us.
Our lives can be expressions of his love and goodness, rather than examples of human
wickedness—for all time!

TO READ: *2 Samuel 11:1-27*

A SEDUCTIVE GLOW

*The following Spring, the time of year when kings go to war, David sent Joab and the
Israelite army to destroy the Ammonites. In the process they laid siege to the city of
Rabbah. But David stayed behind in Jerusalem. Late one afternoon David got out of
bed after taking a nap and went for a stroll on the roof of the palace. As he looked
out over the city, he noticed a woman of unusual beauty taking a bath.*

2 SAMUEL 11:1-2

A temptation is an opportunity to go wrong. It is also a chance to do right. A temptation is a potential seduction, but handled correctly it results in an actual strengthening. This can be seen clearly when we compare similar incidents in the lives of Joseph and David. Both of these men were presented with adulterous opportunities. Both knew that adultery was wrong. Joseph accordingly resisted the temptress's advances and, at great cost to himself, preserved his integrity. David, on the other hand, not only succumbed but caught himself in a spiral of selfish decisions that sucked him into ever-deepening culpability.

David's fall was not sudden. Apparently, he had been undisciplined for some time. He was not leading his men into battle but was staying home and letting them fight his battles for him. And it does seem odd that he was getting out of bed in the evening. Whatever had happened to the dashing young warrior, the devoted servant of the Lord, the man after God's own heart? Had he grown careless? Had he become fat and feckless in his advancing middle age?

Perhaps he did not know that Bathsheba would be bathing in full view—and her motivations may well have been impure—so he could not be held responsible for seeing her. But he certainly was responsible for gazing, lusting, sending for her, and engaging in adulterous sex with her. At any point he could—and should—have said no. But the erosion of principle and discipline had already taken place, and the moral failure concluded in disaster.

We can all learn from mistakes, but learning from the mistakes of others is less painful than living with the consequences of our own. David's fall tells us that failure to reverse spiritual erosion leads to undermining moral principle. Then, when we are subjected to the stress of temptation, failure and collapse quickly result.

Strong men know how to stand firm, but even the strongest man becomes a weakling if he ignores basic prudent precautions and begins to play with temptation on the assumption that he can break off at any time.

Moths love candlelight. They are attracted to its seductive glow and flirt with its warm embrace. Closer and closer they are lured until their wings are singed and they crash and burn. Learn the lesson from David or, if you prefer, behold the disaster of the moth. Be prepared to stand against temptation or you, too, may crash and burn.

TO READ: *1 Kings 2:1–12*

LAST WORDS

"I am going where everyone on earth must someday go. Take courage and be a man."

1 KINGS 2:2

How a man dies says a lot about how he lived. His last words speak volumes. John Wesley's final words were, "Best of all, God is with us." Ludwig van Beethoven, as he died, said, "The comedy is over." Quite a difference! Wesley died, not only conscious of where he was going, but also vividly aware that the One with whom he had lived so long would pass through the waters of death with him. Beethoven died with no such assured statement, only with words that hint that his life had been a cynical disappointment.

King David, lying on his death bed, said a lot in a few words to his son Solomon. "Take courage and be a man" he said, summarizing his own life and identifying his desires for his son (2:2). But what would it take to "be a man" in David's estimation?

First and foremost, being a man requires being courageous enough to recognize that success is dependent upon obedience to God's will and purpose. David commanded his heir to obey God and promised that if he did so, he would be successful (2:3). It takes a brave man to take a stand on God's ways, particularly when he is subjected to conflicting opinions and pulled by contrary forces. "Doing it my way" is a much more common and popular slogan than "Doing it HIS way," but the latter is the pathway to lasting success.

Second, being a man includes trusting in God's promises. David pointed his son to the promises of God as the source of assurance and strength (2:4). The man who knows how to "trust and obey" can be confident that God will be proactive in his affairs and deeply involved in his life.

Third, being a man includes administering justice (2:5-9). It may appear that David was urging Solomon to take vengeance on his enemies in order to resolve personal grudges, but it was actually a matter of administering God's justice rather than getting even. This same concern for justice led David to press on Solomon the responsibility to show kindness to those who deserved it (2:7).

Last words carry extraordinary weight because they are memorable; and because they often summarize a life lived, they pack an extra punch. So let us ensure before we die, and before our children do too much living, that they see and hear what they should hold as highest priorities.

TO READ: *1 Kings 3:1-15*

THE GREAT OCEAN OF TRUTH

*"Give me an understanding mind so that I can govern your people well
and know the difference between right and wrong.
For who by himself is able to govern this great nation of yours?"*

1 KINGS 3:9

Sir Isaac Newton, the brilliant scientist, said toward the end of his life, "I feel like a little child playing by the seashore while the great ocean of truth lies undiscovered before me." Despite his accomplishments in the fields of mathematics and the physical sciences, Newton was aware that what he did know was infinitesimal compared to what he did not know. And humility was the only appropriate response.

King Solomon, as he embarked on the task of governing God's people, was also aware of how much he did not know about ruling and reigning. Humility was appropriate in his case, too. Some men in similar situations crumble under the crushing feelings of inadequacy and distinguish themselves by their ineffectiveness. Others try to hide their ignorance and convince themselves of their independence. Not Solomon. He knew what to do with his limitations and where to take his shortcomings. He worshiped! He turned to the One in whom all knowledge is found, the fount of all wisdom. The Lord responded by inviting Solomon to ask for whatever he wanted, promising it would be given to him. This would appear to be a dangerous thing for God to do, but God, having seen Solomon at worship, knew his heart. And when Solomon responded by asking for wisdom, "the Lord was pleased . . . and was glad" (3:10).

Solomon was not interested in self-aggrandizement. His prime concern was that he should be equipped to do what God had called him to do. He had enough wisdom to know that he needed wisdom, and he was smart enough to know that he wasn't smart enough. He also knew that receiving wisdom from the Lord was more important than getting more wealth or more power. Wealth and power without wisdom to administer them can lead to all kinds of evil, and even long life without wisdom can be bitter or futile.

Wealth, power, and longevity have their attractions for men in all ages, but the smart ones ask God for wisdom to live as they should. Like Solomon, many of them discover that God, having granted them wisdom, also gives them the other things as a bonus, because he knows they will be smart enough to handle them properly. So get smart, and seek wisdom!

TO READ: *1 Kings 19:1–18*

"I'VE HAD ENOUGH"

Then he went on alone into the desert, traveling all day. He sat down under a
solitary broom tree and prayed that he might die. "I have had enough, LORD,"
he said. "Take my life, for I am no better than my ancestors."

1 KINGS 19:4

E very man has his breaking point. At some point, under the right circumstances, a man
will say, "I've had enough." Often when it comes, it is something of a surprise, and the
sudden feelings of discouragement can be crushing, even to the point of wanting to die.

This was certainly the case with Elijah. He had handled the powerful king Ahab
without any problem, had confronted and routed the 450 prophets of Baal with ease, and
had fearlessly challenged an apostate nation in the name of the Lord. No sign of a breakdown, no hint of impending emotional collapse. But collapse he did.

It was Jezebel, a formidable woman with ferocious habits and far-reaching influence,
who proved to be the last straw for Elijah. Jezebel made no attempt to have him killed,
although it was undoubtedly within her power. She simply threatened him and gave him
twenty-four hours to get out of town, which he did in a hurry.

We can only surmise why Elijah became so frightened. No doubt the years of tension
had taken their toll. The emotional struggle with the priests of Baal would have drained the
most resourceful person. The spiritual high of the mountain left him vulnerable to a spiritual
low in the valley, and the sheer output of spiritual energy over an extended period had no
doubt left him depleted. Then the physical strain of running before the king's chariot could
not have helped. But perhaps the straw that broke Elijah's back was when God did no
miracle to eradicate Jezebel, and Elijah realized that this enemy was not going away. She was
his thorn in the flesh.

Finally Elijah lay down, disgruntled, dejected, and depressed, and announced that
he was through. But the Lord cared for him tenderly and treated him to an unforgettable
object lesson. A miraculous meal, a supernatural strengthening, a mighty windstorm, a
violent earthquake, a raging fire, and a gentle breeze showed Elijah that God is not limited
to what is mighty and spectacular. He can be equally effective through what is weak. After
this object lesson, God told Elijah to get up, get going, and get on with the job. And that
he did, understanding at last that the Lord does mighty things through meager means and
miserable men.

When Elijah said, "I've had enough!" he was ready to learn that God is enough.
When he thought, "I can't!" he discovered that God can. So his depression was not all bad.
In fact, it was only as he sank lower that he was raised higher. And the message for all men
at all times is still, "The way to up is down."

TO READ: *2 Kings 1:1-18*

HAIRY AND SCARY

One day Israel's new king, Ahaziah, fell through the latticework of an upper room at his palace in Samaria, and he was seriously injured. So he sent messengers to the temple of Baal-zebub, the god of Ekron, to ask whether he would recover. But the angel of the LORD told Elijah, who was from Tishbe, "Go and meet the messengers of the king of Samaria and ask them, 'Why are you going to Baal-zebub, the god of Ekron, to ask whether the king will get well? Is there no God in Israel? Now, therefore, this is what the LORD says: You will never leave the bed on which you are lying, but you will surely die.' " So Elijah went to deliver the message.

2 KINGS 1:2-4

At times life gets hairy and scary. How a man behaves at such times speaks volumes about what he believes. Take Elijah and Ahaziah for example. Their reactions to a tense situation provide great insights into what they were made of.

Elijah was "a hairy man" (1:8), and he lived in scary times. King Ahab had led Israel to reject Yahweh and embrace the religion of Baal. Then Ahaziah succeeded Ahab his father as king and perpetuated the apostasy. When he was seriously injured in a fall, he immediately turned for spiritual help to Baal-zebub, not to the Lord. In response, God sent Elijah to intercept the king's messengers with a prophetic message rebuking the king and predicting his death. The king did not receive the message well, but angrily sent a detachment of soldiers to arrest Elijah. To the king's threats Elijah responded cooly, giving God's anger room to burn.

The contrast between the prophet and the king is stark. Elijah trusted implicitly in God's word and in his power to intervene in the affairs of the king. Ahaziah dismissed the Lord as irrelevant. Two contrasting worldviews were on display. One was based on the recognition of Yahweh as God the Creator, who had chosen the people of Israel as his precious treasure, had given them the land in which they lived, and had promised to bless his people and the world as they responded to him in loving obedience. The other worldview was based on the worship of Baal, a nature and fertility god, whose worship demanded appeasement if the people were to prosper. The former approach believed that Yahweh was sovereign and trustworthy, while the latter believed that Baal was in charge. It was a matter of either/or, not both/and. There was no room for compromise. Either Yahweh was God, or Baal was. Elijah left no room for doubt whose side he was on—and neither did Ahaziah! Confrontation resulted—a hairy, scary scene. And Yahweh proved, once again, that "the Lord is God!" (1 Kings 18:39).

Men today are often in similar situations. Alternatives to worshiping the Lord abound. Some dismiss him as irrelevant, and some reject him out of hand. Others wish to embrace both him and the gods who stand in opposition to him, seeing little contradiction and caring even less. But a man must address the issue of who is truly the Lord, because one day he will fall through his lattice and need someone to help and somewhere to turn. The one he trusts at such a moment will either support him or collapse like a rotten lattice. That's scary!

TO READ: *2 Kings 19:1–19*

NO TIME
TO GO WOBBLY

*"Now, O LORD our God, rescue us from his power; then all the kingdoms
of the earth will know that you alone, O LORD, are God."*

2 KINGS 19:19

This is no time to go wobbly, George." That was the message Margaret Thatcher, prime minister of the United Kingdom, sent to George Bush, president of the United States, at the height of the Gulf War. She was right, of course. In times of national distress, resolute leadership is desperately needed. But leaders, too, are human, subject to doubt and vulnerable to threat.

King Hezekiah needed the same kind of encouragement to stand strong when Jerusalem was besieged by Sennacherib and his Assyrian armies. The people were in dire straits, their leader under severe pressure. But he handled it well. Sennacherib arrogantly, belligerently called into question both the capabilities of Hezekiah and the relevance of Yahweh. Hezekiah promptly discarded his royal regalia and donned sackcloth, the dress of the distraught and devastated. He made no attempt to put on a brave face, he issued no propaganda for the masses. The situation was critical, he knew it, and he let the people know it. Suitably clad, the king made his way to the house of prayer and sent messengers to call on the prophet Isaiah for counsel and support. He rightly saw that the situation was more than a mere military or political issue; it was a spiritual matter, requiring a spiritual response. It was also a direct affront to the Lord. Since God's own reputation was at stake, Hezekiah urged the Lord to deliver his people.

And what a response he got! In effect, Isaiah told Hezekiah not to "go wobbly," because Yahweh was in charge. Sennacherib had claimed that all gods were irrelevant in comparison with his power. But Isaiah reminded Hezekiah that Yahweh is far from being an impotent irrelevance—Yahweh is the Creator and Sustainer of all things, the Lord of history, and the covenant God of his people. Because of who he is, God would defy the defiant and defend the defenseless. He would prove his power on behalf of his people.

Leaders, under the pressure of giving direction to beleaguered believers, aware of their own weakness and the immensity of their adversity, need to know where their resources lie. Like Hezekiah, they need to face reality and to seek the Lord, looking for a word from him indicating the right path. And they must gather round them those who will support and strengthen them in leadership's lonely hours. Such encouragers can remind them that, because of who the Lord is in the situation, there is "no time to go wobbly."

GOD'S SHINING FACE

Turn us again to yourself, O God. Make your face shine down upon us.
Only then will we be saved.

PSALM 80:3

H umans have ingeniously devised a multitude of impersonal ways to communicate with each other. Telephone, telegraph, fax, E-mail, and the old-fashioned post all serve to pass on information. But without exception they lack the personal touch, the intimacy of presence. They tell us only what the sender wants to tell us, leaving us to guess at what he feels. To really know the whole story we need more—we must meet face-to-face!

The face is controlled by a mass of muscles. It can be contorted in a thousand different ways, reproducing a plethora of images. Frowns and grimaces, impassivity and rapt attention, snarls or smiles. Smiles! That is what we long to see.

God commanded Aaron and the rest of the priests to pronounce a specific blessing on the children of Israel (Num. 6:22-27). This blessing included the words "May the Lord smile on you" (Num. 6:25). Older versions of the Bible say, "The Lord make his face shine upon thee" (KJV). Shine or smile—the picture is wonderful. It conveys the beaming, approving look of the Lord, showing his deep satisfaction with his people.

But the writer of this psalm lamented that he could see no smile on the face of the Lord (80:3). The people were not basking under his approving gaze—they were estranged from him. And they were not smiling themselves—they were drinking "tears by the bucket-ful" (80:5). So what could be done? They needed to ask the Lord, "Turn us again to yourself, O God. Make your face shine down upon us. Only then will we be saved" (80:3).

It is physically impossible to gaze on a smile if you turn your back on the one who is smiling. You need to turn in his direction to see him face-to-face. Likewise, you cannot experience God's approval if you are heading in your own willful direction. The smallest child soon learns that smiles from a parent are much to be preferred over frowns, so he adjusts his behavior accordingly. Grown men need to remember that they are God's children, if they have faith through Christ. So before they act they should think, "Will this action bring my Father delight or anguish? Will it elicit a smile or merit a frown?"

Most of us know in our hearts what pleases the Lord. Should we have any doubts, we can always refer to Scripture. How wonderful it will be for us to experience God's shining, smiling face!

TO READ: *1 Chronicles 28:1-21*

CHIP OFF THE OLD BLOCK?

*"And from among my sons—for the LORD has given me many children—he chose
Solomon to succeed me on the throne of his kingdom of Israel. He said to me,
'Your son Solomon will build my Temple and its courtyards, for I have chosen him
as my son, and I will be his father.' "*

1 CHRONICLES 28:5-6

Some fathers do not hesitate to tell their children what to do with their lives—and
they're often wrong. One father who has worked hard to build his business assumes
his son will be eager to take over, only to discover that the son has neither the heart nor
the head for such a task. Another father, frustrated in his own athletic career, pushes his
son to excel so that he may vicariously enjoy what he has personally been denied, only to
discover that his son prefers footlights to football and plays by Shakespeare to plays from
scrimmage.

David, too, had designs for his son Solomon. But there was a difference. God had told
David what he wanted his son to do—even giving David detailed instructions! (28:19).
David then drew up the blueprints and began collecting the raw materials for his son's work
(22:1-5), and he spoke to his son with certainty and authority concerning the work that he
would do (22:6-19; 28:20-21). David was not just laying his own plans on Solomon, as
many fathers do. He was laying God's plans on his son, in accord with God's will. And it
was exactly the right thing.

Fathers today can still discover God's plans for their children, they can begin collecting
the "materials" that will help their children fulfill those plans, and they can instruct their
children in those plans. By prayerfully and carefully studying God's word, fathers can find
general principles of guidance for their children; and by carefully and prayerfully observing
their children's aptitudes, abilities, opportunities, and interests, they can help their children
discover more specific details of God's plans. Today's fathers should remind their children
that, whatever their occupation, their calling is to be the Lord's servants; and whatever their
success, their abilities are God-given. They should remind their children that everything they
have received comes from God, and that their lives on earth will prepare them for the
experience of eternity. Fathers should tell their children that, whatever their field of
endeavor, if they pursue the Lord's will with enthusiasm, they can count on the Lord's
presence and enabling.

Shame on fathers who impose their own will and ignore God's will in their
children's lives. But blessed is the man who watches his children carefully and pursues
God's path for them wholeheartedly. Those men understand the difference between
imposing their will and influencing their children, the difference between intimidation
and inspiration.

TO READ: *2 Chronicles 1:1–13*

IF ANY MAN
LACKS WISDOM . . .

"Now, LORD God, please keep your promise to David my father, for you have made me king over a people as numerous as the dust of the earth! Give me wisdom and knowledge to rule them properly, for who is able to govern this great nation of yours?"

2 CHRONICLES 1:9-10

I f you inherited a million dollars, what would you do with it? If you could have anything you asked for, what would it be? Questions like these are rarely asked seriously and therefore seldom answered sensibly. But Solomon received a serious invitation from the Lord to respond to just such a question.

When the Lord invited the new king to ask for whatever his heart desired, the response was memorable. Solomon did not ask for personal enrichment, safety, or longevity but for the tools he would need to be what God had called him to be. "Now, Lord God, please keep your promise to David my father, for you have made me king over a people as numerous as the dust of the earth! Give me wisdom and knowledge to rule them properly, for who is able to govern this great nation of yours?" (1:9-10). So unusual was Solomon's request that the Lord not only commended him and gave him what he asked for, but also showered him with unsolicited bonuses.

Solomon's request for wisdom and knowledge was indicative of his maturity. Knowledge is the accumulation of information, whereas wisdom is knowing how to apply the information and make good decisions. Solomon needed no one to tell him that the task he had been given was more than he could handle on his own. He was in touch with his own inadequacy. So he specifically asked for knowledge to understand the problems, and wisdom to know what to do about them. Many men have been too smart for their own good, too impressed with their own abilities to be aware of their deficiencies. Solomon was nobody's fool. He was already wise enough to know he needed help, and smart enough to know where to find it.

Every man must recognize the peculiar and special challenges of his calling. And each man must be aware that in his own strength he does not have what it takes to be all that God calls him to be. Smart men know their limitations and know where their help comes from. They catalogue their deficiencies and turn to the Lord, the source of wisdom and knowledge, finding in him resources for the work at hand. And they find that "if you need wisdom—if you want to know what God wants you to do—ask him, and he will gladly tell you. He will not resent your asking" (James 1:5). Smart men know how smart they aren't. Wise men know how desperately short of wisdom they fall, and they are wise enough to ask for more.

NOVEMBER

TO READ: *2 Chronicles 7:11-22*

THE WAILING WALL

Then if my people who are called by my name will humble themselves and
pray and seek my face and turn from their wicked ways,
I will hear from heaven and will forgive their sins and heal their land.

2 CHRONICLES 7:14

T he wailing wall in Jerusalem is one of the saddest places on earth. Day after day faithful Jews stand before its imposing ruin, pouring out their souls to the Lord, asking him to send the promised Messiah. Quite apart from the sadness of their failure to recognize that Jesus is Messiah, the wall itself, the sole remnant of Israel's majestic temple, speaks a solemn sadness of its own. It speaks silently of former glories long gone, of broken covenants and shattered dreams, of sin and judgment, and of false hopes.

When Solomon had finally completed the temple and his own palace, the Lord appeared to him one night. He told Solomon that if the people of Israel ever turned away from the Lord, he would send a series of increasingly alarming calamities (7:19-22). If the people refused to respond to the Lord and abandoned him, in the end they would be uprooted from the land and the temple would be destroyed. Then people would pass by for generations to come and wonder at the devastation of such a magnificent edifice. The people of Israel did turn away from the Lord, God's promise of judgment was fulfilled, and the temple is no more—the Wailing Wall alone remains. Every day it stands in mute testimony to the consequences of Israel's refusal to honor the Lord.

But the Lord did not only promise judgment on sin. He also offered a way to forgiveness and cleansing. The purpose of the promised calamities was not just to punish God's people for their disobedience. God designed the disasters to precipitate repentance. If at any time the people would turn back to God in humility and true repentance, God would restore his blessings to them (7:14). This kind of repentance would not just consist of tearful promises, but of genuine sorrow, heartfelt grief, thorough forsaking of sin, and earnest calling on the Lord. This kind of repentance would release the promised blessings, not only for the repentant individuals but also for the communities of which they were a part.

Similar principles apply today. Willful sin is an affront to God, and it bears grave consequences. These consequences constitute divine judgment, which should lead to repentance and restoration. Many people recognize the need for a reversal of moral trends in their communities but fail to recognize the part God's people must play. For there to be reversal in the community, there must be revival in the church. For revival in the church to happen, there must be renewal in the Christian. Reversal, revival, and renewal all stand waiting in line—for repentance!

TO READ: *2 Chronicles 34:1–13*

YOUTHFUL VIGOR

*During the eighth year of his reign, while he was still young, Josiah began to seek
the God of his ancestor David. Then in the twelfth year, he began to purify
Judah and Jerusalem, destroying all the pagan shrines, the Asherah poles,
and the carved idols and cast images.*

2 CHRONICLES 34:3

M ost sixteen-year-old boys are not known for their piety. Immaturity, irresponsibility, or mischief, perhaps—and voracious appetite, energy, activity, even industry—but not usually piety, even if they are reigning monarchs.

Young King Josiah was different. We are not told what led Josiah to earnestly desire an experience of the Lord. It certainly was not the example of his father, King Amon, or his grandfather, King Manasseh, both of whom were wicked kings. Something was born in Josiah's heart that led him to take seriously both his own spiritual well-being and his royal obligation for the well-being of his people. In a few short years, he used his royal power and prestige to rid his territory of the infamous idolatry that plagued his people and to commission the refurbishing of the neglected temple (34:8). All this by the time he was twenty-six years of age!

Josiah's devotion to the Lord and spiritual leadership were developed without the benefit of the Scriptures, which makes his accomplishments even more remarkable. Then, when Hilkiah the priest discovered the lost Scriptures (34:14), Josiah was horrified to discover how far he and his people had strayed from the Lord's commands. He immediately ordered further study and inquired of the prophet Huldah. When he understood the significance of the word of the Lord, he put it into practice and called the people to follow his lead.

Prior to the rediscovery of the Scriptures, Josiah had known enough about the Lord to know that he needed to know more, and he had seen enough of idol worship to know that it was clearly wrong. Acting on the limited information available to him, he achieved great things. But when he received the word of the Lord, his vision was expanded and his experience enlarged.

Every man is called not only to respond to what he knows but also to ensure that he knows what he should. To know the word and not to obey it is wrong. To have the word and not to read and know it is no better. To paraphrase Mark Twain, "He who does not read and obey has no advantage over he who cannot read or respond." Josiah could not know what was hidden in the lost book. Modern man has no such problem—the Book is available. So we must do what we know, and read the Book. Those who read it will be called to make some changes, some of which will be uncomfortable. But every step we take toward God will lead to blessing.

TO READ: *Ezra 3:1-13*

ENTHUSIASM AND EXPERIENCE

Many of the older priests, Levites, and other leaders remembered the first Temple,
and they wept aloud when they saw the new Temple's foundation.
The others, however, were shouting for joy.

EZRA 3:12

Young people look forward; old folks look back. Youth embraces the future, where most of its life lies; old age reveres the past, where most of its life has gone. Youth has little in the past to which to refer; old age has not much in the future for which to plan. So when youth and old age stand together in the same place, they look in opposite directions and see different scenarios. Old folks see the good old days; the young see only bright horizons. Little wonder they often disagree and not infrequently clash!

On the day when the new foundations of the ruined temple were laid in Jerusalem after seventy years in exile, the reactions of the generations were markedly different. The young people were so excited about what was new and fresh that they sang and shouted and danced for joy. Their faces were wreathed in smiles. But the shouts were mingled with sobs because, while the young were delighted, the old were dismayed. *Their* cheeks wore no smiles, but were bathed in tears (3:12). They remembered and mourned the old temple, the old days, the way things were. And they looked with dismay at what was destined to take its place. In their minds the new was far inferior to the old.

The mingled sounds of delight and dismay were apparently indistinguishable from a distance (3:13). That was good, because it would have been unfortunate if only the shouts of youth had been heard, and it would have been unforgivable if the moans of the old had prevailed. Both had a point. The old had experience, which gave insight to what had been; the young had enthusiasm, which promised momentum for what was to come.

Enthusiasm without the cautions of experience can lead to projects crashing in flames. Experience without the fire of enthusiasm can lead to projects never leaving the ground. Old people harping on the way things were can kill the hope of the future, while young people worshiping the way things will be can be wounded if the lessons of history go unheeded.

God made youth and old age for a reason—they need each other! So let's thank him for youth and praise him for old age, and let us pray that enthusiasm and experience will kiss each other, and that they will live happily together.

TO READ: *Ezra 4:1-5; 5:1-5; 6:1-18*

THE FACES OF EVIL

So the Jewish leaders continued their work, and they were greatly encouraged by the preaching of the prophets Haggai and Zechariah son of Iddo. The Temple was finally finished, as had been commanded by the God of Israel and decreed by Cyrus, Darius, and Artaxerxes, the kings of Persia.

EZRA 6:14

E vil has many faces. On some occasions it smiles seductively and lures the unwary. On other occasions it scowls fiercely and intimidates the insecure. Sometimes evil talks sweetly with offers of helpfulness and cooperation, while at other times it shouts its demands and dire threats of doom. Because evil appears in differing forms, it must be countered in different ways. But first it must be recognized for what it is.

Evil has many faces, but only one goal—to thwart the purposes of God. Evil and opposition sometimes wear a friendly face. The rebuilders of the temple were offered the cooperation of their enemies. These enemies claimed to worship the Lord, but they failed to mention that they also worshiped many other gods (see 2 Kings 17:24-34). Letting them help would have given them equal access to the temple and would have compromised the purity of the people's worship of the Lord. The leaders of Judah and Benjamin rightly recognized that these enemies had "nothing in common" with them (Ezra 4:3), and gave them "no stake or claim in Jerusalem" (Neh. 2:20).

Thus rebuffed, the enemies of Judah and Benjamin became even more overt in their opposition (Ezra 4:4-5). Sterner threats required stronger responses. Later, when the building work was stopped by order of King Artaxerxes in response to spurious statements concerning the builders, it took the challenging preaching of the prophets to counter the evil and get the work moving.

When Tattenai the governor arrived on the site to question the rebuilders about their activities (5:3-5), he was civil and courteous, but committed to stopping the building nevertheless. He took down the names of the builders—an officious act with threatening overtones—and dispatched letters to King Artaxerxes to check out the returned exiles' story. When the reply came that the Jews were indeed authorized to rebuild the temple, Tattenai had no alternative but to allow them to continue. Although he wanted to terminate the restoration of the temple, he was prepared to work within the framework of the law. So the danger passed. God's people have sometimes benefitted from the fact that some of God's enemies do respect law and order.

Wise men recognize evil in a smile or a sneer, and they tear off its mask and meet it face-to-face. But such is the subtlety of evil that wise men are well advised to take counsel with others of like mind, lest they mistakenly call evil good and good evil.

WHOLEHEARTED DEVOTION

I long, yes, I faint with longing to enter the courts of the LORD.
With my whole being, body and soul, I will shout joyfully to the living God.

PSALM 84:2

M en can really get into sports. Just watch them as the winning three-point shot finds nothing but net at the buzzer. Leaping to their feet, arms raised, they shout and holler—jumping, grinning, and hugging the nearest fan. Unrestrained delight! Uninhibited joy! Unabashed emotion! It's all there. Meanwhile, back at the church . . . a different story. The enthusiasm is not always transferable.

The psalmist, however, is an exception. He seemed to get into his worship in a big way: "With my whole being, body and soul, I will shout joyfully to the living God" (84:2). He looked with such longing at the Temple and its courts, the symbols of God's presence (84:3-4), that he even envied the birds who made their nests there! So hungry was he for the opportunity to worship and to share in the fellowship of God's people that he could honestly say, "A single day in your courts is better than a thousand anywhere else! I would rather be a gatekeeper in the house of my God than live the good life in the homes of the wicked" (84:10).

The writer of this psalm was not unaware of the attractions of the life that the wicked live. He was even prepared to describe it as "the good life"!—a life of ease and enjoyment, entertainment and excess. But it held little attraction for him, because he had discovered the good things that the Lord lavishes on his servants (84:11)—grace to live each day wisely and well, and the promise of glory in the age to come.

The psalmist chose well. So often "the good life" lacks depth and purpose and ultimately leaves an empty feeling of disappointment, a bitter taste of disillusionment. The "good life" offers champagne in the evening but says nothing about real pain in the morning. In marked contrast, the psalmist preferred the rugged lifestyle of a pilgrim, and he courageously faced the realities of the Valley of Weeping rather than crafting escapist entertainment designed to help him deny reality. He knew "the good life" is not all that good!

The psalmist was enraptured with the Lord, and with his whole being he let it be known. So it is for the man today who does what is right, who trusts in the Lord and nourishes his spirit in glad worship, adoration, and praise. For him there is no reticence and no reluctance, but lots of rejoicing with his "whole being, body and soul"!

TO READ: *Nehemiah 1:1–11*

"I WAS WRONG"

*Listen to my prayer! Look down and see me praying night and day for your people Israel.
I confess that we have sinned against you. Yes, even my own family and I have sinned!*

NEHEMIAH 1:6

M en do not find it easy to say, "I was wrong," and, "I'm sorry." But we need to learn. Unless we admit culpability and offer apologies, our relationships will suffer.

Nehemiah was the king's cupbearer. Much more than a glorified wine steward, he was a member of the king's inner circle, a trusted aide, a key man in the affairs of state. He was also a deeply spiritual man who knew how to pray to the God of heaven. When he heard about the sad state of affairs in far-off Jerusalem, Nehemiah made use of both channels (1:4; 2:1-8). The cultured man who knew how to present wine to an earthly king also knew how to to present prayers to the heavenly Lord, with dramatic effect.

Nehemiah's prayer was deeply emotional, springing from a recognition that the situation in which God's people found themselves was directly attributable to their own actions. No whining came from his lips, no questions sprang from his heart, no recriminations found their way into his thinking. God had said clearly and unmistakably that if his people obeyed they would be blessed, and if they disobeyed they would suffer the consequences. The mess they were in was simply the accumulation of consequences for which they were responsible. Nehemiah's prayer reflected this insight.

Nehemiah confessed sin on behalf of the people as a whole. In itself, this could have been too vague, too fuzzy, too out-of-focus. True, the people had sinned collectively; but, as Nehemiah recognized, collective guilt is the sum total of individual guilt. Israel's guilt included Nehemiah's own guilt. Collective confession has its place—right alongside individual, personal confession. It is the logical response to individual guilt, not a convenient substitute for admission of personal culpability.

The same Lord who has promised that actions have consequences has also guaranteed that confession leads to forgiveness and that forgiveness is the pathway to restoration. Nehemiah knew this well. So his prayer, which was deeply confessional, was also quietly confident.

We men should be as eager to approach the Lord as we are to make business contacts, and as well-versed at presenting our heart concerns to God as we are at offering our products to potential customers. And like Nehemiah, we, too, should be ready to confess our sins, confident that God will hear and forgive. Then, when we present our requests, we can have confidence that God will hear us and answer.

TO READ: *Nehemiah 4:1-23*

FINISHING THE JOB

*Then as I looked over the situation, I called together the leaders and the people
and said to them, "Don't be afraid of the enemy! Remember the Lord, who is great
and glorious, and fight for your friends, your families, and your homes!"*

NEHEMIAH 4:14

M ore jobs get started than get finished. More projects are conceived than are completed. Initial enthusiasm gets drained, capital gets exhausted, energy gets dissipated. Unforeseen obstacles rear ugly heads, unanticipated problems loom large, unwelcome factors prevail. People get tired, bored, disgruntled, disappointed, dishonest, angry, envious, jealous, fractious, competitive, combative. Projects die on drawing boards. "I quit" becomes a mantra.

All of that could have been Nehemiah's experience. If ever there was a project designed to discourage its workers and deplete its resources, Nehemiah's rebuilding project was it! Poor pay, long hours, constant problems, dangerous working conditions, understaffing, shortage of materials, a nonexistent benefits package, limited supervision, little job satisfaction—you name it, it was all there. But somehow Nehemiah got the job done. How did he do it? Nehemiah only succeeded because God empowered him and protected him. He continually relied on God for help and strength, and he was not disappointed (4:4-5, 9, 14-15, 20).

Nehemiah also instilled in his workforce a concern for the well-being of the community. The project in which they were involved was significant because it served more than personal interests. More than pay and perks, Nehemiah focused his workers' attention on the well-being of those for whom they were responsible—their families and their homes (4:14). They should work hard to provide for and protect those whose care was their concern.

In addition to these motives, there was a higher vision, a nobler goal. "Remember God," Nehemiah said. He knew that the rebuilding project ultimately served God. He knew that rebuilding the city would fulfill the divine objective. So he and his workers were enrolled together in providing the sweat and muscle that would result in God's will being done on earth as it is in heaven.

Workers whose focus is narrowly self-centered struggle when conditions are less than ideal and quickly jump ship if they can improve their own situation and get what they imagine to be their just desserts! But men and women inspired with a cause that transcends purely personal preference endure more and are satisfied with less. They finish the job they are given, because they know that doing the will of God and providing for the needs of others gilds the mundane realities of work with a glory that makes it all worthwhile.

TO READ: *Esther 1:10-20; 3:1-6; 4:1-17*

RESPECT MUST
BE EARNED

"Go and gather together all the Jews of Susa and fast for me. Do not eat or drink for three days, night or day. My maids and I will do the same. And then, though it is against the law, I will go in to see the king. If I must die, I am willing to die."

ESTHER 4:16

R espect must be earned. It may be demanded, but it can never be imposed. Fear may be coerced, and obedience may be enforced; but respect flows freely from a heart full of appreciation for admirable qualities and behavior.

King Xerxes of Persia apparently did not know this. He was incensed when Vashti, his beautiful queen, refused to be paraded before his majesty's drunken friends (1:10-12). In his opinion, Vashti did not show him proper respect, so she was deposed as queen and banished for life (1:19). This, the king and his advisers decided (1:20), would ensure that men would be respected by their wives! It is a rare woman who respects such a man.

Some time later a shady character by the name of Haman was elevated to the number-two position in the kingdom (3:1-6). He demanded respect and expected everyone to bow before him. But a feisty official, a Jew called Mordecai, had no respect for Haman and refused to bow. Haman's response was to order the annihilation of all Jews! This, he determined, would teach the Jews the meaning of respect! It is a warped mind that orders "ethnic cleansing" as a response to an insult.

Some leaders have egos that cannot bear the slightest slight. They abuse power, and their punishments bear no resemblance to the imagined crimes. Such leaders receive only hatred and disdain.

But then there was Esther. Esther was Vashti's successor as queen of Persia. She was also Mordecai's cousin. As queen, she remained a closet Jewess because Mordecai had told her to keep her nationality a secret (2:10, 20). Esther was informed of the imminent destruction of her people, and she was reminded that she was in a position to do something about it. She must approach the king, an illegal and dangerous act (4:11). She must use her exalted position as a platform for righteousness. She must disclose her ethnicity and perhaps sign her own death warrant. She knew how desperately she needed both her kinsmen's support and the Lord's enabling (4:16).

Xerxes and Haman, with their small minds and fragile egos, craved respect but generated only fear. Esther, with her quiet courage, sense of duty, and simple faith, rescued her people and earned their respect. Leaders who demand respect often do not receive it. But you can respect a leader who leads by example and demonstrates dignity.

TO READ: *Job 1:6-22*

BAD THINGS HAPPEN

"All right, you may test him," the LORD *said to Satan. "Do whatever you want with everything he possesses, but don't harm him physically." So Satan left the Lord's presence.*

JOB 1:12

I n a perfect world all would be sweetness and light—or so we fondly imagine. But our world is often ugly and dark. We dream and work to bring about our utopia, but it never comes. Bad things happen. And they happen continuously, relentlessly, and cruelly, to bad people and also to the good. Sometimes, it seems they happen more to the good than to the bad. Why?

Job's world was sweetness and light. He had lots of money, a successful business, a great family, recognition, and a good reputation. And with all of this, Job was a righteous and deeply religious man—the best of the best. Then came calamity upon calamity, until he was left only with fresh graves, shattered barns, decimated herds, chronic illness, and a bitter wife. God's best had been dealt life's worst. But why?

A skeptic would quickly answer, "Bad things happen because there is no good God to keep them from happening." The skeptic thinks he has an incontrovertible point. But surely, if it be argued that the presence of bad things points to God's absence, it must be conceded that the presence of good things points to God's presence. "Yes," the skeptic might reply, "and what kind of God is he if he exists? If he is all good, why does he tolerate evil? If he is all-powerful, why doesn't he stop it?"

The story of Job points in another direction. God, our creator, rules all things by his mighty power, and he is good. Satan, our accuser, is evil. For reasons that we don't understand, God allows Satan to engage in evil functions, but only under tight divine control; yet God makes *everything*, even evil, serve his purpose, and he brings eternal good out of temporal evil.

It may be a hard truth to embrace, a bitter pill to swallow. But ultimately, God's ways are beyond our comprehension. "There are secret things that belong to the Lord our God" (Deut. 29:29). At some point we have to humbly accept what God has told us and trust that he is doing what is right. Even though "clouds and darkness surround him," we can trust that "righteousness and justice are the foundation of his throne" (Ps. 97:2). And there is no getting away from the fact that good can come out of evil.

Look at the cross of Jesus Christ. It was temporal evil, but from it came eternal good. Satan did his worst. God did his best! What gross evil, but what glorious good! Best of all, God does not watch our pain dispassionately—in Christ he endured it himself.

TO READ: *Job 22:1-30*

AT ODDS WITH GOD

"Stop quarreling with God! If you agree with him, you will have peace at last, and things will go well for you. Listen to his instructions, and store them in your heart. If you return to the Almighty and clean up your life, you will be restored."

JOB 22:21-23

Job's friend Eliphaz was remarkably good at jumping to conclusions—and landing in the wrong place. For example, when he witnessed Job's sufferings, he assumed that his friend must have been doing some terrible things to warrant such catastrophe (22:6-7). "You must have" done this and "you must have" done that, he reasoned, despite that there was no basis upon which to construct such an indictment. For it appears that Job was innocent of everything of which he was accused.

Eliphaz didn't get everything wrong, though. If Job had indeed been guilty of the things of which he was accused, he should have taken Eliphaz's words to heart, because these instructions provide the right direction for a guilty man to take. "Stop quarreling with God! If you agree with him, you will have peace at last, and things will go well for you. Listen to his instructions, and store them in your heart. If you return to the Almighty and clean up your life, you will be restored" (22:21-23). Good advice, especially for those at odds with God.

I doubt very much that Job needed this advice, but I am certain that many men *do* need it. Many a man is at odds with himself and the world because he's at odds with God. Nothing goes right for him. He's out of sorts and bent out of shape, and he doesn't even know what bothers him. He experiences inner turmoil, his relationships are tenuous, and he derives little or no satisfaction from all that he does. He may interpret the problem as a physical issue and determine to take more time off and get some rest. Or he may decide the roots of his restlessness are relational, so, accordingly, he changes his job or his wife or both. But such a man needs to recognize that his lack of outer order arises from a lack of inner peace. And that is evidence that he has a broken relationship with the Lord, from whom he came, to whom he will go, and through whom and for whom he exists. Without the Lord, there is little left, and the inner vacuum produces a lack of peace.

A decision to "agree with" God (22:21), the source of all truth and wisdom, is common sense; and to "stop quarreling with God" is obviously the smart thing to do. You cannot win an argument against God. Ceasing to try leads to the inner peace from which a deep-rooted sense of order takes hold. Then contentment and satisfaction are not far behind. Paul called it "peace with God" (Rom. 5:1).

TO READ: *Job 40:1-14*

BRACE YOURSELF
LIKE A MAN

"Brace yourself, because I have some questions for you, and you must answer them."

JOB 40:7

C hildren love to ask their fathers *why*, but fathers are not always able to answer. God *is* always able to give an answer, but he does not always choose to. This poses problems for men. Like their own children, men not only expect an answer to every query, they expect the answer to meet with their approval.

God's silence had been unbearable for Job. With no answer to his questioning *why* and his beseeching *please*, Job resorted to drawing his own conclusions while his friends resorted to their own theories. Both got it wrong. There were flashes of insight, there were elements of truth. Yet in the end Job accused God and the friends abused Job.

At last it was time for God to speak. "Brace yourself," God told Job, and it's a good thing he warned him. Job's request for an audience with the Lord had been granted, and it was overpowering—Job was engulfed in a torrent of questions. The Maker made it clear that Job's questions, as well as his friends' explanations (42:7), had been full of foolishness. God is God—he alone has the power, wisdom, and justice necessary to be God. In response, Job recognized his impudence and put his hand over his mouth in silence. At the end, as at the beginning, silence was the best posture in the presence of almighty God.

Modern man is not always so reticent. Has he not explored the galaxies with his telescopes, trod on the moon, and sent his ingenious machines to rove on Mars? Certainly he has!—only to find that the more he discovers, the more lies undiscovered. His accumulated knowledge serves to demonstrate the depth of his ignorance; his examination of creation's mechanics simply plunges him further into the darkness of creation's mysteries. Modern man should brace himself for questions about the gaps in *his* knowledge and the limits of *his* experience, and then learn humbly to bow himself at God's feet. Sadly, more often than not man wants to brag about himself than to brace himself, to say, "Wow is me!" rather than "Woe is me!"

When the great Creator questions one of his tiny creatures about how much the creature knows or can do in comparison with God, the only appropriate response is to humbly bow in total recognition of one's own nothingness. As the great wise man, Solomon, once said, "God . . . is in heaven, and you are only here on earth. So let your words be few" (Eccles. 5:2).

TO READ: *Psalm 95*

LITTLE GODS AND
THE GREAT CREATOR

*Come, let us worship and bow down. Let us kneel before the LORD our maker, for he
is our God. We are the people he watches over, the sheep under his care. Oh, that
you would listen to his voice today!*

PSALM 95:6-7

O ur world is full of little gods. These gods are not only to be found in temples in the
East—they reside in garages in the West, on beaches in the south, and in ski lodges
in the north. You can find them hidden in vaults, stored in musty attics, hung on walls,
and draped around shoulders. Some of them are tied up alongside a dock, and others wrap
their arms around our neck. That doesn't make sense, you say? Consider this: gods are
objects of veneration, articles that demand and receive our unbridled adoration. They are
things and people that take our mind off God himself and usurp his place in our life.

What exactly is his place? It is the central place, the superior position, the ultimate
throne of authority in the core of our being. Why should he expect the superior place? The
answer is, because he is superior to all things. God made all things; he is as superior to all
things as a craftsman is superior to his tools. He towers above all things, including the tiny
people that have made themselves gods. He created them to be his servants! —not to
worship things or people, but to worship him, their Creator! People have the temerity and
audacity to accept veneration and the idiocy to worship created things. They should know
that the Creator is greater by far.

Our world, which is full of little gods, needs to heed the call, "Come, let us worship
and bow down. Let us kneel before the Lord our maker, for he is our God. We are the
people he watches over, the sheep under his care. Oh, that you would listen to his voice
today!" (95:6-7). But there is a reluctance to do that. Not only will it mean tearing some
little gods from the positions they have usurped, but there is also a general feeling abroad
that if you become too involved with God you might find him tyrannical and you may
become fanatical.

Fortunately those who know God know better. They know him not only as the great
King but also as a loving shepherd who "watches over, the sheep under his care" (95:7).
Who could possibly care for God's creation more than God, the Creator? Who can be
trusted more than he can? And who is worthy of our adoration and veneration more than
he is? So let us be done with the little gods; "Come, let us worship and bow down. Let us
kneel before the Lord our maker"—the Creator who cares!

TO READ: *Job 42:1-17*

QUESTIONING GOD IN IGNORANCE

"You ask, 'Who is this that questions my wisdom with such ignorance?' It is I. And I was talking about things I did not understand, things far too wonderful for me."

JOB 42:3

God believes in freedom of speech. He made us capable of thinking and gave us the tools to articulate our thoughts, and he expects us to use these divinely imparted gifts. He allows us to say what we think about him, even uncomplimentary and erroneous thoughts. Incredibly, he gives us the freedom to blaspheme him and to question his justice, righteousness, and integrity. But he also holds us accountable for what we say.

Having listened to Job's questions and complaints, and having endured the answers of Job's friends, God pointedly asked, "Who is this that questions my wisdom with such ignorant words?" (38:2). The question required an answer, and Job's reply was brief and to the point: "It is I. And I was talking about things I did not understand. . . . I take back everything I said, and I sit in dust and ashes to show my repentance" (42:3, 6).

God's powerful self-revelation served to show Job the depth of his ignorance: "I had heard about you before, but now I have seen you with my own eyes" (42:5). It isn't simply that God is too big to be contained in one man's intellect, even though he is. But the way God does things is so different from the way we think he should do things, that when we begin to grasp the fringes of his workings we ought not think that we understand the wonder of it all. As Job said, "I was talking about things I did not understand, things far too wonderful for me."

There was no point in Job's denying that he had been questioning God or, more importantly, that the questions were the queries of ignorance. Even though Job did not get a complete answer to the *why* of his predicament, he did get a revelation of *Who* is in control. And his response was appropriate—humble submission to the God whom he now knew much better, but whom he knew he would never fully understand.

Like Job, we can speak with seeming authority from the depths of our ignorance, and we can utter profundities that further revelation shows to be false. That is why we should be slow to speculate and cautious about questioning God. It is right and proper for us to speak with authority when Scripture speaks with clarity, but on other subjects we should exercise a becoming modesty of opinion. Otherwise, we can all too easily drift into subjects "far too wonderful" for us.

TO READ: *Proverbs 1:1-9*

GETTING WISE

These proverbs will make the simpleminded clever.
They will give knowledge and purpose to young people.

PROVERBS 1:4

The information age has dawned. So now, we can "surf the Web." Not long ago, surf was something bleached-blond youths rode to shore, and webs were things that spiders worked hard to create. But now one surfs the Web from the comfort of home to seek information. We "access" it, "download" it, and store it in computers that allow us to gather vast amounts of information about the world in which we live.

But amassing information is not the same as being wise. Information informs us, to be sure, but wisdom tells us what to do with the information. Collected information tells you what is possible, while wisdom tells you what is prudent. Not all knowledgeable people are wise—sometimes they do bad things with good information. Not all wise people are among the world's most knowledgeable—some of them don't know much, but they do wonderful things with very little. Wisdom cannot operate without information; but information does not guarantee wisdom.

Proverbs are pithy sayings that stick in the mind, conveying a needed truth. Proverbs lead to wisdom. Some of them beget discipline. For example, "If you search for good, you will find favor; but if you search for evil, it will find you!" (11:27). Good information there; but wisdom says, "Aha! I'd better watch what I'm looking for!" Other proverbs teach good conduct. Here's a proverb that helps in this regard: "It is better to be poor and godly than rich and dishonest" (16:8). A wise man takes that to heart, sees the truth of it, and decides that honesty is not only the best policy but the only policy for the wise. And so he deals honestly.

Proverbs need to be read, remembered, meditated upon, and performed. They impart pure knowledge, they offer sweet rewards, they administer stern warnings, and they demand disciplined responses. When proverbs are considerd carefully and embraced wholeheartedly, they nourish deeply, redirecting convictions and dramatically changing lives.

Man is in danger of becoming a giant in information and a pygmy in wisdom: as he concentrates on assimilating facts, he runs the risk of neglecting matters of faith. He is at risk of dressing himself in information with nothing to clothe his life. That is why we need to learn the proverbs: they "will make the simpleminded clever. They will give knowledge and purpose to young people" (1:4). Wisdom will crown us with grace and clothe our lives with honor (1:9). That's much better than bare information!

TO READ: *Proverbs 5:1–23*

SEXUAL FREEDOM

An evil man is held captive by his own sins; they are ropes that catch and hold him.
He will die for lack of self-control; he will be lost because of his incredible folly.

PROVERBS 5:22-23

I ncredible folly"! That is how adultery is described in Proverbs 5:23. But in secular society, adultery is characterized in more glowing terms: "sexual freedom," "adult entertainment," "mature adventure," "free love." Who is right about adultery? Is it something to be embraced, or something to be avoided?

Look at the facts. Adultery can mean that "you will lose your honor" as well as your fortunes (5:9). Having spent years building a solid reputation for integrity and generating respect in the community, the adulterer finds himself exposed as a cheat. He's cheated his wife and kids, and he has shown that he is not above lying to save his own skin. Should his wife react by legitimately terminating the marriage, "strangers will obtain [his] wealth, and someone else will enjoy the fruit of [his] labor" (5:10). His "free love," he discovers, is not at all cheap!

Then there is the unpalatable truth that sexually transmitted diseases are common among the unfaithful, so the adulterer may "groan in anguish when disease consumes [his] body" (5:11). He will no doubt bear his share of shame and find reason to reflect on his own lack of discipline. He may even be wise enough to admit, "I have come to the brink of utter ruin, and now I must face public disgrace" (5:14).

Modern society is certainly blasé about adultery, but shame and stigma, ruin and regret are still part of the package. The allure of adultery masks the reality of moral, social, spiritual, and financial ruin. He therefore takes steps to avoid the adulterous path, to banish the adulterous thought, and to discipline the adulterous desire. He will also nurture the romantic and sexual love of his wife, so that adulterous attraction is not so alluring because his desires are being appropriately sated and his commitments are being totally fulfilled.

Selfishness is the main reason for stress in all aspects of marriage. Unselfishness is the best cure for marital ills. Selfish people want their sexual needs fulfilled, while unselfish people desire to meet the needs of their partner. Selfish people make sexual demands, unselfish people give sexual satisfaction. Any man whose wife meets his sexual needs as he meets hers will find he has no desire to stray, and adultery will be far from his mind. He will cherish his wife and be cherished in return. His honor will remain intact; his integrity will be unsullied. Anything less is "incredible folly."

TO READ: *Proverbs 7:1-27*

SEDUCTION

Love wisdom like a sister; make insight a beloved member of your family.
Let them hold you back from an affair with an immoral woman, from listening
to the flattery of an adulterous woman. . . . Her house is the road to the grave.
Her bedroom is the den of death.

PROVERBS 7:4-5, 27

Seduction wears many dresses, all of them attractive. Sometimes her dress is sexy. Other times it reeks of money. Some days she wears her power suit. Seduction is all about money, sex, and power.

Seduction has to wear heavy makeup to hide the blemishes. She wishes to convey a message that is fundamentally false. She presents her message well—sweet as honey, smoother than oil, laden with flattery, and offering great reward for little expense.

"Come with me," says seduction in her pricey dress. "I can offer you a deal that will make you rich. No risk, no questions asked, no downside, only profit. Together we'll laugh all the way to the bank." And the seductive words work. Hadn't he been particularly chosen for this opportunity because of his unique abilities? Wasn't this deal especially for him because he had been such a good friend? The offer is too good to be true—because it isn't true. Smart as he is, seduction makes him like a "simpleminded young man who lacked common sense" (7:7).

Later, seduction comes to the man dressed to kill, alluringly perfumed and whispering promises of unimaginable delights. Does he need to be assured that his manhood is not diminished, that he is still attractive? She says she finds him irresistible, and her husband is away so nobody will know. To salve his conscience, she assures him that she, too, is religious: "I've offered my sacrifices and just finished my vows" (7:14). So he goes with her, "like a bird flying into a snare, little knowing it would cost him his life" (7:23).

Later, seduction comes offering power at a bargain price. Just cut a couple of corners and the resulting prestige and position will place him among the movers and the shakers. Just think how much good he can do there! It's an offer he cannot refuse.

But he should refuse, because embracing seduction leads to sin. And "the wages of sin is death" (Rom. 6:23). So seduction's pretty dress becomes a burial shroud. "Her house is the road to the grave. Her bedroom is the den of death" (Prov. 7:27).

The wise man knows enough to refuse seduction's blandishments. He embraces God's instructions, he orders his life according to the dictates of his Lord, and he stands strong in the power of the Spirit. In standing, the wise man is strengthened in resolve and character, in reputation and honor.

GETTING RICH

Lazy people are soon poor; hard workers get rich. A wise youth works hard all summer; a youth who sleeps away the hour of opportunity brings shame.

PROVERBS 10:4-5

Lazy people are soon poor; hard workers get rich" (10:4). Proverbs like this are generally true, but there seem to be exceptions to every rule. There are some lazy people who seem to have the Midas touch: they do very little but what they touch turns to gold. By the same token, there are hard workers who never seem to be able to dig themselves out of the hole of their financial misfortune.

That said, there is great wisdom in reminding people who choose not to work that the result will be poverty, and "the poverty of the poor is their calamity" (10:15). The lazy person may blame his calamity on everything but himself. But the root of his problem lies between his two ears: his attitude toward work is all wrong. He neither sees work as a privilege nor recognizes the nobility of labor. He doesn't like work, and he feels obliged to avoid everything he does not like. It matters not to him that God worked and that Jesus spent the bulk of his life in honest toil. He is oblivious to the benefits of using his God-given time and talents, and he is not interested in producing something of value that will enrich the life of a needy person. Truly, a man "who sleeps away the hour of opportunity brings shame" (10:5).

On the other hand, the man who sets about his work with energy and determination usually provides abundantly for his dependents and produces enough to give generously to those in need. "The earnings of the godly enhance their lives" (10:16). He has the means to offer to the Lord the fruit of his labor, and in the glow of this worshipful activity, the Lord's work prospers through the work of his hands. Such a man is aware that, while his work is productive, "the blessing of the Lord makes a person rich" (10:22)—it is the Lord who gives a man the ability to get wealth! The wise man knows it, utilizes the abilities he has been granted, and mingles his sweat with praise and his energies with thanksgiving.

So while there are noble poor people and rich rascals, as a general rule the lazy languish and the productive prosper. Those who work hard can take delight in a job well done, and they enjoy the benefits of things well earned. But those who lie lazily in self-induced poverty take delight in very little, for they have little that is delightful to enjoy.

TO READ: *Ecclesiastes 2:1-12*

MONEY AND MEANING

But as I looked at everything I had worked so hard to accomplish,
it was all so meaningless. It was like chasing the wind.
There was nothing really worthwhile anywhere.

ECCLESIASTES 2:11

M en are more than animals—but that doesn't mean we are happier. Animals search for food, while men search for meaning. Animals are driven by instinct, men by desire. Animals forage happily in the mud, while men look to the stars and ponder existence. Animals sleep peacefully in holes in the ground, while men toss and turn fitfully on beds of ease. Animals find contentment in little, but men find dissatisfaction in plenty. What are we missing?

Men find *some* satisfaction in working hard, but we always look for something more. We translate work into money and channel money into everything our heart desires. With money a man can put food on the table and a roof over his head. With more money he can fill his belly with delicacies, his home with treasures, his garage with vintage cars, and his cellar with vintage wine. Money will buy him abundant pleasure. But pleasure generates an appetite for more—grander experiences, bigger thrills, costlier adventures. Then, after desperately pursuing pleasure and purchasing all that money can buy, he retires to his bed and wonders why he is still unfulfilled, why life seems so meaningless.

These are often the musings a successful man has in his heart. Remarkably, these were the same questions that Koheleth, which means "the Teacher," had about his experiences in antiquity. The questions are not new—they bothered men in bygone yesterdays as much as they do today. This suggests that these struggles for meaning and fulfillment are not the products of circumstances so much as the results of a common human experience of dissatisfaction.

It is true that God "richly gives us all we need for our enjoyment" (1 Tim. 6:17). Then why is it that man has difficulty finding that enjoyment? It is because he forgets the God who gives the things, and he substitutes the things for God! Man too often trusts in temporal things that pass away, rather than in the eternal Lord from whom all things come.

So what should a man do? He should work as an act of worship to the Lord, who gives him the ability to work. Then he should treat his earnings as treasures that God has committed to him to manage, and he should administer these resources in a way that pleases the Lord. He will discover that the purpose of life is not to make money but to serve and enjoy the God who made everything!

TO READ: *Psalm 103*

GOD'S TENDER MERCIES

Praise the LORD, I tell myself, and never forget the good things he does for me.
He forgives all my sins and heals all my diseases. He ransoms me from death
and surrounds me with love and tender mercies.

PSALM 103:2-4

G enuine appreciation is enthusiastic—it eagerly enrolls others in joyful acknowledge-
ment and celebration. David is a good example. He said, "The Lord has made the
heavens his throne; from there he rules over everything" (103:19). David found this so
encouraging and such a reason for rejoicing that he took delight in praise and exhorted the
whole created order to recognize and rejoice that God is firmly on the throne.

The only problem with visions of God, high and lifted up on his throne, is that he
can appear to be remote and inaccessible, removed from us and unmoved by the vicissitudes of life that we endure. But nothing could be farther from the truth. In fact, the
wonder of the divine-human relationship is that the transcendent Lord is immanent (close
by). He who rules the heavens and the earth is neither unaware of nor unconcerned about
the intimate details of our lives.

So tender are God's thoughts toward us that he continually bears in mind that we
are frail, fallen, and finite. "The Lord is like a father to his children, tender and compassionate to those who fear him. For he understands how weak we are; he knows we are only
dust" (103:13-14). God is painfully aware of our limitations. He knows all about our
sinful disposition, and he recognizes how tenuous our hold on life is. So he deals with us
accordingly—both firmly and tenderly.

This does not mean that God overlooks our failings or excuses our sin. On the
contrary, he holds us responsible, but he makes a way for us to be forgiven through the
gracious work of Christ on the cross. In fact, "He forgives all my sins and heals all my
diseases" (103:3). We should remember that our sins will finally be forgiven, our diseases
will finally be healed, and we will be finally ransomed from death when we are finally
with him in heaven. All this is because of Christ. In the meantime, we can say with David,
"He fills my life with good things" (103:5)—and we can be grateful.

We need to keep telling ourselves of God's tender mercies because we have an
ingrained tendency to forget. We must take steps to "never forget the good things he does"
for us (103:2). As we consider these things, each of us, whatever his frame of mind, should
stop and say, "As for me—I, too, will praise the Lord" (103:22). Recollecting God's tender
mercies makes for warm hearts, and warm hearts warm up other hearts to "praise his holy
name" (103:1).

TO READ: *Song of Songs 4:1–5:1*

INTIMACY AND ECSTASY

"Awake, north wind! Come, south wind! Blow on my garden and waft its lovely perfume to my lover. Let him come into his garden and eat its choicest fruits." Young Man: "I am here in my garden, my treasure, my bride! I gather my myrrh with my spices and eat my honeycomb with my honey. I drink my wine with my milk." Young Women of Jerusalem: "Oh, lover and beloved, eat and drink! Yes, drink deeply of this love!"

SONG OF SONGS 4:16–5:1

M en are aroused by what they see, while women are more often awakened by what they hear and feel. Masculine arousal is much closer to the surface, and men's sexual appetites are more rapidly satisfied than those of their loved one. To the extent that these generalizations are true, the possibilities for misunderstanding, disappointment, and frustration abound.

The young man in this poem is entranced with the physical endowments of his wife and is eager to tell her all that he feels about her. The very recital of his appreciation warms her heart and stirs her desire for him.

Men today can learn a lesson at this point. Rather than embarking on lovemaking without preamble, warning, or preparation, the caring husband will take the time to understand his mate and to bring her along with him in intimacy and ecstasy. He does not assume she will move at his speed and be satisfied as he is satisfied. He knows better than to rush her before she is ready and to roll over and go to sleep just as she is getting interested.

In the poem, the young woman is without doubt interested in her lover's lovemaking. In response to him she exclaims, "Awake, north wind! Come, south wind! Blow on my garden and waft its lovely perfume to my lover. Let him come into his garden and eat its choicest fruits" (4:16). There can be even less doubt that the man will readily respond to the invitation! She is ready, and he is ready, to enjoy mutual fulfillment and satisfaction. "Oh, lover and beloved, eat and drink! Yes, drink deeply of this love!" (5:1).

The language of the poem may not be exactly to our taste (4:1-11, for example). It is unlikely that most modern western women would be excited to hear that their teeth remind their lover of shorn sheep or that their hair is reminiscent of flocks of goats! We need to employ erotic language of our own. But there is no mistaking the ancient lovers' legitimate eroticism. Neither is there any confusion about the limits of their sexual enjoyment. They regarded each other as the "private garden" reserved exclusively for the other (4:12). No one else was allowed to enjoy the fruits.

Intimacy in marriage is all about unreserved enjoyment, unabashed expression, and unequivocal exclusiveness. In this kind of marital intimacy, lasting, mutual satisfaction is to be found. Without such intimacy, the experience of marriage can be more martial than marital.

ADMITTING WEAKNESS

*Then I said, "My destruction is sealed, for I am a sinful man and a member
of a sinful race. Yet I have seen the King, the LORD Almighty!"*

ISAIAH 6:5

Most men are aware of their weaknesses. They may not spend a lot of time beating their breast over them, but if confronted with obvious evidence that they have failed they will usually admit that they are not perfect and may even reluctantly concede that they have a problem in that area. Even a strong man, in his nobler moments, will confess to an Achilles' heel.

Isaiah was different. He confessed he was deficient in what others probably regarded as his greatest strength, his speech. Isaiah was a reputed wordsmith, a skilled communicator, a man capable of sublime statement and exquisite poetic expression. From his lips and quill flowed truth and beauty. But Isaiah confessed he had a problem with his lips! "Woe is me! . . . because I am a man of unclean lips" (6:5, KJV). Even his strength was flawed with weakness!

Apparently Isaiah was aware that his lips were capable of saying "unclean" things—unkind, untrue, unhelpful, and unacceptable things. There were at least two reasons for this sad state of affairs. First, by Isaiah's own admission, he was "a sinful man" (6:5)—he had an inbuilt tendency to deviant behavior, a tendency that his lips expressed. Second, he lived in a society where sinful speech was accepted: "and I dwell in the midst of a people of unclean lips" (6:5, KJV)—and he had acquiesced in the wrongdoing. As a result, Isaiah's guilt was not so much in his weaknesses as in his strength!

But this realization did not come to Isaiah as he compared himself with his contemporaries. It could not, for they were no better than he. He needed an external reference point, and he got it in his vision of the Lord (6:1-4). Seeing the Lord in his holiness helped Isaiah see his own fallenness.

Repentance comes in different shapes and sizes. Some "repentance" is nothing more than being sorry that I got caught. Some is a matter of being sorry that I am suffering because of what I did. Some is regret that I do bad things. But deep-down repentance—real repentance—goes beyond being chagrined about what I've done to being distressed about what I am. This kind of repentance recognizes that I am a fallen man, shot through with deviancy. Deep-down repentance leads me to say not just, "I've done some bad things," but to confess, "I am a sinful man." It involves acknowledging that I am fallen—*especially* in my strengths.

TO READ: *Isaiah 9:1–7*

GOD'S NO POLITICIAN

For a child is born to us, a son is given to us. And the government will rest on his
shoulders. These will be his royal titles: Wonderful Counselor, Mighty God, Everlasting
Father, Prince of Peace. His ever expanding, peaceful government will never end. He
will rule forever with fairness and justice from the throne of his ancestor David. The
passionate commitment of the LORD Almighty will guarantee this!

ISAIAH 9:6-7

When politicians run for office, few but the most fervent partisans take their promises seriously. A great gulf often separates political promises from reliable guarantees.

We do not know whether the people in Isaiah's time had arrived at such a point of skepticism, but we do know that they had little reason for confidence. The glory days of David and Solomon were long gone; the Assyrian hordes were knocking on the door. The future looked gloomy. Then the Lord spoke through Isaiah.

God promised his people that their land would be overrun and that the formerly great nation of Israel would be left like "a stump" in the land (6:13). But the term *stump,* while full of dire predictions, held a glimmer of hope: The people knew that a pruned stump would in time sprout, flourish, and bear fruit. "The stump will be a holy seed that will grow again" (6:13).

Later, God promised that the dynasty of David would not disappear—it would be overrun, but it would be resurrected and would spread across the world, bringing peace and prosperity, stretching into eternity (9:1-7). A universal, everlasting kingdom! The government of this new kingdom would "rest on" the shoulders of a "child," a most unusual child who would be "Wonderful Counselor, Mighty God, Everlasting Father, Prince of Peace" (9:6).

The Israelites might have been tempted to think that Isaiah had lost touch with reality. They could expect not only survival but revival? This would happen through a child who would demonstrate divine qualities? Unbelievable. But Isaiah had not lost touch with reality—he had been in touch with the author of reality! And the reality is that this child's "ever expanding, peaceful government will never end. He will rule forever with fairness and justice. . . . The passionate commitment of the Lord Almighty will guarantee this!" (9:7).

When God makes passionate guarantees, sane people sit up and take note. God is not a politician running for office—his pronouncements warrant a better response than skepticism or dismissal. When he speaks, men should listen. History shows that God does what he says he will do—when he guarantees something with "passionate commitment," he comes through. Unlike any politician, God has the power to accomplish what he promises. In his guarantee we find the confidence to banish the darkness of despair—we find hope in an otherwise hopeless world.

THE POSTGAME SHOW

*Say to those who are afraid, "Be strong, and do not fear, for your God is coming
to destroy your enemies. He is coming to save you."*

ISAIAH 35:4

S ports fans set aside a major portion of their lives to follow the fortunes of the team
of their choice. It is not enough for them just to watch the game. Fully involved fans
must give careful attention to the "pregame show," in which they indulge themselves with
speculation and anticipation. Then follows the game itself, in which they involve themselves as if something of significance is taking place. And then, the final whistle is only the
signal for the "postgame show" to begin. To this postmortem the fan gives himself with
earnest devotion as he analyzes and criticizes the game. The game begins before it starts
and continues after it has ended. The fans can't get enough of it!

Our salvation also began long before we were born, and it will continue far beyond
our earthly end. Salvation has three tenses, and history has three phases. Salvation lets us
contemplate the past, looking back over what God has done. We can also celebrate the
present, savoring what God is doing. And on the basis of God's promises we can anticipate
the future, looking forward to what he will yet do. The three tenses of our own salvation
also tie into the three phases in the history of salvation. In the past the prophets predicted
that Christ would come again; that we can contemplate. Now Christ has come; this we can
celebrate. And in the future, Isaiah reminds us, Christ will come again; that we can
anticipate.

We contemplate the beginnings of our salvation because of what Christ did when he
came, and we anticipate the conclusion of our salvation, which he will accomplish on his
return. When Christ returns in great glory he will consummate all that he has begun. Not a
few blind eyes, lame legs, and deaf ears were healed when he came the first time, but these
were simply foretastes of what he will do when he comes again (35:5-6). Then he will
make all things new.

Armed with anticipation, we should encourage each other. There are tired hands that
need to be strengthened, weak knees that need to be encouraged. The fearful need to be
told, "Be strong, and do not fear, for your God . . . is coming to save you" (35:4). However,
unlike sports fans, we can enjoy our postgame show now—we know who wins, and we
can savor his victory even while the "game" is still in progress.

TO READ: *Isaiah 40:1-31*

FLY HIGH

He gives power to those who are tired and worn out; he offers strength to the weak.
Even youths will become exhausted, and young men will give up. But those who wait
on the LORD will find new strength. They will fly high on wings like eagles.
They will run and not grow weary. They will walk and not faint.

ISAIAH 40:29-31

S ome men start well and finish badly. Others make a slow start and finish in grand
style. Hezekiah was one of the former. Granted, he was confronting monumental
problems. But he did have Isaiah at his side preaching no shortage of messages concerning
what the Lord would do on Hezekiah's behalf. Yet after his miraculous healing, Hezekiah
turned away from the Lord and lapsed into self-absorption, which reached its nadir when
Isaiah predicted that all Hezekiah's possessions would eventually be carried off to Babylon
(39:5-7). Hezekiah casually thought, "At least there will be peace and security during my
lifetime" (39:8).

Hezekiah's tragic about-face was probably stimulated by his inadequate knowledge
of the Lord. This was certainly the case with many of Hezekiah's subjects. Isaiah asked
them, "How can you say the Lord does not see your troubles? How can you say God
refuses to hear your case? Have you never heard or understood?" (40:27-28). They may
have heard about God, but they apparently had not understood. Inadequate knowledge of
the Lord led to an insufficient grasp of his purposes and an inferior experience of his love.

What was Israel—and Hezekiah—missing? "Don't you know that the Lord is the
everlasting God, the Creator of all the earth? He never grows faint or weary. No one can
measure the depths of his understanding" (40:28). They needed to be reminded that the
Lord is the Creator of all things—including Israel! Wherever the people of Israel looked
there was evidence of the majesty and glory of God the Creator. They should have
remembered that the glorious Creator had crafted them, his people, as surely as he had
created the sun, moon, and stars. This should have been sufficient for them to trust him
implicitly and serve him gladly. But such was not the case, and calamity was about to
follow their faithlessness.

The great Creator also wanted his people to understand, even as they went through
the deep trials that were heading their way, that "he gives power to those who are tired and
worn out; he offers strength to the weak. But those who wait on the Lord will find new
strength. They will fly high on wings like eagles. They will run and not grow weary. They
will walk and not faint" (40:29, 31).

These are encouraging words for all who have eyes to see the wonders of the Creator
in the creation, who have ears to hear that their Creator stands ready to bless and provide.
Those who believe this "fly high on wings like eagles." Others wander as sheep without a
shepherd.

TO READ: *Isaiah 48:12-22*

PEACE AND ORDER

*"The LORD, your Redeemer, the Holy One of Israel, says: I am the LORD your God,
who teaches you what is good and leads you along the paths you should follow.
Oh, that you had listened to my commands! Then you would have had peace flowing
like a gentle river and righteousness rolling like waves."*

ISAIAH 48:17-18

Diplomats work toward a "lasting peace" in the trouble spots of the world. Worried parents long for "peace of mind" when their children are in trouble. And the harried businessman sailing his yacht wants nothing more than "a little peace." There is nothing more attractive to the human race than peace—and nothing more elusive.

God had problems with his chosen people. He could not always get them to listen to him, and when they did listen they were often incapable of understanding what he was saying. Even when they understood, they did not necessarily do what he said. So the result was chaos. Now, we know that God is not a God of confusion but a God of order (1 Cor. 14:33, 40). So the chaos is not by his desire or design.

God addressed the issue through his prophet Isaiah: "Oh, that you had listened to my commands! Then you would have had peace flowing like a gentle river and righteousness rolling like waves" (48:18). God's promise of peace is directly related to observance of his principles. If the human race wants peace they can have it, but it comes at a price. The price is refusing to do things man's way and being willing to do things God's way.

This message to God's ancient people should be heeded today. We have engineered much chaos, and God calls us to order—to peace. We tend to question what God says is "good" and to doubt the path he chooses. So we go our own way and do our own thing, which results in varying degrees of chaos. We tend to regard God's commands as onerous and his dictates as restrictive, if not destructive, of human happiness. People expend vast energy resisting God's commands—arguing with them, breaking them, and enthusiastically engaging in activities and attitudes that fly in the teeth of them. A brief review of the commandments will confirm this to be true! Yet when God gave the commandments to his people, Moses told them, "Obey the Lord's commands and laws that I am giving you today for your own good" (Deut. 10:13). God's commands are for our good!

When things are done God's way, that's the right way, and things run as he intended, like a well-maintained machine. But disobedience throws a wrench into the works and puts sand in the gears. Profound disorder ensues! And disorder is the antithesis of peace. But where does order come from? From ordering our life according to the orders of the God of order—and that's an order!

TO READ: *Psalm 104*

EVERYTHING BEAUTIFUL

O LORD, what a variety of things you have made! In wisdom you have made them all. The earth is full of your creatures.

PSALM 104:24

Our summer skies used to be filled with multicolored butterflies. They flitted and flirted with soft-winged abandon. But now many of them are in danger of becoming extinct. What a shame! Our grandchildren may never chase them as we did. Some things are being irretrievably lost from our world, never again to grace the sky. And who's to blame? "Magnificent man," who failed to be what he and woman were created to be: "masters over all life" (Gen. 1:26).

The mandate was clear. God delegated the oversight of his bewildering and beautiful creation to humans and told us to "be masters over the fish and birds and all the animals" (Gen. 1:28). Perhaps we thought being masters meant being tyrants and exercising brute force. And maybe we misconstrued the mandate to "multiply and fill the earth and subdue it" (Gen. 1:28) as giving us a free rein to pursue our own purposes without thought to the well-being of God's handiwork. Not so!

But all is not lost. There is still time for us to look again with wonder on the fish, the birds, and the animals; to study them as our first father who named them did (Gen. 2:19-20); and then to see them as the psalmist did: "O Lord, what a variety of things you have made! In wisdom you have made them all. The earth is full of your creatures" (Ps. 104:24). The oceans teem with life; the forests are full of his creatures; pastures and mountains are the habitations for his handiwork. Storks among the firs, badgers among the rocks, young lions in the bush, and goats in the mountains (104:17-22)—all these things silently testify to the wonders of God's creative mind, the glory of his wondrous skills, and the beauty of all that he has made.

Seeing this, man should learn to worship (104:33), joining with creation in acknowledging the one from whom we come and through whom "we live and move and exist" (Acts 17:28). This attitude will not only lead to the preservation of that which was entrusted to our care but will also contribute to our adoration of God as we exercise our God-given ability to see something of the wonder of him who is hidden from the natural eyes but who shines forth for the eyes of faith in the things he has made.

Each time the man of faith sees a butterfly flutter by, he should see a revelation of God's wonder and raise his "Praise the Lord!" (104:35).

GOD'S PLAN AND SUFFERING

But it was the Lord's good plan to crush him and fill him with grief. Yet when his life
is made an offering for sin, he will have a multitude of children, many heirs.
He will enjoy a long life, and the Lord's plan will prosper in his hands.

ISAIAH 53:10

W hen tragedy strikes and people suffer, the inevitable question is *Why?* Pain and suffering are so contrary to our wishes that when they arrive we are surprised and even affronted that such things could happen to us. But happen they do, and happen they will. Often the *why* question will not be answered to our satisfaction. Are we then to assume that suffering is meaningless? Should we conclude that we live in a ludicrous world that lacks rhyme or reason and scream our resentment or adopt stoicism with a stiff upper lip?

Scripture, while not giving all the answers we would like, certainly gives enough to assure us that suffering is neither meaningless nor without value. The greatest example of the deepest suffering is found in Isaiah's account of the Suffering Servant (52:13–53:12). In the midst of this catalogue of the servant's agony we are told, "It was the Lord's good plan to crush him and fill him with grief" (53:10). The sheer brutality and obscenity of the servant's suffering makes us shudder, but the thought that it was "the Lord's good plan" certainly raises the question *Why!* Fortunately, we are not left to speculate. His life was "an offering for sin" (53:10). There was a reason for the suffering of the servant: to take care of the problem of sin.

While sin is often passed off as unimportant, Scripture shows that sin is an affront to God, meriting death and eternal separation from him. No human being could suffer the consequences of sin—eternal death—and survive to be introduced to fellowship with God. So it was necessary for a sinless substitute to bear the penalty in order that sinful man might be forgiven and reconciled to God. That is what the servant, the Lord Jesus Christ, accomplished when he died on the cross to take away our sin. It was agony producing atonement. And the benefits have flowed to all the redeemed and will continue to flow until time is no more.

No suffering of ours will ever procure redemption for another (see Ps. 49:7-9, NIV); no pain we endure will ever cleanse another sin-stained life. But if God intended the suffering of the servant, perhaps we can perceive the possibility that God will bring good that we would not otherwise have experienced out of our suffering (see Rom. 8:28). This should drive us deeper into dependence on God and stimulate in us a deeper compassion for those who are suffering.

TO READ: *Isaiah 55:1-13*

FOOD FOR THE SOUL

Why spend your money on food that does not give you strength?
Why pay for food that does you no good? Listen, and I will tell you
where to get food that is good for the soul!

ISAIAH 55:2

There is food, and there is junk food. There is food that builds the bones and muscles, and there is food that clogs the arteries. There is food that provides energy, and there is food that adds fat. In short, there is good food and bad food. Why would people spend good money on bad food? Presumably they like the flavor and discount the consequences.

God asked a similar question twenty-seven hundred years ago about how his people were feeding their soul. They seem to have been more interested in tickling their palate than in eating a healthy spiritual diet. So God asked them, "Why spend your money on food that does not give you strength? Why pay for food that does you no good? Listen, and I will tell you where to get food that is good for the soul!" (55:2).

But where specifically is this "food that is good for the soul" to be found? In the word of God! Where God's word is taken seriously—where God's people turn to it constantly, hungrily feed on it, inwardly digest it, and allow it to generate its life-transforming energy in their lives—it will prosper, and so will they (55:10-13). When we come to the Lord eagerly, unreservedly, expectantly, repentantly, and trustingly, we can partake of the rich food of his word. The food is not cheap—it is free! Someone else paid for it. Access to God and his provision has been provided and paid for, and the valued benefits are available to all—free of charge!

The delicious menu includes an everlasting covenant, mercies, and unfailing love (55:3), the promise of a fruitful life (55:10-12), and a "glorious" experience (55:5). But to benefit from this rich fare, we must abstain from the junk food of wrong thinking, from "the very thought of doing wrong" (55:7). It is in the womb of the thoughts that sin is conceived. So, "Let the people turn from their wicked deeds" (55:7). We must embrace a new regimen of turning to the Lord and discovering his thoughts and desires. The change in diet will quickly generate fresh nourishment, new energy, and vitality.

When the arteries of the soul are clogged through a bad spiritual diet, cardiac arrest of the spirit happens. Instead of beating regularly and powerfully with love for God, the heart becomes cold and heavy, the flow of energy becomes lethargic, and spiritual activity stops. There's a better way, through a healthy diet of divinely provided "food that is good for the soul." So think clearly, and eat wisely.

WHEN I RUN, I FEEL HIS PLEASURE

"I knew you before I formed you in your mother's womb. Before you were born I set you apart and appointed you as my spokesman to the world."

JEREMIAH 1:5

E ric Liddell was one of the greatest athletes Scotland ever produced. An international rugby player, Olympic champion, and world-record-holding sprinter, he was also a man of profound spiritual conviction. He attributed his speed to the fact that God had made him fast, and he knew that God was smiling upon his athletic prowess and success. He said, "When I run, I feel his pleasure." Eric Liddell was a born athlete.

Jeremiah was a born prophet (1:5). Jeremiah won no races and wore no victor's crown. No smiles of victory wreathed his face. Instead, tears of anguish coursed his cheeks. Yet he, too, felt God's pleasure when he did what he was born to do. Even in the darkest days he basked in the assurance that "the unfailing love of the Lord never ends," and that "the Lord is my inheritance" (Lam. 3:22-24).

Without this deep sense of divine purpose, it is unlikely that Jeremiah would have ever embarked on his life work, let alone completed it. Jeremiah's work of announcing God's judgment inevitably produced more cold shoulders than warm embraces. No one relishes unpopularity; everyone prefers acceptance to ostracism. But Jeremiah knew that he had been appointed for the task.

Jeremiah's calling was one thing; his equipping was another. The Lord touched his mouth, gave him words to speak, strengthened his resolve, granted him immunity from the attacks he would face, and above all promised to stand by him to take care of him (Jer. 1:9-10, 18-19). Armed with such assurances, Jeremiah faced the foe and ran his race.

God calls and equips. Never the one without the other. No one would expect God to call a man to be an Olympic sprint champion while omitting to make him fast. Neither would God call a man to be a prophet without giving him words and will, courage and constancy.

Not many of us are born athletic champions, and even fewer of us are called to be prophets of doom. But we were all born for something. We are to believe, discover, and embrace it, whatever it is. Should we initially find the calling not to our liking, we should remember that the one who calls is the one who creates. In his providence God made us just right for what he had in mind. For us to be and do something else would not be right. Running the race set before us means knowing where we're going. And we feel his pleasure.

TO READ: *Jeremiah 3:6-25*

WAYWARD
HEART DISEASE

"My wayward children," says the LORD, *"come back to me, and I will heal
your wayward hearts." "Yes, we will come," the people reply,
"for you are the* LORD *our God."*

JEREMIAH 3:22

U ntreated, heart disease can prove fatal. Symptoms of the disease are not always apparent. Superb athletes, apparently fine specimens of health and vigor, have been known to collapse and expire in the midst of the stadium. Tanned and well muscled, highly trained and conditioned, they had given every indication of being in the best of health. But they were unaware of the silent killer—undiagnosed, untreated heart disease.

There is another killer heart disease that can go undetected. Only God, the great physician, can unerringly diagnose the condition, as he did in ancient Judah. They suffered from "wayward heart" disorder (3:22). Judah gave every outward indication of being in good spiritual health. Like their sister Israel, Judah had been unfaithful to the Lord, but they had professed to return to him in repentance. Yet they had "only pretended to be sorry" (3:10).

The northern kingdom, Israel, was much more blatant about her behavior. She was utterly faithless and made no secret of it; it was obvious she was sick. But Judah was like a tanned, well-conditioned athlete with a sick heart—outwardly in great shape, inwardly at risk. God's concern was evident when he compared the two and said, "Even faithless Israel is less guilty than treacherous Judah" (3:11).

Fortunately, there is hope for those who are sick from a wayward heart, because God not only diagnoses the condition, he offers healing. "Come back to me, and I will heal your wayward hearts," he promises (3:22). For Judah to do this required a great degree of honesty—they had to admit that they had only been pretending allegiance to the Lord. By contrast, the northern kingdom simply had to confess their obvious waywardness and turn from their wicked ways.

The healing of a wayward heart can only be done by the Lord, and only when men and women crave his healing touch. The Great Physician stands willing and able to heal, but the patient must be ready and willing to present himself for surgery—to respond to the Lord's invitation, "Come back to me, and I will heal your wayward hearts." So whether our symptoms are overt or hidden, we need to search our heart for signs of waywardness. We need to stop pretending and offer ourselves to his healing touch. The surgery may be unpleasant, the recovery painful. But the healing is deep and profound, and robust spiritual health is the result.

DECEMBER

TO READ: *Jeremiah 10:1-16*

CONFUSION

LORD, there is no one like you! For you are great, and your name is full of power.

JEREMIAH 10:6

L eft to his own devices, man is like a blind person alone in a thick forest on a starless night. Governed by his own instincts, he couldn't be more confused.

Man is confused about God. How confused is he? He reads his future in the stars. Then he cuts down a tree, carves out an idol, dresses it in finery, and nails it to the wall to ensure that it will not topple over. Then he worships it! There it stands "like a helpless scarecrow in a garden" (10:5), and in front of it stands man—a hopeless supplicant in a quandary. You don't need to be very smart to recognize that is not very smart. Man knows instinctively that God is the Creator, nevertheless he goes ahead and adores the things that he himself has made rather than the One who made him.

If it be protested that modern man would do no such thing, one need only look at the devotion lavished upon automobiles and computers, medicine and technology, to see that even today man tends to look for saving grace in his own handiwork. We might be tempted to say that man today is not so stupid as to distrust the Lord and trust what has repeatedly failed him. But knowing the frailty of politicians, man still looks to them to solve his problems. And aware that the stock market is driven by such shaky dynamics as fear and greed, man still looks to it for his security. That's confusion!

Fortunately, God does not leave man to his confusion. Jeremiah reminded his contemporaries, "Lord, there is no one like you" (10:6); and when Christ came he said, "I am the light of the world. If you follow me, you won't be stumbling through the darkness, because you will have the light that leads to life" (John 8:12). Christ in his earthly life unerringly cast light on who God is and what he is really like.

At the same time, Christ banished the darkness in men's minds concerning their true condition, and he revealed unmistakably that man is both precious and perverse, both fallen and forgivable, reprobate but redeemable. When a man knows this, he finally gets his bearings, and he steps out into life knowing God and knowing himself, understanding where he came from and where he's going, recognizing that the Lord is master and he is servant. He becomes bent on following the Lord rather than on meandering in the morass of his own mistaken ideas and destructive desires. That's a whole lot better than living in perpetual confusion.

WATCH YOUR BACK

*This is what the LORD says: "Cursed are those who put their trust in mere humans
and turn their hearts away from the LORD."*

JEREMIAH 17:5

I n our culture one is constantly advised to watch one's back and cover one's tail. The
conventional wisdom is that people cannot be trusted and will abuse any trust another
may place in them. This is a sad state of affairs, but there is nothing new about it. God
himself expressed such a view when he told Jeremiah, "Cursed are those who put their
trust in mere humans and turn their hearts away from the Lord" (17:5). Modern man
thinks it is smart not to trust mere humans. He's right—he will be cursed if he does!

This does not mean that no one should ever trust anyone. Rather, it is a condemnation of transferring trust away from the Lord and putting it in humans, as though there
were nowhere else to turn for support but to humans.

The issue is the human heart—people cannot be trusted because they have sinful
hearts. Man roundly resists and resents this idea—even while working hard to protect
himself from those he cannot wholly trust! But the Lord says, "The human heart is most
deceitful and desperately wicked. Who really knows how bad it is?" (17:9).

The Lord answered his own question: "But I know! I, the Lord, search all hearts and
examine secret motives. I give all people their due rewards, according to what their actions
deserve" (17:10). If people do not trust the Lord and if they do not commit their actions to
his evaluation, their human relationships will be deficient—or, more accurately, "cursed."

Fortunately, the Lord does more than search hearts—he changes them too. That is
why Jeremiah called on the Lord to bless him in his difficult and dangerous situation.
"O Lord, you alone can heal me; you alone can save" (17:14).

In this world it is a good idea to watch your back. We all have wicked hearts, so it is
not stupid to be on your guard. But to be really blessed, you need to trust the Lord—like a
tree by a riverbank, to put your trusting roots deep into the fresh waters of his unfailing
trustworthiness (17:7-8). That means trusting that he is right in what he says, right in what
he does, right in what he promises, and reliable—reliable to reveal your own twisted
motives, and reliable to alert you when you begin to place unwarranted confidence in man
and deficient confidence in God. Him alone you should fully trust. So watch your back—
and watch your heart!

TO READ: *Psalm 110*

THE VICTORIOUS LORD

The LORD said to my Lord, "Sit in honor at my right hand until I humble
your enemies, making them a footstool under your feet."

PSALM 110:1

K ing David and his successors lived in a volatile part of the world. Their reigns more
often than not saw them take up the weapons of war. But there was something
different about the way they went into battle. They exhibited assurance. As the Lord's
anointed king had been reminded by the psalmist, he sat in a place of unique honor at
God's right hand from which he could watch Yahweh win the victory. In addition, the king
knew it was only a matter of time until he would win because the battle was the Lord's.
This did not mean, of course, that he and his people would not be involved—in fact the
king was told, "your people will serve you willingly" (110:3). Nor did it mean that the
king could be complacent, lazy, or self-willed and get away with it. After all, sitting at
God's right hand implies being completely in harmony with God's plan.

But this psalm is much more than a promise to the king of a physical nation. In fact,
it holds the distinction of being one of the passages of the Old Testament most quoted in
the New Testament. (See, for example, Matt. 22:43-45; Heb. 5:6; 7:17, 21; and 10:12-13.)
The apostles were not at all reluctant to see in this psalm a prediction of the way that the
Lord Almighty would eventually win total victory through his Son, our Lord Jesus. The
apostles saw in Christ's death, resurrection, and ascension the fulfillment of all God's
claims to ultimate, universal victory over his enemies. Our risen Lord is now seated at the
Father's right hand—the place of prestige and authority. And he is not only praying for his
children, but also waiting until the day for his triumphant return in glory.

This understanding greatly heartens the believer. As the believer lives today in a
volatile world full of dangers and distractions, he bears in mind that Jesus his Lord is in
the immediate presence of the Father, with unhindered access to him, able and willing to
call heaven's resources to the beleaguered man's aid. And the believer need never forget
that enemies are defeated foes—it is only a matter of time until they will be routed. He
can go confidently on his way, day by day anticipating the return of the victorious King.

It is good to know who wins in the end. It's even better to know you're on his side—
and if you're not, you'd better get there!

TO READ: *Lamentations 3:1-24*

START THE DAY FRESH

*The unfailing love of the LORD never ends! By his mercies we have been kept from
complete destruction. Great is his faithfulness; his mercies begin afresh each day.*

LAMENTATIONS 3:22-23

There is nothing quite so welcome as a bright, fresh dawn after a dark, stormy night. Peace and tranquility take the place of turmoil and stress, and all seems right with the world. Frayed nerves are calmed, troubled spirits are soothed, trepidation steps aside, and hope is restored. A fresh start is at hand!

The darkness of the prophet Jeremiah's night was terrifying. Not only had he suffered the abuses and indignities of cruel men, but his sufferings had led him into the deepest spiritual gloom and the darkest night of the soul. His pain was intensely physical and emotional, and the anguish of his tormented spirit was well-nigh unbearable. But after his description of his turbulent, stormy, fearsome night comes a remarkable statement about God's mercies morning by morning: "The unfailing love of the Lord never ends! By his mercies we have been kept from complete destruction. Great is his faithfulness; his mercies begin afresh each day" (3:22-23). Fresh mercies every day! These mercies are not listed, but we know they stem from God's faithfulness and are hidden in God himself.

Jeremiah insisted, "The Lord is my inheritance; therefore, I will hope in him" (3:24). Apparently Jeremiah had discovered the secret of being able to return morning by morning to renew his relationship with the Lord and to drink deeply of his "unfailing love." This love was unfailing because it was the source and the substance of the covenant that God had made with his people. This covenant was an agreement and promise never to leave them or forsake them—a commitment guaranteeing that God would be nothing less than God to his people, at all times and in all circumstances.

Like Jeremiah, men today need to start each new day on a fresh note, reminding themselves of the unfailing love of their covenant-making and promise-keeping God, whose mercies are fresh each morning. Some men try to make it through a stormy week on the basis of mercies delivered fresh from the pulpit on Sunday morning, which unfortunately have become stale by Wednesday. For the rest of the week they struggle to remember what they heard and how it relates to the latest storms of life. God offers fresh mercies each morning which are to be found in communion with him through his word, through prayer, and through fellowship with his people. Dark nights then give way to fresh mornings, and God's mercies bring fresh energy and vigor with which to meet the day. So smart men start the day fresh!

TO READ: *Ezekiel 3:16-27*

GOD'S ADVANCE WARNING SYSTEM

"If I warn the wicked, saying, 'You are under the penalty of death,' but you fail to deliver the warning, they will die in their sins. And I will hold you responsible, demanding your blood for theirs."

EZEKIEL 3:18

It is now possible with satellites to track a developing hurricane heading for a densely populated area and to calculate accurately the estimated rainfall. Given this information and the means to communicate it, great loss of life can be averted—provided the people listen and take action.

In Ezekiel's day there were no satellites but there were prophets—God's special gift to his people, although the people did not always regard them so highly. A prophet was a watchman, appointed to warn the people of impending danger, so his messages were often full of foreboding. But people don't always like to hear about judgment, so they often ignored the message or abused the prophet.

God gave Ezekiel a message of impending judgment for the people of Israel, and he told Ezekiel that he must deliver the message, even if the people would not listen (3:17, 27). How did God impress on Ezekiel the urgency of his message? The well-being of countless people was at stake, and Ezekiel was responsible for whether he delivered God's message to them: "If . . . you fail to deliver the warning, they will die in their sins. And I will hold you responsible, demanding your blood for theirs" (3:18). Not that he bore all the responsibility alone—the people were responsible for how they responded to the message.

There is a parallel between the ancient prophet/watchman and the modern-day believer. Once a believer's eyes have been opened to the truth in Christ Jesus—truth that includes the appealing message of sins forgiven and the unappealing forewarning of judgment to come—that believer is responsible to share what he knows with those who don't know. This can be unnerving—there certainly is a challenge involved—but the believer should see his role as a gracious appointment, a privilege as well as a duty.

Ezekiel was dramatically bound with ropes and his tongue was stuck to the roof of his mouth once he had received his commission (3:24-26). The only time Ezekiel could speak was when God gave him a message for the people (3:27). The believer today should not anticipate such treatment. The point for both Ezekiel and the believer is this: don't rush out and say whatever comes into your head. Wait until the impulse of the Spirit directs you, and then tell those in your sphere of influence what he has told you.

If people can say to me, "You never told me," I am responsible. If on the other hand the truth is that they never listened, the responsibility is all theirs.

SOUR GRAPES

"Why do you quote this proverb in the land of Israel: 'The parents have eaten sour grapes, but their children's mouths pucker at the taste'?"

EZEKIEL 18:2

W hen bad things happen the usual question is *Why?* It is usually assumed that bad things happen because of somebody's actions. Very often this is the case—cause and effect can be traced. But while this is true, we should not blame everything on somebody else.

That is what the people of Israel tended to do. As they sat in exile, they recited the ancient proverb, "The parents have eaten sour grapes, but their children's mouths pucker at the taste" (18:2). They were saying, in essence, "We are in this predicament because of what our forebears did. Where's the justice in that?" At its root this question challenged the Lord's justice and impeached his holiness. The Lord, through Ezekiel, had an immediate answer. He instructed his people: "As surely as I live, says the Sovereign Lord, you will not say this proverb anymore in Israel" (18:3). Why not? Because, as God then explained, "All people are mine to judge. . . . And this is my rule: The person who sins will be the one who dies. . . . Righteous people will be rewarded for their own goodness, and wicked people will be punished for their own wickedness" (18:4, 20). No doubt this instruction came as a shock to the people of Israel, especially because the Lord had taught them, "I do not leave unpunished the sins of those who hate me, but I punish the children for the sins of their parents to the third and fourth generations" (Exod. 20:5).

There is some comfort in being able to blame someone else for your misfortune. And because our lives are inextricably bound up in each others', there is a sense in which the actions of one will inevitably affect the experience of another. The actions of a parent will no doubt contribute to the makeup of the child, and this makeup will include tendencies that may lead to wrong actions. But this does not absolve an individual from the consequences of his own sin. Each person is fully responsible for what he chooses to do.

We need to understand this principle clearly. In our day we see the link between our genetics, our environment, and our behavior—and we tend to blame everything on genetics and environment! Yet whatever our "nature or nurture," the bad news is that we are individually responsible for our actions. But the good news is we can be individually forgiven! If you accept individual responsibility, you can enjoy personal forgiveness. This God offers because he is not only just, but gracious, too.

TO READ: *Ezekiel 36:16-38*

CHARACTER AND REPUTATION

"Then I will sprinkle clean water on you, and you will be clean. Your filth will be washed away, and you will no longer worship idols. And I will give you a new heart with new and right desires, and I will put a new spirit in you. I will take out your stony heart of sin and give you a new, obedient heart. And I will put my Spirit in you so you will obey my laws and do whatever I command."

EZEKIEL 36:25-27

There's a big difference between character and reputation. Character is what you are, reputation is what people believe you are. Reputation is less important than character, but it is important. What people believe about you might be totally false, but it can be damaging nevertheless.

God's character is beyond reproach. But in Ezekiel's time, God's reputation was being impugned among the nations, owing to what his people, Israel, had done (36:16-20)—they had soiled his reputation by their evil behavior. In keeping with his promise, God had "scattered them to many lands to punish them for the evil way they had lived" (36:19). But the surrounding nations had interpreted this as a sign of weakness on God's part. God's reputation was suffering, so he told his people, "I am bringing you back again . . . to protect my holy name, which you dishonored" (36:22).

But God would not just bring Israel back to return to their old ways. He would change their hearts. "When I reveal my holiness through you . . . , then the nations will know that I am the Lord" (36:23). But how would God effect such a drastic change? God would carry out his program of restoration, which included washing their "filth" away, imparting to them a "new heart with new and right desires," taking away their "stony heart of sin," and promising them, "I will put my Spirit in you so you will obey my laws and do whatever I command" (36:25-30).

Ever since the Holy Spirit came at Pentecost, he has been doing this work in people's lives. God "[washes] away our sins and [gives] us a new life through the Holy Spirit" (Titus 3:5). As we trust God to save us from our sins "because of what Jesus Christ our Savior did," God "generously [pours] out the Spirit upon us" (Titus 3:6). He gives us a new heart and a new Spirit so we can obey him and do his will (see Rom. 8:1-17; 12:2). God does all of this for us, not because we "deserve it" (Ezek. 36:32), but to demonstrate his holiness, power, and mercy.

If God's reputation is to remain untarnished among the nations, his people need to live in accord with his character. This can happen when they have been transformed through the regenerating power of the Holy Spirit, who takes up residence in the inner recesses of their spirits and enlivens, enraptures, energizes, and empowers them. Their lives then give them delight and bring the Lord honor.

THE MAKING
OF A MAESTRO

But when Daniel learned that the law had been signed, he went home and knelt down as usual in his upstairs room, with its windows open toward Jerusalem. He prayed three times a day, just as he had always done, giving thanks to his God.

DANIEL 6:10

The society lady told the brilliant pianist, "Maestro, you're a genius." The maestro replied with a smile, "Thank you, madam, but before I was a genius I was a bore." His apparently effortless artistry was the product of hours and hours of unseen, disciplined practice. Our world applauds the glitter of genius, but it does not always appreciate the drudgery of discipline.

When trouble comes we react—sometimes with courage, sometimes with cowardice. Occasionally when the pressure is on we instinctively know exactly what to do. At other times we flounder. To a large extent our reaction has been determined before the pressure arrives. As with the artist who has practiced, it is the hidden hours of discipline that determine our performance under pressure.

Daniel was under the gun. His impeccable behavior and outstanding abilities, his disciplined commitment to principle, and his remarkable success had made him plenty of friends—and not a few enemies. His enemies, out of anger and jealousy, manipulated the king to get rid of him. Daniel was subjected to persecution when his freedom of religion was taken away with the stroke of a pen (6:6-9).

But Daniel was conditioned by disciplined practice. While he was concerned for the well-being of Babylon, his exile home, he had made no secret of his commitment to Jerusalem. Three times a day he opened the windows of his prayer room to face the city of his heart and publicly expressed his devotion to Yahweh, the Lord, who had chosen Jerusalem to be the center of his earthly activities. So when trouble came, discipline took over: "When Daniel learned that the law had been signed, he went home and knelt down as usual in his upstairs room, with its windows open toward Jerusalem. He prayed three times a day, just as he had always done, giving thanks to his God" (6:10). In Daniel's hour of challenge, it was the habit formed by disciplined practice that kept him faithful.

We may minimize the dangers Daniel faced, because we know he escaped death at the jaws of the lions. But the reality is that Daniel confronted prejudice, intolerance, hatred, persecution, and injustice without sacrificing an ounce of faithfulness. And he did it because discipline had produced habits, and habits had been transformed into character. He knew how to stand tall and firm on well-worn knees!

TO READ: *Daniel 9:1-19*

PROMPTED PRAYER

During the first year of his reign, I, Daniel, was studying the writings of the prophets.
I learned from the word of the LORD, as recorded by Jeremiah the prophet,
that Jerusalem must lie desolate for seventy years.

DANIEL 9:2

O ccasionally people talk about "wrestling in prayer." They are referring to the fact that prayer is not easy. Saying prayers may not be difficult if it means simply reciting what we learned as children. But really praying, really laying hold of God, really pouring out the soul fervently and earnestly, does not come without a struggle. So we need help.

Daniel identified the great resource for stimulating prayer: it was as he was "studying the writings of the prophets" that he was prompted to turn to the Lord and plead with him (9:2). Daniel read Jeremiah's prediction that the Exile would last seventy years (Jer. 25:11-12). Daniel did not understand what this meant, so he prayed. As he did so, he began to think about the behavior of God's people, which had led to divine retribution, and his heart was moved to confess the sins that had led them into their predicament of exile.

It is worth noting that Daniel's prayer was sprinkled with allusions to the Scriptures that he had been reading. For instance, when he exclaimed, "We have sinned and done wrong. We have rebelled against you and scorned your commands and regulations" (Dan. 9:5), he may have been thinking of Jeremiah 14:7. And when he affirmed, "Lord, you are in the right; but our faces are covered with shame, just as you see us now" (9:7), he may have had Jeremiah 3:25 and 23:6 in mind. Daniel's talking to God was a direct result of God talking to him. This is exactly how it should be, for in no other way can we be confident that we are praying as we ought.

It may strike us as odd that Daniel should include himself in the prayer even though he had led such an exemplary life. But we should remember that while we are individually responsible for our actions, we are also products of our culture, and if that is corrupt, then we are corrupted.

Daniel prayed from a heart touched by the Scriptures. He was conscious of God's righteousness and human sinfulness because of what the Scriptures teach, and he was looking for God's promises in the word to be fulfilled. His praying was not shooting from the lip; it was responding to God's word.

The relationship and fellowship between God and his children, like all relationships, needs communication, and communication involves listening and talking. In the divine-human relationship God talks to us in his word, and we should listen. Then we talk to him in prayer—and he *does* listen!

TO READ: *Psalm 119:1-24*

WONDERFUL TRUTHS

Open my eyes to see the wonderful truths in your law.

PSALM 119:18

C losed eyes and sightless eyes have something in common: neither can see beauty. The beauty is there for the seeing, but with no eyes beholding it the beauty shines on unappreciated, like a diamond in the desert sand.

Hearts have eyes, windows letting in the light of life. But if the eyes of the heart are closed, truth shines on, unobserved. The heart is darkened, the mind is confused, desires are twisted, and wrong decisions are made. The difference between right and wrong becomes blurred and indistinct until right seems wrong and wrong seems right. Eventually the very existence of objective truth is questioned and the person stumbles into a subjective morass of sensuality and sin. Meanwhile, truth shines on unabated—and unappreciated.

Any man, young or old, who is concerned that his life is heading downhill, his principles compromised and his morality eroded, at least has the eyes of his heart opened partially. But he needs to ask the Lord to open his eyes fully to the "wonderful truths" found in God's word (119:18)—truths that have shone brightly through the centuries, pointing unerringly to who God is, who we are, what he expects, what we have done, what God has done about it, what we should do, and how we should live as a result. These are wonderful truths!

Once a man's eyes are opened to the truth of God's word, the man thus begins to perceive vistas of truth formerly undreamed of—mysteries previously hidden, insights formerly never imagined. He discovers answers to questions he never thought to ask, and he questions opinions never previously examined. More wonderful truths!

These truths are carefully hidden in the heart and are pondered (119:11, 15). As a result, the mind becomes educated in God's principles and promises (119:7), the emotions are stimulated to wholesome delight and godly desire (119:16), and the will is moved to make decisions that consistently reflect the divine principles. Thus might a man live life to the full.

Happy is the man who has eyes wide open to discern, desire, and do God's will.

TO READ: *Amos 5:18—6:7*

ALARMISTS

*How terrible it will be for you who lounge in luxury and think you are secure
in Jerusalem and Samaria! You are famous and popular in Israel,
you to whom the people go for help.*

AMOS 6:1

A larmists see danger and conspiracy at every opportunity. Their alarms are dismissed with a wave of the hand, and complacency settles like a warm blanket over chilling predictions. But when alarmists are right, they are very right. And when the complacent are wrong, they are very wrong! God's prophets, like Amos, were often regarded by the people as alarmists, and the people perfected complacency to a fine art. But God's prophets were always very right.

In the time of Amos the people living in Jerusalem (in the southern kingdom) and those who resided in Samaria (in the northern kingdom) felt perfectly secure. Were they not the people of God? Were they not the foremost nation? Did they not have systems of religious observance second to none, and had not God rewarded their hard work with prosperity and abundance? Were they not assured that God would judge their enemies and bring well-deserved punishment on their enemies' heads? Life was good, and prophets who said otherwise were at best a nuisance and at worst disturbers of the peace.

But Amos was right: all was not well. The day of judgment, which the people anticipated would fall on their enemies, would also fall on them. And it would be a calamity; there would be no escape. And the reason for this? They had grossly mismanaged their blessings, robbing the needy of justice and the oppressed of mercy (5:7; see 5:24). They had developed a religion long on ritual and short on reality. They had replaced God's revelation with their own speculations and had substituted the worship of their own deities for the worship of God (5:25-26). They had been blinded by their self-sufficiency and had become deaf to the prophets' warnings.

The God of grace, mercy, and love is also the God of righteousness, holiness, and judgment. When his mercy is abused, his grace despised, and his love taken for granted, then his holiness is offended, his righteous indignation provoked, and his judgment assured. We need not embrace every alarmist's predictions of gloom and doom, but God's warnings of the consequences of sin should not be dismissed. Complacency takes for granted what he never grants, while trusting confidence embraces all that he offers, listens to all that he says, and takes seriously all that he predicts and proclaims. In that position we can rest, as Elisha Hoffman said, "safe and secure from all alarms."

TO READ: *Jonah 3:1–4:11*

CHOOSE YOUR ENMITIES

So he complained to the LORD about it: "Didn't I say before I left home that you would do this, LORD? That is why I ran away to Tarshish! I knew that you were a gracious and compassionate God, slow to get angry and filled with unfailing love. I knew how easily you could cancel your plans for destroying these people."

JONAH 4:2

We can choose our friends, but we must accept our relatives. And our enemies often appear on the horizon unexpected and unbidden. The question then becomes, Now what do we do? Enemies, like friends and relatives, rarely go away on their own.

The city of Nineveh was full of "people living in spiritual darkness" (4:11), which is why God sent Jonah to preach to them and to warn them of the consequences of their actions. The people responded and repented, and the Lord stayed his hand of judgment. And Jonah was furious. "So he complained to the Lord about it: 'Didn't I say before I left home that you would do this, Lord? That is why I ran away to Tarshish! I knew that you were a gracious and compassionate God, slow to get angry and filled with unfailing love. I knew how easily you could cancel your plans for destroying these people' " (4:2). We should note that in the biblical languages *slow to get angry* means "patient." Jonah was angry because God was not angry enough! God was too patient for Jonah's taste. Yet God was not overlooking sin or ignoring unrighteousness. He was withholding his judgment to give the Ninevites the opportunity to put their lives in order. That is what patience does! But Jonah was so hostile to the Ninevites that he wanted them to be punished as they deserved. This attitude was understandable, given the Ninevites' reputation for cruelty and their antipathy toward Jonah's people, Israel. But this is where the patience of God and the attitudes of men part company.

God will eventually judge if people persistently turn down his offer of mercy. But our role when dealing with a nagging wife, an obstreperous boss, or even a recalcitrant teenager is to see that we do not deny them what God grants them—the opportunity to be forgiven and the chance to put things right. We need to recall God's patience with us. Instead of hoping that people who make life difficult will "get theirs," let us patiently encourage them to "get his"—his forgiveness. Those who get what is coming to them because of their misdeeds will find their lives blighted. Those who appropriate God's patience as a golden opportunity for a new start will find their lives blessed. One mark of spiritual maturity is the desire to see enemies blessed, not blighted.

TO READ: *Habakkuk 3:1–19*

CHOOSING JOY

Yet I will rejoice in the LORD! I will be joyful in the God of my salvation.

HABAKKUK 3:18

S ome people are incorrigibly cheerful. Troubles roll off their backs, and nothing darkens their dawn or casts shadows on their noonday. But for the rest of us, joy and cheerfulness do not come so easily. So what should we do?

Habakkuk had been given insights into God's purposes, which showed quite clearly that he and his compatriots were in deep trouble. God had determined to hand his people over to the Babylonians—that bitter and relentless nation that had devised methods of cruelty never seen before. The judgment of God on the people of God was in the plan of God to be carried out through the enemies of God! Habakkuk's courage understandably faltered when he considered these things (3:16), and the questions mounted in his mind.

Habakkuk had prayed, "I have heard all about you, Lord, and I am filled with awe by the amazing things you have done. In this time of our deep need, begin again to help us, as you did in years gone by. Show us your power to save us. And in your anger, remember your mercy" (3:2). Habakkuk's fears were not immediately assuaged, and his vision of what was going to happen did not change. But his confidence in a righteous God dealing in justice and mercy remained strong, prompting him to say, despite all the hardships and calamities he knew would come his way, "Yet I will rejoice in the Lord! I will be joyful in the God of my salvation" (3:18).

There are many days when we cannot possibly rejoice in our circumstances. Ask Habakkuk! But on those days we can remember to "rejoice in the Lord." There's a big difference between rejoicing in the Lord and rejoicing in our circumstances! If circumstances dominate our thinking, we will exhaust our energy with efforts at changing our circumstances, and we will find ourselves joyless and despairing. But if we perceive God, who transcends our circumstances and works through our circumstances, to be in control in the midst of our circumstances, then *he* will fill our mind. The trust and assurance that result become the womb of our renewed joy. But it doesn't just happen automatically. Like Habakkuk, we have to make a choice and say, "I will rejoice in the Lord! I will be joyful in the God of my salvation." Being joyful is a choice.

TO READ: *Haggai 1:1-15*

FIRED WITH ENTHUSIASM

Now go up into the hills, bring down timber, and rebuild my house. Then I will take pleasure in it and be honored, says the LORD.

HAGGAI 1:8

Vince Lombardi, legendary coach of the Green Bay Packers, once told his players, "If you are not fired with enthusiasm, you will be fired—with enthusiasm!" Nothing of substance can be accomplished without enthusiasm.

After seventy years of exile in Babylon, the people of Judah returned to their homeland, led by Zerubbabel the governor and Jeshua the high priest. As soon as the people had settled in, they immediately set about rebuilding the temple (Ezra 3:1-7)—with enthusiasm! They believed they were called to do something significant, and with great energy they set to work. But the initial enthusiasm for the rebuilding program slowly drained away. The people had volunteered for a project that was as demanding as it was worthwhile. As time went by, discouragements came, and sacrifice began to be less appealing than self-interest. *Why, they may have pondered, should we expend so much effort on building a place of worship when we don't have adequate living accommodations for ourselves?* So they stopped building the temple and started building their own fine abodes (Hag. 1:2-4).

This went on until Haggai came along and roundly condemned the people's failure to complete the work they had begun. Recognizing that their enthusiasm for the temple had waned in direct proportion to the waxing of their self-interest, Haggai addressed that same self-interest. He pointed out that everything they were interested in was turning out to be a disappointment (1:5-11). There was a shortfall in their experience, and Haggai saw a definite cause in their self-absorption. The remedy he prescribed was quite simple: Get your priorities right and put the Lord first. "Now go up into the hills, bring down timber, and rebuild my house. Then I will take pleasure in it and be honored, says the Lord" (1:8).

Haggai's message fired up the leaders and the people. Their enthusiasm was rekindled, they "worshiped the Lord in earnest" (1:12), and they began again the work of rebuilding God's temple (1:14). And the work was finished (see Ezra 6:15).

In the community of believers, people are motivated in different ways. It is a challenge for leadership to know how to kindle enthusiasm and maintain it. Some will work hard motivated by a grand vision, others are less nobly motivated. Wise leaders know how to keep the fires of enthusiasm burning while avoiding burning people out with exhaustion.

TO READ: *John 1:1–18*

THE INCARNATE WORD

*For the law was given through Moses; God's unfailing love and faithfulness
came through Jesus Christ. No one has ever seen God. But his only Son,
who is himself God, is near to the Father's heart; he has told us about him.*

JOHN 1:17-18

The more sophisticated man becomes, the more fascinated he is with origins. He peers with ever increasing erudition into the universe and discovers new galaxies and unheard-of wonders. The question "How did it all begin?" grips man's attention. The scientific answer is, "We don't know exactly." So the search goes on—for origins and significance and meaning.

What science and speculation are not equipped to determine, divine revelation reveals with certainty. Divine revelation announces, "In the beginning the Word already existed." This "Word" was God, and he "created everything there is" (1:1-3).

The Jews reading "the Word" would think of authority. When "God said," "it was so." When God would say, "This is what the Lord says," it would be so. The authority of the Word! But Greeks reading about the "Word" would think of "reason" being communicated, which is what words are supposed to do. The Word is authoritative reason communicated to men.

But who is this Word? He became human, lived among men, was full of unfailing love and faithfulness, and was identified by the apostle John as Jesus Christ, the Son of God (1:17-18). The Word was eternally God. Through him and for him, the world was created. Then he came into the world, populated by men who have never seen God, to tell them what God is really like. Science cannot do that. Speculation cannot do that. Only God can show God to man—and he did it. But would you believe that men in large measure have rejected the revelation, preferring to live in the darkness of their established beliefs? Yet Jesus, still full of unfailing love, still offers, to those who believe him and receive him, "the right to become children of God" (1:12).

We admire members of the armed forces who sacrifice their own comforts and safety, leave home and hearth, and head for foreign lands to defend what is dear to them. We respect courageous missionaries who brave loneliness, disease, unknown perils, and misunderstanding to take the message of hope and deliverance to people in bondage. How much more should we revere Jesus, the Word who became flesh, who knew glory in eternity with the Father and gladly laid aside all privilege, assumed our humanity, bore our sorrows, truly felt our pain, and died our death! How sad that so many have neither recognized him nor revered him. How glad are those who do!

THE SON OF GOD

But Jesus replied, "My Father never stops working, so why should I?"
JOHN 5:17

The history of the church is littered with embarrassments such as the Great Inquisition and the Crusades. There have been many well-documented failures on the part of individual professing Christians as well. While we must not summarily brush aside failures and contradictions, it is important to remember that the validity of Christianity depends only on the validity of Jesus Christ. Men need to consider him—his claims, his life, his deeds, his death, his resurrection, and his impact on human history.

One day Jesus visited the pool of Bethesda, a place where crowds of sick people waited to be assisted into the waters. They believed the waters would heal them on certain occasions (see 5:3-4, footnote). Jesus approached one man and asked a penetrating question. "Would you like to get well?" (5:6). Why else would the man have been there? But it was an astute inquiry. Perhaps the man had gotten used to being carried around. Perhaps he had become so accustomed to begging that he would not have known how to earn a living. The man's answer is no answer—he simply complained. But when Jesus authoritatively commanded him to rise, he did—and was healed!

But it was the Sabbath. The rules said no working on the Sabbath. In the minds of Jesus' opponents, healing was work, so Jesus had profaned the Sabbath and must be held responsible (5:16). In an instant the situation took a dramatic turn. Jesus asserted, "My Father never stops working, so why should I?" (5:17). This thinly veiled assertion was not at all unclear to Jesus' listeners. They recognized it as a claim to equality with the Father—a claim to deity. That deserved death!

Undeterred, Jesus insisted that he was only doing what he saw his Father doing (5:19). The Father had sent him (5:30), the Father had given him a ministry of raising people from the dead (5:21), the Father had promised or given eternal life to those who believed his message (5:24), and the Father had authorized him to be the ultimate judge of mankind (5:26-27). Superlative claims!

Some men to this day insist that Jesus never claimed to be God. If this discourse is not a claim to deity, what is it? The answer to such a question is critical. Christianity is nothing if Christ is not God incarnate; but if he is God, Christianity is everything. God came looking for us, showed himself to us, died for us, rose again, and one day will take us to himself!

TO READ: *Psalm 119:89-112*

TRUST AND OBEY

How sweet are your words to my taste; they are sweeter than honey. Your commandments give me understanding; no wonder I hate every false way of life.

PSALM 119:103-104

Words are like people. They have relatives that look like them, and sometimes they share common concerns. Take "disciple" and "discipline," for instance. These two words are closely related. A disciple is a person who understands the discipline of obedience. Discipleship is not solely about obedience, though—it is also about trusting the master teacher. Discipleship is not possible without both obedience and trust. The right balance is summed up by the old hymn: "Trust and obey, for there's no other way to be happy in Jesus, but to trust and obey."

Obedience doesn't always make people happy—just the opposite! Obedience sometimes means doing exactly what we don't want to do, and that can make us very *un*happy. So the question is, can you be a happy disciple when you are disciplined to be obedient and when being obedient is not pleasant? The psalmist apparently thought so! He said, "How sweet are your words to my taste; they are sweeter than honey. Your commandments give me understanding" (119:103-104).

Commandments sweeter than honey? How can this be? First, the psalmist said, "I will never forget your commandments, for you have used them to restore my joy and health" (119:93). When God's commands seem onerous, men often cast them aside and experience a sense of freedom as they do what they want rather than what God wills. But such joy is short-lived as the negative consequences to health and well-being become apparent. Lasting joy and well-being are found by doing things God's way.

Obeying God's commands gives men an edge! Seeing things from a divine perspective is clearly superior to the limited vision of the secularist. As the psalmist said, "Your commands make me wiser than my enemies" (119:98). That's a great position to be in!

It's all too easy to take a wrong turn in life (119:104). But God's commands help us see the right course and avoid the wrong track. That knowledge can save us a lot of grief. God's commands are indeed sweet, and obeying them is really the way to go!

God's commandments are undeniably sweet, but they can be hard, too. Fortunately, God never issues a command without enabling its performance. With one hand he holds out the command, with the other he extends the power. So we trust him for the power as we obey his command. That's how the disciple who is disciplined to obey learns to be happy!

FULCRUM OF FAITH, LEVER OF LOVE

"You are the salt of the earth. But what good is salt if it has lost its flavor? Can you make it useful again? It will be thrown out and trampled underfoot as worthless. You are the light of the world—like a city on a mountain, glowing in the night for all to see."

MATTHEW 5:13-14

Archimedes said that if he were given a fulcrum, a long enough lever, and somewhere to stand, he could move the world. But he never did it. Jesus showed that if he was given the wholehearted devotion of an insignificant group of ordinary people, he, too, could move the world. And he did it!

When vast crowds were attracted to Jesus as a result of his dramatic healing ministry, he set about teaching them the message he had come to deliver. But he didn't teach them in the way we might have expected. He started by taking a small group of men off to one side and training them.

At first sight this looks like a slow and cumbersome approach. Jesus could have reached more people, personally, if he had gone to the masses rather than spending so much time on a small group. But he knew he had only a limited time on earth, and his technique was to mobilize people who would not only carry on where he left off but would train future generations who would continue the proclamation down through the centuries.

While Jesus was investing in "a few good men," he was looking for quality and quantity through them. The quality would be in their blessedness, which would come through their attitudes to the Lord, to themselves, and to others. Jesus' description of blessed attitudes or "Beatitudes" became one of the cornerstones of his teaching and remains to this day a fundamental statement of discipleship.

If the quality would be seen in the disciples' blessed attitudes, the quantity would be seen in the way their blessedness was scattered like salt among others and diffused like light in the darkness as they lived out their lives in the world. Jesus didn't call his disciples to be blessed in a box; he told them that they were called to be the salt of the earth and the light of the world. They would be his chosen means to get the Good News out. Men who know God's blessing, who have the "blessed attitudes," and who band together for the good of the Kingdom become like salt that adds flavor to society and light that lightens the darkness and shows other men the way to go. This way Jesus gets quality *and* quantity.

When Jesus takes his stand in the hearts of men, he receives the fulcrum of devotion in their lives. Then, as he wields the lever of his all-powerful love, he moves the world in which his disciples live—and the movement is always upward.

TO READ: *Matthew 20:1–16*

AN HONEST DAY'S PAY?

"He answered one of them, 'Friend, I haven't been unfair! Didn't you agree to work
all day for the usual wage? . . . Is it against the law for me to do what I want
with my money? Should you be angry because I am kind?' "

MATTHEW 20:13, 15

D iscrimination, differentials, and arbitration are hot topics in today's labor market. We don't have to look far for the reasons! People have a tendency to be selfish, greedy, lazy, dishonest, and a host of other things that make life in the workplace a challenge. So over the years a vast body of legislation has been put in place in an effort to deal with these issues. How successfully it does so is a matter for debate.

Given all these concerns, Jesus' story about working conditions in his day sounds strangely out of date and totally out of touch with modern workplace realities. But what he had to say is relevant nevertheless.

Jesus told the story of a vineyard owner who hired laborers in the morning at the going rate, then hired others later in the day at nine o'clock, noon, three o'clock, and five o'clock, and promised to pay them at a rate that would be fair. At the end of the day, as the law of the land required, he gathered the men together to pay them. The five o'clock crew were paid first and were given a full day's pay, so the others assumed they would get a bonus. But none was forthcoming, and they objected. The owner challenged his disgruntled workers to explain why they should be angry simply because he was being kind (20:13). He said that he had paid what he promised to pay, and if he wanted to be gracious to someone it was his prerogative, as he was spending his own money (20:15).

Therein lies the point of the story: God deals with everybody on the basis of his justice, and as he chooses he adds extra doses of kindness that are totally undeserved. Who can quarrel with that? We can be very thankful that God does not "pay" us what we deserve—that he gives us freely the gift of eternal life (see Rom. 6:23).

A man who sees his work experience as part of his discipleship will acknowledge the validity of the old adage, "An honest day's work for an honest day's pay." This adage applies to both employers and employees. Employers should make sure they pay their employees fairly for the work they have done, and employees should make sure they do fairly the work for which they are paid! Then justice will be done.

In the workplace, justice must be done. But grace in the workplace should never be far from the believer's mind, and kindness at work will never be out of place.

PROGNOSTICATION AND PREPAREDNESS

"So stay awake and be prepared, because you do not know the day or hour of my return."

MATTHEW 25:13

E very generation of Christians has expected Christ to return in their lifetime. And they have had one thing in common: They have all been wrong.

The Lord Jesus did promise to return to take his people home. But he did not say when the event would take place. In fact, he told his disciples specifically, "You do not know the day or hour of my return" (25:13). This has not stopped some prognosticators from saying that they may not know the day or hour, but they have figured out the month and year! They've all been wrong, too.

Why did Jesus compare his return to the Flood of Noah (24:37-39), when despite countless opportunities to hear and see that something was going to happen, Noah's contemporaries studiously avoided responding to his warnings and carried on life as usual? Why did Jesus compare his return to the arrival of a thief (24:43-44), explaining that his return would not be advertised any more than the arrival of a burglar is publicized in advance? His multiple illustrations were designed to hammer home both the inevitability of the event and the uncertainty of the *when.*

Supposing Jesus had said, "I'll give you three millennia to evangelize the world, and then, on January 1, A.D. 3001, I will return at precisely 9:00 GMT." What would the promise of his return have meant to generations of believers who lived in the preceding centuries? In the midst of their sufferings, exiles, and martyrdom, what comfort would they have derived from his promise, knowing that he would not come soon? And what would have been the effect on the church if they had known that they still had a little time to do what they wanted to do before getting around to doing what he had told them to do? Where would have been the sense of urgency, the challenge to holiness, and the keen sense of tiptoe anticipation?

Jesus' point was that all his disciples should be living in a sense of anticipation, actively on the job, working hard to bring about the consummation of his purposes and living consistent lives so they would not be ashamed at his coming. His instructions could not have been more clear: "So stay awake and be prepared, because you do not know the day or hour of my return" (25:13).

Speculating about Christ's return is intriguing but not unproductive. Participating in preparing for his return is imperative and pays lasting dividends.

TO READ: *Mark 16:1-20*

THE EMPTY TOMB

But the angel said, "Do not be so surprised. You are looking for Jesus, the Nazarene,
who was crucified. He isn't here! He has been raised from the dead!
Look, this is where they laid his body."

MARK 16:6

Ractically everybody puts Jesus in the category of "best man who ever lived"; many agree that he's "the greatest teacher the world has known"; not a few insist he "showed us how we ought to live"; and some believe he "demonstrated how to face death." But however true these opinions may be, they all fall short of what the Scriptures say about him.

After Jesus' crucifixion, his body was reverently laid in a tomb. Courageous women realized that his body had not been treated properly with burial spices, so early on Sunday morning, in fear and trembling, they went to the tomb to lovingly administer appropriate care. When they arrived they were confronted with an empty tomb and an angelic messenger who proclaimed, "He isn't here! He has been raised from the dead!" (16:6). After the angel had given them further instructions and a promise that they would see Jesus, the women left the scene "too frightened to talk" (16:8). But talk they did when they met the disciples. Quickly the word spread, the Lord appeared, and the evidence mounted that Jesus, who had truly been dead, had been literally raised from the dead and was very much alive. Even the disciples, who had forsaken Jesus and were understandably reluctant to believe the women's report, eventually were persuaded by Christ's personal appearances to them, and they "went everywhere and preached" the good news of the Resurrection (16:20).

Even a moment's reflection will show that this series of events immediately lifts Jesus beyond the opinions mentioned above into a position that only he can occupy. He is infinitely more than revered teacher, glowing example, courageous facer of death, and unimpeachable role model. His resurrection is seen to be the Father's endorsement of all Jesus' claims and the seal of validation that his death takes away our sins. His life after death is a statement concerning the reality of eternal existence, and his conquering of death is a robust reminder that death need hold no fear for those who trust their eternal destiny to Jesus.

The bottom line is that approving opinions about Jesus' life miss the point unless married to joyous belief in his resurrection. Reverence, however sincere, for a dead Christ, however noble, will do nothing for a sinner headed toward a lost eternity. Only a personal experience of the risen Lord will suffice.

STREET SMARTS

I tell you, use your worldly resources to benefit others and make friends.
In this way, your generosity stores up a reward for you in heaven.

LUKE 16:9

People get uneasy in the pews when preachers talk about money, and many preachers get uneasy in the pulpit when it is time to talk finances. Jesus had no such reluctance. He spoke openly, unapologetically, trenchantly, and not infrequently on the subject! More often than not, he concentrated on showing how the pursuit and possession of money could have a negative effect on a person's life. But he did not always regard money negatively—while it can become a spiritual trap and liability, it can also be a useful tool and asset. To illustrate the point, he told a story that raised both eyebrows and hackles—the eyebrows of the modern reader, the hackles of his contemporary listeners.

The story recounts the shady dealings of a rich man's manager. When the manager realized that his embezzlement was about to be discovered, he went about making some deals that would make things easier for him when he found himself out of work. The deals were fundamentally dishonest, and when his boss found out about them and the original embezzlement, he shook his head admiringly and admitted that his manager was nothing if not smart when it came to handling finances to his own advantage. This response, rather than outrage, suggests there is reason to believe the rich man was no paragon of virtue either!

This story raises eyebrows because, while Jesus never endorses the dishonesty of the manager, he does use him as a positive role model for disciples with regard to shrewd money management. He appears to be mourning the fact that his disciples are not smart enough in handling their money. They don't see the positive benefits of proper financial management. The shady manager knew how to use money to make friends. Jesus wants his disciples to use money to make friendships that last for eternity.

But how? Money invested in introducing a tribal group to the gospel, leading them to eternal salvation, will make for a lot of eternal friendships, and money invested in the lives of orphans that leads to their temporal and eternal well-being is money well spent.

It's a matter of serving God with your money or serving yourself with it—and you serving your money! You manage your money or your money manages you. Sure, you can invest in Wall Street, but make sure you invest in the streets of gold, too. You'll be surprised by the friends you meet up there that you never knew down here!

TO READ: *Acts 1:1-11*

MEN, MOVEMENTS, AND MONUMENTS

*"But when the Holy Spirit has come upon you, you will receive power
and will tell people about me everywhere—in Jerusalem, throughout Judea,
in Samaria, and to the ends of the earth."*

ACTS 1:8

I n the history of human endeavors, there is a natural progression from "man" to "movement" to "monument." A charismatic individual typically comes on the scene, mobilizes others to join him, and achieves great things. When the leader dies or leaves, his followers continue for a while in his spirit. But the movement generally lacks the founder's dynamism and eventually loses momentum. Subsequently, it either fails outright or becomes only a monument to its former, departed glory. Man, movement, monument.

Christianity did not follow the "man-movement-monument" scenario. Jesus' charisma cannot be denied. But when he died, he died alone. And after he rose from the dead, he had to appear to his disciples repeatedly to convince them that he was truly risen from the dead (1:3). He had to explain to them again that his kingdom was far different from the one they imagined (1:3, 6; see John 18:36). Even when he made his dramatic exit to heaven, they stood staring into the sky (Acts 1:11)—they apparently still misunderstood that his departure was planned and his return was inevitable!

Not a very promising beginning! And yet Jesus' "cause" not only survived but has even thrived, so that the four corners of the globe and the most remote stretches of the world resound to the praise of the Lord Jesus two millennia later. What happened?

Prior to his departure Jesus told his disciples, "In a few days you will be baptized with the Holy Spirit. . . . You will receive power and will tell people about me everywhere" (1:5, 8). This power of the "Spirit of God, who raised Jesus from the dead" (Rom. 8:11) imparted to them supernatural power that made them compelling witnesses for Christ.

Rather than losing momentum after the first generation, this movement of the Holy Spirit has continued, empowering Christ's followers to serve him. The Holy Spirit has winged their message to many hearts and has performed mighty works of grace, turning people "from the power of Satan to God" (Acts 26:18).

There is no denying that Christianity has in some instances degenerated into a monument, and its places of worship into museums. But it is equally true that, where ordinary men and women in the power of the Spirit have proclaimed the Good News of Christ's saving grace, the church has continued to grow and thrive. When this happens, there is no man-movement-monument syndrome. The Man, Christ Jesus, is still at work through the Holy Spirit, doing what only he can do—and doing it well!

"PLEASE HURRY, LORD!"

O LORD, I am calling to you. Please hurry! Listen when I cry to you for help!
PSALM 141:1

Temptations come when you least expect them: when you're off guard, when you're feeling down, when you're rejoicing in a triumph, or when you're licking your wounds in defeat. Without warning, without consideration, without compunction, and without asking permission, they come roaring in like a whirlwind or sliding in like a serpent. Overt or covert, obvious or insidious, temptations have only one goal: to bring you down.

When temptations come, reaction time is cut to a minimum. That is why prayer must be instantaneous and urgent. "O Lord, I am calling to you. Please hurry!" (141:1).

"Please hurry, Lord, because if you delay it might be too late. I may already have said what I ought not to have said. Out of malice I may have spoken a half-truth, out of anger I may have retorted viciously. My words may already have been fired at their target without any chance of recall, arrowing their way to an unsuspecting heart. They may already have poisoned someone's thoughts about an innocent person, ruined a reputation, or opened a barely healed wound.

"Please hurry, Lord, or I may already have entertained such lustful desires that I have actually fed on the delicacies of evil. How could I do it, Lord? How could I think such desires were delicious and partake of such evils, knowing how wrong they are? But I'm capable of this, Lord. I need your help because, after I've tasted what seemed delicious, I can scarcely rid my mouth of the lingering, loathsome taste.

"Lord, my prayer is urgent to the point of being abrupt, but it comes from a heart that trusts you to see it as a pleasant offering of need and desire. A declaration of dependence!

"Lord, should you see fit to answer my prayer by sending a brother who will put me straight, that will be fine. It may hurt, it will probably sting, but it will save the day. I'll accept what he tells me as being a word from you, and I'll do what he says as if you were standing right there. But please send him quickly. Reaction time is desperately short."

When temptations rear their ugly heads, if God doesn't make haste the devil will wreak havoc. But the only reason he would not make haste is because we haven't made a point to cry for help.

TO READ: *Acts 19:21-41*

THE WAY TO A MAN'S HEART

"As you have seen and heard, this man Paul has persuaded many people that handmade gods aren't gods at all. And this is happening not only here in Ephesus but throughout the entire province! Of course, I'm not just talking about the loss of public respect for our business. I'm also concerned that the temple of the great goddess Artemis will lose its influence and that Artemis—this magnificent goddess worshiped throughout the province of Asia and all around the world—will be robbed of her prestige!"

ACTS 19:26-27

M any are of the opinion that "the way to a man's heart is through his stomach." According to this theory, if you keep a man's basic needs met, he'll be pretty docile and amenable! There is, however, a quicker way to a man's heart, and that is through his wallet. Few things can be counted on to make a man passionate more quickly than money. Paul certainly discovered this during his ministry in the great city of Ephesus.

A number of lucrative businesses had sprung up around the temple of Artemis in Ephesus. A craftsman called Demetrius had a lucrative business making the silver shrines of the goddess (19:23-24). When Paul's teaching was turning people away from worshiping Artemis, Demetrius was incensed that his business was in jeopardy. He called together his craftsmen, along with other men whose businesses were likewise suffering (19:25), and he complained about what Paul's teaching was doing to their business and to the prestige of their goddess (19:27). At this the anger of the men boiled over, a demonstration took place, and crowds joined in, even though "most of them didn't even know why they were there" (19:32). An ugly, dangerous situation developed, but the mayor handled it superbly and averted a disaster.

Demetrius was at least honest enough to say that he was worried first about his wallet, then about his prestige, and then about the status of Artemis! Granted, the crowd did not chant, "Great is the wallet of Demetrius!" Their rallying cry was, "Great is Artemis of the Ephesians!" But behind the solidarity for the goddess was a profound concern for threatened wallets.

It is certainly appropriate for a man to react passionately if he is in danger of losing his livelihood. But many men have the same problem as Demetrius—their passionate concern for their wallet overrides all other interests and priorities. Such men may make appropriate religious noises, but their underlying interests are financial rather than spiritual. They may show some interest in the things of God, but little passion. Passion is reserved for the wallet. They devour the Dow with relish, show off their possessions with delight, and revel in the good of their goods.

Sadly, these men have forgotten "that it is the Lord your God who gives you power to become rich" (Deut. 8:18). Perhaps if they could recover that insight they might get passionate about him!

TO READ: *Acts 26:1–32*

TAKING
OPPORTUNITIES

Agrippa interrupted him. "Do you think you can make me a Christian so quickly?"
Paul replied, "Whether quickly or not, I pray to God that both you and everyone here
in this audience might become the same as I am, except for these chains."

ACTS 26:28-29

T he difference between an optimist and a pessimist is that the pessimist sees a difficulty in every opportunity, while the optimist recognizes an opportunity in every difficulty.

When Paul faced difficulty, he recognized opportunity, and he was not slow to grasp it. His difficulties were many and serious. He had been within an inch of losing his life at the hands of the mob in Jerusalem. Rescued by Romans and smuggled out of the city, Paul was detained in prison. One day he was summoned before King Agrippa. Surrounded by his retinue, the king sat in splendor. Before him stood the apostle—in chains! In such an intimidating situation, Paul was totally unintimidated. His primary concern was not to save his own skin but to save his hearers' souls.

The way Paul snatched an opportunity from the jaws of difficulty is instructive. He was unfailingly courteous, he spoke with deep conviction, and his message was focused on Christ. He commended the king for his expert knowledge of "Jewish customs and controversies" (26:3), and he expressed appreciation for the opportunity to speak to him. When Festus rudely accused him of being insane he responded courteously: "I am not insane, Most Excellent Festus" (26:25). Paul's defense was not a dry theological or political oration but a heartfelt explanation of personal experience. He pointed everyone's attention to the Lord Jesus, with particular emphasis on his death and resurrection.

Jesus appointed his disciples "to tell people about [him] everywhere" (1:8). The message and its presentation have not changed. A courteous respect for the feelings, opinions, objections, and misunderstandings of the person being addressed must not be lost in the enthusiasm or stress of the moment. And there is no substitute for the compelling simplicity of an account of saving grace in the life of the witness. But everything must be centered in an explanation of who Jesus is, what he has done, what he offers, and what he desires, deserves, and demands.

Agrippa walked away from the encounter with Paul knowing exactly what the apostle was aiming at (26:28). The witness is not reponsible for his hearer's reaction, but only for presenting his hearer with an unmistakable and clear account. With this in mind, we should recognize opportunities and learn to grasp them, like Paul—with clarity, courtesy, and conviction.

TO READ: *Romans 1:1-5, 16-20.*

THOSE WHO
WILL NOT SEE

From the time the world was created, people have seen the earth and sky and all that God made. They can clearly see his invisible qualities—his eternal power and divine nature. So they have no excuse whatsoever for not knowing God.

ROMANS 1:20

"There are none so blind as those who will not see," my mother used to tell me when I couldn't find something. She imagined that I did not *want* to find the offending article! At times she implied that it was a peculiar masculine aberration. She may have been right!

God has a similar complaint about humanity. All people can "clearly see [God's] invisible qualities—his eternal power and divine nature" (1:20) in the creation all around them. The creation abounds with clear evidence of God's being and character. As a result, "the truth about God is known to them instinctively" (1:19). But men reject what is clear to them—they push the truth away from themselves. It is not that man *cannot* know God— it is that he *will* not respond to the knowledge available on every hand. There are none so blind as those who will not see.

There is more. Man has taken his refusal to see God a perverse step further. He has crafted alternative theories about reality that deny and reject God. He has put in God's place things that could never be responsible for creation (1:23). Man prefers what God has made to the God who made it! Throughout the world man is guilty of worshiping materials and rejecting the Maker. This is the ultimate folly, but man does not see it. Man regards this foolishness as evidence of the superiority of human wisdom! There are none so blind as those who will not believe!

A wise man will examine the intricacy of all creation and determine whether it looks like an accident or a created order. He should then ask if the order suggests an intelligence behind the order. God apparently expects man to see enough in creation to convince him of God's existence and power. Should a man arrive at the conclusion that there is a Creator, he should then see if there is further information available about the Supreme Being. If he reads, learns, and inwardly digests the Scriptures, he will find the answers to questions about his origin, purpose, reason for being, personal longings, and much, much more—and all in Christ our Lord!

Nothing is more crucial for man's well-being in life and eternity than finding God. The God who revealed himself partially in creation leads the seeking man to discover more of his self-revelation in Christ. Eventually the man comes to see the truth in Christ and to experience the salvation found only in him.

There are none so blind as those who will not see—and none so blessed as those who will—and do!

TO READ: *Romans 15:1–13*

DEVOTION

So I pray that God, who gives you hope, will keep you happy and full of peace as you believe in him. May you overflow with hope through the power of the Holy Spirit.

ROMANS 15:13

The man who is devoted to fishing knows that if he wants the delights of catching fish he must accept the demands of getting up before dawn, braving the elements, and spending long hours catching nothing. But the devoted fisherman regards it all as worthwhile.

There are untold delights in being devoted to Christ. Those who "believe in him" can anticipate God keeping them "happy and full of peace" and can "overflow with hope through the power of the Holy Spirit" (15:13). But devotion to Christ has its own demands.

Christ was so devoted to the Father's will that he "didn't please himself" (15:3). The Father's will was intensely challenging at times—the Garden of Gethsemane comes immediately to mind. There Jesus shrank from the horror of his assignment, but he devoted himself to the Father and did his will nevertheless.

Jesus also devoted himself to the needs of those around him. Even the outcasts of society found in him a friend and support. His arms were open wide to those who responded to his invitation, and he turned no truly repentant person away (Matt. 11:28-30). So Paul could say, "Christ has accepted you" (Rom. 15:7), and he stressed that the Lord Jesus "came as a servant" (15:8).

Devotion to the Lord requires that the devotee have "the attitude of Christ Jesus" (15:5). We demonstrate this attitude most clearly when we are devoted to the well-being of others—even those with whom we disagree! We should reach out to those who don't know Christ so that they "might also give glory to God for his mercies to them" (15:9).

If the believer becomes nervous about the demands of devotion, he should remember that among the delights of devotion is the experience of being kept happy and full of peace! Serving others, reaching out, accepting people, and not pleasing yourself certainly does not sound like a recipe for happiness to secular man. But for the one who has studied the life of Christ and has devoted himself to his cause, there is assurance enough that this is the way to fullness of life.

The devoted fisherman who reels in his fish counts the demands of fishing as nothing. The believer who finds his happiness in bringing glory to God and blessings to mankind regards the demands of devotion to Christ a delight.

TO READ: *Philemon 1:1–25*

PEACE BROKERS

My plea is that you show kindness to Onesimus. I think of him as my own son
because he became a believer as a result of my ministry here in prison.

PHILEMON 1:10

S ome people are task oriented, while others are people oriented. While we all have our inclinations and proclivities, we all need to be both task and people oriented, to an extent. A well-rounded life is one in which the things that need to be done get done. This includes seeing that the relationships that should be nurtured get nurtured.

For the most part, Paul was task oriented; his stated ambition was "to preach the Good News where the name of Christ has never been heard" (Rom. 15:20), and he pursued that ambition relentlessly. Nevertheless, he also poured himself into developing and maintaining lasting relationships.

Paul's relationship with Philemon, the godly Colossian businessman, is a case in point. Perhaps Philemon had treated Onesimus in ways that fractured their relationship. Or perhaps Onesimus simply longed to run his own life. Whatever the case, now Paul asked Philemon to "show kindness to Onesimus" (v. 10), to restore their broken relationship. In asking this, Paul was relying heavily on his own relationship with Philemon.

Some people do things that break the peace. Those of us who have been disappointed at times with our efforts at peacemaking may be inclined to ask, Why should I expend a lot of effort in trying to make peace between people who aren't interested? Two answers are readily available. First, "As members of one body you are all called to live in peace" (Col. 3:15). Second, "God wants his children to live in peace" (1 Cor. 7:15). God has made peace with those who are his children, and their lives should be characterized by peaceful relationships. God's deep desire for his children is that they should not be known as contentious people but as peace-makers. This is reason enough for us to expend the energy.

Not everybody will be responsive to our peacemaking overtures. Scripture takes this into account and instructs us, "Do your part to live in peace with everyone, as much as possible" (Rom. 12:18). Here is a recognition that not all attempts at peacemaking will succeed; but it is also a clear directive for us to do our part. Even Jesus did not have success with those who were in total opposition to him, but that did not deter him from giving himself to the task of reaching out to them. His responsibility was to reach out. They were responsible for their own failure to respond.

There is no shortage of peace breakers. We need people who, like Paul, will be peace brokers.

TO READ: *2 Peter 3:8–18*

THE DAY OF THE LORD

But the day of the Lord will come as unexpectedly as a thief. Then the heavens will
pass away with a terrible noise, and everything in them will disappear in fire,
and the earth and everything on it will be exposed to judgment.

2 PETER 3:10

When Saddam Hussein, the Iraqi dictator, decided to occupy Kuwait, a coalition of nations decided he should be evicted and punished. The ancient city of Baghdad was subjected to a massive aerial bombardment, and television showed pictures of "smart bombs" hurtling with devastating accuracy into selected targets. People around the world watched from the comfort of their own homes. But there was little comfort in the homes of Saddam's troubled people—for them, the "fireworks display" was destruction and devastation.

So it will be in the "day of the Lord." The prophet Joel said the day of the Lord will be "an awesome, terrible thing" (Joel 2:11). But Peter, preaching in Jerusalem, called it "that great and glorious day of the Lord" (Acts 2:20). Which will it be—great and glorious or awesome and terrible? It will depend entirely where you're sitting. Those who are safe and secure in Christ's salvation will rejoice as they are introduced to the full glory of his presence for all eternity; those who are not in Christ will experience the awesome, terrifying judgment of God.

Many men struggle when faced with these weighty truths. Will God really bring fiery judgment on his own creation? Does he intend to create "new heavens and new earth?" Will people really perish in the coming judgment? When will all this happen?

The timing of the "day of the Lord" is a secret known only to God. We are certain that the great day will happen. We are uncertain about the timing (2 Pet. 3:10). Why the uncertainty? Why didn't God tell us when it will happen? Perhaps because he knows human nature! Those people who have suffered for the sake of God's Kingdom and who have endured because they have hoped for his speedy return would likely have despaired. And those who have had little interest in reaching the perishing would have had even less interest if they had known that the Lord was not about to return. And since we are selfish people, we might have lived as we wished until the last minute before getting around to being what we should have been!

These things seemed to be on Peter's mind when he said that the promise of the day of the Lord, and the uncertainty of its timing, should stimulate us to "holy, godly lives" (3:11). We should "look forward" to this great event, and the anticipation should inspire us to "hurry it along" (3:12). Of one thing we can be sure—"the day of the Lord will come"!

TO READ: *Psalm 147*

NATURE'S GOD

How great is our Lord! His power is absolute!
His understanding is beyond comprehension!

PSALM 147:5

O ne of the advantages of living in a relatively undeveloped country like ancient Israel was that the people, of necessity, lived close to nature. They knew that milk does not originate in cartons, that bread does not come sliced, and that hens lay eggs. Not for them endless hours spent watching television or surfing the net! There was work to be done, and it had to be done outside, in the elements. They looked at the clouds, not CNN, to discern the weather. And they saw God send the rain, without which they would not survive. When the snow and ice came they did not head for the slopes: they watched God break up the stubborn soil, without which they would not be able to sow and reap. And when the thaw came, they embraced the spring and headed for the fields, anticipating a harvest that only the Lord could make possible. Close to nature, they were close to nature's God. In the minute, mundane details of life they had cause for rejoicing.

Not for ancient Israel was the power of electricity, internal combustion, or the atom. Their biggest power source was six horsepower—literally! When the horses strained at their tasks and moved their loads, people were thankful for God's provision of such a magnificent animal, but they knew that even the horse was powerless compared to their God. And if the horse was unimpressive relative to God, then man was simply puny (147:10). So they had nowhere to turn but to the Lord, and they found in him the resources for life that only he could give.

We are more civilized but less smart, more educated but less astute. The ancient agriculturalists knew the One on whom they were dependent, whereas we forget. They knew whom to thank, but we get confused. We need to take a few moments—or hours, or days! —to reflect on creation and remember the One through whom all power flows and from whom all creativity originates. If we'll leave for a moment our sophisticated tools and toys and consider the lilies and study the birds, if we'll listen to the wind in the trees and smell the fragrance of the lilac in the evening air, then we'll be able to remember God's powerful work and humbly sing, "How great is our Lord! His power is absolute! His understanding is beyond comprehension!" (147:5). As the psalmist declared, "How delightful and how right!" (147:1).

references

BELLAH, ROBERT, ET AL. *Habits of the Heart.* New York: Harper and Row Publishers,1985.

BLOOM, ALLAN. *The Closing of the American Mind.* New York: Simon & Schuster, 1987.

BONHOEFFER, DIETRICH. *The Cost of Discipleship.* New York: Simon & Schuster, 1995.

DAVIES, NORMAN. *Europe: A History.* Oxford: Oxford University Press, 1996.

ELLIOTT, ELISABETH. *The Shadow of the Almighty.* New York: Harper & Brothers, 1958.

_____. *Through Gates of Splendor.* Wheaton, IL: Tyndale House Publishers, 1981.

Encyclopaedia Brittanica. 15th ed.

GUINNESS, OS. *The Call.* Nashville, TN: Word, 1998.

HERBERT, GEORGE. *Selected Poems.* Edited by Gareth Reeves. New York: Barnes and Noble, 1971.

HARMAN, CARTER. *A Popular History of Music.* New York: Dell Publishing, 1969.

JOHNSON, SAMUEL. *Letters of Samuel Johnson.* Edited by Bruce Redford. Vol. 1. Princeton: Princeton University Press, 1992.

JOHNSON, SAMUEL. *The Rambler,* No. 2. <http://etext.lib.virginia.edu/toc/modeng/public/Joh1Ram.html>.

LACTANTIUS, *Divine Institutes.* Washington: Catholic University of America Press, 1964.

LEWIS, C.S. *Surprised by Joy.* New York: Harcourt Brace, 1955.

MOTYER, ALEC. *The Prophecy of Isaiah.* Downers Grove, IL: InterVarsity Press, 1993.

Oxford Dictionary of Quotations, 2nd ed. Edited by Elizabeth Knowles. Oxford: Oxford University Press, 1999.

PASCAL, BLAISE. *Pensées.* trans. by W. F. Trotter. 1660. <http://www.ccel.org>.

POPE, ALEXANDER. *The Dunciad in Four Books.* Edited by Valerie Rumbold. New York: Longman, 1999.

RUSSELL, BERTRAND. "A Free Man's Worship." In *Bertrand Russell on God and Religion.* Edited by Al Seckel. Buffalo: Prometheus Books, 1986.

SANTAYANA, GEORGE. *Life of Reason,* vol. 1. Buffalo: Prometheus Books, 1998.

STOTT, JOHN R. W. *God's New Society.* Downers Grove, IL: InterVarsity Press, 1979.

TANNEN, DEBORAH. *That's Not What I Meant!* New York: Morrow, 1986.

_____. *You Really Don't Understand.* New York: Morrow, 1990.

TOCQUEVILLE, ALEXIS DE. *Democracy in America.* Translated and edited by Harvey C. Mansfield and Delba Winthrop. Chicago: University of Chicago Press, 2000.

TWAIN, MARK. *The Unabridged Mark Twain.* Edited by Lawrence Teacher. Philadelphia: Running Press, 1976.

WESLEY, JOHN. *The Journal of John Wesley.* ed. by Percy Livingstone Parker. Chicago: Moody Press, 1951.

WORDSWORTH, WILLIAM. *William Wordsworth: Selected Poems.* Edited by Walford Davies. London: Everyman's Library, 1975.

reference index

topical index

FAILURE
Jan 14, 25, Feb 14, 20, Apr 8, June 22, Aug 23, 25, 26, Oct 8, 9, 23, Nov 1, Dec 16

FAITH
Jan 16, Feb 4, 5, Mar 13, Apr 7, 12, 14, May 4, 9, 13, 23, June 4, 7, 13, 21, 26, Aug 10, 17, 20, Sep 14, Oct 9, 14, 17, 18, 19, Nov 26

FAITHFULNESS
Jan 1, 3, 10, 15, 18, 21, Feb 26, Mar 19, Apr 8, 17, June 26, 29, Aug 4, Sep 3, 26, Oct 2, Dec 4

FAMILY
Jan 11, 27, Apr 11, July 28, Aug 15

FATHERHOOD
Jan 28, Feb 6, July 17, Oct 30

FEAR
Jan 18, 31, Feb 22, 23, 25, 28, Mar 4, 14, Apr 8, May 27, 28, June 7, 9, 11, 21, July 22, 23, Aug 20, Sep 12, 22, Oct 10, 19, 27, Nov 8, 23, Dec 13, 21

FOCUS
Jan 29, Apr 2, 12, 13, May 13, Aug 19, Sep 19, 20, Nov 7

FOOL/FOOLISH
Jan 15, 19, Feb 25, Mar 20, Apr 1, 14, Sep 3, Dec 27

FORGIVENESS
Jan 12, 16, 28, Feb 2, 5, 15, 21, Mar 3, 12, Apr 15, 25, May 5, 13, June 11, 12, 16, 17, 22, July 9, Aug 2, 18, Sep 27, 28, Oct 3, 5, 8, 15, Nov 1, 6, 19, Dec 6, 12

FREEDOM
Feb 2, Mar 11, 20, Apr 14, 24, 26, May 12, June 16, July 20, 21, 26, Aug 22, 29, Sep 2, 18, Oct 16, Nov 13, 15, Dec 17

FRIENDSHIP
Jan 18, Mar 21, May 21, 23, June 11, 24, 25, July 28, Aug 4, Oct 20, Nov 11, Dec 12, 22

FUTURE
Jan 5, 19, Feb 3, 18, Mar 3, May 9, 28, June 3,

10, 21, July 8, 11, 14, 29, Aug 9, Sep 3, 22, Oct 9, Nov 3, 23

GENEROSITY
Aug 2, Sep 23, Oct 12, Nov 17, Dec 22

GENTLENESS
Jan 18, Feb 18, May 7, 31, Aug 2

GOD'S AUTHORITY
Feb 17, Mar 27, Apr 13, July 6, 10, 11, 12, 24, 26, Aug 5, 30, Sep 27, Nov 12, 13, Dec 15

GOD'S PROVISION
June 9, July 4, Sep 5, Nov 28

GOD'S SOVEREIGNTY
Jan 17, Feb 17, May 4, 17, July 9, 11, 23, Aug 8, 26, 30, Sep 9, Oct 17, 22, 27, Nov 9, 11, 12

GOD'S WILL
Feb 16, 17, Mar 19, May 2, June 3, 6, Dec 10

GOD'S WORD
(see Bible)

GODLINESS
Jan 8, Feb 12, 19, 23, 26, Mar 7, 15, 18, Apr 2, May 21, 31, June 29, July 30, Aug 6, 23, 25, Oct 14, 17, Nov 14, 17, Dec 10, 30

GRACE
Jan 5, Feb 2, 4, 10, 11, 14, Mar 4, 12, Apr 3, 4, 6, 21, 22, May 3, 6, 16, June 4, 10, 12, 24, July 7, 12, Aug 3, 14, 18, 31, Sep 7, 11, Oct 11, 14, 15, 16, Nov 5, 14, Dec 11, 19, 23, 26

GREATNESS
Apr 6, May 7

GUIDANCE
Jan 7, Feb 22, Mar 23, Apr 9, June 20, Oct 21, Dec 5

GUILT
Feb 5, 10, May 5, June 11, 16, Aug 18, Sep 3, Oct 8, Nov 6

HABITS
Mar 2, July 4, Dec 8